STUDIA
ETYMOLOGICA
CRACOVIENSIA

S T U D I A
ETYMOLOGICA
CRACOVIENSIA

14 (2009)

CONDIDIT ET MODERATUR
MAREK STACHOWSKI

KRAKÓW 2009

This volume has appeared thanks to the financial support of the Jagiellonian University's Faculty of Philology and the Institute of Oriental Philology at the Jagiellonian University.

We would ask for all references to be encompassed by the abbreviation *SEC*.

The contents and style of the articles remain the sole responsibility of the authors themselves.

All unpublished non-commissioned works will not be returned.

On editorial matters please contact the Chief Editor: Prof. Dr. Marek Stachowski, ul. Barska 1/4, PL – 30-307 Kraków; e-mail: stachowski.marek@gmail.com; fax: (+48) 0-12 422 67 93.
Books for review and contributions for publication should be sent to the Editor.

ISBN 978-83-233-2758-5

Jagiellonian University Press
ul. Wrocławska 53, 30-011 Kraków, Poland
tel. 0-12 631 01 97, fax 0-12 631 01 98
mobile 0-506 006 674
e-mail: sprzedaz@wuj.pl
http://www.wuj.pl
Bank account: Pekao SA, 80 1240 4722 1111 0000 4856 3325

This volume is dedicated
to the memory of
Professor Eugene Helimski

CONTENTS

Studia Etymologica Cracoviensia
vol. 14   Kraków 2009

Александр Е. АНИКИН (Новосибирск)

ВМЕСТО НЕКРОЛОГА:
ИЗ ВОСПОМИНАНИЙ О Е. А. ХЕЛИМСКОМ

1.

Как минимум года за два до своей кончины Е. А. Хелимский (Е.) стал говорить о том, что я должен буду написать о нем некролог. "О тебе писать я не стану, – будь добр жить подольше!"

Когда спустя год в Новосибирске началась подготовка "Сибирской энциклопедии", и в ней было решено поместить небольшую статью, посвященную Е., я ознакомил его с ней. Он уже чувствовал себя плохо, но причина еще не была известна. Обсуждение (по телефону) касалось и жанра текста: "Статья или сразу некролог?" Такой юмор не казался чересчур черным: еще была уверенность, что путь к выздоровлению найдется. Смерть Е. положила конец всем надеждам и подвела итоги его жизни и деятельности. Масштабы его фигуры в науке впечатляющие, что можно видеть даже по упомянутой статейке.

Выдающийся лингвист. Специалист в области исторической и описательной самоедологии, диалектологии уральских языков и общей уралистики, тюркологии и алтаистики, славистики, ностратического языкознания, этнолингвистики и исторической антропологии, языковых и культурных контактов в Сибири и Евразии, исследования ранних источников по Сибири, проблем языковой политики и языкового строительства. В 1968-1999 гг. – участник и организатор полевых исследований в районах обитания коми, ненцев, селькупов, энцев, нганасан и кетов (более 20 экспедиций). Автор основополагающих исследований в области ранней этнической и языковой истории прауральцев, самодийцев и финно-угров (проблемы прародины), древних контактов уральских народов, уральской и самодийской реконструкции на всех ее уровнях и диалектного членения самодийских языков (в том числе на основе анализа рукописных архивных материалов по вымершим южносамодийским языкам), описания самодийских языков (словарь, фонология, морфология, социолингвистика) и культур (фиксация и анализ устной традиции – метр и ритм северносамодийского стиха, поэтика шаманских песнопений и др.). Автор многочисленных работ по истории и диалектологии других уральских языков, ранним славяно-венгерским и славяно-финским языковым отношениям, славянской и русской этимологии, исторической фонетике тюркских языков, языку аваров и другим проблемам уралистики, славистики, алтаистики, сибиреведения и общего языкознания.

По кругу собственных интересов мне ближе всего знакомы научные достижения Е. по русской и славянской этимологии, хотя в его деятельности они занимают скорее маргинальное положение. Тем не менее, его вклад в эту область науки весьма значителен. Сюда относятся анализ прибалтийско-финского и иного языкового материала в новгородских берестяных грамотах, а также ранних славянских заимствований в финно-угорских языках; этимологическое описание ранних топономастических и апеллятивных данных по истории русского освоения севера Восточной Европы и Сибири (например, убедительные этимологии слов *Енисей*, *мамонт*); существенное расширение сведений об истории русских сибирских слов по архивным материалам XVIII в. (Г. Ф. Миллер и др.); исследование русской субстратной топонимии севера Европейской части России, повлекшее важные выводы о раннем диалектном членении уральских языков; выявление ранее практически не изученного пласта селькупских заимствований в русских говорах Западной Сибири. Представленные на люблянском съезде славистов (2003 г.) аварско-славянские этюды Е. продемонстрировали правдоподобные свидетельства доминирующей роли тунгусо-маньчжурского компонента в Аварском каганате, а вместе с тем — несколько красивых и убедительных этимологий важных и трудных для объяснения русских слов (*объре*, *бояре*, *хоругвь* и др.). Его обращения к теме ранних венгерско-славянских связей дали кроме прочего существенные уточнения, касающиеся реконструкции и этимологии ряда праславянских лексем resp. соответствующих русских лексем (*берцовая кость* и др.).

Обратившись к лексике собственно славянского происхождения, он разработал богатый перспективными идеями этюд об этимологии слав. *velje*, *bolje*, проанализировав возможность трактовки этих и ряда других лексем как сложений частиц.

Очень ценивший «задачность», как он выражался, этимологии (и вообще лингвистики), Е. А. Хелимский с огромным интересом и удовольствием углублялся в конкретные задачи истолкования многих русских (конечно, и не только русских) слов.

Масштабам Хелимского-ученого вполне соответствует его необыкновенная личность.

Мне довелось быть близко знакомым с Е., особенно в последние годы его жизни. Судьба, щедро наделившая его незаурядными дарованиями,[1] была к нему беспощадна, подвергая его – и чем дальше тем больше – тяжелейшим испытаниям: потери близких людей, долгая мучительная болезнь с заранее предрешенным итогом. Все это не могло не сказаться на его настроениях и на внешности. Е. образца 2001 г. (особенно памятный по его приезду в Новосибирск в феврале), Е. после смерти единственного сына в 2002 г. – совсем не одно и то же.

Становившиеся с начала 2006 г. все более явственными боли, казавшиеся сначала (что способствовало грубой врачебной ошибке) рецидивом случившейся еще в 90-х г. болезни костей, к осени 2007 г. стали совершенно невыносимыми. Боли лишали всякой возможности работать и доводили до мысли о самоубийстве. "Привези мне из Парижа маленькую гильотинку" – шутил он в апреле 2006 г., когда самое худшее было еще впереди.

Адекватный диагноз (cancer), поставленный, с непростительным опозданием, в декабре 2006 г., казался новым и последним ударом судьбы. Однако Е. было по силам превратить его в сильнейший мобилизующий фактор. Тайный враг, отравлявший жизнь, был разоблачен, и Е., пребывавший в депрессии и страданиях от мучительных болей, бесстрашно вступил в последний отрезок своего жизненного пути, без остатка посвятив последние месяцы своей жизни только служению науке. Один из врачей довольно точно определил оставшийся ему срок жизни – около года. Удивительно, что он сумел столько продержаться: в феврале 2007 г. случился микроинфаркт и лишь присутствие О. Дорофеевой, поддерживавшей Е. в последние месяцы его жизни (и оказавшей ему большую помощь также в научной работе), отсрочило его кончину, которая могла наступить уже тогда. Среди моря страданий он ни йоту не терял своей обычной корректности, высоты и почти нечеловеческой твердости духа, не изменяя своим принципам и главному устремлению. "Спасти свою душу значит для компаративиста – придумать хорошую реконструкцию" (октябрь 2007 г.).

Последний разговор с Е. по телефону был у меня 22 ноября 2007 г. – он, видимо, чувствовал, что болезнь берет свое и конец уже совсем близок: речь зашла о др.-рус. *билинчь*, и в голосе Е., звучавшем так, будто у

---

[1] Е. кончил школу в Одессе с золотой медалью, поступил на математическое отделение Московского университета и успешно учился, но нашел лингвистику более "задачной" (см. выше) и сменил специальность. Он был одаренным шахматистом, имел несомненные литературные, а также педагогические способности, что проявилось в его работе как научного руководителя и просветителя (научно-популярные статьи). У него были и задатки крупного политического деятеля. Этот перечень нетрудно продолжить.

него была очень сильная простуда,[2] чувствовалась тоска от сознания того, что он лишается радости обсуждать такие предметы, как происхождение слов.

Сознавая всю серьезность своего положения и мужественно смотря в лицо смертельной болезни, он сумел низвести ее до положения надоедливой посетительницы, лишь мешающей работать и вынуждающей идти на всякие ухищрения. Как ослабить боль (завязывание пальцев и головы; перемена позы при сидении и подкладывание подушек; подбор лекарств, инъекции морфия и проч.) и при этом по возможности не терять ясности сознания и не впадать в сон; как набирать текст, когда правая рука перестает действовать, а левая не хочет ее заменять, а в глазах все двоится – ежечасно и ежеминутно ему приходилось решать эти и подобные почти неразрешимые проблемы. Последняя проблема такого рода, о которой я услышал, была почти трагикомическая – как приблизить свое тело к столу с компьютером, если выросший из-за лекарств живот не дает этого сделать, а опухоль вынуждает сидеть только боком и только обложившись подушками? Различия между днем и ночью стерлись. Многие часы он проводил в полусне, и лишь 3-4 часа в сутки (если везло, то 5-6) могли быть использованы по назначению. Тем не менее, даже в этих условиях за 2007 г. было сделано немало.

Осенью 2006 г. он не без горечи показал мне довольно толстую пачку карточек, на которых его превосходным почерком был записан перечень задач, мелких и более крупных, которые он был в состоянии при благоприятных условиях решить в ближайшем будущем, но уже почти не надеялся с этим справиться. И через год выяснилось, что пачка уменьшилась больше чем наполовину (многое все-таки осталось нереализованным). Меня утешает мысль, что к ее уменьшению был причастен и я. На одной из карточек было написано "инвестировать больше времени в Самодийско-тунгусские связи" – и этот проект удалось завершить,[3] поскольку Е. действительно "инвестировал" в него немало времени. Как сейчас представляю Е., диктующего мне в октябре 2007 г. "Введение" к "Marginalia ad UEW" – часа так в 3 ночи, среди табачного дыма (курил он много до самого конца[4]), с перерывами на кушанье – кексы и пирожные – а иногда также

---

[2] По его объяснению, это было одним из следствий нового увеличения опухоли, которое было обнаружено при последнем обследовании.

[3] Аникин А. Е., Хелимский Е. А. *Самодийско-тунгусские лексические связи.* Москва, 2007. Я был по преимуществу техническим секретарем-исполнителем этой книги. Но Е. настоял, чтобы фамилии авторов были поставлены по алфавиту.

[4] "Я завоевал право курить дорогой ценой"; "как только помру, сразу брошу". Он конечно, сознавал, какую роль в развитии его болезни сыграло курение (по несколько пачек в день многие десятилетия – немногие такое выдержат). Будучи в больнице (Эппендорф в Гамбурге), он шокировал других курильщиков, в

на выражение неудовольствия по поводу своего слишком однообразного немецкого языка.

2.

Сделав усилие, чтобы не сосредотачиваться на одних только печальных воспоминаниях о последнем периоде жизни Е. (он же Женя, также Евгений Арнольдович или просто Арнольдович; для любимой кошки Ксюши – "дедушка"), попробую назвать некоторые свойства его личности и поведения, которые делали его таким, каким он остался в нашей памяти. Сделать это нелегко. Я никак не могу претендовать на сколько-нибудь полный словесный портрет Е. Но все же попробую. Многое дается со слов самого Е.

• *Свободолюбие и свободомыслие.* Е. были чужды любые предрассудки, всякая косность и робость мысли. Он был независим и внутренне свободен, а его активность и энергия обусловливали его стремление к свободе и в окружающем его мире. В этом один из важных мотивов его политической деятельности в конце 80-х – начале 90-х гг. XX в.

• *Оригинальная внешность, соединявшая интеллект и культуру с ориентальным колоритом* (многие дамы считали его красавцем). Один бывший коллега Е. в Москве, известный анекдотическими поступками и изречениями, как-то по секрету сообщил ему: "Вы очень похожи на автопортрет Пушкина".[5] Е. действительно немного походил на великого русского поэта (имевшего эфиопского предка) – и на его автопортрет тоже.

• *Благоприятно влияющая на других личность.* Его успокаивающий и вразумляющий голос, разумные и мягко-остроумные речи, вежливо-трогательные манеры и чуткость к собеседнику могли заменить визит к невропатологу. Во всяком случае, для меня. То, что могло бы раздражать в других людях, в его исполнении выглядело скорее приятно и/или забавно. Он довольно громко чавкал во время еды, но его чавканье производило такое же впечатление, как веселое чавканье собаки или кошки. Было необыкновенно приятно видеть и слышать, как он ест! Он имел обыкновение трепать себе ухо, и смешные звуки от такого трепания разносились довольно далеко.

основном медиков: "Смотрите на меня – вот что бывает с теми, кто много курит!" А еще в 2004 г. он хвалил Германию как "последнюю страну, где можно жить по-человечески" (т.е. курить где угодно).

5   По рассказу Е., этот коллега, выслушав пространный доклад гостя из Голландии о славистике в этой стране, задал лишь один вопрос: "Есть ли в Амстердаме зоопарк?"

У Е., кстати, совсем не было музыкального слуха, но он был не прочь петь и поучаствовать в хоровом пении[6] (не говоря о готовности поплясать), и слушать его было гораздо интереснее, чем многих певцов со слухом и голосом. Это была своего рода пародия на пение – талантливая, от души и веселая. Как-то раз, в феврале 2007 г., поздним вечером, с высокой температурой и с повязкой на голове, он сидел за компьютером и пел – даже горланил – известную песню про героя гражданской войны на Украине Щорса, идущего под красным знаменем:

Голова обвязана, кровь на рукаве,
След кровавый стелется по сырой траве.

• *Естественная потребность быть всегда в центре событий и способность влиять на их развитие.* Это касалось не только его основной специальности – уралистики и самоедологии, где он задавал тон в решении важнейших проблем. Так памятны его великолепные выступления на различных научных форумах – особенно тогда, когда надо было выступать с ходу, без подготовки и вступать в дискуссии. Нельзя не напомнить, что его деятельность касалась не только науки. Бродя по Вене перед началом симпозиума по славянской этимологии памяти Ф. Миклошича (осенью 1991 г.), некоторые его участники стали свидетелями импровизированного выступления Е. на митинге в поддержку хорватов. В конце 80-х и до падения СССР митинги вообще были его стихией, и мне довелось пару раз участвовать с ним в этих мероприятиях. В январе 1991 г., когда вся прогрессивная Москва вышла протестовать против действий советских войск в Вильнюсе, мне выпала честь нести с Е. написанные им ночью плакаты. Один из них гласил: "Долой банду горбачевцев-ленинцев!"[7] При этом Е.

---

[6] Он был не чужд музыкальных интересов и разбирался в музыке, насколько я успел убедиться по немногим разговорам на эту тему. Для него отнюдь не было пустым звуком, например, имя Р. Вагнера. Он, помнится, рассказывал о различиях восприятия венграми музыки Ф. Листа и Б. Бартока. И прекрасно знал песенный репертуар так называемых бардов (независимых от власти сочинителей и исполнителей песен) советского периода – Б. Окуджава и др.

Вообще, его культурные запросы и познания (кино, театр, поэзия) были весьма широки. Он хорошо знал, например, поэзию украинского гения – Т. Шевченко. Как-то раз мы гуляли по парку недалеко от Winterhudemarkt в Гамбурге и Е., на которого вдруг снизошло вдохновение, целый час оглашал аллеи парка громким чтением стихов Кобзаря наизусть.

[7] Читавшие изготовленные Е. плакаты участники митинга говорили: "Ну, ребята, за такое могут и посадить!" Но со стороны властей явно был приказ никого не трогать. После митинга плакаты пришлось оставить на станции метро "Библиотека имени Ленина", прямо у панно с изображением Ленина. Рядом стоял

имел обыкновение пробираться к самой трибуне (а при случае и выступить), получая затем из разных стран сообщения о том, что тот или иной знакомый видел его по телевизору. На похоронах акад. А. Д. Сахарова Е. был одним из тех, кто нес крышку гроба и так попал на страницы газет.

Он принял активное участие в острейшей политической борьбе, развернувшейся в Москве на закате СССР, сначала как представитель кандидата в народные депутаты СССР (затем и депутата), известного ученого Вяч. Вс. Иванова. "Я хочу оставить моему сыну свободную страну" – так говорил Е. об этой своей деятельности, отнявшей у него много времени, сил и здоровья.[8] Перед ним открывалась карьера профессионального политика, но он, к счастью, не воспользовался этим шансом. И именно тем путем, каким мог пойти Е., когда-то пошел депутат Государственной Думы России С. Юшенков, не так давно застреленный киллерами в Москве.

• *Неукоснительное выполнение задуманного независимо от обстоятельств.* Никаких отступлений от принципа, если только он не будет признан нецелесообразным! Приближавшаяся смерть и неопределенные перспективы уралистики в гамбургском университете ни в коей мере не заставили его отступить от практики пополнения и собственной и инсти-

---

милиционер, и он не сказал ни слова. Помнится, на том митинге Е. между делом долго говорил с кем-то о местоимениях в венгерском.

Впрочем, отношение Е. к коммунистическим идеалам, Ленину могло быть и миролюбиво-юмористическим. Вот два образца то ли сочиненных Е., то ли записанных им от кого-то текстов, посвященных В. И. Ленину:

"Не ест, не пьет, в сердце живет" – загадка (имя Ленина, как утверждала советская пропаганда, живет в сердце каждого советского человека);

"Дедушка умер, а дело живет, лучше бы было наоборот" ("имя и дело" Ленина, по утверждению советской пропаганды, "будет жить в веках"; детям Ленин нередко преподносился как "дедушка").

[8] Воодушевление эпохи "Долой КПСС" сменилось затем глубоким разочарованием и даже чувством вины (не говоря о том, что сыну борьба отца не пригодилась: он был увезен из Москвы в Израиль, где впоследствии и ушел из жизни – почти на шесть лет раньше Е.). "Нашкодил и уехал" – как-то раз из уст Е. прозвучала, уже в Германии, и такая оценка итогов собственной политической деятельности в России. Мнение Е. о политической, культурной и т.п. эволюции посткоммунистической России – и во времена Ельцина и в нынешние времена – было сугубо пессимистическим. Впрочем, об августе 1991 г. он сохранял самые светлые воспоминания. Очень жаль, что взгляды Е. остались известны, в общем, лишь сравнительно узкому кругу людей. Боюсь, что и сейчас вполне актуальны такие, например, его мысли (высказанные в конце прошлого века в связи с обсуждением проблем выживания самодийцев): "В самые последние десятилетия развернулась добыча нефти и газа в Сибири, ведущаяся с нарушением всех экологических и моральных норм... О правовых нормах в СССР и современной России, к сожалению, нельзя говорить всерьез" (Хел. 2000: 33).

тутской библиотек. Еще в октябре 2007 г. он с большим интересом знакомился с поступавшими к нему книгами и просил о доставке новых. В собственно научной работе принцип неукоснительности проявлялся, в частности, в том, что он всегда до конца бился за каждую свою этимологию, неустанно усиливая ее новыми аргументами, вплоть до полного исчерпания ресурсов. "Мы еще можем спасти эту этимологию" – много раз я слышал от него при работе над книгой о самодийско-тунгусских связях. "Спасение", однако, немедленно прекращалось, если обнаруживались неопровержимые свидетельства неправильности этимологии. В сфере политики рассматриваемый принцип Е., пожалуй, был близок к "Pereat mundus, fiat democratia".

За неукоснительностью задуманного стояла твердая и сильная воля Е., временами делавшая общение с ним, несмотря на всю его корректность, не столь уж безоблачным. Общение с ним осложнялось и его склонностью к тому, чтобы озадачить собеседника парадоксальным суждением или неожиданным вопросом, задачей. Поспеть за его быстрым умом было непросто.

• *Чуткость критика.* Подобно тому как хороший дирижер слышит всякую фальшивую ноту, Е. чутко улавливал и отмечал, часто не без сатирического оттенка, всякую лингвистическую (и иную) несуразицу. Вот он читает толкование в русском диалектном словаре: *дугудушка* 'любовница (о женщине)'. На полях появляется его пометка: "А как будет 'любовница (о мужчине)'?".

Его точные и остроумные критические замечания нравились не всем, а кое-кого выводили из себя. Делавший как-то раз доклад о самодийской ономастике известный этнограф, слушая раз за разом подобные замечания, стал терять самообладание. В итоге он стал называть Е. Евгением Абрамовичем. "Я не Евгений Абрамович, я Евгений Арнольдович" – прозвучал наконец протест. Побледневший докладчик вконец утратил контроль над собой: "Извините, Евгений Абрамович, я не хотел Вас обидеть!"

А изредка бывало и так, что критические наклонности Е. переходили в возмущение и он со всей силой своего темперамента обрушивал на голову "провинившегося" нешуточный гнев – в устной или письменной форме. Такое случалось, когда затрагивались особенно важные для Е. научные и прочие ценности. Примером может служить поистине уничтожающая критика Е. в адрес исследования, затронувшего проблемы этнического самосознания обитателей Таймыра.[9]

---

9   "Этническая рознь" на Таймырском Севере (кто ищет, тот всегда найдет...). Рецензия на книгу: Д. Дж. Андерсон. Тундровики: Экология и самосознание таймырских эвенков и долган. Новосибирск, 2000 // *Этнографическое обозрение.* № 5. Москва, 2001. Стр. 173-180.

Уместно сказать, что он был, пожалуй, патриотом малых народов, особенно сибирских. При этом он в целом весьма отрицательно (если не резко отрицательно) относился к самой идее патриотизма – русского или иного – оправдывая ее лишь в той мере, в какой затрагивались язык и культура народа, а также экологической среды его обитания.

Он резко отрицательно относился к попыткам некоторых археологов отстаивать концепцию северного происхождения самодийцев ("маразм"), очень не одобрял часто встречающуюся в научной практике этническую привязку археологических культур на основе одних только археологических данных. Считал методически уязвимыми разработки генетиков по древнейшей этнической истории Сибири.[10] Категорическое неприятие вызывала у него нередкая в советско-российской историографии тенденция отсчитывать культурную историю Сибири только с появления там русских, чему противоречит уже тот факт, что русские города нередко строились на месте поселений аборигенов. Ему была совершенно чужда и попросту враждебна чрезвычайно популярная в России фигура акад. М. В. Ломоносова. Е. видел в Ломоносове не более чем противника ученого с большой буквы – акад. Г. Ф. Миллера, исследованию наследия и вклада которого в разные области науки (история, историческая этнография и топономастика Сибири, формирование научно-интеллектуальной среды в России и проч.) он посвятил очень много времени. Такие взгляды диаметрально противоположны нередкому в России представлению о Миллере-немце – недоброжелателе русского титана мысли и патриота Ломоносова.[11]

Е. считал, что Российская Академия наук должна была бы отмежеваться от посвященной русско-еврейским отношениям в России книги А. И. Солженицына (члена Академии) "200 лет вместе", полагая, что этот труд не безупречен с нравственной точки зрения.[12]

---

[10] Единственный разговор на эту тему возник у нас в связи со статьей: Володько Н. В., Дербенева О. А., Уйнук-Оол Т. С., Сукерник Р. И. Генетическая история алеутов Командорских островов по результатам изменчивости *HLA*-генов II класса // *Генетика*. Том 39. № 12. М., 2003. Стр. 1710-1718.

[11] Е. видел в выступлениях Ломоносова против Миллера предвестие гонений сталинской эпохи на ученых – генетиков, лингвистов и др. Надо заметить, что Е., несомненно, был крупным знатоком истории Российской Академии наук, особенно в XVIII в. О коллизиях между академиками того времени он рассказывал так живо, будто был их современником.

[12] Хотя Е. бесспорно был одним из крупнейших российских лингвистов, его трудно представить членом Российской Академии наук – слишком сильно его взгляды на науку и ученых отличались от характерных для большинства ее членов. Едва ли случайно то, что его попытка баллотироваться в Академию в 2003 г. закончилась ничем: Он выбыл из голосования уже в первом туре.

Способность критически и оригинально мыслить делали взгляды Е. по любому вопросу достойными внимания. К борьбе "сексуальных меньшинств" за свои права он относился без всякой симпатии, как и к самим этим меньшинствам. "Я могу признать их права, но лишь при условии, что будут сначала узаконены многоженство и многомужество – они гораздо более естественны!"

Собственное мнение, существенно отличавшееся от мнения врачей, Е. имел и по поводу собственной болезни и ее лечения. Это приводило к трениям с врачами и к неоднократным побегам из больницы.

• *Глубина и компьютерная скорость умозаключений.* Всегда поражало, что при обращении к любому вопросу он обнаруживает знание и понимание самой сути дела, сути любой проблемы – этимологической или иной. Факты языка (русского, самодийских – любых) он видел как бы в объемном изображении, рассматривая их одновременно в хронологической перспективе, совокупности линий фонетической эволюции, географических координат, особенностей диалектной фиксации и проч. И все это с быстротой компьютера.

Умея тонко понять индивидуальность отдельного слова (факта), он вместе с тем умел видеть его как частичку языка в целом и очень высоко ценил фактор системности. Критические выступления против достижений в изучении древненовгородского диалекта (полученных А. А. Зализняком, С. Л. Николаевым и другими, включая самого Е.) он упрекал как раз в нежелании или неспособности увидеть за отдельными чертами специфическую языковую систему. Сходным образом он относился к критике (Б. И. Татаринцев) в адрес его этимологий, посвященных проблеме тюркского "ротацизма-зетацизма".

Идеи рождались одна за другой. Каждая зажигала Е., который стремился безотлагательно превратить ее в отточенную формулировку. Этот процесс мне посчастливилось не раз видеть. Знакомясь как-то раз с существующими объяснениями слова рус. *аист*, он задумался. Его отрешенный взгляд устремился сначала куда-то в потолок, затем на одну из полок его огромной библиотеки. Через несколько секунд в его руках оказалась монография А. А. Зализняка "Древненовгородский диалект". Последовало восклицание "Ну конечно!", а еще через одну-две минуты он уже излагал содержание своей этимологии: *аист* может быть дериватом от слав. **aje* 'яйцо' с отсутствием йотации,[13] как и в древненовгородском ругательстве *аесова*, букв. 'сователь яйца'.

---

[13]   Эта этимология изложена в книге: Аникин А. Е. *Русский этимологический словарь.* Вып. 1. М., 2007. Стр. 117. Вместе с тем, Е. посвятил ей специальную публикацию (см. в очередном выпуске *Балто-славянских исследований*, посвященном памяти В. Н. Топорова; находится в печати).

Болезни не удалось ни йоту подорвать мощь интеллекта Е., который перестал действовать лишь тогда, когда его тело пришло к окончательному упадку.

• *Новаторство в рамках академической строгости.* Оставаясь верным лучшим традициям академической строгости в уралистике (славистике и др.), Е. был выдающимся новатором в науке, настойчиво развивавшим взгляды, уточнявшие и дополнявшие – не разрушавшие! – существующую систему знаний. Его вклад в уралистику оценят его коллеги-уралисты. Мне довелось стать свидетелем создания научного завещания Е. в области уральской реконструкции и этимологии – "Marginalia ad UEW", где боровшийся со смертельной болезнью автор четко очертил новые перспективы во всех отраслях этой области знания resp. для всех уральских языков. Он не пожалел немалой части оставшегося ему скудного срока жизни, чтобы переписать всю самодийскую часть упоминавшейся книги о самодийско-тунгусских связях на основе уточненной концепции прасамодийского вокализма.

Новизна его взглядов и решений нередко шла вразрез с существующей исследовательской практикой. Здесь уместно привести пространные цитаты из представляющихся весьма важными суждений Е. относительно того "распространенного направления этимологического поиска в индоевропеистике (славистике, германистике, балтистике, кельтологии),[14] которое ориентировано на поиск индоевропейских этимонов для максимального числа (в идеале, пожалуй, для всех) слов, представленных в древних и современных языках".[15] Ср. далее: "При этом остается неучтенным то обстоятельство, что все индоевропейские языки Европы впитали в себя огромную массу доиндоеропейского субстрата, и поэтому для любого слова без очевидных индоевропейских связей (особенно если оно относится к сферам названий растений и животных, ландшафтной терминологии, экспрессивной лексики…) субстратное и вообще контактное происхождение a priori намного более вероятно, чем исконное. В итоге можно заподозрить, что, например, более или менее правдоподобной индоевропейской этимологией уже снабжено в полтора-два раза больше славянских слов, чем имеется слов индоевропейского происхождения в славянском. Можно, конечно, психологически понять нежелание из раза в раз повторять на страницах этимологических словарей комментарий типа "Скорее всего, заимствование из несохранившегося доиндоевропейского языка Ев-

---

[14] К сожалению, мне не довелось поинтересоваться у Е. относительно его мнения по поводу "праевропейского субстрата" В. Махека и сходных идей у других ученых.

[15] Хелимский Е. А. Трансъевразийские аспекты русской этимологии // *Русский язык в научном освещении.* № 2(4), 2000. Стр. 84.

ропы, непосредственный источник не поддается установлению и анализу", хотя именно такого рода комментарий должен, на мой взгляд, во многих случаях предварять все дальнейшие гадания на индоевропейской гуще".[16]

Не знаю, изложил ли Е. в какой-либо своей публикации свои взгляды на развитие индоевропейского языкознания, которое, как ему представлялось, эволюционирует "куда-то не туда". Его настораживало буйное развитие ларингалистики, создававшей, наряду с другими ресурсами индоевропейской этимологии, возможности для разного рода искусственных построений в области изучения индоевропейско-уральских связей.

• *Импульсивность – основательность.* "Я никогда не вымучиваю то, что пишу. Или получается сразу или не получается совсем. Изредка я начинаю что-то делать повторно, но если и тогда не выходит, бросаю окончательно" – так Е. примерно за год до кончины говорил о своей манере писать статьи. Его импульсивность проявлялась не только в осуществлении научных замыслов, но и в быту. Он мог, например, прямо посреди улицы упасть на колени перед встречной собакой и вступить с ней в дружескую беседу.

Эмоция, как и идея, могла захватить Е. целиком и сразу, с огромной силой. Я хорошо помню вечер 30 сентября 2005 г., кафе "Бочка" на Миллионной улице в Петербурге после заседания типологической конференции в Институте лингвистических исследований. Дегустация сочетания "водка с перцем + пиво" (до этого – большое возлияние в Институте), и вдруг звонок на мобильный телефон (В. В. Напольских) и сообщение о смерти С. А. Старостина. На Е., еще минуту назад пребывавшего в состоянии спокойствия и умиротворения, было страшно смотреть. Он сотрясался от рыданий и долго не мог вымолвить ни слова.[17]

Ему было скорее чуждым стремление к крупной форме сочинений и уж тем более довольно распространенная тенденция усматривать в количестве написанного (в толщине книги) едва ли не основной критерий оценки работы ученого.[18] Сформулировать замысел (мысль) и отдать его

---

[16] Там же. "Индоевропейская гуща" отсылает к выражению "гадать на кофейной гуще". Не могу сказать, случайно ли у Е. совпадение с "кофейной гущей" в известной статье И. В. Сталина 1952 г., где разоблачалось учение акад. Н. Я. Марра о языке.

[17] Е. рассказывал, что познакомился со Старостиным будучи первокурсником, во время дня открытых дверей, когда будущие абитуриенты приходят знакомиться с университетом. Получилось так, что Е. подал школьнику Старостину пальто. Е. очень любил его, чрезвычайно высоко ценил его лингвистический талант, хотя и расходился с ним в понимании методов реконструктивно-этимологической работы.

[18] Однажды я поделился с Е. соображением, что Ф. де Соссюр мог бы не пройти в советском научном институте аттестацию, и Е. со мной согласился.

для реализации подходящему соавтору – такова была тенденция последних лет жизни Е., чему способствовали частые депрессии. И приводить лишь необходимый и достаточный минимум материала – этот принцип отчетливо проявился, например, в его книге "Die matorische Sprache", которую при желании легко было бы сделать намного толще. Упомянутая книга о самодийско-тунгусских лексических связях, если бы Е. писал ее в одиночку, скорее всего была бы не книгой, а статьей. Он был автором и соавтором более чем десятка монографий, но все-таки именно сотни статей и тезисов докладов к конференциям, т.е. более или менее краткие воплощения различных его идей, составляют основное содержание его научного наследия.

И вместе с тем он мог годами вести научные разыскания по одной и той же теме (например, по рукописному наследию Г. Ф. Миллера). Не спеша с завершением, годами тщательно накапливать материал по множеству тем и классифицировать его. Результатом такой работы стал огромный архив, содержащий обширные данные по множеству задуманных, начатых или незавершенных проектов. Некоторые, как можно надеяться, еще будут завершены. А были и такие проекты, от реализации которых он отказался – например, от доказательства связи между латышскими интонациями и эстонскими степенями долготы. А сколько идей и замыслов он унес с собой… В октябре 2007 г. он всерьез собирался заняться, например, анализом отношений славянских имен и глаголов типа *гной – гноить* и с одобрением вспоминал в этой связи работы по словообразованию Ю. В. Откупщикова ("Откупщиков – это голова!").[19]

• *Эстетически совершенная форма выражения* смелой и размашистой мысли, нередко (при наличии критического заряда) окрашенная иронией – яркая черта стиля научных работ Е.

Вот характерный пример: "пресловутые *нарцы* Нестора – не народ и не племя, а союз, причем союз не племенной, а грамматический" (Хел. 2000: 333).[20]

Аналогом стиля Е. является его удивительный почерк[21] – быстрый, разборчивый, без излишеств и в то же время изящный.

---

19 См. в особенности: Откупщиков Ю. В. *Очерки по индоевропейскому словообразованию*. Ленинград, 1967. Правда, к разысканиям того же автора по субстратной балтийской гидронимии Е. относился весьма критически.

20 Этот образец страдает тем недостатком, что как раз в данном случае Е., по-видимому, был неправ, хотя и не признал этого.

21 К осени 2007 г. Е. полностью потерял способность писать правой рукой и с трудом осваивал левой рукой искусство подписываться.

• *"Говорит, как пишет"*.[22] Я как-то поделился с Е. наблюдением, что его манера говорить напоминает известного скрипача Гидона Кремера. Е. ответил, что сходство действительно есть, и состоит оно в книжности устной речи. Он мог обратиться к кошке Ксюше со следующей речью: "Очередная порция «Феликса» или «Юлии»[23] может быть положена в блюдечко лишь при том условии, что предыдущая съедена полностью. Исключения невозможны, как и увеличение размера порции. Но есть возможность воспользоваться тем блюдечком, где лежит сухая пища". Все это произносилось так, как если бы он выступал с официальной речью.

Конечно, при необходимости и желании Е. мог говорить проще – но всегда изящно и остроумно, часто переиначивая сказанное собеседником. Вот два образца диалогов с участием Е. в качестве отвечающей стороны:

– Наверное, руководство университета было бы неприятно удивлено, если бы узнало, что прибывший на стажировку в университет сотрудник побывал на Репербане?[24]

– Оно было бы неприятно удивлено, если бы узнало, что он там не побывал!;

– Тебе приходилось иметь отношения с антисемитами?

– Я имею отношения с моей женой Ирмой, она со мной, я антисемит,[25] – значит, я постоянно имею отношения с антисемитом!

• *Аскетизм & гедонизм*. Е. всегда мало ел и (в лучшие годы) довольно мало спал, и в этом смысле был аскетом. Вместе с тем, он был не чужд удовольствий, связанных с пищей и особенно с питьем. "Немецкое пиво оно и в Израиле немецкое пиво" – говорил он после поездки в эту страну в 2005 г.

Понятие завтрака было ему чуждо. День начинался с сигарет, придатком к которым часов в 8-9 утра становился стакан кофе без сахара, причем, кофе растворимого и довольно посредственного. Часов в 11-12 он мог съесть, скажем, одну-две ягодки (малина, клубника) или виноградины. Обеда, в общем, тоже как правило не было – чаще бутерброд или сладости. Ужин, правда имел место, – в последние годы это было что-нибудь вроде котлеты или гамбургера. В целом, прием пищи воспринимался им как тягостная необходимость или даже зло. Тем, кто, по его мнению, много ел (например, автору этих строк), он сочувствовал.

Имея обыкновение работать чуть не до утра, он любил ночью подкрепиться десертом. Дома было всегда полно конфитюров, сладкого сгу-

---

[22] Ср. в знаменитой комедии А. С. Грибоедова *Горе от ума*: "Что говорит! И говорит, как пишет!".

[23] Известные марки кошачьих консервов, которыми Е. кормил свою кошку.

[24] Район Гамбурга, где расположены публичные дома.

[25] См. прим. 26.

щеного молока, шоколада, кексов, пирожных, сладких булочек, йогуртов. Случалась халва, желательно российская. Все это съедалось с большим удовольствием. И конечно, любимое блюдо – мороженое, которое настолько благотворно действовало на Е., что выступало фактически и в качестве лекарства.

• *Хитрость.* В начале 90-х гг. я жил в общежитии Академии Наук СССР в Москве, и однажды мой сосед по комнате, особенно не скрывавший свои националистические воззрения, не без язвительности сообщил мне: "К тебе приходил какой-то хитрый еврей".[26] Е., который и был тем самым евреем, по-видимому, нашел эту спонтанную характеристику проницательной и не возражал против нее, – как и против еще одной, прозвучавшей при мне однажды (1993 г.) из уст Надежды Костеркиной, дочери нганасанского сказителя Тубяку Костеркина: "Ты, Женя, прямо как старый еврей".[27] Ответ Е. был "Почему «как»?".

Ум и хитрость – не одно и то же. Хитрость у Е. была, хотя и не относилась к наиболее важным чертам его характера, и жизнь иногда вынуждала его пользоваться этой чертой. Вот пример. В начале 90-х гг. он приобрел квартиру в Солнцево под Москвой, но получилось так, что на эту квартиру появился еще один претендент, отчество которого было не какое-нибудь, а Рюрикович. Ни о планах его действий, ни о нем самом ничего, кроме адреса, не было известно, и Е. придумал разведку с моим участием: я прихожу к Рюриковичу домой, представляюсь социальным работником и узнаю, что могу, о его намерениях. Хитрость в целом удалась. Главное было в том, что у противника совсем не такие уж плохие квартирные условия (совсем не бедствует), в то время как Е. ничего кроме упомянутой квартиры не имел. Правда была на стороне Е. и борьба Рюриковича с Арнольдовичем закончилась в конечном счете в пользу последнего.

• *Гусарские замашки.* В лучшие годы жизни – когда было здоровье – Е. часто демонстрировал гусарскую лихость. Вот лишь один эпизод его гусарства, связанный с его последним приездом в Новосибирск в феврале 2001 г., главным образом для приобретения селькупских материалов А. И. Кузминой.

Дорога из аэропорта в гостиницу шла по отдаленным районам Новосибирска ("Затулинка"). Был поздний вечер, холодно и темно, мела

---

[26] Об антисемитизме Е. однажды высказался примерно так: "Это как инвалидность. Будто у человека нет руки или ноги". Для лучшего представления об упомянутом "антисемитизме" Е. уместно процитировать сочиненную им притчу. "Эйнштейн и Гитлер не были современниками: Эйнштейн раньше родился, а Гитлер раньше умер. Поэтому Гитлер мылся по нескольку раз в день, а Эйнштейн совсем не любил мыться. Dirty Jews live long – long live dirty Jews!".

[27] И Надя, и ее муж Толя, и Тубяку Костеркин – люди, близкие Е., – все уже отошли в мир иной.

метель. В тесном автобусе появился сомнительного вида гражданин, который вскоре извлек из кармана пистолет, явно настоящий.[28] Он хотел развлечься, привлечь к себе внимание, попугать пассажиров. "Вот, зарплату получил, купил пушку!" Всем стало не по себе, – только не Е. Он был в веселом расположении духа. Подобно революционному матросу, он рывком расстегнул пальто. "Стреляй, сволочь!" – крикнул он ровно так, как это сделал бы герой какого-нибудь советского фильма про революцию и гражданскую войну, подставляющий грудь под вражеские пули. С его стороны это была бравада, шутка. Дядька с пистолетом растерялся. Вскоре он вышел из автобуса и исчез со своим пистолетом в снежной мгле.

И еще один эпизод, – связанный с путешествием по Оби на теплоходе (начало сентября 2005 г.) по давнему маршруту Г. Ф. Миллера и параллельной конференцией на борту. На пристани Октябрьское неожиданно для всех и для себя самого Е. был принят в местное казачье войско. Атаманом оказался директор рыбозавода, великан с громовым голосом. "Кто у вас старший!? Ты, Евгений? Давай выпьем с тобой по стакану водки и ты станешь нашим казаком!". Атаман вручил Е. казацкую шашку и совершил обряд посвящения в казаки. Е. затем передал оружие в музей Ханты-Мансийска. И хорошо сделал, поскольку и он сам, и его попутчики так интенсивно им размахивали, что добром бы история с шашкой не кончилось. Но в памяти своих попутчиков Е. остался с шашкой в руках, посреди множества бутылок. Он мог пить много и водки и пива и чего угодно, все подряд, изумляя окружающих тем, что нисколько не теряет самоконтроля, ясности мыслей и речи. На теплоходе он сорил деньгами, так что его банковский счет в конце поездки заметно уменьшился. Сидящий среди бутылок довольный Е. изображен на многих фотографиях разного времени. Да и я сам впервые в жизни увидел его в начале 80-х гг. за стаканом ракии.

Проявлением гусарства у Е. было, конечно, и несколько бесшабашное отношение к своему здоровью ("меня никакая хворь не берет") и такое же – и даже несколько циничное – отношение к смерти. Вот об этом стоит пожалеть…

• *Любовь к животным*. В наследство от погибшего сына Е. досталась кошка Ксюша – изящное и весьма своенравное существо, которое он боготворил. Конечно на его отношении к ней сказалось то, что она олицетворяла память о сыне. В последние годы Е. жил довольно замкнуто, и кошка в немалой степени заменяла ему общество людей. Хотя она и содержалась довольно строго в том, что касалось пищи (здесь сказывались и привычки самого Е., которые, кстати, кошке шли только на пользу), во всем осталь-

---

[28] Для желающих поехать в Новосибирск специально сообщаю, что описываемый случай с пистолетом не типичен. Других таких случаев на моей памяти нет.

ном ей, как священному животному, предоставлялась полная свобода – например, в праве ходить по клавиатуре компьютера или немножко подрать какую-нибудь книгу. Разговоры с кошкой[29] и игры с ней, совместный отдых на диване или в кресле занимали много времени. "Ух, поймаю эту кошку! Сейчас поймаю!" – и начиналась игра в прятки до упаду.

"Ксюша, обрати, пожалуйста, внимание, на сумку Александра Евгеньевича![30] Неужели тебе не хочется узнать, что в ней? Наверняка там, если покопаться хорошенько, можно найти много интересных вещей. Я очень рекомендую тебе заняться сумкой и как следует подрать ее и содержимое когтями! И вообще, ты уделяешь Александру Евгеньевичу слишко мало внимания. Почему бы тебе не попробовать, насколько у него крепкие штаны?!"

Над миской с кошачьей едой висел листик со стихами от лица Ксюши:

> В блюдечко положено
> То, что мне положено.
> А что не положено,
> То мне не положено.

При отсутствии Е. Ксюша не находила себе места, а по его возвращении домой не оставляла ни на минуту. Подходя (особенно вечером, когда все стихало) к своему дому на Alsterdorferstrasse в Гамбурге, Е. поднимал взгляд на третий этаж, к окну своей квартиры и еще с улицы вступал в общение с кошкой, нарушая покой тихой улочки и громко крича на кошачий лад: "Мяу-мяу, Ксюша!". Можно было услышать и ответное мяукание. Увы, когда Е. в ноябре 2007 г. слег и потерял способность ходить и говорить, Ксюша перестала отождествлять его с прежним своим хозяином и пребывала в состоянии постоянного стресса – пока ее не забрали Паула и Уве,[31] в доме которых она бывала и раньше и где чувствовала (и чувствует) себя очень хорошо.

Разумеется, отношение Е. к Ксюше было проявлением его любви к животным вообще, которая проявлялась и в теории. Он возмущался, например, тем, что для кошек и собак существуют ограничения при переездах самолетом. "Животные куда менее опасны, чем люди!"

---

[29] Речи, обращенные к кошке, были постоянными и отличались от разговоров с людьми лишь использованием междометий: "Мяу, Ксюша, мяу, – ну конечно ты права!".

[30] Т.е. автора этих строк, приехавшего в Гамбург.

[31] Paula Jääsalmi-Krueger (Institut für Finno-Ugristik/Uralistik, Universität Hamburg) и ее муж, Uwe Krueger.

Е. был готов признать, что привязанность к кошке в ущерб отношениям с людьми ненормальна ("живу бирюком"[32]), но не мог ничего с этим поделать, Стремление уединиться с кошкой, заменившей ему семью, шло от депрессивных состояний, которые начались еще в 90-х гг., но стали особенно частыми после смерти сына в 2002 г. Е. говорил, что склонность к депрессиям наследственная – от отца.

*   *
*

Что сказать в заключение этих отрывочных заметок? Е. ушел из жизни рано, и эту утрату ничем не заменить. Его отъезд из России стал потерей для России,[33] его смерть стала потерей для европейской и мировой науки. И его жизнь и его смерть оказались полны трагизма. Он не осуществил множества замыслов, на нем прервался род его предков. Он один из ученых тех поколений, которое состоялись в науке в первые послевоенные десятилетия – и смогут ли будущие поколения дать адекватные замены таким крупным фигурам, как Е.? Что ждет в будущем те научные направления, которые он развивал?

Сам он смотрел вперед с оптимизмом. Уже будучи больным, он был не прочь порассуждать насчет того, что лет через 200 историческое языкознание будет жить, и, скажем, его аварско-славянские разыскания сохранят свою значимость.

Нам остается зарядиться этим оптимизмом и верой Е. в лучшие судьбы науки. Нам остается его научное наследие и его образ – единственное в своем роде сочетание мощного интеллекта, темперамента и обаяния, прогонявшее прочь рутину, косность и нелепицу.

Vitabit Libitinam.

Александр Е. Аникин
ул. Жемчужная, д. 28, кв. 28
RUS – 630090 Новосибирск

---

[32] Едва ли нужно говорить, что в лучшие годы круг общения Е. был чрезвычайно широк.

[33] Он уехал из-за безденежья, плохих жилищных условий и т.п. Отчего случилось так, что Россию покинули большинство крупных ученых?

Studia Etymologica Cracoviensia
vol. 14   Kraków 2009

Michael KNÜPPEL (Göttingen)

ERINNERUNGEN AN EINEN GROßEN SIBIRISTEN – ZUM TODE VON E. A. HELIMSKI

Überschattet wurden die Weihnachtsfeiertage des Jahres 2007 von einem traurigen, jedoch nicht ganz unerwartet eingetretenen Ereignis – dem Verscheiden des in Hamburg lehrenden Uralisten Prof. Dr. Eugen Helimski (Jevgenij Arnoľdovič Chelimskij) in der Nacht vom 24. auf den 25. Dezember. Es war dies ein Heimgang, durch den freilich nicht nur die Uralistik eines ihrer bedeutendsten Vertreter beraubt wurde, sondern vielmehr auch die Sibiristik in einer sehr viel umfassenderen Breite – war Prof. Helimski doch über die Uralistik hinausgreifend auf den Forschungsfeldern der sogenannten "Paläoasiatik" und der Altaistik ebenso wirksam wie an über eine reine Linguistik hinausreichenden historisch-vergleichenden Fragestellungen – etwa zu kulturhistorischen und religionswissenschaftlichen Zusammenhängen – interessiert und in der Lage auch hier Bemerkenswertes zu leisten. Der Vf. des vorliegenden Beitrags möchte an dieser Stelle nicht bei den zahllosen Verdiensten des Verstorbenen in so unterschiedlichen Bereichen wie der Samojedologie, der allgemeinen Uralistik, der Altaistik, ling. Rekonstruktionen, der Nostratik etc. etc. verweilen (diese mögen anderenorts gewürdigt werden), sondern bloß einige vereinzelte persönliche Erinnerungen Revue passieren lassen.

Gern erinnert sich der Vf. dieser Zeilen zurück an die vielen interessanten und fruchtbaren Begegnungen mit Prof. Helimski, der mit diesem das Interesse an den Sprachen und Kulturen des nördlichen Eurasien in ihrer faszinierenden Vielfalt teilte. Niemals war hier der Blickwinkel des Verstorbenen "nur" auf die ural. Völker und Sprachen beschränkt, nie erblickte er – ganz im Gegensatz zu bedauerlich vielen anderen – in Sibirien ein zusammenhangsloses Nebeneinander verschiedener Völker, Sprachen und Kulturen. Und selbst dann, wenn Prof. Helimski sich zu rein uralist. Fragestellungen äußerte, war sein Blick stets über den engeren Gegenstand hinausgerichtet und der Fundus, auf den er hier zurückzugreifen vermochte, wirklich beeindruckend.

Mit Dankbarkeit erinnert sich der Vf. an die zahllosen Ermutigungen, sich weiter und immer eingehender mit den Völkern Nordeurasiens, ihren Sprachen, Religionen und Kulturen auseinanderzusetzen und die unzähligen Anregungen, die hier stets von dem leider viel zu früh Verstorbenen kamen. Dies umso mehr als die Befassung mit den Völkern und Sprachen allzu vielen anderen "Kollegen" als geradezu befremdend erschien und bisweilen noch immer erscheint. Das babylonische Sprachengewirr an den Rändern und in den sibirischen Eiswüsten und die Namen von Völkern in diesem geographischen Großraum, die nur wenigen "Eingeweihten" bekannt zu sein scheinen, mußten jeden Türkei-Kundler, der sich für einen Turkologen hielt, natürlich ebenso abschrecken, wie jene Hungarologen und Fennisten, die in der ural. Verwandtschaft im Osten allenfalls so etwas wie ein Ärgernis erblickten. Nicht selten wurde die Befassung auch des Vf.s dieser Zeilen mit den Völkern und Sprachen Sibiriens in armseliger Begrenztheit und vollkommener Verkennung der Bedeutung dieses Raumes für die Turkologie, wie auch für nicht gerade wenige andere Forschungsrichtungen, als "abwegig", "zu weit am Rande liegend" oder gar als "reine Zeitverschwendung" abgetan. Welch einen Gegensatz zu solcher Ignoranz bildete doch die Haltung Prof. Helimskis, der nicht nur stets unterstützend wirkte und interessiert war, sondern zudem durch einen beeindruckenden Erfahrungsschatz und einen bisweilen übermenschlich erscheinenden Fleiß dazu befähigt war, hier in einer Weise disziplinenübergreifend Hilfestellung zu leisten, wie dies nur ganz wenigen Vertretern der verschiedenen, von seinen Interessen berührten Forschungsfeldern möglich gewesen wäre und möglich ist!

Nicht selten waren die Vorträge Prof. Helimskis auf diversen Tagungen und Symposien einer der Höhepunkte – wenn nicht gar *der* Höhepunkt – der betreffenden Veranstaltung und mitunter waren die Plaudereien mit dem Verstorbenen am Rande dieser Veranstaltungen – etwa am Buffet oder beim Kaffee – lehrreicher und fruchtbarer als die Vorträge aller übrigen Referenten. Der Vf. erinnert sich hier an die von ihm häufig nach erfolgten Einladungen gestellten Fragen, die etwa lauteten: "Kommt Helimski auch dort hin?" oder "Wird Helimski einen Vortrag halten?". Stets waren diese Begegnungen dann *die* Gelegenheit, sich entweder über die jeweils eigenen laufenden Arbeiten und zukünftige Projekte oder gerade aktuelle Entwicklungen, Neuerscheinungen oder die Ergebnisse der Arbeiten der Kollegen aus den verschiedenen Disziplinen, die selbst keine Gelegenheit fanden, teilzunehmen, auszutauschen. So erinnert der Vf. sich noch der mit dem Verstorbenen am Rande der Jahrestagung der SUA im Göttinger Michaelishaus lebhaft geführten Diskussion hinsichtlich des in einem seiner jüngsten Beiträge (cf. *Komparativistika, uralistika. Staťi i lekcii.* Moskva 2000, pp. 243-266) gewählten methodischen Zugangs zur altaischen Frage. Eine faszinierende Diskussion, über die beinahe die folgenden Veranstaltungsteile vergessen worden wären. Es war eine wirkliche Freude, mit Prof. Helimski solche Diskussionen zu führen. Einerseits, weil dieser die Diskussion und Kontroverse ja offenkundig schätzte (so ließ er den Vf. bei einer Gelegenheit einmal wissen, daß eine erfolgreich angeregte Kontroverse, eine "kleine Provokation", die den wissenschaftlichen Diskurs in Gang bringt, häufig mehr wert sein kann, als die – oftmals nur vermeintliche – Lösung eines Problems, was zweifellos zutreffen dürfte) und andererseits weil der Verstorbene ein wirklich angenehmer Diskussionspartner war – offen für andere Ansichten, stets in der Lage seinen Standpunkt mit gewichtigen und messerscharfen Argumenten, ohne jeden Anflug von Überheblichkeit, zu verteidigen und vor allem stets kompetent! Wie lehrreich und unterhaltsam zugleich konnte dieser Austausch doch immer wieder sein. Um wie Vieles werden in dieser Hinsicht künftige Veranstaltungen ärmer sein? – Und dies dürfte sicher nicht nur eine Befürchtung des Vf.s sein.

Bemerkenswert war freilich auch der Umstand, daß mit Prof. Helimski ein ausgedehnter Austausch auf Forschungsfeldern möglich war, für die es ja sonst so gut wie keine Ansprechpartner außerhalb Rußlands gab. Der Vf. möchte hier bloß an die jukagirischen Studien erinnern – eines der zahllosen gemeinsamen Interessen. Gerade hier bestand ein besonders für den Vf. lehrreicher und interessanter Kontakt, obgleich Prof. Helimski und selbiger etwa in der Frage der "uralo-jukagirischen Frage" bekanntlich recht unterschiedliche Auffassungen vertraten: war die genet. Verwandtschaft des Jukagirischen mit den ural. Sprachen vor rund 5-7.000 Jahren für Prof. Helimski eine konkrete Möglichkeit, stand (und steht) der Vf. solchen entfernten Verwandtschaftsverhältnissen schon aus prinzipiellen Gründen skeptisch bis ablehnend gegenüber. Die recht unterschiedliche Sicht des Problems der Verwandtschaftsverhältnisse der jukag. Idiome (wie auch die Haltung zu anderen Forschungsrichtungen, welche "entferntere Verwandtschaftsverhältnisse" zum Gegenstand haben) hat den Austausch jedoch in keinerlei Weise getrübt – dies nicht zuletzt, da Prof. Helimski über dem kleinlichen Gezänk stand, in welches sich die meisten Verfechter wie Gegner der "uralo-jukag. Frage" so gern verzettelt haben (für die altaische Frage gilt im Übrigen Ähnliches). Stets war Prof. Helimski an allen Neuigkeiten interessiert und bereit seine teils überragenden Kenntnisse und Erkenntnisse in Bezug auf das Jukagirische zu teilen. Wohl nur ganz wenige dürften auf diesem Felde Vergleichbares vorweisen können. So ließ er dem Vf. stets Kopien neuerer (zumeist eher schwer zugänglicher) Beiträge zum Jukagirischen ebenso zukommen, wie die Unterrichtsmaterialien und Tischvorlagen seiner eigenen Veranstaltungen im Hamburger Institut. Darüber hinaus fand Prof. Helimski immer auch die Zeit zu wahrhaft ausgedehnten Behandlungen interessanter Einzelprobleme der jukag. Idiome über Telephon und Internet. So erinnert sich der Vf. noch mit großer Freude an Prof. Helimskis Ausführungen hinsichtlich seiner Betrachtungen zum jukag. Satz-Focus-System – ein Telephonat von mehr als zweieinhalb Stunden! Wer findet heutzutage – trotz flatrate – noch die Zeit für solche "Fernseminare", von dem Problem, daß sich ja offenbar kaum jemand näher mit dem Jukagirischen befaßt hat oder befassen möchte, einmal ganz abgesehen. Welchen Verlust die jukag. Studien mit dem Tode Prof. Helimskis – nicht nur in Deutschland, sondern ganz allgemein – erlitten haben, wird sich wohl nur den wenigsten erschließen.

Ähnlich wie mit der Teilnahme an diversen Tagungen und Kongressen verhielt es sich mit den jeweils neuesten Publikationen Prof. Helimskis, denen der Vf. – ebenso, wie zahlreiche Kollegen – mit Spannung und großen Erwartungen entgegensahen. Erwartungen, die dann nicht enttäuscht wurden. Und nach der Lektüre jedes Beitrages, dessen Erscheinen so sehr entgegengefiebert wurde, stand für den Vf., wie für viele andere, stets fest, daß Warten wie Lektüre sich unbedingt gelohnt hatten. Sehr gut noch vermag der Vf., der der Lektüre russischer Texte nur bedingt befähigt war, sich an die für ein wirkliches Verständnis der russ. Arbeiten Helimskis erforderlichen Übersetzungsarbeiten mit der Hilfe "Pawlowskis" zu erinnern. Aufwendige und bisweilen zeitraubende Unternehmungen, die nach dem Empfinden des Vf.s ohnehin nur die Publikationen einiger bestimmter Sibiristen – unter diesen natürlich jene Prof. Helimskis – zu rechtfertigen schienen. War die Arbeit dann vollbracht, so stellte sich niemals das Gefühl ein, Zeit vertan zu haben. Wenn nun auch hoffentlich noch für die folgenden Jahre mit posthum erscheinenden Beiträgen Prof. Helimskis zu rechnen sein wird, so wird dies doch niemals mehr dasselbe sein können wie zuvor: fehlt doch zum einen der in der Vergangenheit häufig folgende Austausch mit dem Vf. derselben und werden zum anderen mit künftigen posthumen Schriften wohl kaum noch Anstöße zu Kontroversen gegeben, "die den wissenschaftlichen Diskurs in Gang bringen" (dies entweder aus falsch verstandener Pietät oder aus schlichter Ignoranz).

All jenen, die das Vergnügen der Diskussion mit dem Verstorbenen hatten – und wohl mehr noch jenen, die in einem sehr viel unmittelbareren Kontakt mit ihm gestanden haben, als der Vf. dieser Zeilen, war der Verlust, den das Verscheiden Prof. Helimskis für die verschiedenen Forschungsfelder, auf denen er lange Jahre gewirkt hat, bedeutet, ohnehin schon beim Empfang der betrüblichen Nachricht gegenwärtig – vielen anderen wird sich dieser wohl erst allmählich offenbaren. Ohne in die bei solchen traurigen Anlässen leider allzu üblichen Lobhudeleien verfallen zu müssen, kann an dieser Stelle der Heimgang eines großen Sibiristen bedauert werden.

Michael Knüppel
Seminar für Turkologie und Zentralasienkunde
der Georg-August-Universität Göttingen
Waldweg 26
D – 37073 Göttingen

Studia Etymologica Cracoviensia
vol. 14   Kraków 2009

Anna WIDMER (Hamburg)

ERINNERUNG AN EUGEN HELIMSKI

Obwohl ich von Erinnerungen an Eugen Helimski auch vier Monate nach seinem Tod unverändert durchflutet bin, fällt es mir schwer, von ihm zu schreiben, ohne seine Laufbahn und die Ergebnisse seiner wissenschaftlichen Arbeit zu fokussieren. Er war einfach durch und durch Wissenschaftler.

Ende der 80er Jahre bin ich dem Namen Evgenij Arnoľdovič Chelimskijs zum ersten Mal begegnet, im Selkupisch-Unterricht meines damaligen Lehrers Hartmut Katz an der Universität München – sein samojedologisches Werk wurde von Hartmut Katz, ebenfalls Spezialist der samojedischen Sprachen, hoch geschätzt und immer wieder zitiert. Bald darauf, im Sommer 1990, beim *Congressus Septimus Internationalis Fenno-Ugristarum* in Debrecen/Ungarn, bin ich ihm auch persönlich begegnet: Es ergab sich, daß wir bei einem Vortrag nebeneinander zu sitzen kamen, und Hartmut Katz sagte mir, um wen es sich beim jungen, schlanken, schwarzlockigen, bärtigen Mann mit der fein geschnittenen Nase und den großen, leicht schräg stehenden Augen handelte. An den Vortrag selbst erinnere ich mich nicht mehr, aber an Eugen Helimski in der betreffenden Situation umso deutlicher: Nach dem Vortrag meldete er sich zu Wort und lieferte einen seiner Diskussionsbeiträge, die ich noch so oft in ähnlicher Weise erleben durfte. Er erhob sich mit einer leichten Bewegung zur Seite hin und sprach, unbeirrt durch seine Suche nach Wörtern in der entsprechenden Fremdsprache, mit ungeheurer Autorität, Dynamik, Energie und Konzentration.

Ein Jahr später, im November 1991, sahen wir uns in Groningen wieder, bei dem *Symposium aus Anlass des 25-jährigen Bestehens der Finnougristik an der Rijksuniversiteit Groningen* mit dem Titel "Finnisch-ugrische Sprachen zwischen dem germanischen und dem slavischen Sprachraum". Wir wurden einander vorgestellt und zu viert – mit ihm, Hartmut Katz und meinem späteren Kollegen Tiborc Fazekas, der damals schon am Finnisch-Ugrischen Seminar in Hamburg arbeitete, wo Eugen Helimski fast zehn Jahre später mein Vorgesetzter werden sollte – gingen wir in ein Restaurant. Die Samojedologen bestellten status- und standesgemäß gleich mehrere der winzig kleinen Gläser niederländischen Bieres gleichzeitig, um nicht so lange aufs nächste warten zu müssen, und rauchten die stärksten Zigaretten, die im Handel erhältlich waren. Mangels Pa-

pier wurden die Bierdeckel zweckentfremdet und mit Etymologien vollgekrit-
zelt, man tauschte sich über die letzten Vorträge aus und über finnougristische
Werke, die in letzter Zeit erschienen waren. Ich war von der Gesellschaft und in
erster Linie von Eugen Helimski so fasziniert, daß Hartmut Katz nach dieser
Kongreßreise im Unterricht über ihn zum Vergnügen meiner Kommilitonen und
zu meinem Verdruß immer nur als "dein Eugen" sprach.

Gespräche wie dieses erste in Groningen, bei Bier und dichtem Tabakrauch,
sollten zwischen uns noch öfter stattfinden – über Sprachwissenschaft, seine
Forschungsreisen, Literatur, Musik, Religion, Politik, Geschichte, Fußball, seine
Familie und Freunde, Emanzipation – und nicht zuletzt über die moralische,
motorische und ästhetische Überlegenheit der Familie der Felidae. Auch als ich
seine Assistentin am IFUU Hamburg war, bedienten wir uns im nahegelegenen
Restaurant "Backatelle" häufiger der polyfunktionalen Bierdeckel. Da wurden
nun auch weniger erfreuliche Sachen skizziert als Etymologien, manchmal ver-
suchten wir so naiverweise den herangaloppierenden Amts- und Verwaltungs-
schimmel zu zähmen.

Das deutsche Universitätssystem, das er im Anschluß an seine diesbezüglich noch idyllisch angenehmen Forschungsaufenthalte in Berlin mit seiner Be-
rufung auf den Hamburger Lehrstuhl im Jahre 1998 noch sehr gut kennenlernen
sollte, war ihm in vielen Punkten zuwider. So klagte er auch zunehmend über
die bürokratischen Pflichten, die er als Institutsvorstand zu erfüllen hatte und
die ihn daran hinderten, seine Forschungen im gewohnten Ausmaß weiterzutrei-
ben. Den Unterricht hingegen genoß er und er investierte viel Zeit in die Vorbe-
reitung seiner Veranstaltungen.

Diese für ihn nach seiner Tätigkeit in Rußland ungewohnten Pflichten in
der Institutsverwaltung und den universitären Gremien – er hatte zunächst als
Wissenschaftlicher Mitarbeiter der Akademie der Wissenschaften in Moskau
(1978-1997) und dann als Professor an der Russischen Staatlichen Universität
der Geisteswissenschaften (1992-1998) gearbeitet – zehrten zusehends an seinen
Kräften. Er empfand seine neue Situation als belastend und teilweise sogar
lähmend, er fühlte sich regelrecht hineingeworfen in das deutsche universitäre
System mit seinen – in Hamburg jedenfalls bis Ende 2006 – vergleichsweise
antiautoritären Strukturen, und merkte zugleich, daß es für Außenstehende praktisch unmöglich war, die lebensnotwendigen Seilschaften an den Universitäten
zu durchschauen, geschweige denn sich mit der nötigen Chuzpe einzuklinken.
Die deutsche Gesellschaft mitsamt ihren politischen, wirtschaftlichen und sozia-
len Hintergründen blieb ihm bis zum Schluß suspekt, was jedoch keineswegs
bedeutet, daß er sich mit ihr nicht weiterhin gründlich und kritisch auseinander-
gesetzt hätte. Das hat er im übrigen auch mit dem politischen Leben in Rußland
getan, an dem er bis Ende der 90er Jahre aktiv teilnahm. So groß der wissen-

schaftliche Respekt auch war, der ihm von der internationalen Fachwelt entgegengebracht wurde, seinen Platz in Hamburg fand Eugen Helimski nie wirklich.

Diese Verlorenheit verschwand jedoch schlagartig in wissenschaftlichem Kontext. Bei Tagungen lösten die Vorträge und Fachgespräche bei ihm schon fast eine Art Euphorie aus. Er blühte auf, wirkte ausgesprochen selbstsicher, stürzte sich in Diskussionen, und er tat dies, seinem bemerkenswert breiten wissenschaftlichen Spektrum entsprechend, zu unzähligen Themen. Dies zeichnete ihn aus bei seinen öffentlichen Auftritten: fokussierte Konzentration, Zielstrebigkeit, autoritäre Beiträge. Von seiner Meinung ließ er sich denn auch selten abbringen. So vertrat er auch diejenigen seiner Thesen, die von vielen seiner Kollegen heftig kritisiert worden waren, unbeirrt weiter, so seine Erklärung des Stufenwechsels in verschiedenen uralischen Sprachen als Zeugnisse eines gemeinuralischen Stufenwechsels, oder bestimmte Phänomene des Ungarischen als Merkmale einer Tonsprache, oder auch zu Fragen benachbarter Disziplinen wie der Indogermanistik, der er stets über die Maßen kritisch gegenüberstand. Zugleich wies er aber z.B. im Unterricht darauf hin, daß die nostratische Theorie, die er ebenfalls vertrat, nicht der communis opinio der Finnougristik entspräche und auch aus seiner Sicht nicht völlig gesichert wäre.

Zum Teil wurde er in der Diskussion – anders als im Privatleben, in denen er Konflikten eher aus dem Weg ging – überdeutlich, es entwickelten sich hitzige Streitgespräche, v.a., wenn er das Gefühl hatte, daß der Vortragende seine intellektuellen Kräfte nicht so nutzte, wie er es seinen Fähigkeiten nach hätte tun können und, der wissenschaftlichen Ethik folgend, auch müssen. Er faßte Oberflächlichkeiten dieser Art als eine Beleidigung der Wissenschaft auf, und fühlte sich gewissermaßen auch persönlich angegriffen, wohl weil er sich so sehr mit den wissenschaftlichen Inhalten identifizierte.

Diese Phasen außergewöhnlicher mentaler Aktivität bei Tagungen und Kongressen wirkten sich auch auf den zwischenmenschlichen Bereich aus. Sein Selbstbewußtsein blühte in der fachlichen Umgebung auf und in der Folge entfaltete sich bei Tagungen oder in sonstigen wissenschaftlichen Kontexten auch sein Charme in nicht-fachlichen Bereichen. Seine sonst im allgemeinen zurückhaltende, teilweise sogar schüchterne Art wich einer von Geisteswitz sprühenden Offenheit. Er entpuppte sich als Mensch mit außergewöhnlichem Humor, oftmals jagte ein Witz – überwiegend politischer, aber meist politisch gar nicht korrekter Art – den nächsten, und man lachte Tränen.

In den letzten Jahren, in denen er durch Krankheits- und Todesfälle in seiner nächsten Umgebung gebeutelt war und zeitweise mit starken Selbstzweifeln zu kämpfen hatte, zog er sich zurück, nahm auch seltener an Konferenzen teil, aber nur um die Energie, die ihm die Schicksalsschläge übrig ließen, in die Forschung zu investieren. Auch in seinen letzten Monaten zeigte sich deutlich, daß er buchstäblich für die Wissenschaft lebte. Wohl wissend, daß er nicht mehr lange zu leben hatte, nahm er sich mit fast übermenschlicher Anstrengung der Arbeiten an, die er noch nicht abgeschlossen hatte, ordnete seinen Nachlaß minutiös, bestimmte bis in alle Einzelheiten die Fortführung seiner Projekte durch seine Mitarbeiter und Kollegen. Ich glaube, es ist sehr bezeichnend für ihn, daß er auch in dieser letzten Phase seines Lebens keine "Schwäche" zulassen wollte, sich nicht scheute, unerträgliche Schmerzen auf sich zu nehmen, nur um seine Arbeiten weiter voranbringen zu können. Systematisch nahm er nacheinander, in der von ihm nach Dringlichkeitsgrad festgelegten Reihenfolge, noch nicht abgeschlossene Arbeiten hervor, sein wertvolles Feldforschungsmaterial aus Sibirien, Notizen und Aufsätze zu etymologischen Fragen, zum Schamanismus, zu Sprachkontaktphänomenen, alten Quellen, Ortsnamen und auch zu nicht-finnougristischen Disziplinen wie der Slavistik und Turkologie.

Weit überdurchschnittliche Intelligenz, Eigenständigkeit, Unbeirrbarkeit, mal unübertrefflich gründlich, mal – völlig begeistert von den neu zu beackernden Feldern – zu Schnellschüssen neigend, witzig, wißbegierig, sich selbst und anderen gegenüber streng, aber auch voller Liebe und Verständnis, konsequent und widersprüchlich wie alle Menschen, die ich schätze – so wird er mir in Erinnerung bleiben.

Man kann über die Trinkgewohnheiten der einzelnen Völker und Völkerschaften gewiß geteilter Meinung sein. Zhenja stammt aus einer Sozialisierung, die diesbezüglich eindeutig ist. So möchte ich ihm diese letzte Ehrerweisung nicht vorenthalten und erhebe hier ein virtuelles Glas und lade alle Leser dieser Zeilen ein, in memoriam suam anzustoßen oder zumindest ihm im Geiste das Trinkopfer zu spenden.

Anna Widmer
Institut für Finnougristik/Uralistik
Johnsallee 35/37
D – 20148 Hamburg

Studia Etymologica Cracoviensia
vol. 14   Kraków 2009

Marek STACHOWSKI (Kraków)

EUGEN HELIMSKIS MATERIALIEN ZUR ERFORSCHUNG DER ÄLTESTEN SLAWISCH-UNGARISCHEN SPRACHKONTAKTE

Inhalt: Einleitung. – Eugen Helimskis hungaro-slawistische Publikationen. – Wörterverzeichnis. – Anhänge. – Index der slawischen Etyma. – Abkürzungen. – Bibliographie.

Einleitung

Schon als junger Mann kam Eugen Helimski auf die Idee, ein allumfassendes historisch-etymologisches Wörterbuch der slawischen Lehnwörter im Ungarischen zu schreiben. Ungefähr Anfang der 80er Jahre des 20. Jh.s begann er damit, Materialien für das geplante Werk zu sammeln, doch bald mußte er sich auch mit anderen Aufgaben beschäftigen, so daß die Arbeit an den ungarischen Slawismen nur langsam voranschritt. Daß ihm das Thema der slawischen Lehnwörter im Ungarischen weniger dringend erschien, lag zum einen am enorm breiten Interessenkreis Helimskis, zum anderen aber auch an seiner Überzeugung, man müsse in erster Linie die aussterbenden samojedischen Sprachen für die Wissenschaft retten, weswegen er es immer wieder nur am Rande anderer Aufgaben, wenn auch stets mit viel Eifer bearbeitete. Wie wichtig ihm die eilige, aber solide Feldforschung war, zeigt die Tatsache, daß er mir einmal, kurz nachdem mein *Dolganischer Wortschatz* (Kraków 1993) erschienen war, zum Teil im Scherz (denn er liebte paradoxe Formulierungen), zum Teil aber mit einem gewissen Kummer sagte, daß ich das Glück gehabt habe, den *Dolganischen Wortschatz* veröffentlichen zu können, bevor ich nach Tajmyr reisen und dort erfahren konnte, daß in dem und dem Dorf noch ein weiterer alter Mann lebt, der viele Märchen kennt und altertümliche Wörter, die heute allenfalls noch in alten Liedern vorkommen, versteht und erklären kann. Er selbst hatte dieses "Glück" nicht, er kannte die Dörfer und die alten Männer, und er wollte sie noch alle besuchen, solange sie lebten. Es war ihm sehr wohl bewußt, daß er die Arbeit mit ihnen nicht ohne weiteres auf später verschieben konnte. Das slawisch-ungarische Wörterbuch mußte warten. Ein Teil seiner Materialien konnte

Helimski jedoch in Form von Artikeln veröffentlichen, die zeigen, daß er das Thema gründlich verstand. Mit der Zeit spielte er mit dem Gedanken, auf ein Wörterbuch ganz zu verzichten, und stattdessen das Problem der slawisch-ungarischen Sprachkontakte in zwei Monographien darzustellen. Die eine würde dann das Thema von der ungarischen Seite darstellen ("Slawisches im Ungarischen"), die andere – von der slawischen Seite ("Slawisches anhand des Ungarischen"). Auch diesmal gab sich Helimski nicht mit bloßer Träumerei zufrieden, sondern bedachte den Inhalt und die Struktur der beiden Monographien ganz genau – so hat er Konzepte ausgearbeitet, und in einem dieser Konzepte sogar bereits die ungefähre Seitenzahl der einzelnen Kapitel geplant (s. Anhang 1). Heute können wir nur bedauern, daß er es nicht mehr geschafft hat, die beiden Bücher zu schreiben.

Als er mir im Februar 2007 seine slawisch-ungarischen Materialien übergab, wußte er schon, daß er sie nicht mehr zu Ende wird bearbeiten können. Ich meinerseits konnte seinen Vorschlag, daß ich das Thema unter Mitheranziehung dieser Materialien bearbeiten und als meine Arbeit veröffentlichen sollte, nicht akzeptieren. Helimski selbst wäre es, meinte er, genug gewesen, im Vorwort genannt zu werden. Das konnte ich, wie schon gesagt, nicht akzeptieren – und so habe ich ihm versprochen, zumindest das zu edieren, was seinen Standpunkt präsentiert. Solange er noch lebte, wollte ich die Materialien gar nicht berühren, denn ich hätte mich gefühlt, als schriebe ich seine Todesanzeige schon zu seinen Lebzeiten. Jetzt aber scheint die Zeit gekommen.

Es ist mein Ziel, Eugen Helimskis Etymologien, Notizen und Kommentare an dieser Stelle in einer Form darzustellen, die es möglich macht, seine Ideen und zum Teil auch den Forschungsprozeß zu verstehen. Die umfangreichste Quelle dieser Publikation ist Helimskis Kartei, aber ich habe in das Wörterverzeichnis auch seine Notizen, die er auf losen Blättern und teilweise in Heften gemacht hat, eingearbeitet. Ob er selbst all diese Notizen hier ebenfalls in dieser Form darstellen würde, wird sicherlich für immer unbekannt bleiben.[1]

---

[1]   Man darf höchstens hoffen, daß er diese Arbeit billigen würde. Jedenfalls schätzte Helimski selbst Arbeit mit Archivmaterialien sehr hoch und er hat sich auch in dieser Hinsicht verdient gemacht, so z.B. durch größere Artikel wie "Архивные материалы XVIII века по енисейским языкам" (*Палеоазиатский сборник*. Ленинград, 1986, 179-212) und eine ganze Reihe von Monographien: [zus. mit U. Kahrs] *Nordselkupisches Wörterbuch von F. G. Maľcev (1903)* (Hamburg 2001); [zus. mit H. Katz (†)] *Gerhard Friedrich Mueller – Nachrichten über Völker Sibiriens (1736-1742)* (Hamburg 2003); *Г. Ф. Миллер и изучение уральских народов & Г. Ф. Миллер: Описание живущих в Казанской губерни языческих народов, яко то черемис, чуваш и вотяков... (репринт издания 1791 г.)* (Hamburg 2005); *Южноселькупский словарь Н. П. Григоровского* (Hamburg 2007). Obwohl es sich dem Titel weniger eindeutig entnehmen läßt, stützen sich auch seine Monographien *The language of the first Selkup books* (Szeged 1983) und *Die matorische Sprache* (Szeged 1997) hauptsächlich auf Archivmaterialien.

Ein Teil der Materialien wurde aus der Publikation ausgeschlossen. So z.B. diejenigen Zettel, die keine eigenen Ideen von Helimski beinhalten, sondern lediglich Angaben aus fremden Werken (meistens Kn., TESz oder Györffy). Unberücksichtigt geblieben sind weiterhin alle Notizen von klarem Arbeitscharakter (Sätze wie "zu überprüfen ist noch, ob..." u.a.) sowie Fragen, Kommentare, Sätze usw., die von Helimski gestrichen wurden.

Eine Mahnung bei der Wahl des zu veröffentlichenden Materials war mir das Schicksal der Zettel aus der koreanischen Kartei von G. J. Ramstedt, der sie in seinem koreanischen etymologischen Wörterbuch nicht berücksichtigt hat. Ihre unkritische Veröffentlichung durch Songmoo Kho (*Paralipomena of Korean etymologies*, Helsinki 1982) war ein wahrer Bärendienst. Von den von Ramstedt gesammelten ca. 5000 Stichwortzetteln wurden nämlich von ihm selbst für sein Wörterbuch nur knapp 2000 herangezogen, und er hatte offensichtlich seine Gründe, die übrigen 3000 auszuschließen. Die Tatsache, daß sie 30 Jahre nach seinem Tod ungesichtet veröffentlicht wurden, bedeutete daher, daß auch diejenigen ediert wurden, die Ramstedt zwar (vermutlich in der Anfangsphase seiner Arbeit) notiert, dann jedoch als unsicher oder gar irrtümlich aus der Publikation ausgeschlossen hat. So wurde z.B. korean. *maịl* 'village, settlement' mit nur einem Wort, und zwar mit kirg. *māl* 'квартал, селение' zusammengestellt. Das kirgisische Wort ist natürlich ein Reflex des arab. *maḥalla(t)* (> osman.-türk. *mahalle* 'Stadtteil, -viertel'). Offensichtlich wurde Ramstedt das erst später klar, denn er hat diese Zusammenstellung in seinem Wörterbuch nicht berücksichtigt – schade nur, daß er den entsprechenden Zettel nicht vernichtet hat.

Um Situationen dieser Art zu vermeiden und den Autor nicht (ungewollt) zu blamieren, wurden hier alle unsicheren Notizen ignoriert, obwohl man sich denken kann, daß die Tatsache allein, daß Helimski selbst sie nicht vernichtet hat, eher darauf hinzuweisen scheint, daß er sie nicht unbedingt alle für wertlos hielt. Jedoch noch einmal: ob Helimski genau dieselbe Wahl treffen würde (auch im Fall des Umschlags mit der Aufschrift "Ошибочные этим."), werden wir wohl nie erfahren.

Mein eigenes Eingreifen in die Materialien wurde hier auf ein Minimum reduziert. Der russische Text stammt prinzipiell von Helimski, der deutsche von mir. Wo dies eventuell zu Mißverständnissen hätte führen können, steht mein Text in { }, und dem Text von Helimski ist die Abkürzung "Hel." vorangestellt. Die Fußnoten stammen immer von mir. Die Sternchen vor rekonstruierten slawischen Etyma stammen von Helimski. Ungarische historische Angaben werden nur teilweise angeführt, denn sie wurden alle von Helimski aus TESz oder OklSz exzerpiert. Die ältere Literatur wird im Stichwortartikel in [ ] angegeben; nach der Quellensigle dagegen steht in ( ) eine von Helimski formulierte kurze Inhaltsangabe zu dieser Quelle – gegebenenfalls mit Helimskis Kommentar. Die von Helimski im Manuskript hie und da abgekürzten Wörter (wie z.B. *происх.*

= 'происхождение') werden im Abkürzungsverzeichnis nicht aufgelöst, denn sie bilden kein System. Sie sind im Text einfach ohne Lösung gelassen, wo sie leicht verständlich sind, oder aber in { } direkt im Text mit einer Lösung versehen. Die einzelnen Stichwortartikel sind fast alle nach einem einheitlichen Schema strukturiert worden, es sei denn, Helimski hat einen Artikel selber anders gebildet (was sehr selten der Fall war).

Dem Wörterverzeichnis folgen die nachstehenden Anhänge:

Anhang 1: Inhaltsverzeichnisse von zwei geplanten Monographien (s.o.).

Anhang 2: Eine kurze Liste von Wörtern, die Helimski für aus der Sicht der ungarischen Sprachgeschichte besonders interessant hielt.

Anhang 3-24: Listen mit Beispielen für verschiedene Lauterscheinungen. – Diese stammen von Helimski. Nur relativ wenige dieser Wörter befinden sich auch im Wörterverzeichnis. Andererseits lassen sich im Wörterverzeichnis wiederum zusätzliche Beispiele finden, die in den Listen fehlen; ich habe die Listen jedoch nicht vervollständigt, um so das Originalbild zu erhalten. – Vgl. Anhang 25.

Anhang 25: Wörter mit Reflexen des slawischen Suffixes -ica. Auch an dieser Stelle haben wir es mit keiner vollständigen Liste zu tun (so fehlen hier z.B. ung. *gërlice* 'Turteltaube' < slaw. *gъrlica*; ung. *kabóca* 'Heuschrecke' < slaw. *kobylica*, u.a.m.). – Vgl. Anhang 3-24.

Anhang 26: Notizen oder fertig redigierte Fragmente, die vermutlich Teile von Kapiteln der geplanten Monographien sein sollten. – Der Gebrauch der 2.Sg. ("твоя система", "думаешь ли ты...", usw.) macht den Eindruck, die Notizen seien für eine dritte Person geschrieben worden. An wen genau sich hier Helimski wandte, bleibt unbekannt. Oder war das eine Art Dialog mit sich selbst? Aber dagegen spricht der Umstand, daß die 1. und die 2.Sg. auch in ein und demselben Abschnitt gebraucht werden können.

Eugen Helimskis hungaro-slawistische Publikationen

1988

1. [abstract] Венгерский язык как источник для праславянской реконструкции и реконструкции славянского языка Паннонии. – *X Международен конгрес на славистите: Резюмета на докладите.* София, 1988, 78.

2. Венгерский язык как источник для праславянской реконструкции и реконструкции славянского языка Паннонии. – *Славянское языкознание. X Международный съезд славистов: Доклады советской делегации.* Москва, 1988, 347-368 [nachgedruckt in Хелимский 2000 (s. Bibliographie): 416-432; auch: www.helimski.com].

3. *Király* и *olasz*. К истории ранних славяно-тюрко-венгерских связей. – *Славяне и их соседи. Место взаимных влияний в процессе общественного и культурного развития. Эпоха феодализма: Сборник тезисов.* Москва, 1988, 53-55 [nachgedruckt in Хелимский 2000 (s. Bibliographie): 433-435; auch: www.helimski.com].

4. Славянский интердиалект в Венгрии Арпадов? – *Славяне и их соседи. Место взаимных влияний в процессе общественного и культурного развития. Эпоха феодализма: Сборник тезисов.* Москва, 1988, 63-66.

1989

5. Славянское койне в Венгрии Арпадов и происхождение славяно-венгерских топонимов в Трансильвании. – *Материалы к VI Международному конгрессу по изучению стран Юго-Восточной Европы. Лингвистика.* Москва, 1989, 48-55 [nachgedruckt in Хелимский 2000 (s. Bibliographie): 462-466; auch: www.helimski.com].

6. Изучение ранних славяно-венгерских языковых отношений (Материалы и интерпретации. Вопрос об этноязыковых контактах венгров с восточными славянами). – *Славяноведение и балканистика в странах Зарубежной Европы и США.* Москва, 1989, 184-198 [nachgedruckt in Хелимский 2000 (s. Bibliographie): 404-415; auch: www.helimski.com].

1990

7. К корпусу ранних славянских заимствований венгерского языка. – *Uralo-Indogermanica. Балто-славянские языки и проблема урало-индоевропейских связей: Материалы 3-ей балто-славянской конференции,* I. Москва, 1990, 76-82 [auch: www.helimski.com].

1991

8. [abstract] Slavic/Latin/German stress and Hungarian vowel harmony. – *Finnisch-ugrische Sprachen zwischen dem germanischen und dem slavischen Sprachraum: Symposium aus Anlaß des 25-jährigen Bestehens der Finnougristik an der Rijksuniversiteit Groningen.* Groningen, 1991, 14.

1992

9. Slavic/Latin/German stress and Hungarian vowel harmony. – *Finnisch-ugrische Sprachen zwischen dem germanischen und dem slavischen Sprachraum. Vorträge des Symposiums aus Anlaß des 25-jährigen Bestehens der Finnougristik an der Rijksuniversiteit Groningen.* Amsterdam – Atlanta, 1992, 45-54 [nachgedruckt in Хелимский 2000 (s. Bibliographie): 456-461; auch: www.helimski.com].

1993

10. [abstract] Ранняя славянская христианская терминология в венгерском языке. – *XI Medzinárodný zjazd slavistov: Zborník resumé.* Bratislava, 1993, 117-118.

11. Ранняя славянская христианская терминология в венгерском языке. – *XI Международный съезд славистов. Славянское языкознание: Доклады российской делегации.* Москва, 1993, 46-64 [nachgedruckt in Хелимский 2000 (s. Bibliographie): 436-451; auch: www.helimski.com].

1998

12. [Diskussionsbeiträge]. – *XI Medzinárodny zjazd slavistov. Záznamy z diskusje k predmeseným referátom.* Bratislava, 1998, 32-35, 63-65, 82-84, 136-137, 443-444 [auch: www.helimski.com].

2000

13. Лексико-семантические раритеты в ранних славянских заимствованиях венгерского языка. – [Ursprünglich auf dem Symposium zum 100. Todestag von F. Miklosich (Wien 1991) vorgetragen. Publiziert erst in Хелимский 2000 (s. Bibliographie): 452-455; auch: www.helimski.com].

2003

14. *Bécs* und *Pécs* vor dem Hintergrund der ungarischen Vertretung der slawischen Nasalvokale. – Bakró-Nagy M. / Rédei K. (ed.): *Ünnepi könyv Honti László tiszteletére.* Budapest 2003, 181-193 [auch: www.helimski.com].

Wörterverzeichnis

abajdoc *dial.* (1320/1325) (vgl. auch 1590: *abajnac; abajnoc* (ÚMTSz) u.a.) '1. смешанный; 2. смесь ржаного и пшеничного зерна; 3. замусоренное зерно' [Kn. 1: 55 und TESz 1: 88 (< **oba/idvojьcь*); EtSz 1: 34]. – **Hel.:** {EtSz, Kn., TESz:} < *obojьпьсь, ср. слвц. диал. *obojenec* 'гермафродит', ст.-слав. обоинъ *obojnъ*; слн. *obôjen* 'zu beiden gehörig'. – {Dazu Hel. noch:} или < *obojǫdьcь через *abajondoc, abajndoc*; ср. ст.-слав. обоюждоу 'ἑκατέρωθεν', слн. *obojód* 'по обе стороны', др.-р. обоюду, рус. *обоюдный* – Фасм. 3: 106. – {Später ohne Kommentar darunter dazugeschrieben:} *obojedьпьсь*. – {Auf der Umseite:} См. еще: Трубачев in Езиковедско-етнографски изследвания в памет на акад. Ст. Романски, С. {= София}, 1960, 142-143.

abajnac, abajnoc – s. *abajdoc*.

abál (1580) ~ **abárol** (1561) ~ **abáll** (dial. 19.Jh.) 'обварить' [EtSz 1: 5 (схрв. или слн., где долгий *a*); Kn. 1: 55-56 (долгота вторична и ее возраст неизвестен); TESz 1: 89]. – **Hel.:** < slaw. *obari* < *obvari-*: схрв. слн. *obáriti*, слвц. *obarit'*.

abárol – s. *abál*.

Ablánc(-patak) (1233: in vallem ... Ablanch) 'приток р. Репце в м. Ваш' [Stan. 2: 8 & Kiss 37 – оба из *Jablonьcь*; Moór 1936: 19]. – **Hel.:** < ? slaw. *obьlanicy*. Ср. Фасм. 3: 103 *obьlъ* < *obvьlъ*.

ábráz (< altung. **abráz**) (1372/1448 bis 1617) 'образ' [RMGl. 62 (ca. 1560: ‹abraaz› – *ábráz* фактически неизвестно; *ábra*, *ábrázat* – основа для такого написания; диал.: *abrázat* Gyergyó, Секейфёлд); Kn. 1: 57-58 (с предл. об ассим. – излишне); TESz 1: 90-91]. – **Hel.:** < slaw. *obrazъ*. – Vgl. *rásza*.

abrosz (1372/1448; ca. 1395; ca. 1405: abruʒ [!, mit -*u*-]) 'скатерть' [Kn. 1: 59; TESz 1: 92-93]. – **Hel.:** < slaw. *obrusъ* id.

agár (1193: Agar hn.; ca. 1395: agar) ~ *dial.* **ogár** 'гончая собака' [Kn. 2: 584-585; TESz 1: 101]. – **Hel.:** < ? slaw. *ogarь*. – Zu diesem Wort s. heute Stachowski 1995 (2003).

Aka (seit 1437) Ortsname, Komitat Komárom-Esztergom [Kiss 43 (zum Personennamen *Ok* oder Ortsnamen *Akes*). – **Hel.:** < slaw. *oko*.[2]

akal – s. *akol*.

akna (1197/1337: Acnahege; 1222: Akana (сол. {= соляная} копь); 1621: akonájá) ~ *dial.* **akona** 'шахта, мина; (ст.-венг.) соляная копь и др.' [EtSz 1: 48-49 (гласный в *akana*, *akona* – на венг. почве и не подтверждает *okъno*); Kn. 1: 60-61 (нет, подтверждает)]. – **Hel.:** < slaw. *okъno* – обычно 'окно', но ср. чеш. *okna* Pl. 'ямы, шахты'; схрв. *òkno* тж. 'шахта'; болг. *óкнó* тж. 'сол. {= соляная} копь'. – Фасм. 3: 128: не *okno*.

akol (*akal) (*akolok*, *akola* → *aklok*, *akla*) (1037: Okul город; 1130-40: Ocol город) 'овчарня, хлев' [EtSz 1: 49-50; Kn. 1: 62; TESz 1: 118 (Сущ. ошиб. этим. {= существенно ошибочная этимология} из тюрк. (Munkácsi NyK 27, 161). Но ср. в. *ól* < тюрк. *aɣul* (TESz 2: 1072-1073) 'хлев', отраженное в ст.-венг. как 1211 Bureu*ohul* hn., Lu*oul*. Т.о., контаминация *akal {i *aɣul → akul > akol. Возможно, исходный в-т {= вариант} сохранен в *akal*)]. – **Hel.:** < slaw. *okolъ* (слн. *okòl* 'овчарня, загон', чак. *okol* 'свинарник', ст.-польск. *okół* 'загон, овчарня', укр. *óкіл*, *óколу* 'загон'.

---

[2] Wörtl. 'Auge', aber das Wort wird im Slaw. auch als Bezeichnung von Teichen, Seen und Quellen gebraucht, vgl. poln. *Morskie Oko*, See im Tatragebirge; ukr.dial. *вóко* 'углубление в скале, из которого течет вода'; sonst vgl. auch den krimtat. Ortsnamen *Karagöz*, urspr. sicherlich 'Schwarze Quelle' (Jankowski 2006: 824f.) sowie estn. *silm* '1. Auge; 2. Meeresarm, Meerenge'; für andere Beispiele s. auch Helimski 2008.

akona – s. *akna*.

alaj – s. *olaj*.

alé(jos) – s. *olaj*.

Aranyosgadány – s. *Gadány*.

atracél (1401: Atrochel szn) 'растение Anchusa' [Kn. 1: 67; TESz 2: 196 (*j-* >
∅- в венг.)]. – **Hel.**: < slaw. *ǫtrocělъ*. – Ср. ЭССЯ 6: 72-73 (**ǫtro*) и 3:
179-180 (**cělъ*); чеш. *jitrocel* 'Plantago', слцк. *jitrocel ~ jatrocel* id. (Machek 229 с указ. на предл. F. V. Mareš'ем **jędro-čelъ*).

babona (1533: babonakual; 1697: bábónás) 'суеверие; (ст.-венг. тж.:) колдов-
ство, ворожба' [Kn. 1: 70-71; TESz 1: 211]. – **Hel.**: < slaw. *bobona*. Ср.
ЭССЯ 1: 111 **bobonъ / *babunъ / *babona* с недооценкой форм с *bo-*:
слвц. *bobona* 'суеверие', польск. *zabobon*, укр. *забобóн, бобóна*, рус.
забобóны, см. ЕСУМ 1: 106 и 2: 214; Фасм. 2: 70; SP 1: 288 (*bo- ~ ba-*).
– Поздн{ее}?

Babót (1217: Bobeth) Ortsname, Komitat Győr-Moson-Sopron [Kiss 71 (дета-
ли ненадежны); Stan. 2: 15]. – **Hel.**: < slaw. *Bobovьcь*.

Bag Ortsname. – Др.-венг. *Båg* (1278 Bog), венг. *Bag* < слав. *bogъ?* – В качестве славянского источника можно предполагать либо **bogъ* (> мак.
бог 'tumor', укр.диал. *бог* 'желудок; первое отделение желудка жвач-
ных животных, рубец', ср. также схрв. *bŏgav* 'отекший, набухший',
слн. *zbogati se* 'испортиться', *bogor, -orja* 'tumor, чирей'; см. ЭССЯ 2:
159-160 и ЕСУМ 1: 219-220), либо аналог (или перенос) гидронима
*Bogъ 'Южный Буг' (др.-рус. **Бог**, укр. *Бог*, польск.[3] *Bóg* > рус. *Буг*,
ср. также *Βογοῦ* в Const. Porph. DAI 42; см. Фасм. 1: 227). Значительно
менее вероятно слав. **bogъ* 'deus'. – По всей вероятности, того же
происхождения и МН *Bag* в медье Пешт, которое Л. Кишш возводит к
др.-венг. ЛИ *Bogu* (1138/1329) и далее предположительно сравнивает
с ст.-польск. ЛИ *Bog* (Kiss 73). Однако не меньшие основания имеет
под собой сравнение ЛИ *Bogu* с венг. *bog* 'узел', словом финно-угор-
ского происхождения (так в TESz 1: 321).

Bagamér (1281: Bagomer; 1225: Bagamerium) Ortsname, Komitat Hajdú-Bihar [Kn. 73 (выводит из Богомир, etc.); Stan. 2: 17 (**Bugumir, -měr*, со
ссылкой на Морошкин 16)]. – **Hel.**: < ? slaw. *Bogoměrъ (Bogoměŕъ)*.
Почему не {ung.} *Bagmér*? – Vgl. *Budmér*.

Bagota – s. *Bakta*.

Bajót (1202: Boiotth; 1244: Bayoth) Ortsname, Komitat Komárom-Esztergom
[Stan. 2: 20-21; Kiss 75 (иначе, но неубед.: *bajat* 'род огузов')]. – **Hel.**:
< ? slaw. *bojevьcь*.

---

[3]   Hier wurde vermutlich poln. *Boh* (Kiss[2] 1: 262) mit poln. *Bug* verwechselt. Zu dem
letzteren s. insb. Babik 2001: 104-106.

Bakóca (1332: Bokolcha) Ortsname, Komitat Baranya [Stan. 2: 22 und Kiss 76: < *Bukovica*]. – **Hel.:** < ? slaw. *bekovica* или *bokovica* (ЭССЯ 1: 183 *beka* – ива Salix vitellina или Salix viminalis).

Bakta Ortsname. – Др.-венг. *Bågotå* (1232/1360 Bagotha, 1338-1339 Bokcha [э: Boktha]), венг. *Bakta* (Nagy-, Kisbakta) < слав. *bogata* (ж.р.) (ЭССЯ 2: 158) или *Boguta* (гипокористическая форма к ЛИ типа *Bogъdanъ*, *Bogumilъ*, *Boguslavъ* и под.). К фонетическому развитию (во втором открытом слоге слав. *a* > др.-венг. *ā* > *o* > *∅* или слав. *u* > др.-венг. *u* > *o* > *∅*) ср. венг. *pajta* (др.-венг. *payata*- 1363) 'сарай' < слав. *pojata*, венг. *szolga* (др.-венг. *zuluga* 1222) 'слуга' < слав. *sluga*. – На территории Венгрии представлены еще по крайней мере 4 топонима *Bakta* (бывш. медье Саболч, Абауй, Хевеш, Гёмёр), см. Stan. 2: 23-24 (с произвольной этимологией от *bak*- + -*ta*); Kiss (sub *Baktakék*, *Baktalóránthá-za*, *Egerbakta*, дается сравнение со ст.-схрв. ЛИ *Bokta*). Кроме того, имеется *(Pécs)bagota* в медье Баранья (1262/1413 Bagatha), см. Stan. 2: 17-18 (слав. *bogata* или, скорее, *Boguta*); Kiss 505 (слав. *Boguta*, что хуже согласуется с др.-венг. написанием Bagatha); Györffy 1: 275.

Balástya (seit 1760) Ortsname, Komitat Csongrád [Kiss 80: < dial. *balustya* 'együgyű' ?]. – **Hel.:** < ? slaw. *boltišče* (ЭССЯ 2: 179).

Balsa (seit 1291/1383) Ortsname, Komitat Szabolcs-Szatmár-Bereg [Kiss 86: < *bal* 'левый', *Balázs*? ~ схрв. *Balša*?]. – **Hel.:** < slaw. *bolъša*.

bán (1116: banus (лат.); 1146: ban) 'бан, правитель' [Kn. 1: 74-75; TESz 1: 236 (< авар.: EtSz 1: 267-269)]. – **Hel.:** < схрв. *bân*, болг. мак. *бан* (или непоср. из авар.?).

bánya '1. dial. целебный источник (1577), ванна (1585) и др.; 2. шахта (? 1240; 1332)' [Kn. 1: 76-77; TESz 1: 241; EtSz 1: 151-152]. – **Hel.:** < slaw. *baňa* (ЭССЯ 1: 151-152 страдает от неучета венг. материала!).

Barad – s. *Borod*.

Baranka (1273: Borynka, 1274: Baranka) Ortsname (= slowak. *(Suchá) Broňka /Bronka*. – **Hel.:** < slaw. *bronьka* (от цветообозначения *bronъ*, см. ЭССЯ 3: 41-42; украинским диалектам неизвестно).

barázda (1130-40: brazda) ~ *dial.* **berázda, bërázda, borázda, borozda** etc. 'борозда' [Kn. 1: 81; TESz 1: 247 (труднообъяснимо *borozda*)]. – **Hel.:** < slaw. *brazda* < *borzda*.

barkóca *dial.* (1257: Burcolcha (лес); 1279/1380: borcolcha; 1325: Borkoucha-fa 1350: Barkolchafa) 'берека; Sorbus terminalis {= poln. *brzęk* ~ *(jarząb) brekinia*; dt. *Elsbeere*}' [EtSz 1:294-295; Kn. 1: 82 (развитие как в *parlag* < *prělogъ*); TESz 1: 252]. – **Hel.:** < {ung.} *barkovca* < slaw. *barākovica* < *berēkovica* < панн. *brěkovica* < *berkovica* (ЭССЯ 1: 194-195 *berka*, *berkъ*, *berkovьcь* – а это {= die Form *berkovica*, rekonstruiert anhand des ung. *barkóca*} недостающий ж.р.). – Спец. это: Hadrovics 1960: 6.

Baskó (seit 1467) Ortsname, Komitat Borsod-Abaúj-Zemplén [Kiss 94: слав. *Baškov или от ст.-венг. Bas ЛИ]. – **Hel.:** < slaw. božьkovъ.

Battyán Ortsname, belegt in verschiedenen Komitaten seit 1198 [Kniezsa 1943: 195 (неизв. происх.); Kiss 589 (от имени Bothan ~ Botond; ? от кабарского плем. названия, менее вер. слав. происх.); Berrár StSl. 12: 54 (!)]. – **Hel.:** < slaw. botьjanъ '(большой) аист' (ЭССЯ 2: 226-227); ст.-чеш., польск. (> слцк.), с сомнениями в общеслав. произн. – SP 1: 342-343.

bazsár – s. *bazsa-rózsa*.

bazsa-rózsa (ca. 1577: baʃaroʃa) 'пион, Paeonia' [EtSz 1: 316-317; Kn. 1: 85; TESz 1: 262-263]. – **Hel.:** < slaw. boža; болг. (БЕР 1: 62) бóжа 'див мак, Papaver rhoeas' (ср. ЭССЯ 2: 228 в статье božurъ), ю.-слав. božurъ 'пион, (болг. тж.) дикий мак' (ЭССЯ 2: 228). – Контаминация и на слав., и на венг. почве? Отсутствие совсем ранних фиксаций. Ср. ca. 1470: baʒar 'Peoniaca'; 1520-30: bozsir; 16.Jh.: basal Rosa ~ busia Rosa, buʃir roʃa, Buser; 2. Hälfte des 16.Jh.: buzser; 17.Jh.: Baʃur; 1807: Bazsál, Bazsál-rózsa. – {Auf einem anderen Zettel:} Заслуживает внимания также ст.-венг. вариант **bazsár** (ок. 1470: baʒar 'Peoniaca'), который может отражать *božarъ или *božarь.

Bégány (*Kis-, Nagybégány*) (1332/1335: Bygan, Bekan) Ortsname (= slowak. [< ung.] *(Malá, Veliká) Běhaň*). – **Hel.:** < ? slaw. *běganъ (< *běgati, s. ЭССЯ 2: 58-59).

*bélc *altung.* (1521: belch; 1635: belcs) 'белый, светлый (масть)' [Kn. 2: 595 (sub *belc*; вслед за Zolnai Nyr 35: 198 сопост. также с слн. *bêlec*, схрв. *bélac* < *bělьcь*, что не проходит)]. – **Hel.:** < altung. *bélca* < slaw. *bělica* (ЭССЯ 2: 64-65). – Ср. диал. *belice* (с 18 в.) 'белая овца' < румын. *belíţă* < слав. (TESz 1: 27).

berázda – s. *barázda*.

bërce *dial.* (seit 1816 – не может быть старое!) 'Jochscheide, Rippenbein, Netznadel, Wagenschwengel – валек повозки' [Kn. 1: 88-89; TESz 1: 282-283]. – **Hel.:** < slaw. *bьrdьce* (ЭССЯ 3: 166; ЕСУМ 1: 169-170; SP 1: 429-430 (бéрце < *bьrdьce)). – Фасмер 1: 159: бéрце, бéрцо 'берцовая кость', диал. 'свая для укрепления рыболовной снасти'. Этимологии удовл. нет. – {S.u. *borda*}.

Bereg (1214/1550: Beregu; 1232/1360: Beregh; 1233: Bereyg; 1323 und 1327: Bereegh) Ortsname (= slowak. *Břehy*). – **Hel.:** < slaw. *brěgy (< *bergъ, см. ЭССЯ 1: 191-192). – Исходный облик венгерского топонима *Berég* отражают написания Bereyg, Bereegh. Современная форма с кратким гласным второго слога отражает вторичное восточнославянское влияние, отчасти, возможно, и контаминацию с венг. *berek* 'роща' (что особенно вероятно для топонима *Beregszász* [произносится *Berekszász*], сложение < *Bereg* и *szász* 'саксонец'). – В свете предложенной выше интерпретации, укр. *Бéрегове*, рус. *Бéрегово* могут непосредственно продолжать слав. **Bergovo* (см. ЭССЯ 1: 189). чеш. слвц. *Berehovo* < вост.-слав. (иначе ожидалось бы **Břehovo*, **Brehovo*).

Beregdaróc – s. *daróc.*

Beregszász – s. *Bereg.*

bërëna – s. *borona.*

*Bernece (1245: Burnuce; 1281: Bernechepataka), in: **Bernecebaráti** Ortsname, Komitat Pest [Kiss 107]. – **Hel.:** < slaw. *brьnьce* или *brьnica* (Ср. ЭССЯ 3: 69-70 **brьna*); или *bъrna*.

Berzence (ca. 1228/1230: Burzence {sic!, Bu-}) Ortsname, Komitat Somogy ~ **Börzönce** (1234: Bezenche; 1261: Berzencha; 1320: Berzence) Ortsname, Komitat Zala [Stan. 2: 48 und Kiss 107, 125-126: < **berzьnica* (к *береза*)]. – **Hel.:** < slaw. *bъrzьnica* oder *bъrzinica* oder *bъrzanica* (ср. болг. *бързàница* от *бърз* [БЕР 1: 102], *Бързина* река [ibid.]). – Ansonsten s. ЭССЯ 3: 136 für **bъrzina* (укр. *борзикá* 'быстрина'), ЭССЯ 3: 139 für **bъrzъnъ* (схрв. *бр̀зан*, *бр̏зан* 'быстрый').

beszéd (1318: Bezedkeu hn.; 1372/1448: beʒedekett; 1416/1450: èbèzëd) ~ *dial.* **beszéd** [bɛ-] 'речь' [Kn. 1: 90-91; TESz 1: 289]. – **Hel.:** < slaw. *besěda* (ЭССЯ 1: 211-213; на с. 213 явно ошибочно **besědъ/*besědь* на основе схрв.диал. *bècjed*, *bëcjēd* [Hel.: схрв. < венг.]). – **sěd-*, если к *sěsti.*

Bilke (1338-1339: Bylke) Ortsname. – Согласно {hier Platz für bibliographische Angaben frei gelassen} название этого {???, = dieses Ortes} (и одновременно реки, притока Боржавы) отражает слав. **bělъka* (см. ЭССЯ 2: 81-82), укр. *бíлка*. По крайней мере столь же правдоподобны и другие варианты славянской этимологии – например, от **bylъka / *bylьka* 'стебель, трава' (см. ЭССЯ 3: 149). При любом решении нужно предполагать вариативность и взаимовлияние венг., слвц. и укр. названий.

bocs *altung.* (nur 1444: boch) 'большой сосуд для вина' [Kn. 1: 95]. – **Hel.:** < slaw. *bъči* (ЭССЯ 3: 107-108) или *bъčь* (ЭССЯ 3: 108 – только слн. *bùč, bòč, bèč*).

bocska (seit 1587) 'бочка' [Kn. 1: 95; TESz 1: 316]. – **Hel.:** < slaw. *bъčьka.* – Может быть новым заимств.

Bodmér – s. *Budmér.*

bolgár (1138/1329: Bulgar szn.; 1356: Bolgar szn.) 'болгарин' [Kn. 1: 98; TESz 1: 332]. – **Hel.:** < slaw. *bъlgarъ* (или из тюрк. *bulγar*, ? букв. 'смесь').

Bolkács (1319: Bolkach) Ortsname in Siebenbürgen, Komitat Kis-Küküllő = рум. Bălcaciu, нем. Bulkesch [Kniezsa 1943: 223 (неизв. происх.)]. – **Hel.:** < slaw. *bъlkačь* '*борматун, заика', ср. ЭССЯ 3: 117-119.

borázda – s. *barázda.*

borda (1355: Bordas szn.; ок. 1405: bõda) 'бёрдо (гребень в ткацком станке); (с 1578:) ребро' [Kn. 1: 100-101 (без увер. в возм. отожд. 'бёрдо' и

'ребро'); TESz 1: 343-344 (сходство бёрдо и гр. {= грудной} клетки)].
– **Hel.**: < slaw. *bьrdo* 'бёрдо' (ЭССЯ 3: 164-166). – *бёрдо* 'часть тк. {=
ткацкого} станка в виде гребени, служит для прибив. утка, напр. чел-
нока и определ. расст. нитей основы'. Отсюда, – 'устой, остов, опорная часть, стержень' → {???} {польск.} диал. *na jedno brdo* 'на один
манер',[4] ? словин. *bjȁrdo* 'дюймовые доски в лодке', рус.диал *бёрдо*
'щит для установки берданок еза {= запруды} для ловли рыбы зимой',
укр. *бéрдо* 'каменистая земля, твердый грунт', *бóрдо* 'мертвая рука,
мертвая нога' [ЕСУМ 1: 169: неясно]. Еще более отчетливо эта семантика в *bьrdьce*, см. ЭССЯ 3: 165 и *berce* {s. hier oben: *bёrce*}.

Borod *nur altung.* (1264/1270: Borod; 1357: Brod). – **Hel.**: < slaw. *brodъ* (см.
ЭССЯ 3: 36-37). В современном венгерском языке топоним, вероятно,
имел бы вид *Barad*.

borona *dial.* ~ **bёrёna** *dial., altung.* (1406: Berena; 1510: Borona) {'Holzstück,
Balken'} [OklSz. 88; Kn. 1: 103 (перв. в-т {= первичный вариант} *bёrёna*,
другой в-т – в рез-те {= в результате} смешения с *borona* 'борона');
TESz 1: 347 (как и Kn.; < слав. *brъvьno*, ср. ст.-слав. **брѣвьно** [в ЭССЯ:
бровьно!]); Ашбот 246 (м.б. и **бърно* паралл. ф. {= форма}? → рус.
берно, румын. *birnă*)]. – **Hel.**: < slaw. *brъvьno*, *bьrvьno*? (ЭССЯ 3: 72-
73); и *brъvьno/bъrvьno*?; ср. ЭССЯ 3: 71: *brъvь* (откуда *-no*) < *brъvь*
через ассимиляцию. – {Auf einem getrennten Zettel mit dem Titel: "**bьrvьno*":} Отметим, что в пользу подобной реконструкции {d.i. **bьrvьno*},
наряду с выдвигавшимися ранее аргументами (J. Rozwadowski RS 1:
251; Фасм. 1: 209), свидетельствует венг.диал. *bёrёna, borona* [...], как,
по-видимому, и румын. *birnă*. Эти формы без затруднений выводятся
из **bьrvьnó* (с предположением об упрощении $Cv > C$ {d.i. $rv > r$}, ср.
csütörtök, диал. *csёtёrtёk* < *četvьrtъkъ*; диал. *csёtёrt* < *četvьrtь*), в то
время как при исходном слав. **brъvьno* (Bern. 1: 92) или **brъvьno*
(ЭССЯ 3: 72-73) ожидалось бы развитие такого типа, как в *bürü* 'мостик' < *brъvь*. – Vgl. *bürü*.

borozda – s. *barázda*.

Borsova ~ **Borsva** ~ **Borzsova** ~ **Borzsva** ~ **Bózsva**, Flußnamen. – {In dieser
Skizze wurde an einigen Stellen Platz für bibliographische Ergänzungen
frei gelassen. Die Stellen werden hier nicht gekennzeichnet.} Я. Мелих
усматривал в топонимах типа *Borsova / Bózsva* заимствованные вен-

---

[4]   Die Notation *(na jedno) brdo* ist vermutlich defekt, denn das Wort liegt in dieser
Form in poln. Dialektwörterbüchern nicht belegt vor. Wie mir der Krakauer Dialek-
tologe, Józef Kąś dankenswerterweise berichtet, ist das Wort in südpoln. Dialekten
(sowie in der Weberfachsprache) als *bardo* 'Geschirr im Webstuhl' bekannt. Der
Ausdruck *na jedno bardo* bedeutet also wörtlich 'nach ein und demselben Geschirr',
d.h. 'in ein und dieselbe Weise'.

герским языком славянские образования от древневенгерского имени
Bors (~ венг. *bors* 'черный перец'), отраженного также в многочисленных топонимах типа *Bors, Borsi, Borsod.* Э. Моор трактовал их как
отражения слав. **Borišova*, от ЛИ *Boriš* (< **bor* 'битва') (UJb 7: 438).
Эту точку зрения поддержали И. Книежа и Я. Станислав, который ре-
конструирует славянский источник скорее как **Boršava* от ЛИ **Boгьšь*
(ср. также Šmilauer 1932: 440-441). Л. Кишш склоняется к объяснению
предложенному Мелихом, тогда как Д. Кришто и др. считают этимологию топонима *Borsova* невыясненной и предпочитают отделять это
название от *Bors, Borsi, Borsod.* – Обе представленных в венгерских
работах этимологии, во-первых, игнорируют то обстоятельство, что и
Borsova/Borzsova в Закарпатье, и *Bózsva* – реки, в связи с чем их образование от ЛИ с помощью суффикса принадлежности маловероятно;
во-вторых, не находят объяснения славянские и венгерские формы с *ž*
(zs). С учетом этого следует отдать безусловное предпочтение возве-
дению рассматриваемых топонимов к слав. **Вържava* (букв. 'более бы-
страя'). Укр. *Боржава* непосредственно отражает эту праформу. Для
венгерского следует предполагать закономерное развитие **Вържava* >
др.-венг. **Buršāva* (в период до появления фонемы [ž]) ~ **Buržāva*,
откуда далее *Borsova ~ Borsva ~ Borzsova ~ Borzsva* (с частичной или
полной редукцией гласного во втором открытом слоге трехсложного
слова) и *Bózsva* (из *Borzsva*, с диалектным развитием долгого *ó* из *or*
перед стечением согласных).

Borsva – s. *Borsova.*

Borzs(o)va – s. *Borsova.*

Bózsva – s. *Borsova.*

bödön (1469: ? bodon szn.; 1484: Bodonkwth hn.; 1685: dőbőnőkbe; 1794: bödön) 'бидон; (seit 1484) сруб колодца' [Kn. 1: 106-107; TESz 1: 357-358].
– **Hel.:** < slaw. *вьдьнъ* (ЭССЯ 3: 113-114); формы м.р. – только в ю.-сл.

*Bördőce (1324: Burzeulche; 1381: Berzelche; 1405: Brzelcz; 1524: Berzel-
cze), in: **Iklódbördőce** Ortsname, Komitat Zala [Stan. 2: 68 und Kiss 288:
< slaw. **Berzovica, *Berzьnica*]. – **Hel.:** < ?? slaw. *bьrzd[ovica]* (ЭССЯ 3:
135 – **bьrzdъ* (только др.-рус., белор.), **bьrzdica* (только схрв. *брздù-
ца* 'стремнина').

Börzönce – s. *Berzence.*

Budmér (1291: Budmer), in: **Kisbudmér** Ortsname, Komitat Baranya [Kiss
338 (сравн. с именем *Будимúр* etc.)] ~ **Bodmér** (1311: Budmer) Ortsname, Komitat Fejér [Kiss 114]. – **Hel.:** < slaw. *Budimĕrъ.* – Vgl. *Bagamér.*

burján (1343: Burian szn.; 1673: burjánok) 'бурьян, сорняк' [Kn. 1: 113; TESz
1: 391-392]. – **Hel.:** < slaw. *burьjanъ* (ЭССЯ 3: 99-100, с сомнениями в
общеслав. хар-ре).

buta I *altung.* (1199: ? Butha szn.; сюда ли: 1577 'загнутый кверху'?) 'глупый, тупой (ст.-венг.)' [TESz 1: 395-396 (неизв. происх.; слн. *bútart* 'тупой, глупый' < венг., как и нем. (Транс.) *buta* 'buta'; слав. объясн. ошибочно); EWU: Unbek. Urspr.; см. EtSz!]. – **Hel.:** < slaw. *buta* (ЭССЯ 3: 101-102); польск. *buta* 'Hochmut, Hochnäsigkeit', укр. *бутá*, слн. *búta* 'тупой'.

buta II 'загнутый кверху' – s. *buta* I.

bürü (1322/1364: Munkadbrui hn.; 1673: bŏrǔc) 'мостик' [Kn. 1: 114; TESz 1: 403-404]. – **Hel.:** < slaw. *brъvь* (ЭССЯ 3: 71-72: < *brъvь*). – Vgl. *borona*.

cúca *arch.*, *dial.* < **szúca** *altung.*, *dial.* (1388: Zulchas szn.; ca. 1395: ʒulcha [s-]; ca. 1405: chucha; Mitte 15.Jh.: *szúca*) '1. (*arch.*) копье; горн. вершина; 2. (*dial.*) вязальная игла; заостренная палка etc.' [Kn. 1: 118; TESz 1: 458-459 (вер., с ю.-слав.)]. – **Hel.:** < slaw. *sulica* < *sudlica*.

csahol (? **csáhol**) *altung.* (1458-1560 (OklSz 112): chahol, chyahol) 'вид рубашки' [Kn. 1: 119 (выводит из *čachъlъ*, но допускает и старое заим. из *če-*)]. – **Hel.:** < slaw. *čexъlъ* (ЭССЯ 4: 35-36); др.рус. **чехолъ** ~ **чахолъ**, слвц. удар. на 2-м слоге.

csákány (1393: ? Chakan szn.; ca. 1395: chakan; 1517: chakanyokkal) 'кирка́' [Kn. 2: 604-606; TESz 1: 469]. – **Hel.:** < slaw. *čakanъ* (ЭССЯ 4: 12-13) или непоср. из тюрк. *čakan* – менее вер. {= вероятно} ввиду сем. {= семантики}.

Csala (1356: Chala) '1. с.-в. предместье (ныне часть) Секешфехервара, м. Фейер [смотрит на Будапешт]; 2. ю.-з. предместье Bonyhád'a, м. Тольна [смотрит на Печ] (1299: Chala)' [(ad 1:) Kiss 154, Kiss² 303 (от ЛИ Chala (1211) от *csal* 'обмануть'); (ad 1, 2:) Stan. 2: 100 (с совершенно иными объяснениями)]. – **Hel.:** < slaw. *čelo* (ЭССЯ 4: 45; ср. слн. 'лоб, передняя, выступающая сторона предмета: фронтон, фасад дома').

Csalár (= слвц. *Čeláry*) Ortsname, Komitat Nógrád [Stan. 2: 101 (возводит к *Čalári*)]. – **Hel.:** < ? slaw. *čelar(i)* '≈ жители предгорья'.

Csatár 1. (1141-61: Chitary) Ortsname, Komitat Zala [Kiss 157; Stan. 108-109 (< *ščitarь/i*)]; 2. = румын. *Cetariu* (1213: Catar) Ortsname in Siebenbürgen, Komitat Bihar. – **Hel.:** < ? slaw. *četarь/i* ~ *četarjь/i*; vgl. slaw. *četa* > ung. *csata*.

csáva (1546: Cawaban; 1565: czáua) 'дубильное вещество' [Kn. 1: 123-124; TESz 1: 487-488 (отмечается, что знач. {= значение} = болг., но форма ≠ болг.)]. – **Hel.:** < slaw. *ščava* (Фасм. 4: 495).

csåvkå – s. *csóka*.

csëmër – s. *csömör*.

Csencs(e) Ortsname. – **Hel.:** Весьма вероятно, что слав. *čęstja* > *čęšča* 'чаща' (см. ЭССЯ 4: 109 – рефлексы отмечены только в восточнославянском ареале, начиная с др.-рус. XI в. **чащα**) отражено в топонимах из комитата Ваш: 1401 Czchenczche, 1452 Chenche. Соответствующие формы без конечного гласного: 1359, 1424: Chench, 1486: Chencz, совр. *Német-*, *Horvát-* и *Taródcsencs* (нем. Deutsch-, Kroatisch-Tschan-tschendorf и Tudelsdorf) – названия деревень, *Csencs* – хутор между Nagykölked и Sároslak. Эти формы вторичны и возникли в результате переосмысления конечного *-e* как Px3Sg (*Németcsencse* 'Немецкая Csencse' → *Németcsencs-e* 'Csencs немца' → *Németcsencs*). – См. об этих топонимах Moór 1936: 23, где предлагается объяснение *Csencs* из слав. **Čenčice* или **Čenk-je* от антропонима *Čenko* и под. (диминутив к *Vlčen* или соответствие др.-венг. личных имен *Chenk, Chenka* и т.д.). Однако существование одантропонимических топонимов предполага-емого Моором облика (в отличие от топономив типа чеш. *Čenkov*, хорв. *Čenkovo*, которые дали бы в венгерском **Csenkő* или **Čankó* {!, ɔ: **Csankó*}) представляется маловероятным. – В фонетическом отно-шении обращает на себя внимание отражение **stj* (**šč*) в виде *cs* в постконсонантной позиции. [...] ср. также слав. **-ętj-* > венг. *-encs-* (**lętja* > *lencse* 'чечевица', **sъrętja* > *szerencse* 'счастье'). – Наряду с этим – **Csencsice** (нем. Zunkendorf) в Словакии (область Спиш) < слав. диминутива **čęstjica* > **čęščica*.

Csencsice – s. *Csencs(e)*.

cserény [-ɛr-] *dial.* (1338/1395: ? Cherenthow hn., ок. 1395: cheren) ~ *dial.* **cserín** 'плетеное из прутьев изделие; примитивное жилье пастуха; низкая дверь перед входом в кухню в крестьянскм доме; часть печи или стены возле печи или очага; Flechtwerk; niedrige Flurtür eines Bauernhauses; Teil des Ofens oder der Wand {am} Ofen' [Kn. 2: 813-815 (опровергает слав. этимологию); TESz 1: 507-508 (не принимает ее); EWU: "Abl{eitung} aus einem fiktiven Stamm", zu *serít, sűrű, serény*]. – **Hel.:** < slaw. *čerěnъ/ь* (ЭССЯ 4: 64-65; болг. 'верхняя часть очага').

cserín – s. *cserény*.

csërësznye – s. *csërësznye*.

csërësznye (OklSz) (1256: cheresna(fa); ca. 1395: chereſnÿe) ~ *dial.* **csërësnye**, **cserësnye**, **csörösnye**, **cserösnye** (Hel.: тесная связь *ë* с *sn* вм. *szn*?) 'че-решня' [Kn. 1: 129-130; TESz 1: 509-510 (*cs : s > cs : sz*, как в *csésze*)]. – **Hel.:** < slaw. *črěšьna* (*črěšьńa* ?) < *čeršьna* (ЭССЯ 4: 78-79). – В свете всего сказанного в этим. ист. нельзя исключить заим. и из иного источ-ника, видимо, восходящего к лат. *cerasina* ~ *ceresina* 'вишневая'. – Все шатко. В-т 1256 г. м.б. *-na* или *-ńa*; если *-na*, то разв. в *-ńe* м.б. внутривенг. или рез-том {= результатом} повт. заимств. {= повторного заимствования}; не искл. и заим. венг. > слав. по кр. мере части форм; в-т с *-na* м.б. подтвержд. рек-ции {= подтверждение реконструкции}

*-*nа*, согласно Фасмер ГрСлЭт 3: 224 *-ńа* под влиянием аналогии с *вишня*.

cserösnye – s. *csёrёsznye*.

Csertő (1360: Chertw) Ortsname, Komitat Baranya [Kiss 162: *cser* 'cserfaerdő' + *tő* 'основание']. – **Hel.:** < ? slaw. *čьrtovъ/а/о* (ЭССЯ 4: 165).

csésze [-é-] (ca. 1395: cheʒeu; 1498: Cheze) 'чашка' [Kn. 1: 131-132 (132: в ст.-чеш. *а* внутри слога между 2 первично палат. согл., а в конце слога после первично палат. согл. в XII в. регулярно развился в *е*: **češe*. Дифт-ция {= дифтонгизация (!)} долгого *é* в чеш. произошла в XIV в., т.о. венг. слово могло быть заим. между XII а XIV в. Венг. *-sz-* – рез-т диссим. {= результат диссимиляции}); TESz 1: 512-513]. – **Hel.:** < др.-чеш. *čěše* < slaw. *čaša* (ЭССЯ 4: 30-31).

csobolyó 'бочонок, сосуд для питья'. – **Hel.:** < ? slaw. *čьbVl(j)а*.

csóka (1138/1329: ? Cauka szn.; 1211: ? Choucha szn.; ca. 1395: choka) ~ *dial.* **csávkȧ** (повт. заим.) 'галка' [Kn. 2: 616-617; TESz 1: 547-548 (скл. {= склоняется} к идее о независ. ономат. происх.)]. – **Hel.:** < slaw. *čavъka* (ЭССЯ 4: 31-32), но ср. тж. тат. (миш.) *čawka*, балк. *čauka* etc.

Csoma (1327 Chama) Ortsname (= {slowak.} *Čoma*, {ukr.} *Чома*). – **Hel.:** < ? slaw. **čита*; в этом случае современные славянские формы < венг. Интерпретацию затрудняют этимологические трудности, связанные со слав. **čита* (см. ЭССЯ 4: 133 sub **čиtъ*; также TESz 1: 550 sub *csoma* 'pestis' и TESz 1: 573 sub *csuma* 'почка, кочан, стебель'; последнее несомненно связано с румын. *ciumă* 'побег, росток').

csorda (1282/1325: Charadajaras hn.; 1291: Churda; ca. 1395: chorda, cherda) 'стадо, гурт' [Kn. 1: 141-142 (возм. **čьrda*; или из схрв. **črida*); TESz 1: 555-556 (через *csёrёda*)]. – **Hel.:** < ? slaw. *čerda* (не *črěda*!) (ЭССЯ 4: 60-61; Топ. 4: 315-323), ?*čьrda*. – Ср. *csoroszlya* < *črěslo* < *čerslo*! (Может быть регулярным).

csoroszlya – s. *csorda*.

csorpák (1887, MTSz) 'мялкоячеистая сеть' [Kn. 1: 143 (< укр., польск.)]. – **Hel.:** < slaw. *čьrpakъ* (ЭССЯ 4: 158); укр. *черпа́к* 'вид рыболовной сети', польск. *czerpak* (Linde, ЭССЯ нет: < укр.?). – Скорее всего, новое заим.

csömer – s. *csömör*.

csömör (1135/1262/1566: ? Chemer hn.; 1553-61: csemer; 1563: csömör) ~ *dial.* **csёmёr, csömer** (возможна контаминация с *sömör* 'стригущий лишай' ~ *sömörög* 'сморщиваться' оном.) 'тошнота, отвращение (диал. также 'узелок под кожей')' [Kn. 2: 618-619; TESz 1: 563-564 (преувеличивая семант. трудности)]. – **Hel.:** < slaw. *čemerъ, -ь* (ЭССЯ 4: [-ъ:] 52-53, [-ь:] 53-54). Но ср. *čьтьrъ* (ЭССЯ 4: 146) с отчасти совпад. значением (польск.диал. *czmer* 'мелочь, дрянь' ~ чеш. *čemera* 'гадость, дрянь'; слн. *čemér* ~ *čmér* 'яд, гной; досада etc.') (Венг. → *čьть/еrь/ъ*). Ср. ung.

csöbör ~ *csëbër* 'ушат' < *čьbьrъ* {vgl. poln. *ceber* id.}. – Поздн{ее} ? – {In einer getrennten Notiz heißt es noch:} Вокализм венгерского слова позволяет [...] думать, что славянский источник имел вид **čьtьrъ* или **čьterъ*.

csörösnye – s. *csërësznye*.

Dabrony (1311: Dobrongonusfalu) Ortsname, Komitat Veszprém [Stan. 2: 156-157 (сравнивается с чеш. *Dobřín*, польск. *Dobrzyń* etc.); Kiss 171 (~ чеш. *Dobroň* szn.)]. – **Hel.:** < slaw. *dobryni* (ЭССЯ 5: 46-47).

Dalocsa (1193: Dolosa) 'поле в Bogyiszló, Komitat Tolna, на берегу Дуная' [Stan. 2: 138 (из Dolaša)]. – **Hel.:** ? < slaw. *dolica* (ЭССЯ 5: 61 'долина').

Damak (1279: Domok; 1478: Damak) Ortsname, Komitat Borsod-Abaúj-Zemplén [Stan. 2: 138-139 (так); Kiss 172 (к *Domokos* или к чеш. *Domek* < *Domaslav* etc.)]. – **Hel.:** ? < slaw. *domъkъ*.

*Damás(d) (1138/1329: Damaſa), in: **Ipolydamásd** Ortsname, Komitat Pest [Stan. 2: 139; Kiss 291]. – **Hel.:** < slaw. *Domašь* (≠ ЭССЯ 5: 68 **domatjь*). Ср. чеш. *Domaš* ЛИ; др.-р. **Домаш**.

Darány (1229/1550: Dran; 1437: Daran) Ortsname, Komitat Somogy [Stan. 2: 140; Kis 173]. – **Hel.:** < ? slaw. *dьranь* (ЭССЯ 5: 217-218); ср. др.-рус. **дрянь**; слвц. *draňa* 'бесплодная почва'.

Dargóc (1360: Dorgoch; 1448 Dargocz) Ortsname, Komitat Somogy [Stan. 2: 141]. – **Hel.:** < slaw. *dragovьcь* < *dorgovьcь*.

Darnó (seit 1336; 1341: Darno, Dorno; 1348: Darnow) Orts- und Bergname [Kniezsa 1942b; Stan. 141, 142; Kiss 173, 174: Возводят к **Dьrnovъ* (от *dьrnъ*)]. – **Hel.:** < slaw. *drěnovъ* < *dernovъ* (ЭССЯ 4: 208 'кизиловый'). – Vgl. *Darnóc, Darnóca*.

Darnóc (1446: Darnocz) Ortsname, Komitat Borsod-Abaúj-Zemplén [Stan. 2: 141 (**Drnovec/-vci*)]. – **Hel.:** < slaw. *drěnovьcь* < *dernovьcь*. – Vgl. *Darnó, Darnóca*.

Darnóca (1494: Darnocza) Ortsname, Komitat Tolna [Stan. 2: 141 (< **Drnovica*)]. – **Hel.:** < slaw. *drěnovica* < *dernovica*. – Vgl. *Darnó, Darnóca*.

daróc '1. неясного знач. слово (пыт. {= пытается} объяснить как назв. {= название} профессии) в след. конт. {= следующих контекстах}: de populis nostris, qui *drawc* uulgo dicuntur 1263-70 (ÁÚO 8: 20); populi *drauch* (ibid.); terram Dumuslou (= *Domoszló*) in comitatu de Aba Vyvar, in qua populi *drauch* in antea residebant 1263/94 (ÁÚO 8: 70); 2. ряд топонимов, см. Kiss 103-104 (*Beregdaróc*); Stan. 2: 142 (1284: *Drauch*) [NB! *Daróca*!]; 3. сермяга; сермяжная ткань (1349: darouch' [Kn. 2: 622-623 (*daróc*[1] 'сермяга' < ? *dьravьcь* от *dьrati, dьravъ*; *dároc*[2] {sic!: á – o} – слав., но неизв. {???, = 'происхождения'}); TESz 1:596 ('сермяга' – неизв. происх.)]. – **Hel.:** < slaw. *Drava* п.п. {= правый приток} Дуная (гр. *Δράβος*, лат. *Dravos* ~ *Dravus*; у An. ок. 1150 Droua), схрв. *Dráva*, слн. *Dráva* (> в. *Dráva*). – Среди многочисленных топонимов *Daróc* на территории исторической Венгрии [...] лишь некоторые непосредственно восходят к слав. **dravьсь/i*, другие же отражают др.-венг. *daróc* – название одной из этнопрофессиональных групп (восходящее, вероятно, к тому же славянскому источнику), см. Stan. 2: 142; Kiss 103. Учитывая, что *Beregdaróc* впервые фиксируется в фонетическом облике, сходном со славянским прототипом (Drauch), этот топоним скорее относится к первой из названных групп. – S. auch *Bereg*.

Darza (~ **Darza-patak**) 'приток р. Марцаль, м. Веспрем' [Stan. 1: 142 (**Drza* ∨ **Drzava*, ср. схрв. *Drzava*); Kiss 174 (? слн.диал. *drása* 'вид сорняка')]. – **Hel.:** < slaw. *dereza* (ЭССЯ 4: 205-206).

debre – s. *dobra*.

decka – s. *dëszka*.

degecs – s. *deget*.

degesz – s. *deget*.

deget *dial.* (1767: deget) ~ *dial.* **degett, degecs** (? 1731: gyehecsek), **degesz** (много в-тов типа **dohat** etc.) 'колесная мазь' [Kn. 2: 624; TESz 1: 603-604]. – **Hel.:** < slaw. *degъtь* (ЭССЯ 4: 204-205; все же скорее всего < балт., лит. *degùtas*. В ю.-слав. отсут. {= отсутствует}). – Поздн{ее}? (скорее всего).

degett – s. *deget*.

derce (OklSz 150: [ε – ε]) (1234-70: ? Durche hn.; 1621: derce; 1863: dörczéje) ~ *dial.* **dërce** '1. мука крупного помола; 2. (ст.-венг.) ссора; 3. (1763) кожница и шелуха различных плодов' [Asboth Nytud {= NytudÉrt} 1: 187 – ссылка в Kn. 1: 151, к-рый предпочитает возводить к **tьricę*, болг. *tríci*, схрв. *trĩce*, ст.-слав. **трицѧ**, что фонетич. неправдоподобно; не приниамет этого и TESz 1: 616]. – **Hel.:** < slaw. *dъrtьca* (незасвид.), ср. *dъrtь* (ЭССЯ 5: 227).

Dercen (1321: Derzen; 1332/1335: Dersen) Ortsname (= {slowak.} *Drysina*, {ukr.} *Дрисина*). – **Hel.:** Форма венгерского топонима позволяет предполагать как славянский прототип **drisinъ* или даже **drisina* (откуда непосредственно *Дрисина*), так и некое иное образование, связанное со слав. **driskati/*dristati*, **dristьnъ/*dristьna* (см. ЭССЯ 5: 116-117) и производными фитонимами **drěstъ*, **drěstьnъ* (см. ЭССЯ 5: 110-111). В частности, *Dercen* могло фонетически регулярным образом – через промежуточные формы *Derészen*, *Darszen* – развиться из формы **der-sьnъ/*drěsьnъ*, соответствующей схрв. *дресан* 'Polygonum persicaria', слн. *rdésen* 'горец Polygonum', укр.диал. *дéресень* 'Polygonum minus', *дрясен* 'Polygonum hydropiper L.' (ЕСУМ 2: 38).

dërёk, dërёka (1307: derekes szn.; 1400: derekal) ~ *dial.* **dërík, dërёkát** (-ti), **derík** (-ki) '1. талия, поясница; торс; 2. добрый, сильный, статный'

[Kn. 1: 151-152 (смешаннорядность – из-за исходного -ə), TESz 1: 617-618 (с неопр. сомнениями)]. – **Hel.:** < slaw. *drěkъ* (ЭССЯ 5: 108), ср. *drěčьnъ(jь)* 'достойный, крепкий' etc. (ЭССЯ 5: 107-108) ~ лит. *draĩkas* 'долговязый, стройный'. – {Zur Opposition: slaw. *drěkъ* (Subst.) vs. lit. *draĩkas* (Adj.):} Не было ли Adj. в праславянском?

dërík – s. *dërěk*.

*Dërzs, in: **Nyírdërzs** (1298: Ders) Ortsname [Kiss 472; EtSz 1: 1327; Kniezsa MNNy 4: 223; Kniezsa MagyRom. 1: 295] ~ **Tiszadërzs** (1343: Ders) Orts-name, Komitat Jász-Nagykun-Szolnok [Stan. 2: 149; Kiss 644]. – **Hel.:** < slaw. *dьržь* (ЭССЯ нет, но ср. дериваты от *dьržati* типа рус. *у́держ*, чеш. *nádrž* 'сосуд', польск. *Dzierż* ЛИ). – {Später dazugeschrieben:} **držь* (SP 5: 69).

dëszka (1469: Dezkas szn.) ~ диал. **doszka, decka, dëcka** (в-ты с *do-* – секей-ские {!}) 'доска' [Kn. 1: 153; TESz 1: 622]. – **Hel.:** < slaw. *dъska* (или *dьska*?) (ЭССЯ 5: 183-184). – Венг. слово м.б. заимствовано из формы с уже развившимся из ъ *е*, типа слн. *deskà*, чеш. *deska*, слвц.диал. *deska* – так предп. Kn., TESz – или отражать {sic!; э: может отражать ~ отражает} "исконное", но не засвид. слав. **dъska* из герм. < лат. *discus*, см. ЭССЯ. – {Auf einem anderen Zettel:} Допустимо думать, что именно эта незасвидетельствованная в славянском форма отражена в венг. *dëszka* 'доска' (с XV в.). Напротив, венг.диал. (преимущественно в секлерских говорах) *doszka* 'id.' регулярно отражает **dъska*.

dinnye (? 1093: dinna hn; ca. 1395: dÿne, dÿene; ca. 1405: dinne) 'дыня, арбуз' [Kn. 1: 155-156; TESz 1: 640]. – **Hel.:** < *dynja* (схрв. *dȉnja*, слн. *dínja*, болг. *dínja*) ~ *dyńa* (Фасм. 1: 559; БЕР 1: 393; ЭССЯ не приводит). – Не отражает ли *-ńń-* дифтон. сочетания *-nj-*?

dobra (1891: dobra (Komárom)) ~ *dial.* **debre** (1831: debre, debrő (Bodrog-köz)) 'яма, вымоина, овраг' [Kn. 1: 149 (< слвц. *debra*); TESz 1: 666 (sub *döbör*; < слвц. – отд. заим. {= отдельное заимствование})]. – **Hel.:** < slaw. *dъbra* (ЭССЯ 5: 176-177 sub *dъbrь*).

Dobrony (*Nagydobrony*) (1248/1393: Dobron; 1282/1379: Dubron; 1299: Dub-run) Ortsname (= {slowak.} *(Veliká) Dobroň*, {ukr.} *(Великая) Добронь*). – **Hel.:** Фонетическое тождество современных венгерских и славян-ских названий указывает на то, что одно из них является поздним за-имствованием. Скорее всего, {ukr.} *Добронь* < венг. *Dobrony* < слав. **dъbrinъ* (от **dъbrь*, см. ЭССЯ 5: 176-177; ср. многочисленные дерива-ты типа схрв. *дабрина*, укр. *дебрине́ць*). В пользу этого решения сви-детельствуют др.-венг. формы с *и* (рефлекс слав. **ъ*). Гораздо менее вероятно, что венг. *Dobrony* < *Добронь* < **dobrъ*.

doh (ca. 1456: dohoſba) 'затхлость' [Kn. 1: 156-157; TESz 1: 653]. – **Hel.:** < slaw. *dъxъ* (ЭССЯ 5: 178) или *duxъ* (ЭССЯ 5: 153-154).

dohat – s. *deget*.

Dombró (1330: Dumburou) Ortsname (heute: Mozsgó), Komitat Baranya ~ **Dombró** (1291: Dumburou) Ortsname in Siebenbürgen, Komitat Torda-Aranyos [Stan. 2: 159, 352; Kiss 434 (*dǫbrava)]. – **Hel.:** < slaw. *dǫbrava / dǫbrova / dǫbrovъ*.

***donha** (1458: dωhna; 1604: dunha; 1611: donha) 'перина' [Kn. 1: 164 (все из слав. *duchna ~ duchnja*; не исключено и то, что задун. *dunyha* и трансильв. *donyha* – раздельные заимствования из ю.-слав. *duchnja*); TESz 1: 688]. – **Hel.:** < slaw. *dux(ъ)na* (ЭССЯ 5: 157). – Ср. **dunyha** < схрв. *dȕhnja, dȕnja*, слн. *dunja* < *dux(ъ)n̂a*.

***dosnok** – s. **dusnok*.

doszka – s. *dëszka*.

***Döbör**, in: **Döbörhegy** (1538: Deberhegye) Ortsname, Komitat Vas ~ **Döbrö-köz** (1309: debregzth) Ortsname, Komitat Tolna ~ **Döbröce** Ortsname, Komitat Veszprém [Stan. 2: 143 (*Döbrököz < Dobrogostь*); Kiss 186: {a} < *dobrъ*; {b} < *Dobrogostь* (немыслимо! Ср. 1224: Dobrogozt szn.); {c} < *Dobrica* ∨ *Dubrovica* и под.]. – Сюда же, вероятно, *Döbrönte*. – **Hel.:** *Döbör* < slaw. *dъbrъ* (ЭССЯ 5: 176-177); *Döbröce* < ? slaw. *Dъbrьca*. – О слав. *dъbrъ* в венг.: TESz s.v. *döbör*; Kn. 1: 149, 2: 774.

Döbröce – s. **Döbör*.

Döbrököz – s. **Döbör*.

Döbrönte – s. **Döbör*.

dunyha – s. **donha*.

***dusnok** [? ***dúsnok**, ?? ***dosnok**] (1067/1267: Dusnuky hn.; 1211: ? Dosnuch szn.; 1215/1550: Duʃunic hn.; 1222/1550: duʃinicos; 1335: Dusnok hn. = heut. **Dusnok** Ortsname) 'завещанный церкви слуга, выполняющий обязанности ради души своего бывшего господина (впоследствии tarló)' [Kn. 1: 165-166; TESz 1: 693; OklSz 162]. – **Hel.:** < slaw. *dušь-nikъ*, ст.-чеш. *dušník*. Ср. ЭССЯ 5: 164 *duša*.

eckába – s. *ëszkába*.

ecset [ε – ɛ] (1480: ? Eczethes szn.; 1533: Echeth) 'кисть (малярная), помазок' [Kn. 2: 630-631; TESz 1: 706]. – **Hel.:** < ? slaw. *sъčetь* (Фасм. 4: 505-506 – в пользу ***sčetь*, но ср. *č*- в болг. и полаб. *sacét* 'щетина, щетка, чесалка'). – Венг. форма объяснима из *sčetь*.

Egerbakta – s. *Bakta*.

eplény *dial.* (ca. 1395: eplen 'furale'; nach 1475: epleen) ~ *dial.* **eplíny** etc. 'перекладина между полозьями саней' [Kn. 1: 167-168; EtSz 1588; TSz 777]. – **Hel.:** < slaw. *oplěnъ*; болг.диал. *оплён*, схрв.диал. *òplen, òplin, òpljen*, слн. *oplèn* (dial. *oplìn*), слвц. *oplen*, укр.диал. *оплíн, оплíнь*, чеш. *oplen, oplín*, в.-луж. *woplon*, н.-луж. *hoplon* ≈̃ гр. πλῆμυ.

eplíny – s. *eplény*.

eretnëk [ε – εt-] (1357: Eretnuk szn.; 1456: eretnek) 'еретик' [Kn. 2: 631-632; TESz 1: 785]. – **Hel.**: < slaw. *eretьnikъ*. – {Zwar} ст.-слав. кретикъ, но: схрв.кайк. *(j)eretnik*, рус. *еретник*, слн. *jeretník*.

érsëk (1299: Ersek hn.; ca. 1405: erſeg) 'архиепископ' [Kn. 2: 632-633; TESz 1: 790-791 (допускает, что {слвц.-мор.} *yarssik* < венг.)]. – **Hel.**: < ? slaw. **aršikъ*; слвц.-мор. 1480-90 *yarssik*.

ëszkába (OklSz) (1348: Scaba; 1587: izkaba; 1698: szkábás) ~ *dial.* **iszkáva**, **eckába**, **ëszkóba** 'скоба, застежка' [Kn. 1: 168-169; TESz 1: 801]. – **Hel.**: < slaw. *skoba* (Фасм. 3: 643). – Zu Kn. а.а.О.: *szkaba > iszkaba > ëszkaba* – Нет. В-т с *ë*- фиктивен, а перехода *i > e* (ε) не было – вообще, *i*- сохранялось! Сущ-ло {= существовало} два варианта протезы: *a/e* (ε), как в *asztal* etc., и *i*-, как и в *ispán*. Этот вопрос требует спец. иссл. на всем, не только слав. м-ле {= материале}. Нет ли связи у *i/a* с долг. {= долготой} след. гласного etc.? – {Später dazugeschrieben:} не было ли в слав. *СаСá > СоСá*?

ëszkóba – s. *ëszkába*.

ësztëke – s. *ösztöke*.

ësztërág *dial.* < **ësztërak** *altung.* ([ë] – laut OklSz) (1329/14.Jh.: ? Straak hn.; 1369: ? Eztrak hn.; 1519: eztragoth [acc.]) ~ *dial.* **ësztrag**, **ësztërag** 'аист' [Kn. 2: 633-634; TESz 1: 804-805]. – **Hel.**: < slaw. *stьrkъ* (? ~ *stьrokъ*; ср. схрв. *штрк*, кайк. *štrok*). Выяснить.

Esztergom hn. (1079-80: ſtrigonensis comes; 1146: Estrigun) [Kiss 209 (без увер.)]. – **Hel.**: < slaw. *strĕgomъ < stergomъ* < (?!) *strigomъ*, (?) *strigunъ* – {vgl.} слвц. *Ostrihom*. – {Vgl. dt.} *Gran* 'Esztergom' vs. slaw. **gronъ* > {alttschech.} *Gron* ~ {ung.} *Garam* (Kiss 233).

ësztërha *dial.* (ca. 1405: оʒterha; 1582: eszterhéj; 1893: ësztërhé) 'навес (крыши), стреха' [Kn. 1: 169-171; TESz 1: 805-806 (sub *eszterhéj*)]. – **Hel.**: < *strĕxa* (Фасм. 3: 776-777) (строй?) < *stĕrxa* (схрв. *strĕha*, слн. *stréha*, укр. *стріха*).

eszteze (1522) 'тропинка'. – **Hel.**: < хрв. *steza* < ст.-слав. стьза.

ësztrag – s. *ësztërág*.

gabna – s. *gabona*.

gabona (ca. 1405: gabona; 1549: gobna; ca. 1560: gabnanak) ~ *dial.* **gabna** 'хлебные злаки, зерно' [Kn. 1: 174-175; TESz 1: 1010-1011]. – **Hel.**: < slaw. *gobino* (ЭССЯ 6: 185 – не учитывает значения, к-рое дает Kniezsa).

Gadány (1193: Godan) Ortsname, Komitat Somogy ~ **Aranyosgadány** (1192/1374/1425 Gadan) Ortsname, Komitat Baranya [Kis 60, 229 (ср. болг. *Годán* ЛИ, схрв. *Gudan*)]. – **Hel.**: ср. {poln.} *Gdańsk*.

*Galgó (nur altung. 1290/1342: Golgoua; 14.-15.Jh.: Galgo) Ortsname. – **Hel.**: < slaw. **glogova* (ж.р., см. ЭССЯ 6: 136). В современном венгерском языке топоним имел бы вид *Galgó* (Györffy 1: 539; EtSz 1: 882). – Ср.

Galgó, румын. *Gâlgău*, бывш. м. Сольнок-Добока (1405: Galgo); *Almas-Galgó*, румын. *Gâlgău*, бывш. м. Силадь (1560: Chalgo) [EtSz 1: 882; Stan. 2: 181]. Ср. также шесть топонимов **Galgóc** < слав. **Glogovьcь* [EtSz 1: 882-885; Kiss 554].

Galgóc – s. **Galgó*.

gally (1611) 'вешка (тонкая); der dünne Zweig' [Kn. 1: 177-178; TESz 1: 1023]. – **Hel.**: < slaw. *goljь* [ЭССЯ 7: 16-17] oder *golje*.

galóca I (1371: Galohkatou hn. {EWU: = ? Galohatou}; ок. 1520: Galocza) 'рыба Salmo hucho – дунайский лосось' [Kn. 1: 179; TEsz 1: 1020-1021 – выводят из слав. *glavatica* (схрв. *glavatica* 'Salmo hucho' etc.)]. – **Hel.**: < slaw. *glavica* < *golvica* [ЭССЯ 7: 8-9 (в частности, укр. *головиця* 'Salmo hucho')].

galóca II (1783) 'ядовитые грибы Amanita' [Kn. 2: 638; TESz 1: 1021]. – **Hel.**: возможно, искусств. перенос {= ? Bedeutungswandel von *galóca* I}.

garabla – s. **garáblya*.

*garáblya *altung.*, *dial.* (1319: garabla hn.; 1597: Vas garablia; 1766: geráblya) ~ *dial.* **gerábla**, **gërábla**, **garábla**, etc. 'грабли; Rechen' [Kn. 1: 189-190; TESz 1: 1049-1050 (в обоих местах – вместе с *gereblye*)]. – **Hel.**: < slaw. *grabľa* < *grabja* [ЭССЯ 7: 97-98]. – Vgl. *gereblye*.

Garabonc (1335: Garaboncz; 1432: Gerebench (неясно); 1376: Garabanch) Ortsname, Komitat Zala [Stan. 2: 182 (< *Grabovnica*); Kiss 233 (< *Grebe-nьcь*)]. – **Hel.**: < ? slaw. *grobьnica* (ЭССЯ 7: 134) (*Grabovnica* > **Gar-bónc*; *Grebenьcь* > ? *Gerebnec* и под.).

garággya ~ **garágya** *dial.* (1588: garádgyából) 'ограда, особ. из навоза' [Kn. 1: 183; TESz 1: 1027-1028 (sub *garágya*); EtSz. 1038 (во всех этих источниках допускается, что из *garád-ja*, Px3Sg – что излишне, или выводится из схрв. *grâđa* – что фонетически не объясняет -ggy-)] ~ *altung.* garagya (1277), Gradya (1322) 'огражденное место, садок для рыбы' [OklSz 294; EtSzl 1037]. – **Hel.**: < slaw. *gradja* < *gordja* (ЭССЯ 7: 36-37). – {Zur Herkunft des ung. Wortes: [1] < ung.dial. *garád-ja*, Px3Sg < *garád* 'забор, ограда, рама' < slaw. **gradъ* < **gordъ* oder [2] < "схрв. *grâđa*" heißt es in einer getrennten, aber inhaltlich dazugehörigen Notiz:} Первая версия выглядит излишней и искусственной, второй противоречит то обстоятельство, что *garágya* засвидетельствовано в диалектах той части Венгрии, которая максимально удалена от сербохорватской языковой территории, к востоку от Тисы (Надькуншаг, Бихар, Сабольч) см. EtSz 1038, SzlJsz {= Kn.} 182. […] К фонетическому оформлению заимствования (рефлекс группы *TorT*, отражение слав. **dj*) см. Хелимский 1988: 356-357, 359-360.

garas (ca. 1460: garaσσ) 'грош' [Kn. 2: 639; TESz 1: 1028-1029; Mollay 1982: 283-284]. – **Hel.**: < чеш. *groš*. – Позднее, но свид. {= свидетельствует} о том, что в XIII в. (первый *denarius grossus* 'толстый динарий' появился в 1266 при Людовике IX Святым во Франции – TESz 1: 1028-1029) рефлексация сахраняла 'праслав.' вид.

garázda (1375: Garazda szn.; 1527: garazda) 'сварливый, грубый, хулиганствующий etc.' [(!) EtSz 1056-1059; Kniezsa Pais-Eml. 332 (возражения); TESz 1: 1029 ("Szláv eredete nem valószínű")]. – **Hel.:** < slaw. *gorazda, -ь* (ЭССЯ 7: 32); к семантике ср. *gorazditi (sę)* – {ор. cit.} 7: 31-32. – Vgl. *garázna*.

garázna *dial.* (Трансильв.) (до 1764: garaznalkadasra), {semantisch:} = *garázda* [EtSz 1062-1063; Kniezsa Pais-Eml. 334 (возражения); TESz 1: 1029 (вместе с *garázda*)]. – **Hel.:** < slaw. *gorazdьna, -ъ* (ЭССЯ 7: 32-33). – Vgl. *garázda*.

Gasztony (1269/1271/1759: Goszton, Gosztun) Ortsname, Komitat Vas [Stan. 2: 184; Kiss 234]. – **Hel.:** < slaw. *gostinъ* (ЭССЯ 7: 64-65) (*gostunъ* ?).

gatya (1530: gatÿa) 'белые полотняные штаны' [EtSz 1104-1110 (< серб., не ранее XV-XVI в.), Kn. 1: 186-187 (допускает древность); TESz 1: 1034-1035 (< серб.)]. – **Hel.:** < slaw. *gatja* (ЭССЯ 6: 106-108; схрв. *gȁća, gȁće* (*ɡȁɦe*)). Фонетика – в пользу поздн. происх.

gazda (1372/1448: gaჳda) 'хозяин' [Kn. 2: 640-641; TESz 1: 1037-1038]. – **Hel.:** < slaw. *gospoda* (ЭССЯ 7: 58-59). Kn. {а.а.O.} сомневается, не замечая, что в *gospoda* 2-й слог открытый.

Gelén Ortsname, Komitat Nógrád [Stan. 2: 186 (иначе: **Golan*)]. – **Hel.:** < ? slaw. *glěnъ* (ЭССЯ 6: 120-121). – Vgl. *Gelénes, Gelence*.

Gelence Ortsname, Bezirk Galanta (Slowakei) [Stan. 2: 186]. – **Hel.:** < slaw. *glinica* (ЭССЯ 6: 126). – Vgl. *Gelén, Gelénes*.

Gelénes Ortsname, Komitat Szabolcs-Szatmár-Bereg [Kiss 235 (неправдопод. из имени *Kélianus ~ Gelyanus*)]. – Vgl. *Gelén, Gelence*.

gelyva – s. *golyva*.

gerábla – s. **garáblya*.

gёrcsa *dial.* (1786: gértsája) ~ *dial.* **gircsa, gёrdzsa, girdzsa** 'пер{едняя} часть шеи; спинной хребет; адамово яблоко; зоб' [Kn. 1: 641-642 (позднее, но не < слвк. из-за g, а не h); TESz 1: 1048 (вслед за Benkő StSl {= ?} 12: 44 отрицает слав. происх.)]. – **Hel.:** < slaw. *gъrča* (ЭССЯ 7: 202).

gёrdzsa – s. *gёrcsa*.

geréb [gɛ-, OklSz] *dial.* (1611: geréb) ~ **gёréb** '(1611) запруда, насыпь, дамба, гать, плотина, препятствие; (1742) хребет, позвонок; (1801) сухая ветка; (1864) дверной засов' [Kn. 1: 189 (*geréb* 'хребет' < *gъrbъ* [плохо]); TESz 1: 1048-1049 (без этим.)]. – **Hel.:** < ? slaw. *grěb-*; ср. ЭССЯ 7: 108-109 (*grebati/grěbati*), 109 (*grebja* > рус. диал., укр. *грéбня* 'гать, плотина'), 112-113 (*greby* > макед.диал. *гребен* 'хребет у скотины').

gerebën (OklSz; *gerebent, -(j)e*) (1294: Gerebenes hn.; ca. 1405: gereben) 'чесальный гребень (для льна, конопли)' [Kn. 1: 189; TESz 1: 1049]. – **Hel.:** < slaw. *greby, greben-* (ЭССЯ 7: 112-113).

gereblye [ε – ε – ε] (1319: ? Garabla hn.; ок. 1395: gereblÿe) 'грабли; der Rechen' [Kn. 1: 189-190 (< *grablje*, ср. ЭССЯ 7: 97-98: *grabja*); TESz 1: 1049-1050 (так же)]. – **Hel.:** < slaw. *grebľa* < *grebja* [ЭССЯ 7: 109 (ср. укр. *греблí* 'грабли')]. – Vgl. **garáblʲa.*

gërle (1830: gerle – слово, распространившееся преим. из палоцких говоров) 'горлица, Streptopelia turtur' [OklSz.; Kn. 1: 195; TESz 1: 1054 (считают, что это собств. венг. образ. на основе *gerlice*, вопреки высказ. ранее взгляду); Ашбот 238-239]. – **Hel.:** < slaw. *gъrla* < *gъrdla* (В статье ЭССЯ 7: 204-205 gъrdlo: схрв. *гр̀ља* 'горлица', чеш. *hrdla*, слн. *gŕla*). – {Kommentiert auf einem getrennten Zettel:} Такие названия горлицы как схрв. *гр̀ља* 'горлица', слн. *gŕla*, чеш. *hrdla* приведены в ЭССЯ среди рефлексов **gъrdlo.* По-видимому, здесь все же представлено особое праслав. слово – **gъrdla* (откуда и регулярный диминутив **gъrdlica*, получивший более широкое распространение). Оно отражено и в венг. *gërlɛ* 'горлица' (< **gъ́rla* < **gъrdla*). Вслед за О. Ашботом {Ашбот 238-239}, Kn. 195 и TESz 1: 1054 преполагают, что слово *gërlɛ* проникшее в литературный язык из палоцких говоров (где оно впервые фиксируется лишь в 1830 г.), представляет собой собственно венгерское образование от *gërlice* id. (< слав. **gъrdlica*). С учетом клеющихся слав. данных такое предположение выглядит надуманным и излишним. – Vgl. unten *gërlice.*

gërlice (1372/1448: gerlicʒeket; 1416/1466: gorlicet) (диал. преим. {= диалектально преимущественно} *gë-, gö-, gi-*, так же и Ашбот) 'горлица' [Kn. 1: 194-195; TESz 1: 1054; Ашбот 236-239]. – **Hel.:** < slaw. *gъrlica* < *gъrdlica* (ЭССЯ 7: 203-204). – Für Kommentar s.o. *gërle.*

Gétye (1275: Gegye) Ortsname, Komitat Zala [Kiss 239: слав. *Gotja/Gotje*]. – **Hel.:** < ? slaw. *gatьje.*

gircsa – s. *gërcsa.*

girdzsa – s. *gërcsa.*

godolya *arch.* (1275: Gudulamal hn.; 1290: godolafa; 1287: Gudula) 'груша (дерево)' [Kn. 1: 196; TESz 1: 1068]. – **Hel.:** < slaw. *gduľa* < *kъdulja* (ЕСУМ 1: 487).

golyva (1524) ~ *dial.* **gelyva** (1576) 'базедова болезнь, зоб'. – **Hel.:** < кайк.-хрв. *gljïwa*, чак.-хрв. *gľiva* (в др. слав. яз. нет этого значения).

Gondoc Berg im Komitat Zala [Stan. 2: 195 (< *Gondovьcь* или *Gǫdovcьcь* {sic!, ɔ: *-vьcь*})]. – **Hel.:** < slaw. *gǫdьcь* (ЭССЯ 7: 81).

*Gonszna < *altung.* ⟨Gunzna⟩ (1250) Ortsname, Komitat Komárom [Kn. AECO 4: 321, 401; Stan. 2: 200]. – **Hel.:** < slaw. *gǫsina* (ЭССЯ 7: 83-84).

guzsaly < **kuzsaly** (1346: Gwsalwth hn.; ca. 1405: guʃal; 1602: Kusaly szn.; 1632: kuzsaly) 'ручная прялка' [Kn. 1: 206-207; TESz 1: 1111-1112]. – **Hel.:** < slaw. *kuželjь* < *kǫželь* (ср. ЭССЯ 12: 80-82: **kǫžьlь* / **kǫželь* / **krǫželь*. – Слово указывает на **kǫ́željь*, т.к. имели бы **kǫ́žьljь* > *kuzsoly*, **kǫžéljь* > *küzsely* etc. – Не самое раннее.

*Gyalla, in: **Ógyalla** Ortsname: Hurbanovo (Словакия; слвц. до 1948: Stará Ďala) ~ **Újgyalla** (слцк. Nová Ďala > Dulovce) [Kiss 479 (к тюрк. *jalan*, *jalïn* 'пламя'); Kn. AECO {= ?} 2: 102; Majtán {1972:} 117, 153]. – **Hel.:** < slaw. *jedla* (ЭССЯ 6: 14 – **edla* 'ель'; {aber vgl.:} схрв. *jéla*, *jě̀la*, слн. *jêla*, в.-луж. *jědla*, н.-луж. *jedła* {sowie poln.liter. *jodła* ~ dial. *jedła*}).

Gyalóka (1308: Gyoloka; 1319: Gyaloka) Ortsname, Komitat Győr-Moson-Sopron (= нем. *Jelwicken*) [Stan. 2 : 201; Kiss 250]. – **Hel.:** < slaw. *jelovьka* < *edlovьka* (ЭССЯ 6: 15). – Vgl. *jalóc*.

Halábor (1300: Harabur; 1324: Harabor; 1332: Harabor) Ortsname in Transkarpatien (= {slowak.} *Hrabarov*, {ukr.} *Грабаров*) [Stan. 2: 204]. – **Hel.:** {Auf zwei verschiedenen Zetteln kommentiert:} **[1]** < slaw. **grabrъ* (см. ЭССЯ 7: 99), с отражением перехода *g* > *h* или < слав. **xrabrъ* < **xorbrъ* (см. ЭССЯ 8: 71-72). В последнем случае современные славянские формы представляют собой модифицированные заимствования старо-венгерской формы (до диссимиляции *r* > *l*); **[2]** < slaw. *xrabrъ* < *xorbrъ* (ЭССЯ 8: 71-72). В Закарпатье! Не *Harbor* < *xarbrъ*, не *Harabor* < *xorobrъ*.

halom (1055: holma; 1269: Hulum [!] hn.) 'холм' [Kn. 1: 210 (было бы **hulmu*. Поэтому Melich < рус. *холмъ* → в др.-рус. уже был в IX в.!); TESz 2: 38; Ашбот 261-263 (преобразование как в *malom* < *mъlynъ*)]. – **Hel.:** < slaw. *xъlmъ* (ЭССЯ 8: 138-139).

*hamút (ca. 1395: hamuth; 1566: hamoth (? hamuth); 1579: hamútokban) 'хомут' [Kn. 1: 211-212 (**hamut*); TESz 2: 42-43 (*hamut*)]. – **Hel.:** < slaw. *xomǫtъ* (> *xomutъ*). – Поздн{ее}: *ǫ* > *u*.

Harábor – s. *Halábor*.

harák dial. (seit 1840) 'мокрота', **harákol** dial. (ab 1801) 'харкать, откашливаться' [Kn. 1: 837 (*harákol* ≮ *xrakati*: было бы *harákál*); TESz 2: 53 (оном. ~ слав.)]. – **Hel.:** < ? slaw. *xrakъ* (Ср. ЭССЯ 8: 89 *xrakati*).

haraszt (1225: Horosth; 1227 (OklSz): horost; ca. 1228: chrast; 1231 (OklSz): horozta, charasta; 1238 (OklSz): Hurozt; 1245/1423 (OklSz): horozt; 1257 (OklSz): horost [т.е. много раз *o – o* !]) 'сухая, опавшая листва; (ст.-венг.) дубняк, кустарник etc.' [Kn. 1: 212-213 (в фонет. отнош. удивит. всего др.-венг. *horoszt*); TESz 2: 57-58]. – **Hel.:** < slaw. *xvrastъ* < *xvorstъ* (ЭССЯ 8: 130-131).

Helemba 'о-в на Дунае' (1234: Helumba zygeth; 1270: Helunba) ~ 'Эстергом' (1138/1329: Helenba, Chelemba) [Stanislav 1948 2: 210-211 – "Podľa

osobného oznámenia spisovateľa Domastu, je tu skatočne vodopád na Ko-
váčskom potoku"; На запад нах. {= находится} долина *Chleba* (новое
слвц.)]. – **Hel.**: < slaw. *xlęba* (ЭССЯ 8: 32-33 – с сомн. разделением
xlęba от *xlębь*). – {Vgl. auch Kiss[2] 1: 583 s.v. *Helemba* und 562 s.v. *Ha-limba*}.

Helmec (1299: Hylmuch, Hulmuch; 1334: Helmuch) Ortsname. – **Hel.**: < slaw.
*xъltьсь (от **xъltъ*, см. ЭССЯ 8: 138-139).

Herencsény (1303: Herenchen) Ortsname, Komitat Nógrád [Stan. 2: 212 und
Kiss 272 (от *Chrěnčane* от *xrěnъ* – но ср. *Herény*!)]. – **Hel.**: < slaw.
xręšč(any) (Ср. ЭССЯ 9: 95-96 *xręščь*).

Herény (1265: Heren) Ortsname, heute: *Tormafalu* = dt. *Krensdorf* (!) [Stan. 2:
212-213; Moór 1936: 30]. – **Hel.**: < slaw. *xrěnъ* (Отсюда же и *Herény* –
ныне часть Сомбатхея, 1263 Herin, см. Kiss 272 с той же этим.). – Vgl.
Herencsény.

Hetye – s. *Hetyen*.

Hetyen (1270-1272/1393: Heytin; 1808: Hettyén, Hetény). – **Hel.**: Для близких по фонетическому облику топонимов – **Hetye** (Egyházashetye) в м.
Веспрем (1264: Heghe), **Hetye** (Makkoshetye) в м. Дьёр-Шопрон (1275:
Heghe) – предлагались объяснения из слав. **Xot-ja* или **Xot-je* (Kniezsa StSl. 1: 46; Kiss 199) или из слвц. **Haťe* от слав. **gať* (Stan. 2:
214). Оба эти объяснения вызывают сомнения, в частности потому, что
плохо согласуются со старыми написаниями *gh, g*. (В одном из вариантов ст.-венг. орфографии практиковалась передача *ty* через *gy* (но
обычно не через *gh, g*), причем этот вариант в канцелярских докумен-
тах вышел из употребления в конце XIII в.). Представляется более
вероятным, что топонимы *Hetye* образованы от венг. *hegy* 'гора' (ср.
возможность развития: *hegy-he > hetyhe > hetye*). Топоним *Hetyen*,
судя по ст.-венг. написанию *Heytin*, может быть и иного происхождения, в том числе и славянского (например, из **xotьjinъ*, ср. чеш. *chotin*
'невестин', см. ЭССЯ 8: 85-86); однако неясен статус вариантов *Hettyén*
и *Hetény*.

Hirip (1370: Hyrip), ein Fluß in Siebenbürgen [Kn. MR {= ?} 280: < *herep* 'вид
дерева']. – **Hel.**: < slaw. *xripъ* (Ср. ЭССЯ 8: 978: *xripati, xripěti, xripo-
ta/xripotъ*).

*honszár – s. *huszár*.

hort (1213/1550: Hurt szn.; ca. 1395: horth) 'охотничья собака' [Kn. 1: 217-
218; TESz 2: 149]. – **Hel.**: < slaw. *xъrtъ* (ЭССЯ 8: 148-149).[5]

huszár (1432: huzorones; 1449: hwzar szn.) '*altung.* (верховой) грабитель;
seit 1481: легковооруженный кавалерист, гусар' [Kn. 1: 219-220 (<

---

[5] Zu diesem und einigen anderen Namen für Hunderassen s. auch Stachowski 1995.

схрв.); TESz 2: 174-175 (id.)]. – **Hel.:** < slaw. *xusarь* (Фасм. 4: 285-286; ЭССЯ нет) < *xǫsarь* > ung. ***honszár** (1378: Hunzar) (по TESz м.б. ошибкой).

Ibrány (1310/1408: Ibran) Ortsname [Kiss 286 (arab. *Ibrāhīm*, 1263/1348: Ibrachin szn.); Horger MNy 25: 255; Galambos MNyTK 64: 9; Mikesy MNy 40: 242; BárcziHtört. 101, 102 (видимо, *á > i*?)]. – **Hel.:** < ? slaw. *jьbranъ* (Ср. ЭССЯ 8: 205-206: *jobrъ*, гидроним; БЕР 2: 2 Йбровица; 2: 3 Йбър). Есть и топонимы на -*ábrány* (Bükká., Nyírá.), {???} явно от *Ábrahám*.

Igló (1279: Igloszasza) Ortsname = *Spišská Nová Ves* (Словакия) [Stan. 2: 229; Kiss 287; Majtán 1972: 449; Kniezsa 1942b: 33]. – **Hel.:** < ? slaw. *jьgъlovъ*. – (1) Ср. *jьgъlъ* как редкий в-т к *jьgъla*, ЭССЯ 8: 213-214; (2) М.б. вторично по отн. к *Jihlava* (Моравия), нем. *Iglau*.

Ignéc (1248/1393: Ignech) Ortsname (= {slowak.} *Zňacovo*; {ukr.} *Знячево*). – **Hel.:** < ? slaw. *jьzgъnęcь*. Эта чисто формальная реконструкция, объединяющая глагольную основу *jьzgъnati* (см. ЭССЯ 9: 32) и суффикс *-ęcь* (ср. *месяц, заяц*), позволяет непротиворечивым с точки зрения исторической фонетики образом объяснить как венг. *Ignéc* (< *Izgnéc*), так и славянские формы (*Изгняц > Згняц > Зняц*). Альтернатива состояла бы в том, чтобы объявить венгерское и славянские названия не взаимосвязанными – что неправдоподобно.

***igrëc** *altung.* (1237-42: Hirrich hn.; 1244/1364: Igrech hn.; ca. 1405: igrech; 1416/1466: igrècekè) ~ (OklSz:) **igric**, ? **igröc** 'игрок, актер; бесполезный' [Kn. 1: 221-222 (sub *igric*; почему?); TESz 2: 192 (idem)]. – **Hel.:** < slaw. *jьgrьcь*.

igric – s. **igrëc*.

igröc – s. **igrëc*.

Iklódbördőce – s. **Bördőce*.

imala – s. *imola*.

imely *altung.* (1656) 'омела Viscum' [Kn. 222 (< болг. – **Hel.:** Но как и почему?)]. – **Hel.:** < ? slaw. *jьmelъ*; болг. *имел* (~ *имела* etc.), н.-луж. *jémjoł* (БЕР 2: 71-72; Фасм. 3: 139: *omela ~ *ьmela*). – Поздн{ее}?

imla – s. *imola*.

imoja – s. *imola*.

imola *dial.* '1. тина, болото (1193: imola hn.; 1250: Imulna hn. [-*ln*- !]) = *dial.* **imla, imollya**; 2. василек Centaurea, полевица Argostis alba (1783: Imola; 1792: imla; 1798: imolya) = *dial.* **imoja, imala, ímolya**'; ср. еще 1500 inula = komló 'хмель' [Kn. 843 (отвергает связь со слав., предположенную в Dankovszky, делит на 2 слова); TESz 2: 205 (в 2 статьях, следует Kn.); к семантике тж. OklSz 408]. – **Hel.:** < ? slaw. *jьmela* (ЭССЯ 6: 26-

27 *emela; Bern. 1: 425 imela (omela) 'омела Viscum') = укр. імела́ (ЕСУМ 2: 297). – {Für Varianten mit -ln- s. Топ. 2: 26-28}.

imollya – s. imola.

ímolya – s. imola.

Inota (1193: Jonata; 1220/1550: ynata) Ortsname, Komitat Veszprém [Stan. 2: 231 (< слав. Janota); Kiss 281 (< слав. Janota < Jan или < венг. Jonatas < лат. Jonathas)]. – **Hel.:** < slaw. junota (ЭССЯ 8: 195 'юноша' ЛИ).

Ipolydamásd – s. *Damás(d).

iromba dial. (1790: irombán) 'пестрый, рябой' [Kn. 1: 224 (< др.-слвц.); TESz 2: 234-235 (поздняя фиксация из-за диал. хар-ра {= характера} слова)]. – **Hel.:** < slaw. jaręba, -ъ < aręba, -ъ (ЭССЯ 1: 73-75: arębъ ('рябчик', 'куропатка'); op.cit. 76: arębъjь 'пестрый, рябый' – венг. дает нечл. адьект. ф.).

ispán (1265: ysponlesuy hn.; 1282: Spani (лат.); 1379: Espanlaka) 'жупан' [Kn. 1: 225 (*vári-zsupán > várizspán > vári-spán)]. – **Hel.:** < slaw. špan (ст.-слвц. špán < ? венг.) < žъrapъ < gъrapъ ? Cр. gъrapъ – ЭССЯ 7: 197-198. – Немыслимо: [1] Отрывать *gъrapъ от *žuрapъ (игнорируя špan), как это делает Трубачев Этим. 1965: 72; ЭССЯ 7: 197-198; [2] Считать špán венг. перед. {= переделкой} žuрapъ, см. Zett 1977.

isszop – s. iszap.

iszap altung. (ca. 1395: ÿsop 'glarea'; 1575: iszszopba) 'гравий; ил' [Kn. 1: 226-227; TESz 2: 245]. – **Hel.:** < ? slaw. jьzsъръ (ЭССЯ 9: 75-76). – Возможно, ст.-венг. **isszop**, а **iszap** – повт. заим. под вл. {= повторное заимствование под влиянием} схрв.диал. ùcap (правда, оно изв. {= известно} по ЭССЯ в др. значении – 'сыпь на коже').

iszkáva – s. ëszkába.

Iszkáz (1212: Thetheusizkaz; 1331: Izkazy [!]) Ortsname, Komitat Veszprém [Stan. 2: 232 (*Zkazy / *Skazy); Kiss 294 (ср. ст.-схрв. skaz)]. – **Hel.:** < ? slaw. jьzkazy (ЭССЯ 9: 36 *jьzkaza 'порча, изъян' etc.).

isztëke – s. ösztöke.

***Iva**, in: Ivád (1321) Ortsname, Komitat Heves [Stan. 2: 234 (от ivo); Kiss 295 (от ЛИ Iwa или от ст.-венг. iva 'ива', о к-ром см. Kn. 655); TESz 2: 249]. – **Hel.:** < slaw. jьva (ЭССЯ 8: 248-249).

Ivád – s. *Iva.

izgága (1636: izgágát) 'строптивый, задиристый (ст.-венг.: ссора, перебранка)' [Kn. 1: 228; TESz 2: 252]. – **Hel.:** < slaw. jьzgaga (ЭССЯ 9: 27 'изжога').

***Jalóc** (только 1270/1272: Jolouch) Ortsname, Komitat Arad in Siebenbürgen [Šmilauer 1932: 268; Stan. 2: 237]. – **Hel.:** < slaw. jelovьcь < edlovьcь. – Cр. ЭССЯ 6: 15: edlovъ(jь). – Vgl. Gyalóka.

jászol ~ jászoly (ca. 1395: ÿaʒot [ɔ: -ol]; ca. 1405: iaʒol) 'ясли, кормушка' [Kn. 1: 231-232 (*jászoly*); TESz 2: 284]. – **Hel.**: < slaw. *jasli* < *ědsli* (ЭССЯ 6: 44-45: *ědsla, ědslo, ědslь, ědsli*); но есть и болг.диал. *ėcaл*, м.р.: **ědslъ* ?

jászoly – s. *jászol*.

jegënye (1239: Jeguna; 1247: Jegeniefa; 1255: jegnye) 'пирамидальный тополь, Populus italica' [Kn. 1: 232-233 (*-d* было воспр. {= воспринято} как диминутив в первонач. **jagnyéd*); TESz 2: 268-269 (id.)]. – **Hel.**: < слав. *jagnędь* < *agnędь* (ЭССЯ 1: 56) или < ю.-слав. *jagnjed* (так Kn. 1: 232-233). Согласно ЭССЯ (1: 55-56), дериват от *ǎgnę*. – {Vgl. *jerke*}.

jérce 'молодая курица'. – **Hel.**: < слав. *jarica* (ЭССЯ 8: 172-173, Kn. 233). От *jaro* etc., ср. *jǎrę* 'козленок, ягненок'. (Притом *jérce < jerice*). – Vgl. *jerke*.

jerke 'овца, коза (самка)'. – **Hel.**: В любом случае примеры {*jegënye* und *jérce*, s.o.} непоказательны в связи с судьбой **ja-* (> *je-*) (NB: не *jé*!) в *jerke* 'овца, коза (самка)' < слав. *jarъka* / слцк. *jarka* / укр. *ярка*. Скорее здесь отражено диалектное слав. явление (*ja* > *je*, ср. ряд подобных случаев в слн., чеш.), чем развитие на венгерской почве. Ср., однако, *já* < слав. (*j*)*a* в *jász* (< *jazь*), *jász* (< др.-рус. ιасъı), *jászoly* (< *jasli*), *jávor* (< *javorъ*), *járom* (< *jarьmъ*).

Jolsva – s. *Jósva*.

Jósva *dial.* ~ **Jolsva** (1271: Elswa) Ortsname = *Jelšava* in der Slowakei, hierzu auch der Flußname **Jósva** [Staboslav 1948: 2: 241; Kiss 304, 305]. – **Hel.**: < slaw. *elьšava* (? *elьševa*, ЭССЯ 6: 25).

kabala *dial.* (1208/1373: ? Kobula hn.; 1271: Kabalapataka hn.; ca. 1395: kabala) ~ *altung.* **kabla** (ca. 1405) 'кобыла' [Kn. 1: 235-236; TESz 2: 289-290]. – **Hel.**: < slaw. *kobyla* (ЭССЯ 10: 93-98).

kabóca (1791: Kabótza) < **kabolca** (1808: Kaboltza) 'кузнечик, саранча, Homoptera' [Kn. 1: 236; TESz 2: 292-293 (может быть древним)]. – **Hel.**: < slaw. *kobylica* (ЭССЯ 10: 98-99).

kabolca – s. *kabóca*.

kacsa – s. *kácsa*.

kácsa *dial.* (1333/1468: ? Cachafolyasa hn.; 1548: Kaczath) 'утка' [Kn. 1: 238 (sub *kacsa* < слвц.); TESz 2: 297-298 (sub *kacsa*; 298: "A kácsa akakváltozat *á*-ja magyar nyúlás éredménye")]. – **Hel.**: < ? slaw. *kača* (ЭССЯ нет; см. ЕСУМ 2: 409; Machek 1968: 233-234). – Лит. *kacsa* – позднее из слвц.

kádár (1288: kadar szn.; 1585: kádár) 'бондарь' [Kn. 2: 657-658 (сомнения из-за того, что только в соседних с венг. языках; "все же нельзя думать, что слово возникло в венг., т.к. образование имен с пом. {= помощью} отвременного суффикса *-dr* началось только в эпоху обн. {= обновления} языка"); TESz 2: 300-301 (вер., слав.)]. – **Hel.**: < slaw. *kadarjь*

(ЭССЯ нет; схрв. *kàdār*; слн. *kádar*, диал. *kadár*; ст.-слвн. *kadár* (< венг.?).

kalangya (1370: kalangia; 1825: kalanya) 'скирда, копна' [Kn. 1: 242; TESz 2: 319]. – **Hel.**: < slaw. *kladьńa* < *kladьna* (ЭССЯ 9: 180-181); болг. *клáдня* (dial. *клъдн'ъ*, *кладньá* etc.), схрв.диал. *клáдньа*, *клáньа*, рус., укр. *клáдня*. – {Die Entwicklung im Ung. war wie folgt:} {*}*kládnya* > {*}*klánnya* > {*}*kalánnya* > *kalangya*.

kalitka (1410/1490: kalitkaban; 1533: kaletka; 1552: kalátkába [!]) 'клетка (для птиц, мелких животных)' [Kn. 1: 245-246; TESz 2: 325-326]. – **Hel.**: < slaw. *klětъka*. – Не было ли втор. влияния укр. *клíтка*?

Kámor (1742: Kámor-Vára) 'гора (662 m) в горах Бёржёнь (сев. ч. {= северная часть} м. Пешт у границы Словакии' [Kiss 312 (? к польск. *Kamor* szn., диал. *kamor* 'комар')]. – **Hel.**: < ? slaw. *kamorъ*, ср. ЭССЯ 9: 137 und Трубачев Этим. 1970: 10 (beide: словин. стар. *kamor* 'камень').

kamra '(seit 1198) казна; (seit 1372/1448) каморка; (seit 1405) полость тела; (seit 1754; совр.) палата (адм.); (seit 1797; совр.) коллегия' ~ **kamra** '(seit 1560) кладовая, чулан' [Kn. 2: 660-661; TESz 2: 332 (< чаг., вряд ли через слав.)]. – **Hel.**: < ? slaw. *komora* (Фасм. 2: 305) < греч. χαμάρα 'свод' или из лат. *camera*. – S. Anhang 6.

kápa (са. 1395: сара; 1517: сараat) 'поднятье спереди и сзади части седла; капюшон; монашеская ряса; колпак, прикрывающий глаза лошади, сокола' [Kn. 2: 662-663 ('лука седла' не сюда); TESz 2: 355-356 (< лат., вряд ли через слав.)]. – **Hel.**: < ? slaw. *kapa* (Фасм. 2: 183; ЕСУМ 2: 368 (распростр. указывает на обшеслав. хар-р) или < лат. *cappa* (каппа, вид гол. {= головного} убора).

káposzta (1336 szn.) {'Kohl'}. – **Hel.**: венг. не отражает сокращ. предакут. долготы!

kár (1372/1448: kart) 'ущерб, вред; жаль' [Kn. 1: 253; TESz 2: 370-371]. – **Hel.**: < slaw. *kvarъ* (БЕР 2: 307; ст.-слав. кварь); ? < булг. *kәvar*, ср. тюрк. *qor* – Ligeti MNy 29: 220.

*Karász (1306: Karaz), in: **Nyírkarász** Ortsname, Komitat Szabolcs-Szatmár-Bereg [Kiss 473 (= {ung.} *kárász* 'карась' {< slaw., s. EWU s.v.})]. – **Hel.**: < slaw. *krasъ* (ЭССЯ 12: 105 *krasъjь*; м.б. и от **krasь* – ЭССЯ 12: 106).

karisnya – s. *karosnya*.

karmány '(?) Ärmel' (1543: karman kezthyu [= *karmán kesztyű*] '?', OklSz 457) [см. TESz 2: 383-384 sub *karmantyú* 'муфта' (seit 1708)]. – **Hel.**: < slaw. *korъtanъ* (Фасм. 2: 201: др.-рус. Корманъ (имя); рус. *кармáн*; др.-польск. *korman, korban*.

karosnya *dial.* (1343: corosnis) ~ *dial.* **kasornya** (vgl. 1616: kosornyáiában), **karisnya** 'корзина' [Kn. 1: 256-257; TESz 2: 398 (sub *kasornya*) (контаминация с *kosár* и *kas*)]. – **Hel.**: < slaw. *krošьńa* < *krošьna* (Фасм. 2: 384 *krosnia*. – Ср. тж. *kasolya*.

kasolya *dial.* *Siebenbürgen* (1707: kosolya; MTSz: kasolya, kosoja) 'небольшая корзинка' [Kn. 1: 258 (< укр. [Hel.: где только *košelь*]); TESz 2: 397-398 (< вост.-слвц. *košalka* & укр.)]. – **Hel.**: < slaw. *košeľa* < *košela* (ЭССЯ 11: 187-189 *košelъ* / *košela* / *košelь*). – Vgl. *karosnya*.

kasornya – s. *karosnya*.

katka *dial.* (1887) '4 связанные в виде якоря крюка, с пом. {= помощью} которых ищут на дне донную зацепу' [Kn. 1: 259 (допуская сущ. ю.-слав. живой формы)]. – **Hel.**: < slaw. *kotъka* (ЭССЯ 11: 212-213 – только ст.-слав., др.-рус.).

kelence *dial.* (1462: Kelencze hn.; 1524: kelencze (преим. в вост. диал.); 17.Jh.: kölöncze) 'вид (огороженной) пасеки' [Kn. 1: 261 (с сомн.); TESz 2: 429-430 (с 2 другими, но неприемлемыми объяснениями)]. – **Hel.**: < ?? slaw. *kolьnica* (ЭССЯ 10: 168-169: *kolьna* 'сарай' etc., не учтены южно-слав.: схрв. *kôlnica* 'каретный сарай', слн. *kolnica*, слвц.диал. *kôlnica* 'сарайчик').

kelengye (ab 1787) 'подарки родителей к бракосочетанию, приданое; Heiratsausstattung' [TESz 2: 430 (с 3 возм. объясн. – наиб. удачное из лат. *clenodia* 'сокровище, драгоценность' – и с лит., в т.ч. Hadrovics MNy 51: 340, 52: 358; Kniezsa NyK 65: 98; Úrhegyi MNy 63: 482)]. – **Hel.**: < ? slaw. *koľęda* (ЭССЯ 10: 134-135), в частн., н.-луж. *kóloda* 'подарок на новый год', польск. *koľęda* 'рождественный подарок', *'обряд, связанный с началом года'.

kelepce (ca. 1560: kelepche) 'ловушка, западня' [Kn. 1: 261; TESz 2: 430]. – **Hel.**: < slaw. *klepьca* (ЭССЯ 10: 11-12: *klepьcь*; есть др.-рус. клепьца 'tendicula, πάγε, παγίς, ловушка, силок, капкан').

kemënce [ε – ë – ε] (1156: ? Kemence hn.; ок. 1395: kemenche) 'печь' [Mikl. 110. Иначе Kn. 1: 261-262 (< *kamenica* или *komnica* < *katъnica*; не из *kominica*, т.к. не м. быть ж.р. [но ср. болг.диал. комина 'дупка над пещера'])]; TESz 2: 436-437]. – **Hel.**: < slaw. *kominica* (?) (не засвид. Ср. БЕР 2: 572 *комин* < гр. *κάμῑνος*, лат. *caminus*) → *katmьca* (ЭССЯ 9: 134-135 *katmьсь*), в т.ч. ст.-слвц. *kamenca* 'печь', укр. (закарп. 16-17 в.) *каменця* id., {???} рус. (Ветка) *каменница* 'каменная печь в бане'.

kerecsen – s. *Kerecseny*.

Kerecseny (*Tiszakerecseny*) (1324: Kerechun; 1327: Kerechen). – **Hel.**: Обычно это слово непосредственно объясняется из аппелятива **kerecsen** (**kerecseny**) 'охотничий сокол', преобразованного из ст.-венг. *kerecset* (ок. 1282: kerechet, но 1651: kerechen) < слав. *krečetъ* (см. Kn. 1: 263; TESz 2: 453; ЭССЯ 12: 111). Однако ранняя фиксация форм с -*n* (-*ny*), а также написание *Kerechun*, указывающее на исходно узкий гласный последнего слога, заставляют думать скорее о славянском прототипе в виде *krečinъ (см. ЭССЯ 12: 111, где приводятся зооним ономатопеической природы *krečь, откуда МН ст.-укр. *Кречовъ*, и, наряду с этим, рус. диал. *креча* 'птица чибис'). – Фонетически приемлемо и объяснение из *Krěčin, от слав. *krěkъ* (Bern. 613-614), предлагавшееся Я. Станиславом (Stan. 2: 268). – Ср. *Kerecseny*, м. Зала (1019/1370: Kerechen; 1270: Kerchen; 1320: Alsoukerchyn) [Kiss 329; Györffy 15: 275].

Kisbakta – s. *Bakta.*

Kisbégány – s. *Bégány.*

Kisbudmér – s. *Budmér.*

kolbász (1373: Kolbaz szn.; ca. 1405: colbaʒ) ~ *dial.* **kalbász** 'колбаса' [Kn. 1: 272; TESz 2: 523]. – **Hel.**: < slaw. *kъlbasa* (Фасм. 2: 286), но схрв. *kobása*, чак. кайк. *klobăsa*, слн. *klobása*, чеш. *klobása* < *klobasa*. – Видимо, *kalbász* < *klobasa* (> *kalabász*).

kom *dial.* (seit 1574) 'кум' [Kn. 1: 275-276]. – **Hel.**: < ? slaw. *kumъ*. – Не исключено, что вторично по отнош. к *koma. – Vgl. koma.*

koma (1213/1550: ? Comad szn.; 1478: ? Koma szn.; 1526: komam) 'кум' [Kn. 1: 275-276]. – **Hel.**: < slaw. *kuma. – Vgl. kom.*

komor (1222: ? Chomor hn.; 1372/1448: komorodott; 1532: kumuruk) 'угрюмый, хмурый' [Kn. 2: 671 (вопреки Munkácsi 1897: 19, ≮ *xmura*); TESz 2: 540 (неизв. происх., не < вост.-слав.)]. – **Hel.**: < ? slaw. *xmurъ* (Фасм. 4: 250); ЭССЯ *kmurъ* нет. – {Bezüglich des slaw. Anlauts: *k-* oder *x-* heißt es auf einem anderen Zettel:} Kn. 2: 671 и TESz 2: 540 отклоняют выдвинутое ранее (Б. Мункачи) предположение о заимствовании из вост.-слав. *xmurъ, *xmura (что вполне резонно, т.к. слав. *x-* не дает венг. *k-*) […].

Kóny (1220: Coun) Ortsname, Komitat Győr-Moson-Sopron [Stan. 2: 281; Kiss 351-352 (*konjь)]. – **Hel.**: ? < slaw. *konьnъ* (ЭССЯ 12: 18).

konyha < *altung.* **kohnya** (1206: cuhnamezei hn.; 1327: Kuhnyaheg hn.; ca. 1395: chohўna; 1521: konha; 1585: kohnya ~ konyha) 'кухня' [Kn. 2: 671-672; TESz 2: 558]. – **Hel.**: < slaw. *kuxynja* (< др.-в.-н. < лат.; или прямо из др.-в.-н.?).

kopja (1464: kopya) 'копье' [Kn. 1: 278-279; TESz 2: 564]. – **Hel.**: < slaw. *kopьje/-ja* (ЭССЯ 11: 40-41). – Возм., *-ja* – из венг.; так о слвц. *kopija* Kn. 1: 279 {aber vgl. auch poln. *kopia* id.}. – Поздн{ee}.

korcsolya (1339: Korcholyas szn.; ок. korcyola) '(ст.-венг.) салазки, полозья для скатывания бочек; (совр.) коньки' [Kn. 2: 865-866 (вряд ли слав.); TESz 2: 571-572 (id.)]. – **Hel.**: < slaw. *kъrč[i]dlo ~ krъč[i]dlo* (схрв.диал. *kòčulje* Pl., слн.венг. {sic!} *korcsole*, слвц. *korčuľa*; ? укр. *корчýга* 'сани для дров' < венг.). – Ср. *mocsolya, nyoszolya.*

korhad (1595: kodhadni [э: kor-]) 'становиться гнилым, трухлявым' [Kn. 2: 867 (отвергает ошибочно); TESz 2: 574 (id.)]. – **Hel.:** < {aks.} *krихъ* (Фасм. 2: 387) ~ {aks., altruss.} *krъxa* (Фасм. 2: 384). – Vgl. *torha*.

kormány (1323: Kurmanus hn.; ca. 1405: korman; 1512: Kormanyos hn.) 'руль, штурвал; (поздн.) правительство' [Kn. 1: 282; TESz 2: 576]. – **Hel.:** < slaw. *kъrma* (-*n* мог развиться e.g. в рез-те {= результате} уподобления по форме слову **kormán* 'налучник' < др.-тюрк. (огуз., кыпч.) *qurman*).

kovász – s. *Kovászó*.

Kovászó (1270-1272/1295: Koazou) Ortsname (= {slowak.} *Kvasovo* (1808: Kwasow, Kwásowá); {ukr.} *Квасово*). – **Hel.:** < slaw. **kvasovъ/-a/-o* < **kvasъ* (ЭССЯ 13: 153-155) > ung. **kovász** 'закваска' (ca. 1395: couaз).

Kölcsény (1263/1296: Kulchun, Kulchen) Ortsname (= {slowak.} *Kolčino* (1808: Kolčin, Kolčno); {ukr.} *Кольчино*). – **Hel.:** < slaw. **kъlčinъ/-a/-o* (< **kъlčь*, см. ЭССЯ 13: 184).

kuzsaly – s. *guzsaly*.

laboda (1378: Labada wossyan hn.; 1391: Labdasuuasyan hn.; ca. 1395: laboda; ca. 1405: labda) 'лебеда, Atriplex' [Kn. 1: 299-300; TESz 2: 702]. – **Hel.:** < slaw. *leboda* (?), *lebeda*, *loboda* (Фасм. 2: 469-470); не *olboda*, как Bern. 1: 698.

ladik (1475: ladak; 1560: ladik; 1672: ladikásoc [указ. на **ladika*]) 'плоскодонка' [Kn. 1: 300-301; TESz 2: 704]. – **Hel.:** < slaw. *lod-* < *old-*. – Непоср. источник неясен. Kn. и TESz предпочитают сравнение с болг. *ладийка* (диал.), но ср. и *лодка*.

*lakma (1598: lakmározik 'пирует') [Kn. 1: 301-302 (на *lakoma*, *lakma* 'прожорливый' диал., с XIX в.; с *lakmározik* не отождествляет); TESz 2: 710-711 (так же)]. – **Hel.:** < slaw. *lokoma/ъ* < *olkoma/ъ* (повсюду *la-* в слав.!). Сложно, ненадежно, неубедительно из-за возможности позднего заим. *lakoma*. – {Später dazugeschrieben:} Но ср. схрв. *lōkta* 'кусок' < тур.! (Bern. 729).

lánc (1219/1550: ? Lanczij hn.; 1263: ? Lanch hn.; ca. 1405: Lanch; 1553: lanchorwl) 'цепь' [Kn. 1: 302-303 (*lánc* < *lanьcь*: болг. *лáнец*, схрв. *lánac*, ст.-кайк. *lanc*, слн.диал. *lânec*, вост.-слвц. *lanc*, укр.диал. *ланц*); TESz 2: 714-715 (*лáнец* etc. < венг.)]. – **Hel.:** < ung. *láncó* (*láncók* ?) < slaw. *lancих* ~ *lancug* (< нем. **Lannzug*) (Фасм. 2: 458). – Скорее переосм. {= переосмысление} -*ok* как Pl. – Поздн{ее}?

láncó – s. *lánc*.

lapocka (ок. 1405: lap[i]chka; 1493: lapoczka) 'лопатка (анат.); *уст. тж.* лопатка (инстр.)' [Kn. 1: 305; TESz 2: 722]. – **Hel.:** < ? slaw. *lopatьka*.

lëdnëk (1471: lednyk; 1533: lennôk; 1664: lendeket) ~ *dial.* **lednëk, lendëk lëndëk, lendök, löndök, lennëk, lënnek, lënnëk** 'Lathyrus; вика Vicia'

[Kn. 1: 309-310 (< слвц., после деназализации); TESz 2: 738 (< слвц.)].
– **Hel.:** < slaw. *lędьnikъ* (ЭССЯ 15: 51).

lëndëk – s. *lëdnëk.*

lendök, lennëk – s. *lëdnëk.*

lengyel [ε – ε] < *altung.* **lengyen** (1130-40/12.-13.Jh.: Lengen szn.; 1256: Lengel hn.; ca. 1395: lengel) ~ *dial.* **lengyën** 'поляк' [Kn. 1: 312-313; TESz 2:
751]. – **Hel.:** < slaw. *lędjanъ.* – Фасм. 2: 553 *lęděninъ* (откуда якобы *lengyel*); ЭССЯ 15: 44 *lędjane / lęděne.* – Венг. форма указывает скорее на
*lędjenъ ~ **lędjьnъ* ~ **lędjonъ.* Ср. Konst. Porph. *De adm. imp.* 9, § 37:
Λενζαννήνοι, Λενζενίνοι.

lengyen – s. *lengyel.*

lepény (ca. 1395: lepeўn) ~ *dial.* **lepíny** 'лепешка' [Kn. 2: 684; TESz 2: 756].
– **Hel.:** < slaw. *lepěnъ/ь.* – Ср. Фасм. 2: 484: *лепёха* (? ~ *лепить* [но это
лѣпити]).

lepíny – s. *lepény.*

Lócs (Ende des 13.Jh.: Louch {aber laut Kiss[2] 2: 43 – in dieser Form schon
1239 belegt}) Ortsname, Komitat Vas [Kiss 384 (= *Lóc*, с ранней субсти-
туцией *c → cs*, как в *császár* etc. [Hel.: но в ауслауте ее нет]); Tagányi
MNy 9: 264; Moór Acta Ethn. 12: 38]. – **Hel.:** < ? slaw. *lovъčjь* (< *lovьcь*).

Lónya (1270/1580: Lonya; 1325: Louna) Ortsname [Kiss 386; Kniezsa 1942a,
Nr. 245; Stan. 2: 319]. – **Hel.:** < slaw. **lovVnja* (*V* = ъ, *у* или *i*; от *loviti,
lovъ*).

löndök – s. *lëdnëk.*

Lövő (1265: Lveho) Ortsname, Komitat Győr-Moson-Sopron [Kiss 388-389
(прич. от *lő* 'стрелять'); Tagányi MNy 9: 264; Melich MNy 22: 129, 28:
18], belegt auch in: **Egerlövő** (1221/1550 Luen [ɔ: Lueu]), u.a.m. – **Hel.:** <
?? slaw. *lьvovъ.*

macsója – s. *mocsolya.*

macsola – s. *mocsolya.*

mágla – s. *máglya.*

Maglóca (1220: Magluca) Ortsname, Komitat Győr-Moson-Sopron [Kiss 395
(< *Могилица*); Stan. 2: 326; Moór 1936: 37]. – **Hel.:** < slaw. *mogylovica.* –
Vgl. *Maglód.*

Maglód (< **Maglót** 1380, aber vgl. ca. 1150/13.-14.Jh.: Moglout [Personen-
name]) Ortsname, Komitat Pest [Kiss 395 (< *mag* 'sperma' über einen
Personennamen); Stan. 2: 326]. – **Hel.:** < slaw. *mogylovьcь*; Киш {= Kiss}
совсем отделяет от *Maglóca* – что неправдоподобно. – Vgl. *Maglóca.*

máglya < *altung.* **mágla** (1487: ? Maglas szn.; 1512: ? Magla hn.; 1528: magla;
1551: maglya) '(*altung.*) куча; (*heut.ung.*) костер из больших бревен'
[Kn. 1: 322-323; TESz 2: 815 (совр. значение – nyelújítás (Hel.: м.б., и
форма тоже?))]. – **Hel.:** < slaw. *mogyla* (Фасм. 2: 634-635).

malom < **malon** (1075/1124/1217: ? melinhalmu hn; 1247: molna [3.Sg.]; 1271 /1295: Malomsok hn.) 'мельница' [Kn. 1: 325-327 (с культ.-ист. данными; вероятно < схрв. *molin* – промеж. стадия между *tъlynъ* и *mălin*); TESz 2: 831; ! Ашбот 262 (сходство с *halom*!)]. – **Hel.:** < slaw. *tъlynъ* (< лат. *molina*, через ит. *mulino*?, нем.?, фр.?). – S. *halom*.

malon – s. *malom*.

mancs *dial.* (seit 1792) 'дерев. {= деревянный} мяч' [Kn. 1: 328; TESz 2: 834]. – **Hel.:** < slaw. *męčь*. – Vgl. *Mencshely*.

Markóc (1403: Markochel [э: ? Markolch]) Ortsname, Komitat Baranya [Kiss 407 (от имени типа *Markovec*); Stan. 2: 335]. – **Hel.:** < slaw. *mVrkъvьсь*.

Márok (*Márokpapi*) (1220/1550: Marc; 1248: Mark) Ortsname. – **Hel.:** < слав. ЛИ *Markъ* (< гр.). Встречается и как венг. ЛИ (1211: Marcu; 1214/1550: Marc), см. Fahértói 1983: 213. Судя по отсутствию вставного *о* в совр. венг. ЛИ *Márk*, оно является не продолжением этого ЛИ, а усечением *Márkus* (< лат. *Marcus*) или заимствованием из нем. *Mark* (Ladó 1978: 189).

márna (1590: maarna) 'усач Barbus barbus' [Kn. 1: 329-330; TESz 2: 848]. – **Hel.:** < slaw. *mъrĕna* < gr. μοραίνα, lat. *muraena*.

mátka (1508: matkaiaval 'невеста') 'невеста, суженая; жених, суженый' [Kn. 2: 691; TESz 2: 861-862]. – **Hel.:** < ? slaw. *matъka*. – Поздн{ее}.

Mencshely (1269: Menchel) Ortsname, Komitat Veszprém [Kiss 417 (? < нем. ЛИ *Menzli, Mentzelin*; ?? < роман.: лат. *monticellus* 'холм' + нар. этим.: *hely*)]. – **Hel.:** < ? slaw. *męčь*. – Vgl. *mancs*.

Méra (1256) Ortsname, Komitat Borsod-Abaúj-Zemplén [Kiss 418 (< ЛИ: нем. *Miro, Mero* или схрв., чеш. *Míra*); Stan. 2: 339]. – **Hel.:** < ? slaw. *měra*.

mёrce (ca. 1395: merthe; ca. 1405: merche) ~ *dial.* **mírce, mêrce** (!) 'мера объема (1,5 ведра)' [Kn. 1: 336 (*ĕ* или *ĕ* ?); TESz 2: 898]. – **Hel.:** < slaw. *měrica* (*mě-*).

Mérk (ca. 1290: Merk) Ortsname, Komitat Szabolcs-Szatmár-Bereg [Kiss 419 (? < ЛИ: польск. *Mirek ~ Mirko ~ Mirk*); Stan. 2: 340; Kniezsa MNy 4: 223]. – **Hel.:** < ? slaw. *měrъky*.

merkőce *dial.* (18.Jh.: merkőcze) 'морковь' [Kn. 1: 337]. – **Hel.:** < slaw. *mъrkъvica*; схрв. *mr̂kvica* и др. – Поздн{ее}?

mёszáros (1395: Mezaros szn.; 1438: Manzaros; 1453: Menzarus szn.) ~ *dial.* **míszáros** 'мясник' [Kn. 1: 337-338 (разные объясн. для исчезн. *n*); TESz 2: 906 (2-кратное заимствование)]. – **Hel.:** < slaw. *męsarjь*. – Не могло ли сохранение -*ár*- обусловить развитие из -*еn*- сингармонически не противоречащего -*é*- ?

métej – s. *métely*.

métely ~ *dial.* **métej, mítej** 'сосальщик Trematoda, кожное поражение у овец' [Kn. 1: 338-339 (< ю.-слав. *metyljь ~ метыль, мотыль* 'бабочка'); TESz

2: 909-910]. – **Hel.:** < slaw. *metyljь*; болг. *метúль*, схрв. *mètиль*, слн. *metílj* (БЕР 3: 768). – {Später dazugeschrieben:} "**metyljь*?".

mézga < *mězga*. – S. *mezge*.

mezge *altung. dial.* [= lit. *mézga*, s.o.] (ca. 1560: maghszeyę; 1527: mezge) ~ *dial.* **mezsge**, **mezgye**, **mezga** 'древесная смола' [Kn. 1: 339; TESz 2: 912 (вместе с *mézga*)]. – **Hel.:** <? slaw. *mVzga* {mit einer leeren Stelle für den Vokal}; болг. *мъзга*. – S. *mézga*.

mezgye – s. *mezge*.

mezsge – s. *mezge*.

mírce – s. *mĕrce*.

Misina (1864; ранее *Mecsek* !) Bergname, Komitat Baranya [Kiss 426 (схрв. *Mišina* 'Мишина')]. – **Hel.:** <? slaw. *myšina*. – Поздн{ее}?

Miske (1346: Myske) Ortsname, Komitat Bács-Kiskun [Kiss 426 (< Personenname; 1164: Myske, схрв. *Mĩško* etc.)]. – **Hel.:** <? slaw. *myšьka*.

Miskolc (1150: Miscoucy; 1291: Miskoch; 1293: Myscolch) Ortsname, Komitat Borsod-Abaúj-Zemplén [Kiss 427]. – **Hel.:** < slaw. *Myšьkovьcь (icy)*.

míszáros – s. *mĕszáros*.

mítej – s. *métely*.

mocsila – s. *mocsolya*.

mocsoja – s. *mocsolya*.

mocsolya *dial.* (1138/1329: Machala hn., Maſala hn.; 1156: Mosula hn.; 1260: Mochola hn.) ~ *dial.* **mocsila**, **mocsoja**, **mocsójja**, **macsola**, **macsója** 'лужа; яма для замачивания льна' [Kn. 1: 341; TESz 2: 939]. – **Hel.:** < slaw. *močilo* < *močidlo*. – Ср. венг. *pocsolya* 'лужа' (ономатоп. происх.); явно повлияло. Ср. еще диал. *pocsár* (SzegSz) = *mocsár* 'болото'.

moly (ca. 1395: moÿl; ca. 1405: mol; 1793: Molly) 'моль' [Kn. 1: 342-343; TESz 2: 946]. – **Hel.:** < slaw. *moljь*. – Ср. 2 позиции: Melich 1903: 141: не м. быть болг., т.к. там есть только *molec*, не *moľ*. Asbóth 1907: 81: не потому не может относиться к древнейшему – болгарскому – слою слав. заимствований, что {???, = слова *moľ*} нет в болгарском, поскольку согласно свид-во {!, = свидетельству} *molec* некогда должно было быть, а потому, что на месте слав. *о* в венг. также *о*.

muska *dial.* (1487: ? Muskapathaka hn.; ca. 1560: muska) 'мелкая муха, винная муха' [Kn. 1: 349 (< слав. *muška*, вер. из слвц.); TESz 2: 978-979 (< слвц., ср. ст.-слвц. *vínová muška* 'винная муха', слово в соседних со словаками диал.) – **Hel.:** Все же вероятнее *тъšьka*]. – **Hel.:** < slaw. *тъšьka* (Фасм. 2: 667) (? *mušьka*). – Поздн{ее}?

nadrág (1364: ? Nodrag hn.; ca. 1395: nadrag) 'брюки, штаны' [Kn. 1: 352-353; TESz 2: 992]. – **Hel.:** < slaw. *nadragy* (Фасм. 3: 38). – Поздн{ее}?

Nagybakta – s. *Bakta*.

Nagybégány – s. *Bégány*.

Nagydobrony – s. *Dobrony*.

naszád (1504: ? Nazadiste; ca. 1522: Nazados) 'небольшое, легкое, речное военное судно; (совр.) катер' [Kn. 1: 353-354; TESz 2: 1001 (< др.-рус.)]. – **Hel.**: < ст.-венг. *nászád* < slaw. *nasadъ*; др.-рус. **насадъ** 'вид судна', ст.-чеш. *násadište* и др. (< рус.?); Фасм. 3: 47.

navalya – s. *nyavalya*.

noszolya – s. *nyoszolya*.

nyavalya < altung. **navalya** (1211: ? Neuualeh szn.; 1254/1360: noualyad hn.; 1329/1394: Neualyad hn.; 1854: nyovolya (тж. диал.)) 'хворь; напасть; (ст.-венг.) нужда' [Kn. 1: 356; TESz 2: 1038 (фон. разв. ≈ как в *nyoszolya*, но обобщена др. диал. форма)]. – **Hel.**: < slaw. *nevolja*. – Vgl. *nyoszolya*.

Nyírdërzs – s. **Dërzs*.

Nyírkarász – s. **Karász*.

Nyomja (1272: Namya) Ortsname, Komitat Baranya (seit 1948 – Teil des Dorfes Szederkény) [Kiss 475 (правильно, но также с схрв. *Nemila*); Stan. 2: 356 (к топонимам типа схрв. *Nomanica*)]. – **Hel.**: < slaw. *nemyja*. Ср. болг. *Немúя*; ? укр. *Немúя*.

nyoszolya < altung. **noszolya** (1452: nozolya, 1494: nazolya; 1532: ńozoliaba; 1754: nyaszolyák) 'ложе, кровать' [Kn. 1: 357; TESz 2: 1053 (фон. разв. ≈ как в *nyavalya*, но обобщена др. диал. форма)]. – **Hel.**: < slaw. *nosilo* < *nosidlo*. – Vgl. *nyavalya*.

Ógyalla – s. **Gyalla*.

Ohat < **Ohad** (1220/1550: Vhd; vhudu szn.) Ortsname (heute ein Stadtteil von Egyek, Komitat Hajdú-Bihar) [Kiss 479 (< *oh* {> heut.ung. *ó*} 'alt' + {Diminutivsuff.} -*d*)]. – **Hel.**: < slaw. *vъxodъ*.

ól – s. *akol*.

olaj (1309/1323: oleykutha; ca. 1395: olay) ~ *dial.* **alaj**, **alé**, **aléjos** 'масло (растительное)' [Kn. 1: 359-360; TESz 2: 1073]. – **Hel.**: < ??? slaw. *olějь* (Фасм. 3: 134). – Скорее из др.-в.-н. *olei*, но *alaj* м.б. и старым славизмом!

Ompoly (1271: Onpoy [!]) Flußname in Siebenbürgen, = rum. *Ampoiul* = dt. *Ampoi* [Kiss 482 (румын. < нем. < венг. – слав. поср. {= посредство} не упомин.)]. – **Hel.**: < slaw. **Qpejь* < **Ampeium* (или < румын.?); ср. *Ordo Ampei(ensium)*.

ozsona – s. *uzsonna*.

ösztöke (1275/1323: ? Estuge szn.; 1279: ? Estyuge szn.; 1519: eztǫke, ǫztǫke; 1520: eztekele) ~ *dial.* **ësztëke**, **isztëke**, **üsztöke**, etc. etc. 'палка с жел. концом для очистки плуга; палка, которой поганяют скот' [Kn. 1: 366-367 (-*e* из-за словосоч. *eke-ösztöke*); TESz 3: 43-44 (семантика отчасти из *ösztön*)]. – **Hel.**: < slaw. *styka* (?), *jьztyka* (?) (ЭССЯ 9: 85 *jьztykъ*). – Vgl. *ösztön*.

ösztön (ca. 1405: oȝten; ca. 1490: ǫȝtene 3.Sg.) ~ *dial.* **ësztën** 'палка, к-рой погоняют скот; инстинкт' [Kn. 1: 367; TESz 3: 44]. – **Hel.:** < slaw. *ostьnъ* (Фасм. 2: 165). – Контам. с *ösztöke* (s.o.).

ösztörű (1233: yztru; 1264: vstrov) 'колышек, столбик etc.' [Kn. 1: 367-368; TESz 3: 44-45]. – **Hel.:** < slaw. *ostrvъ* – vgl. Machek 420 (*ostrъvъ*) vs. Kn. (*ostrьvь*).

pajta – s. *Bakta.*

Palkonya (1296: Polkona) Ortsname, Komitat Baranya [Kiss 496 (слав.: ср. рус. *Пулькиня*, чеш. *Plúkoň* ЛИ, польск. *Połkoń ~ Pułkoń* ЛИ); Stan. 2: 388 (*plъkynja* < *plъkъ* 'поле')]. – **Hel.:** < slaw. *polkVnja* (*polkati* 'полоскать') или *plakVnja* (*plakati*).

pánk – s. *pók.*

párna (ca. 1395: parna) 'подушка' (ср. *párnás* 'мягкий, пухлый') [Kn. 1: 393-394; TESz 3: 111]. – **Hel.:** < slaw. *perina.*

paszáta – s. *poszáta.*

pászta (1648: pásztákban) 'полоса поля, постать' [Kn. 1: 398-399; TESz 3: 124]. – **Hel.:** < {ung.} *pasztát* < slaw. *postatь* (-á- вер., под влиянием *pásztor* 'пастух' etc. {Später dazugeschrieben:} Или все же *постать*?). – Vgl. *rásza.*

pëcér I < altung. dial. **pëszér** (1209: pezer hn.; 1416: Ebpezer; ca. 1560: peczer) 'псарь; живодер' [Kn. 1: 407-408; TESz 3: 140]. – **Hel.:** < slaw. *pьsarь.* – Vgl. *peszérce.*

pëcér II – s. *peszérce.*

Pécsbagota – s. *Bakta.*

pele < altung. **peleh** (ca. 1395: peleÿ; ca. 1405: peleh) 'соня (и др. грызуны)' [Kn. 1: 410-411 (против < нем.); TESz 3: 148; Ашбот 264-265]. – **Hel.:** < slaw. *plьxъ* < *pьlxъ* (Фасм. 3: 319-320) или < др.-в.-н. *bilih, pilih*, нем. *Bilch, Pilch* (кот., вер. {= которые, вероятно} < слав.).

pereclen – s. *përëszlen.*

*Perecsen, in: **Szilágyperecsen** (1257: Perchen) Ortsname, Rumänien, früher: Komitat Szilágy; rum. *Periceiu* [Kiss 613 s.v. *Szilágyperecsen* (без реш. {= решения}); Stan. 2: 402; Kniezsa MagyRom. 1: 269 (< *Prečany*)]. – **Hel.:** < slaw. *prěčьnъ.*

përëszlen *dial.* (1291: Perezlen szn.; 1585: perezlen 'веретено (verticulum)') ~ *dial.* **pereclen** 'кружок веретена' [Kn. 1: 416; TESz 3: 163-164]. – **Hel.:** < slaw. *pręslenъ.* – Kn. & TESz: попало после деназализации. Однако вполне мыслимо *prěnslɛn > prěslɛn > përëszlen.*

përzsël (1429: Perzelew szn.) 'палить, опаливать' [Kn. 2: 712; TESz 3: 170-171]. – **Hel.:** < ? slaw. *prъži-*; схрв. слн. *pržiti*, болг. *пръжя* 'варить, жарить' (но ср. венг. *pergel* etc.).

pëszér – s. *pëcér.*

peszérce (ca. 1395: peʒerche) ~ *dial.* **pecér** (!!), **pöczércze** etc. 'растение Ly-copus' [Kn. 2: 714 (с сомн.); TESz 3: 172 ("ism. ered.")]. – **Hel.:** < slaw. *рьsarica* (ср. *рьsarъ* > *pecér*). – Ср. тж. диал. (Csallóköz, seit 1794) *pe-szérce* 'саламандра' (Kn.).

peszmet– s. *poszmat.*

pëszra – s. *piszra.*

pësztërce (ca. 1584: Peztritz; ca. 1600: pisztricz; 1798: pesztertze) 'различные виды съедобных грибов' ~ (спец.) **pisztricgomba** 'Polyporus squamo-sus' [Kn. 1: 419; TESz 3: 173]. – **Hel.:** < slaw. *рьstrica* (Kn.: только **рь-strъcь*). – Поздн{ее}?

pësztra – s. *piszra.*

picke – s. *piszke.*

picsa (ca. 1405: picha) 'cunnus' [Kn. 2: 714-715; TESz 3: 182 (< **piča* – ре-композиция **pičьka*)]. – **Hel.:** < slaw. *pica* (*piča?*); ср. болг. *пи́чка*, слн. *pîčka*, слцк. *pička*, польск. *piczka, picza* (!) ~ *pica, pichna.*

piszke *dial.* (1783: piszke; 1792: Biʃzke, büʃzke, böʃzke; 1808: pöʃzke) ~ *dial.* **picke, püszke** 'крыжовник' [TESz 3: 212-213 (с неудовл. объясн.)]. – **Hel.:** < ? slaw. **рьsika.* – Ср. *псинка* 'паслен' (но ср. тж. *бзинка, бзни-ка, бздика* id.!).

piszra *dial.* (1709: piszra; 1679: piszrang; [стар., но когда?:] pisztra) ~ *dial.* **pëszra, pësztra, piszre, piszráng** 'с белым пятном' [Kn. 1: 424 (< слвц. – ошибочно: слвц. *pestrá*); TESz 3: 214 (< слав.)]. – **Hel.:** < slaw. *рьstra, -ъ.* – Vgl. *pisztráng.*

piszráng – s. *piszra.*

piszre – s. *piszra.*

pisztarang – s. *pisztráng.*

pisztráng < **pisztrang** ~ **pisztrong** (1261: Pistrungus potoc hn.; 1271: Pistrunk hn.; 1364: Pistrongus hn.; ca. 1395: piʃtrang) ~ *dial.* **piszt(a)rang** 'форель' [Kn. 1: 424 (в-т с *á* возникает в Dunántúl в к-це {= конце} XVII в., где рыбы этой нет – он трансформирован); TESz 3: 216]. – **Hel.:** < slaw. *рьstrǫgъ.* – Vgl. *piszráng* sub *piszra* oben.

pisztricgomba – s. *pësztërce.*

pisztrong – s. *pisztráng.*

pitar *dial.* (1795/1844: pitarba) 'сени' [Kn. 1: 425-426; TESz 3: 217-218; Счи-тают преобразованием *pitvar*. Но нет e.g. варианта *udar* у *udvar*! {Später dazugeschrieben:} Но есть *borotva* ~ *borota*]. – **Hel.:** < slaw. *pritorъ* (Фасм. 3: 361-362 & 367), **приторъ** (Зогр.). Из греч. *πραιτώριον* (про-меж. стадия преобразования в *притвор* {'западная паперть церкви, на которой кормят нищих', Фасм. 3: 367}). – Vgl. *pitvar.*

pitvar (ca. 1300: pituaranak) 'сани' [Kn. 1: 425-426; TESz 3: 217-218]. – **Hel.:** < slaw. *pritvorъ* (Фасм. 3: 367). – Vgl. *pitar.*

pluta – s. *póta*.

póc – s. *polc*.

pók (ca. 1395: *pók*; ca. 1405: poukh) 'паук' [Kn. 1: 428; TESz 3: 238-239]. – **Hel.:** < slaw. *paukъ* < *paǫkъ* > *ung. dial.* **pank** ~ **pánk** (1792: pank; 1838: pánk), **ponk** (1831: punkháló; 1863: ponk) id.

póka *dial.* (ca. 1456: pokaȝtath) < **pólka** (ca. 1395: polka) 'пеленки' [Kn. 1: 433 (< *povijalko* кайк.?); TESz 3: 246-247 (ср. ст.-схрв. *povivka*)]. – **Hel.:** < slaw. *povilъka*. – Vgl. (1) *pólya*; (2) *póc* < *polc*.

polc < *altung.* *polca* (1177/1500: ? Pulch hn.; 1343: Poulcha hn.; 1873: póca) ~ *dial.* **póc** 'полка' [Kn. 1: 430-431; TESz 3: 241-242]. – **Hel.:** < slaw. *polica* (-*a* осмыслено как Px). – {Vgl. *póka* < *pólka*}.

pólka – s. *póka*.

pólya (ca. 1480: polalo (глаг.); 1538: pola; 1587: polja; 1890: pólyákban) 'пеленки; бинт' [Kn. 1: 432-433; TESz 3: 246-247]. – **Hel.:** < slaw. *povijalo* < *povijadlo*. – Vgl. *póka*.

ponk – s. *pók*.

poroszka – s. *poroszkál*.

poroszkál (1585: porozkalua; но уже ок. 1395: poroȝka = **poroszka** 'иноходец') 'идти иноходью, семенить, трусить' [Kn. 1: 439; TESz 3: 259]. – **Hel.:** < slaw. *prusa-*, **pruska-*.

poszáta ~ *dial.* **poszta, paszáta** (1590: poszata [долг. не обозн. {= долгота не обозначается} в этом ист. {= источнике}]) 'искалеченный, неуклюжий (особ. ребенок, детеныш); мал. {= маленькая} певчая птичка' [Kn. 2: 922 (считает, что первично 'птичка', другие название к-рой *nyomorék* {???, = eigentlich} 'калека'); TESz 3: 263 (данная этим.)]. – **Hel.:** < ? slaw. *pьsota*; чеш. *psota* 'нужда, бедность', польск. *psota* {'Ulk, Streich'}.

poszmat *dial.* (1739: poszmátos; 1789: poszmatot) ~ *dial.* **peszmet** (1876: peszmet) 'мусор, мусорная куча' [Kn. 1: 440; TESz 3: 263-264]. – **Hel.:** < slaw. *posъmetъ* (Kn. *posъmětъ*: польск. *pośmiat*, укр. *посміт*).

poszta – s. *poszáta*.

póta *dial.* (seit 1887) ~ *dial.* **pluta** 'поплавок' [Kn. 1: 441]. – **Hel.:** < slaw. *pluta* 'пробка, поплавок' (*pluta* > *puluta* > *pulta* > *polta* > *póta*).

pöczércze – s. *peszérce*.

puha (1438: Puha szn.; ca. 1560: pŭha) 'мягкий, пухлый' [Kn. 2: 925-926 (против); TESz 3: 305 (id.)]. – **Hel.:** < slaw. *puxъ* (Adj. Fem. -*a*?); ср. слвц. (Jancs) *puchý* 'мягкий'.

püszke – s. *piszke*.

rab (1498: Raberdeye hn.; 1522: Rab hn.; 1536: rab) 'раб, узник, пленник' [Kn. 1: 452-452 (< схрв., в период турецкого ига); TESz 3: 323-324]. – **Hel.:** < slaw. *robъ* < *orbъ*. Поздн{ее}?

rabota *altung.*, *dial.* (1522: Rabotas szn.; 1577: rabbota) 'работа' [Kn. 1: 453; TESz 3: 325]. – **Hel.:** < slaw. *robota* < *orbota*.

ragya (ca. 1300: ruga; 1416/1450: roga; 1479: Ragyas szn.) ~ *dial.* **rogya** (от Őrség до Szekélyföld) 'оспина; (ст.-венг. и диал. также) ржавчина на растениях, ржавчина' [Kn. 1: 455; TESz 3: 335]. – **Hel.:** < slaw. *rъdja* (ung. *ra-*: возможно влияние e.g. *ragyag* 'сиять'). – Vgl. *rozsda*.

rakonca *dial.* (1287/1296: Rakoncha hn.; ca. 1395: rochoncʒa) 'опорная угловая жердь телеги, саней' [Kn. 1: 457-458; TESz 3: 341]. – **Hel.:** < слн. *rokunica* (схрв. *rukùnica*). – От *rǫka*?

rakottya – s. *rekёttye*.

rásza (1634: rásza; 1662: ráczát [!]) 'рассада' [Kn. 1: 459; TESz 3: 348-349 (*-d* = Dim.)]. – **Hel.:** < slaw. *rozsadъ* < *orzsadъ*. – NB: *rásza* anstatt **rasza* < *raszád*; *ábra* anstatt **abra* < *abráz*; *pászta* anstatt **paszta* < *pasztát*.

rászt *altung.* (ca. 1400 Razth) 'опухоль селезенки' [Kn. 2: 727; TESz 3: 349]. – **Hel.:** < схрв. *râst* 'болезнь селезенки' (слн. *rást* 'рост', слцк. *rast*) < *orstъ*. – Поздн{ее}.

réce (seit dem 14.Jh.) 'утка'. – **Hel.:** ? ⁓ слн. *ráca*, *réca*, схрв. *rȁca*. – {Vgl. EWU 1239}.

Redmec – s. **Regmec*.

*Regmec (in: *Felsőregmec*, *Alsóregmec*) < **Redmec** (1277: Redemech; 1386: Alsowredmech; 1387: Felseuredmech) Ortsname, Komitat Borsod-Abaúj-Zemplén [Kiss 57 (ср. ст.чеш. *Radimice* (Pl.) hn < *Radim* szn.; Hel.: не проходит по фонетике); Kiss 218]. – **Hel.:** < ? slaw. *Rodimьсь*.

rekёttye (OklSz) ~ *dial.* **rakottya** (1181/1288/1366/16.Jh.: Rakathya hn.; 1193: raquatiquerec) ~ *dial.* **rekӧttye** 'дрок Genista; пепельная ива Salix cinerea' [Kn. 1: 460-461 (< *rakytyje*); TESz 3: 371]. – **Hel.:** < slaw. *rokytьje* < *orkytьje*.

rekӧttye – s. *rekёttye*.

rezsda – s. *rozsda*.

rogya – s. *ragya*.

rombol (1621: rombolni) '(ст.венг.) рассекать, разрубать; (совр.) разрушать' [Kn. 2: 731-732; TESz 3: 439 (объединяет с *romlik*, *ront*, etc.)]. – **Hel.:** < slaw. *rǫbi-* {'hauen'} (Слав. заим. попало под сем. {= семантическое} влияние *romlik* 'портиться', *ront* 'портить' etc.).

róna I *книжн.* (1764: rona; 1778: róna) 'равнина' [Kn. 1: 468-469; TESz 3: 440]. – **Hel.:** < slaw. *rovьna* или *rovina* или *rovьnina* < *orv-* (слвц. *rovina* 'равнина'). – Любопытно отсутств. {= отсутствие} слова в стар. письм. {= старой письменности} и в диал.! Искусств. заим. {= искусственное заимствование}? – Vgl. *róna* II.

róna II *dial.* (1774: róna) 'ров (и др.)' [Kn. 1: 468-469; TESz 3: 440 (отграничивают от *róna* 'равнина')]. – **Hel.:** < slaw. *rovina*. – Vgl. *róna* I.

rozsda (1416/1450: roſdatol; 1799: re'sda) ~ **rezsda** 'ржавчина' [Kn. 1: 470 (<
болг.); TESz 3: 453-454]. – **Hel.**: < slaw. *rъžda* < *rъdja*. – Vgl. *ragya*.

ruga (1213/1550: ? Rugas szn.; 1216/1550: ? Ruga szn.; 1270/1355: ruga) 'го-
дичная церк. подать' [Kn. 2: 733; TESz 3: 462]. – **Hel.**: < slaw. *ruga*; ст.-
болг., укр., рус. *рýга* < гр. *ῥόγα* < лат. *rogare*.

sátor (ca. 1150: Saturholmu hn.; 1372/1448: ſatorokot) 'палатка, шатер' [Kn.
2: 939-940; TESz 3: 500-501 (< тюрк.)]. – **Hel.**: < ? slaw. *šatъrъ, šatъrъ*
(Фасм. 4: 413-414) или < тюрк. **čātyr*.

sipőc *altung.* (nur 1587 [OklSz]: "Sypölczöknek az öz ſöwöknek bibalist attak"
– знач. {= значение} недостоверно) [OklSz 846; Kn. 2: 941-942; TESz
3: 546 (попытки сближ. с полск. *siepacz* фон. {= фонетически} недосто-
верны)]. – **Hel.**: < ? slaw. *šipovьcь*. Ср. **šipъ* > слвц. *šíp* 'шип', польск.
szyp 'стрела', в.-луж. *šip*, н.-луж. *šyp* (Фасм. 4: 440).

siska *altung. dial.* (1419: Siska szn.; 1542: syska 'вид пушки'; 1792: siska
'черн. орешки'; 1908: siska 'еловая шишка'; 1915: siska 'желудь') [Kn.
1: 476-477; TESz 3: 548-549]. – **Hel.**: < slaw. *šiška*. – Отчасти позд-
н{ее}. – {Hierzu s. insb. Helimski 1997}.

susnya *dial.* 'боковой побег; хворост, валежник; der Reisig' [Kn. 1: 481 (<
слн. *sušnjâd, x*?); TESz 3: 622]. – **Hel.**: < ung. **susnyák* < slaw. *sušьnjakъ*.
– Поздн{ее}?

szalad *dial.* (ca. 1395: ȝalad; szalad в Трансильв.; szalados в Задун. крае)
[Kn. 1: 485-486 (дет. {= детали} неясны); TESz 3: 657]. – **Hel.**: << slaw.
soldъ (Фасм. 3: 712-713).

szalonna (1249: ? Zolouna, Zolovna hn.; 1546: salonat; 1590: szolonna) 'сало'
[Kn. 1: 487; TESz 3: 665-666]. – **Hel.**: < *szalnna* < *sza|la|nna* < *sza|lán|na*
< *szalánina* < < slaw. *slanina* < *solnina*.

szápa(-keszeg) (1794: száp-keszeg; 1825: szápo-keszeg [Szeged]; 1887: szápa-
keszeg [Szeged]) 'рыба Abramis sapa' [Kn. 2: 750 (лат. *sapa* от Палласа;
но как попало в Сегед?)]. – **Hel.**: < ? slaw. *sapa*; рус. *сáпа* 'лещ Abramis
ballerus; Cyprinus ballerus' (Фасм. 3: 558). – Поздн{ее}?

szekërnye (ca. 1395: ȝekernÿe; 1533: sekőrnie) 'кожаная обувь типа сапог'
[Kn. 1: 495-496; TESz 3: 702]. – **Hel.**: < slaw. *skorьnja* (Pl. *skorьnjě/i* ?).

szëm(ë)rëk *altung.* (1251/1281 Zemeryk, Zimiriktu; 1278/1407 zemerakfa;
1407: zemrekfa) 'вид дерева (*можжевельник)' [Kn. 1: 498; OklSz 908].
– **Hel.**: < slaw. *smrěkъ (smьrkъ?)* (Фасм. 3: 686). – Пример показывает,
что OklSz гораздо лучше рек-ет {= реконструирует} ст.-венг. формы,
чем Kn. – Kn. дает как *szëmërëk*.

szëmrëk – s. *szëm(ë)rëk*.

széna (1055: zenaia) ~ *dial.* **szína** 'сено' [Kn. 1: 499 (! скорее < слвц. вместе
с терминами уборки сена); TESz 3: 720-721 (id.; гл. перв. слога {= глас-

ный первого слога} по всей вер. {= вероятности} удлинился ввиду ударной позиции)]. – **Hel.:** < slaw. *sĕno*.

Szilágyperecsen – s. **Perecsen*.

szína – s. *szĕna*.

szolga – s. *Bakta*.

szomszéd (1322: Zomzed hn; 1345: Zumzed hn.; 1416/1450: Zomzed) ~ *dial.* **szomszíd** 'сосед' [Kn. 1: 510 ("относится к древнейшему слою слав. заим., но непоср. источник не устанавливается"); TESz 3: 781]. – **Hel.:** < slaw. *sǫsĕdъ*. Не может ли быть отражено **somsēdъ*?

sző – s. *szőke*.

szőke < *уст.* **sző** (1130-40: Seide szn.; 1290: zeu; 1211: Zeuke szn.; 1349: Zewka) 'белокурый' [Kn. 2: 757-758; TESz 3: 792-793 (скорее ф.-у.)]. – **Hel.:** < ? slaw. *sivъ*.

szövétnek 1372/1448: ȝewuednekednek; 1590: szeuédnek) 'свеча, светильник' [Kn. 1: 511-512; TESz 3: 799]. **Hel.:** < slaw. *svĕtьnikъ* (возможно влияние *szövendéj* 'вырез платья' и под.).

szúca – s. *cúca*.

tályog (? 1297: Talug hn.; 1516-18: Tharghij; 1551: thaloba (ill.); 1585: talgiu; 1647: tályog – множество вариантов) 'гнойник, абсцесс' [Kn. 2: 957-959; TESz 3: 832-833]. – **Hel.:** < ? slaw. *taljugъ*; ср. ст.-чеш. *talov, tálov* 'гной', н.-луж. *tatug* id., болг. *málog* 'нанос, отложение' etc.

tengelic (seit 1320; ряд вариантов, в т.ч. *tenglic* seit 1357) 'щеголь'. – **Hel.:** (1) slaw. **ščigъlь* – болг. кайк. *štiglec*, польск. *szczygiel*, укр. *щиголь*, н.-луж. *ščigelc*; (2) slaw. **ščegъlь* – слн. *ščĕgljec*, рус. {*щеголь*}; (3) **stegъlь* – чеш. *stehlík*, слвц. *stehlik*.

ténzsola – s. *tézsla*.

terĕm (terme) (1225: ? Terem hn.; 1356: Bankneytereme {sic!, mit -rem-} (OklSz 980); последние данные: 1500; оживлено М. Реваи {= Miklós Révai} (18 в.); оживлено в неправильной форме) 'зал' [Kn. 2: 771-772; TESz 3: 897-898]. – **Hel.:** < slaw. *trĕmъ* < *termъ* (Фасм. 4: 47). – {Laut Róna-Tas (1996: 186f.): ung. < slaw. **term* [wohl ɔ: **termъ*] < türk. **terĕm* < griech. τεραμνα (ibid. 185), τερεμνα (ibid. 186) 'house, habitat', und somit "[…] the existence of the word in Pannonia in the second half of the 9th century demonstrates the cohabitation of Turks with Slavs at the dawn of the Hungarian conquest of the land". – Die türk. Vermittlung ist aber in Wirklichkeit sehr wenig möglich, denn die Belege, auf die sich Róna-Tas a.a.O. beruft, d.h. heut. türkeitürk. *derim* 'a gathering', tschag. *terim* 'die Ähren, die nach dem Mähen auf dem Felde bleiben' können unmöglich von den Verben *der+le-* 'sammeln, zusammenbringen, zusammentragen' und *derin-* 'sich sammeln' (→ **derinek* > *dernek* 'Verein, Verband', *derinti* 'Versammlung, Sitzung', s. Eren 1999: 109) getrennt werden, und weil so-

wohl *der+le-* als auch *der-im* und *der-in-* mit ihrer perfekt klaren morphologischen Struktur auf eine urtürk. nominal-verbale Wurzel √*der± hinweisen, so daß das türkeitürk. *derim* (~ tschag. *terim*) ganz gewiß keine Spur
eines gr. Wortes, sondern eine übliche türk. Ableitung mit dem sehr pro-
duktiven türk. Suffix *-im* von einer urtürk. Wurzel √*der± ist, bleibt jenes
von Róna-Tas angenommene *terĕm* ohne jegliche Unterstützung im türk.
Wortmaterial}.

tézsla [ɛ] *dial.* (1402: ? Tesla hn.; 1577: tẹsola; 1604: tésla) ~ *dial. Siebenbürgen* **ténzsola** 'оглобля плуга' [Kn. 1: 522-523 (секельск. *tánzsola* <
румын. *tânjală*); TESz 3: 916)]. – **Hel.:** < slaw. *tẹžalo.*

Tiszadẹrzs – s. **Dẹrzs.*

Tiszakerecseny – s. *Kerecseny.*

tolmács (1075/1124/1217: talmach hn.; ca. 1430: tolmach) 'переводчик, тол-
мач' [Kn. 2: 772-773; TESz 3: 935]. – **Hel.:** < slaw. *tъlmačь* (Фасм. 4: 72);
или из тюрк. *tylmač?*

torha *dial.* (1694) 'мягкий, рыхлый, дряблый, трухлявый, ломкий; weich,
schlaff, morsch, bröckelig' [Kn. 2: 963 (ошибочное объяснение из слвц.
trhan); TESz 3: 944 (m. fejlemény); EWU: "Unbek{annten} Urspr{ungs}",
(slav{isch} nicht überz{eugend})]. – **Hel.:** < slaw. *truxa* 'Mulm' (Фасм. 4:
111) {vgl. ukr. *труха́* 'сено, солома'}. – Vgl. *korhad.*

Újgyalla – s. **Gyalla.*

*uzsák (ca. 1405: wzak 'austalis') [Kn. 1: 234 (< слав. **užakъ* < **ug-jakъ*, хотя
это слово обнаружить нам не удается. К суффиксу см. Mikl.SlGr 2:
244; рус. *суряк* 'зап. ветер', ibid. 245); RMGl. 731].

uzsonna (ca. 1395: oſſana; ca. 1405: vſunna) ~ *dial.* **ozsona** (долго в ст.-венг.:
ozsonna) 'полдник' [Kn. 1: 543-544; TESz 3: 1044]. – **Hel.:** < slaw. *užina*
(? *užinьna*).

üsztöke – s. *ösztöke.*

vedér, vĕdĕr – s. *vödör.*

Velemér (1273/1349: Welemyr; 1208/1373: Welmer – речка там же) Ortsname, Komitat Vas [Kiss 687 (из имени на *-mir*)]. – **Hel.:** < slaw. *Velimĕrъ.*

venyĕge – s. *venyige.*

venyige [ɛ – ɛ] (1475: zelewenegÿe; 1536: wenyke) ~ *dial.* **venyĕge** 'виноград-
ная лоза' [Kn. 1: 552-553 (< *vinjaga* ◊ *vĕnikъ*); TESz 3: 1115 (id.)]. –
Hel.: < slaw. *vinjaga*, ср. схрв. *вùњага*, слн. *vinjága*, болг. *виня́га.*

verebes – s. *veréb.*

veréb (verebe, verbet) (1330: ? vereb hn.; ca. 1395: vereb; 1416/1466: vèrèbec,
Pl.) ~ *dial.* **veréb, verebes** (OklSz 1082) 'воробей' [Kn. 1: 553-554; TESz
3: 1118-1119 (< др.-рус. **verebъ*)]. – **Hel.:** < slaw. *vrĕbъ* < *verbъ* (в слав.
яз. – только *vorbьcь, verbъjь* etc., но есть фин. *varpu* < *vrabъ* [Kn.]).

verecs – s. *verecsen.*

verecsen *dial.* (seit 1834) ~ *dial.* **verecs, verecseny, verecsöny, verecsű** 'устройство для плетения веревки' [Kn. 2: 780 (≮ *verteno*); TESz 3: 1119]. – **Hel.:** < slaw. *vъrč...* {Auslaut unklar}.

verecseny – s. *verecsen.*

verecsöny – s. *verecsen.*

verecsű – s. *verecsen.*

verőce [vɛ-] (1411: verecke; 1645: verétze; 1750: verőcze) 'калитка; забор; шлягбаум; арена; загородка для зверей' [Kn. 1: 554-555 sub *veréce* < *dvьrьca*; это проходит для диал. *děvércě*, но не для прочих форм; TESz 3: 1121]. – **Hel.:** < ? slaw. *vratica* ⫽ *vrьvica* < *vortica* ⫽ *vъrvica.*

vërsëk – s. *vörsök.*

***vézsnek** *altung.* (ca. 1395: *vesnek* 'i[n]vestigator') 'гончая собака' [RMGl. 771 (sub *vezsnek*); Kn. 1: 556]. – **Hel.:** < slaw. *věžьnikъ*, др.-чешк. *věžník* 'дворовая собака'.

vidér, vidör – s. *vödör.*

vitorla (ca. 1395: vítorla) 'парус' [Kn. 1: 561; TESz 3: 1164-1165]. – **Hel.:** < slaw. *větrilo* < *větridlo.*

vizsla (1350: Vyslasvereb hn.; ca. 1395: viʃla, vyʒla) 'легавая собака' [Kn. 2: 783-784; TESz 3: 1169-1170]. – **Hel.:** < slaw. *vyžьla* (Фасм. 1: 367); ср. слвц. *vyžla.* – {Zu TESz a.a.O.:} Сомнения, затрагивающие и *vizsgál* (< *vizslál*), ввиду неучета *vyga* и слав. этим. *vyžьl-*, см. Трубачев 1960: 24. – {Vgl. oben ung. *hort* und die Anmerkung}.

vöder – s. *vödör.*

vödör (ca. 1165: VVaderei szn.; 1217/1550: ? vederey szn.; ca. 1405: veder; 1511/1593/1681: vödör) ~ *dial.* **vëdër, vedér, vidër, vidér, vidör, vödér, vüdör** 'ведро' [Kn. 1: 562 (< *vědrъ*); TESz 3: 1176 (id.)]. – **Hel.:** < ? slaw. *vъdrъ.*

vörsög – s. *vörsök.*

vörsök *dial.* (1446: ? Weregd hn.; 1829: vörsök) ~ *dial.* **vërsëk** ~ **vörsög** 'узкий проход верши' [Kn. 1: 550 (венг. дериват от *vörse* = *varsa*); TESz 3: 1178-1179 (id.)]. – **Hel.:** < ? slaw. *vъršokъ*, ср. *вершок* 'отверстие в стене избы для выхода дыма'.

vüdör – s. *vödör.*

zabla (1393: ? Zabla szn.; ca. 1395: ʒabla; ca. 1456: ʒaboloʃta) 'удила, узда' [Kn. 1: 564 (sub *zabola*); TESz 3: 1181]. – **Hel.:** < slaw. *zobalo* < *zobadlo.*

zanót (ca. 1395: ʒanolt; ca. 1405: ʒanuth) 'ракитник Cytisus' [Kn. 1: 567; TESz 3: 1186]. – **Hel.:** < slaw. *zanovětъ.*

zsana – s. *Zsana.*

Zsana (seit 1808) Ortsname, Komitat Bács-Kiskun [Kiss 723 (неясно)]. – **Hel.:** < slaw. *žena*; vgl. Kn. 574: *zsana* 'zsémbes asszony'.

zsarátnok *altung., dial.* (ca. 1577: ſaratnak; 1787: zsarátnag) 'горящие углы' [Kn. 1: 574-575 (поздн. < схрв. *žerátak*); TESz 3: 1210-1211]. – **Hel.:** < slaw. **žeratьnikъ* (ср. *žeratъkъ*). – Поздн{ее}?

zsélép ~ zséléb *altung.* (1264: seleb) 'мельничный желоб' [Kn. 1: 577-578 (без разграничения 2 заимствований); TESz 3: 1218-1219 (id.)]. – **Hel.:** < slaw. *žlěbъ* < *želbъ*.

zséllye *dial.* (1519: zsélye; 1575: zéllye) ~ *dial.* **zsélye** 'гроб' [Kn. 2: 975 (считает – вопреки Mikl. 937 и далее Kniezsa MNy 29: 95 – что из лат. *sella*, как и *zsőllye* 'кресло', см. TESz 3: 1226): TESz (нет)]. – **Hel.:** < slaw. *žalьje*. – Только ст.-слав. **жалиκ** 'гробница' (Фасм. 2: 35 *жаль*). – {Auf einem anderen Zettel:} совершенно неоправданы сомнения в Kn. 975, исходящие из отсутствия **žalьje* в живых слав. языках. – {Fazit:} Отражено не только в ст.-слав. **жалиκ** 'гробница', но и в венг.диал. *zsélye*, *zséllye*.

zsolna *dial.* (1759: zsolna) 'зеленый дятел' [Kn. 1: 580 (< слвц.); TESz 3: 1223]. – **Hel.:** < slaw. *žьlna* (ЕСУМ 2: 202).

zsoltina (seit 1798) 'Serratula tinctoria' [Kn. 1: 581]. – **Hel.:** < slaw. *žьltina*.

Anhänge

Anhang 1:
Geplante Monographien

[a]
Общий план монографии
**"Исследование венгерско-славянских
языковых контактов раннего времени"**

1. Славянские заимствования венгерского языка и история их изучения.
   1.1 Предмет исследований.
   1.2 История исследований.
      1.2.1 Изучение топонимов славянского происхождения.
   1.3 Историко-политические аспекты.
   1.4 Лингвистические аспекты.
   1.5 Культурно-исторические аспекты.
2. Проблема венгерско-восточнославянских языковых контактов в эпоху миграций.
   2.1 Леведия и Ателькузу.
   2.2 Изучение археологических данных.
   2.3 Проблема восточнославянского языкового влияния.

3. Проблема венгерско-славянских языковых контактов в Среднем Подунавье.

 3.1 Население Среднего Подунавья в конце IX века.

 3.2 Венгры и славяне в государстве Арпадов.

 3.3 Проблема славянских источников ранних заимствований.

  3.3.1 Словенская версия.

  3.3.2 Чешская версия.

  3.3.3 Словацкая версия.

  3.3.4 Украинская версия.

  3.3.5 Болгарская версия.

  3.3.6 Сербохорватская версия.

  3.3.7 Субстратная версия.

4. Лингвистическая проблематика языковых контактов.

 4.1 Изучение фонетики.

  4.1.1 Глубокоспециальные вопросы.

 4.2 Изучение семантики.

 4.3 Венгерский язык как источник для праславянской реконструкции.

 4.4 Славянские заимствования как источник для исторической фонетики венгерского языка.

 4.5 Проблематика венгерских элементов в славянских языках.

5. Культурно-историческая проблематика языковых контактов.

 5.1 Славянские топонимы и заселение территории Среднего Подунавья.

 5.2 Славянское влияние на хозяйство венгров.

 5.3 Славянское влияние на общественно-политический уклад.

 5.4 Христианская терминология славянского происхождения в венгерском языке.

[b]

Konzept der Monographie

**"Язык паннонских славян
и его субстратное влияние на венгерский язык"**

[Die Ziffern in Klammern beziehen sich auf die ungefähre Seitenzahl
des gegebenen Kapitels (insgesamt ca. 480 Seiten)]

I

*Язык паннонских славян и венгерский язык
(историко-фонетическое и этимологическое исследование)*

Введение. (5)

1. Проблема древнейших славянских элементов в венгерском языке. (60)

 1.1 Венгры и славяне в IX-X вв. (20)

 1.2 Замечания к истории изучения древнейших славянских элементов в венгерском языке и топонимии Венгрии. (30)

1.3 Концепция панноно-славянского субстрата в венгерском языке. (10)
2. Славяно-венгерские фонетические соответствия в древнейших заимствованиях. (80)
   2.1 Принципы выделения корпуса древнейших заимствований. (10)
   2.2 Соответствия гласных. (20)
   2.3 Соответствия согласных. (20)
   2.4 Соответствия в структуре слова. Гармоническое выравнивание слов. (30)
3. Опыт реконструкции славянского диалекта Паннонии. (40)
   3.1 Фонетика и вопросы праславянской реконструкции. (15)
   3.2 Лексика и вопросы праславянской реконструкции. (10)
      3.2.1 Проблема алтаизмов праславянского периода. (5)
   3.3 Диалектологическая характеристика. (5)
   3.4 Социолингвистические аспекты. (5)
4. Древнейшие славянские заимствования и историческая фонетика венгерского языка. (70)
   4.1 Избранные вопросы угорской и правенгерской фонетической реконструкции. (30)
   4.2 Фонетический строй древневенгерского языка. (5)
   4.3 Сравнительная фонетика тюркских и славянских заимствований. (5)
   4.4 Развитие вокализма. (15)
   4.5 Развитие консонантизма. (5)
   4.6 Изменени в структуре слова. (10)
5. Заключение. (5)

II

Приложения

1. Этимологический указатель древнейших славянских лексических заимствований в венгерском языке. (70)
2. Этимологический указатель древнейших топонимов славянского происхождения на территории исторической Венгрии. (150)

Anhang 2:
Interessant für die ungarische Sprachgeschichte:

*akal	gally	kelence
akol	galóca	korhad
barázda	*garáblya	ól – s. *akol*
*bélc	garággya	pitar
buta	gёrcsa	pitvar – s. *pitar*
cserény	gereblye	rombol
daróc	karmány	susnya

szalad verőce vörsök
terëm *vézsnek zsëlép ~ zsëléb
torha

Anhang 3:
Wörter, in denen $V_2 > \emptyset$

apáca < apácca < opatica
Bábca < babica
Bardoc < brodьcь
Bodmér → Kisbudmér
cúca < szúca < sulica < sudlica
Dáka < daleka
Dárza-patak < dereza
esztergályos < ësztërgár < strьgarь
Esztergom < strigunъ (?), stregom (?)
Felső-, Alsóregmec < ? Rodimьcь
Galgo < glogovъ
gálna < kalina
gazda < gospoda
Gilvács < glivačь
Ilva < jьlova
jérce < jarica
Jolsva → Jósva
Jósva, Jolsva < elьšava (? elьševa)
kanca < konica
kapca < kopytьce
kapta < kopyto
Kirva < kriva
Kisbudmér ~ Bodmér < Budimërъ
konyha < kohnya < kuxynja
korpa < krupa
kurca < kurica
máglya < mágla < mogyla

málna < malina
márna < mъrěna
mёrce < měrica
Molvány < milovanъ
pajta < pojata
pálca < palica
párna < perina
Pazsga < požega
pёrnye < pyrьn(ь)ja oder pyren(ь)ja
piszke < ? pьsika
polc < *polca < polica
ponyva < ponjava
póta < pluta
pózna < pauzina < paǫzina
pozsgás < *pozsga < ? požega
rosta, (dial.) rёsta < rešeto
Szaklyán < sokoljanъ
szikla < skala
szilva < sliva
szolga < sluga
*taplya 'тополь' < topolja
tézsla < tęžalo
Ugra < ? u-gora
utca < ulca < ulica
vajda < vajvada < vojevoda
vitorla < větrilo < větridlo
zabla < zobalo < zobadlo

Anhang 4:
Wörter, in denen $V_2 \ngtr \emptyset$

Bagamér < ? Bogomёrъ (Bogomёŕъ)
Bodola < budidlo < budidlo

Galozsa < ? Gložьje
Karakó < krakovъ

Komárom < Komáron < komarьnъ
Komoró < Komarovъ
Szelevény < sloven-

Szomoga < smuga
Vajola < vojidlo
Velemér < Velimerъ

Anhang 5:
Wörter, in denen $V_2 \not> \emptyset$ (Угроза CCC)

Csornata ~ Csernete < čьrnota
Garabonc < ? grobьnica
*Gonszna < gǫsina

Gosztola < Gostilo < Gostidlo
Jároszlófalva < Jaroslavъ
Miriszló < Miroslavъ

Anhang 6:
Wechselfälle $V_2 > \emptyset$

kabala, kabla < kobyla
kabla → kabala
kamra < ? komora
paszáta → poszáta

poszáta, poszta, paszáta < ? pьsota
poszta → poszáta
Vit(e)nyéd < ? Vitońa

Anhang 7:
Wörter mit orT, olT

laboda < ? leboda, lebeda, loboda
ladik < lod- < old-
*lakma < lokoma/ъ < olkoma/ъ
rab < robъ< orbъ
rabota < robota < orbota

rásza < rozsadъ < orzsadъ
rászt < rast < orst
rekettye, rakottya < rokytьje < or-
    kytьje
róna < rovьna/rovina/rovьnina < orv-

Anhang 8:
Wörter mit $TьlT$

alsó-
Csolnok (zusammen mit *csónak* <
    csónok) < čьlnъkъ
csónak (< csónok) → Csolnok

Felsőzsolca < Žьltica
pele < peleh < pьlxъ < pьlxъ
zsolna < žьlna
zsoltina < žьltina

Anhang 9:
Wörter mit *TъlT*

bolgár < bъlgarъ
Bolkács < bъlkačь
dolog < dъlgъ
halom < xъlmъ
kolbász < kъlbasa

oszlop < stlъръ < stъlpъ
tolmács < tъlmačь
Valkó < vъlkovъ/a
Volkán(y) < ? vъlkanъ
Völcsök < vъlčъkъ

Anhnag 10:
Wörter mit *TъrT*

Ágcsernyő → Csörnyeföld
Bakonycsernye → Csörnyeföld
Barnag < bъrlogъ
bërëna → borona
borona, bërëna < brъvъno (? bъrvъ-
        no, brъvъno, bъrvъno)
Csaronda < čъrna voda
Csermely, Csernő < čъrmelь
csërmëlye, csormolya < čъrmVlja
Csernek < čъrnikъ
Csernely → Csörnyeföld
Csernő → Csermely
Csertő < ? čъrtovъ/a/o
csëtër(t) → csötör(t)
Csongrád < Čъrnъgradъ
csorba < ščъrba
csorda < ? čerda, *čъrda
csormolya → csërmëlye

Csorna < čъrna
csorpák < čъrpakъ
Csörnöc-... < čъrnьсь
Csörnyeföld, Bakonycsernye, Cser-
        nely, Ágcsernyő < čъrnь
csötör(t), csëtër(t) < četvъrtь
csütörtök < četvъrtъkъ
ësztërág < ësztërak < stъrkъ (? ~
        *stъrokъ)
morotva < mъrtva
morvány < mъrvanjь
murva < mъrva
Orbó, Varbó < vъrbovъ/a
porga < pъrga
szömörce < ? smъrča
Varbó → Orbó
Varbót < Vъrbovьсь
varsa < vъrša

Anhang 11:
Wörter mit *TъrT*

Berzence < ? bъrzьnica, ? bъrzinica,
        ? bъrzanica < bъrzьnica
Börzönce → Berzence
Csaki-Gorbó < gъrbovъ
gërëncsér < gъrnьčarь
gërëzna < gъrzьno < kъrzьno

gërlice < gъrlica < gъrdlica
gërnye < ? kъrna, -ъ
Gorbó → Csaki-Gorbó
görbe < gъrba
görcs < gъrčь
Görcsöny < ? gъrčьnъ

hort < xъrtъ
horvát < xъrvatъ
hörcsög < hörcsök < xъrčъkъ
kocsma < korcsma < kъrčъma
kocsmáros < korcsmáros < kъrčъ-
    marjь

korcsolya < kъrč[i]dlo, krъč[i]dlo
kormány < kъrma
merkőce < mъrkъvica
murok < mъrky
Szomordok < smъrdъkъ
szömörcsök < smъrčъkъ

Anhang 12:
Wörter mit *TrьT*

bürü < brьvь
görög < görök < grьkъ
kërëszt < krьstъ

kërësztël < krьsti-
kërëstény < kërëstyén < krьstь/i-
    janъ

Anhang 13:
Wörter mit *TrъT*

borostyán, boroszlán < brъščь'anъ/
    brъščьlenъ
boroszlán → borostyán
esztergályos < ësztërgár < strъgarь

ësztërgár → esztergályos
ösztörű < ostrъvъ
përzsël < ? prъži-

Anhang 14:
Wörter mit *TlьT*

bolha < blьxa

kóc < kolc < klъci, Pl. < klъkъ/klъka

Anhang 15:
Wörter mit *TolT*

Baláca < blatьce < boltьce
Baláta-tó < blato < bolto
Balatinca → Palatinca
Balaton < blatьnъ < boltьnъ
Galvács < glavačь < golvačъ
Haláp < xlapъ/y < xolpъ/y
kalász < klasъ < kolsъ

kaláta(-fa) < kolta
kaloda < kláda < kolda
malágy < mladjь < moldjь
maláka < mlaka < molka
maláta < mlato < molto
malogya < mladja < moldja
oláh < vlaxъ < volxъ

olasz < vlasi < volxi
Palatinca < Balatinca < blatьnica <
    boltьnica
szalma < slama < solma
szalonna < slanina < solnina

Szalva < Slava < Solva
szulák < sъvlakъ < sъvolkъ
toklász < stoklasъ < stokolsъ
Zaláta < zlata < zolta
Zalatna < Zoltъna

Anhang 16:
Wörter mit *TorT*

barána (?) < brana < borna
Daráska < dražьka < doržьka
Dargóc < dragovьcь < dorgovьcь
Drág < dragъ < dorgъ
drága < draga, -ъ < dorga, -ъ
garád < gradъ < gordъ
Garadna < ? gradьna < gordьna
Halábor < xorbrъ
haraszt < xvrastъ < xvorstъ
Harmac < xramьcь < xormьcь (?
    xrotьcь)
karácsony < kračunъ < korčunъ
király < kraljь < korljь
maráz < mrazъ < morzъ
Nógrád < Novъgradъ < Novъgordъ
páfrány → páprágy

páprágy, páfrány < *páprát(y) < pa-
    pratь < paportь (oder papratьje
    < paportьje)
paráhol < paráh < praxъ < porxъ
parázna < prazdьna, -ъ < porzdьna, -ъ
parittya < paritya < pratja < portja
pondró < pondravъ < ponorvъ
póráz < povrazъ < povorzъ
szarka < sraka < sorka
varádics < vratičь < vortičь (позд-
    н{ee}?)
varázsol < vraži- < vorži-
Zábrány < ? za brany
zarándok < szarándok < stranьnikъ
    < stornьnikъ

Anhang 17:
Wörter mit *TelT*

bëléndëk < bëlén < blěnъ < belnъ
pëlyva, polyva < plěva < pelva

polyva → pëlyva
szelemën < slěmę < selmę

Anhang 18:
Wörter mit *TerT*

berkënye < brěkyńa < berkyni
csere → cserét
cserё́p < črěpъ < čerpъ

csërёsznyё < črěšьna (črěšьńa?) <
    čeršьna
*cserét (? > csere) < črětъ < čertъ

Cserta < črěta < čerta

csoroszlya < csoroszla < črěslo <
    čerslo

Darnó < drěnovъ < dernovъ

Darnóc < drěnovьсь < dernovьсь

Darnóca <drěnovica < dernovica

marázsa < mrěža < merža (поздн{ее}?)

parlag < prělogъ < perlogъ

Perecsen < prěčьnъ

Poroszló < Prěslavъ < Perslavъ

sёrpenyő < csёrpenyő < csёrpenye
    < črěpьnja < čerpьna

szёm(ё)rёk < smrěkъ (smьrkъ?)

szёmёrke < (1) smrěka [smьrka?];
    (2) < ? smerka

szёmrёk → szёm(ё)rёk

szёrda < srěda < serda

turbolya < trebulja (поздн{ee}?)

vereten (?) < vrěteno < verteno

Anhang 19:
Zum Schicksal des *ě*

acěl < ocělь

bělёzna < blizna, -o

bёrёtva, borotva < britva

bérmál < běrma-

beszёd < besěda

borotva → bёrёtva

csёp < cěръ (? Pl. cěpу)

csésze < čěše < čaša

csёve < cěva

déd < dědъ

dézsa < děža

ebёd < obědъ

eplёny < oplěnъ

eszterha < strěxa

jászol < jasli < ědsli

kalitka < klětъka

kenёz < knēz < kъnęzь (поздн{ee}!)

lép < lěръ

lepёny < lepěnъ/ь

lésza [ɛ́] < lěsa

medve < medvědь

mёh < měxъ

mёr < ? měri-

mёrce < měrica

métely < metyljь (*mětyljь?)

mёzga < mězga

nёma < něma, -ъ

nёmet < němьсь

pёnz < pěnęzь

pёrel < рьrě-

peszérce < рьsarica

repa [ě] ~ [ɛ̄] < rěpa

ritka < rědъka, -ъ (поздн{ee}?)

szégye < sědja

szёlindёk < szёlёndёk < szёlědnёk
    < slědьnikъ

szёmét < sъmětъ ~ sъmetъ

széna < sěno

szín < szёn < sěnь

szővётnek < světьnikъ

szuszёk < susěkъ < sǫsěkъ

tёszta < těsto

věka < věko

vitéz < vitězь < vitęzь

vitorla < větrilo < větridlo

Anhang 20:
Wörter mit *u > u*

(a) Substantive:

abrosz < obrusъ

Budmér (~ Bodmér !) < Budiměrъ

burján < burьjanъ

cúca < sulica

csuka < ščuka

duda < duda (поздн{ee}?)

*dusnok < dušьnikъ

kulcs < kľučь

kulcsár < kľučarь

kurca < kurica

kurva < kurьva

lapu < lapuh < lopuxъ

puzdra < puzdro

ruga < ruga

ruha < ruxo

runa < runo (поздн{ee}?)

suba < ? šuba

sulyok < šuljьkъ

szuka < suka (поздн{ee})

tályog < ? taljugъ

Aber vgl. Esztergom < strigunъ und
s. hier das Wörterverzeichnis.

(b) Adjektive:

buja < buja, -jь

puha < puxъ (Adj. Fem. -*a*?)

puszta < pusta, -ъ

suta < šuta, -ъ

Anhang 21:
Wörter mit *u > o*

Al-Torja < ? Turьja

Bodola < Budilo

csoda < čudo

*donha < dux(ъ)na

káposzta < kapusta

kom < ? kumъ

koma < kuma

konyha < kuxynja

Ro/udna < rudna

szoknya < suknja

toka < ? tuka, -ъ

uborka < ugorka < ugurьka

Vgl. auch *Budmér ~ Bodmér* in Anhang 20(a).

Anhang 22:
Wörter mit *CCu > CoCo*

dorozsba → Kiskundorozsma

Dorozsma → Kiskundorozsma

Golop < glupъ

gonosz < gnusъ

Kiskundorozsma < družьba (zusammen mit altung. *dorozsba*)

komor < ? xmurъ
poroszkál < prusa-, *pruska-
szomoga < smuga
zsolozsma < szolozsma < služьba

Aber vgl. auch: korpa < krupa, póta < pluta, szolga < sluga, turha < truxa.

Anhang 23:
Wörter mit ъ, ь

ablak < oblok < obvъlъkъ
aszat < osъtъ (поздн{ee}?)
dana < dъna < dъbna
debre → dobra
deget < degъtь (поздн{ee}? – скорее всего)
dobra, debre < dъbra (поздн{ee}?)
döbör, töbör < dъbrъ
iga < jьgo
iglice < jьgъlica (поздн{ee}?)

*igrëc < jьgrьcь
ikra < jьkra
imely < ? jьmelъ (поздн{ee}?)
iszap < jьzsъpъ
malom < malon < mъlynъ
mezge < ? m...zga
szikra < jьskra
tiszt < čьstь
tisztel < čьsti-
töbör → döbör

Anhang 24:
Wörter mit Cь/ъC-

ecset < ? sъčetь
márna < mъrěna
pësztërce < pьstrica (поздн{ee}?)
piszke < pьsika
piszra < pьstra, -ъ
pisztráng < pьstrǫgъ
poszáta < pьsota

ragya, rogya < rъdja
rogya → ragya
rozsda < rъžda < rъdja
szulák < sъvolkъ
takács < tъkačь
unoka < vъnukъ

Anhang 25:
Wörter mit -ica

aj(V)nca < ojьnica
Bakóca < bekovica (? bokovica)
barkóca < brěkovica < berkovica
*bélc < *bélca < bělica
*Bernece < brьnьce, brьnica

Berzence < ? bъrzьnica, ? bъrzinica, ? bъrzanica < bъrzьnica
*Bördőce < ? bъrzd[ovica]
cúca < szúca < sulica < sudlica
Dalócsa < ? dolica

Darnóca < drěnovica < dernovica
Döbröce < ? Dobrica
galóca < glavica < golvica
Garabonc < ? grobьnica
Gelence < glinica
Iklódbördöce → *Bördöce
jérce < jarica
Kelence < ? kolьnica
kemënce < ? kominica
Maglóca < mogylovica

medënce < měděnica, ? mědьnica
mẽrce < měrica
pince < pivьnica
polc < *polca < polica
szekerce < sekyrica
szelënce < solьnica
tömlöc < tömnöc < tьmьnica
verőce < ? vratica ◊ vrьvica < vortica ◊ vьrvica

Anhang 26:
Notizen:

(a)

На что надо обратить внимание:

(1) В сущности, венг. *ty/gy*, как алб. *q/gj*, отражает, конечно, не серб. *ħ*, *ħ*, а *tj*, *dj* или, м.б., *kj*, *gj*, т.е. состояние, близкое к праслав. Думаю, однако, что это просто результат того, что в с.-хорв.-словен. развитие *tj > ħ* осуществилось, действительно, <u>позже</u>; к этому времени в болг. <u>уже</u> было нечто вроде *št*. Т.о., в конечном счете, *ty/gy* все-таки не ранние заимств. из слав. языка болг. типа, а заимств. из все того же с.-хорв.-словен., но еще фонетически не продвинутого.

(2) В любом случае, что бросается в глаза, так это то, что твоя {= ? Helimskis} (венг.) система передач передает всегда столь же или более архаичн. слав. язык. Это удивительно, и лишь подкрепляется считанными исключениями. Хронология (относительная) такова:

I. Очень архаичн. заимств. в алб., где *ъ*, *y > u*, *o > a*, *ǫ > o*, *s > sh*. Таких ≤ 10 штук. VI-VIII в.?

II. Твои {= ? Helimskis} венг. слова. X-XI в.?

III. 800 заимств. в алб. с *ǫ > ën, un*, *s > s*, *o > o*, *y > i* etc. Думаю, не ранее XIV-XV в.

(b)

В нек. {= некоторых} случаях я вынужден исходить из слав. формы ≠ ЭССЯ. E.g. *grebьnь* (ЭССЯ *greby/*greben-*, но ср. *гребень*, *гребня*), *grędilь* (ЭССЯ *grędelь*, но ср. *грядиль*). Думаешь ли ты, что при таких отступлениях нужны комментарии? Или можно обойтись краткости ради? Проверь, нет ли этих вар-тов в кн. Варбот. Я бы все-таки оговаривал.

(c)

По венг. данным, в глаг. корне 'мести' жуткое прыганье долготы: *met-/mĕt-*. Потому, что эти глаголы с долготой типа *bĕg-* вообще загадка. E.g. *смёт*. Но венг. *szemét* < *sъmĕtъ*. Но венг. *pemete* < *pometa* (≈ метла).

(d)

Необщеславянские заимствования фиксируемые до 1500 г. (за вычетом турецких заимствований через сербохорватское посредство) (то, что не вошло в картотеку):

balin 'рыба Aspius radax (и др.)'

    ок. 1395 balyn; ряд вариантов

    ~ слав. **bolenъ* / **bolenь* (ЭССЯ 2: 172 "Слово не вполне ясной этимологии, с характерным ограничением ю.-зап. ареалом. Заимствование?".

birka (с 1461) 'овца' < чеш. *birka* (культ.-истор. данные, см. Kn. 1: 92-93; TESz 1: 304-305). Но допустимо думать и о слав. **byrьka* (см. ЕСУМ 1: 184).

cékla (1322 ? szn. Ceclas; ок. 1405 cecla) 'свекла' (диал. *cikla, cvikla* etc.). История распр. {= распространения} культ. термина недостаточно ясна (Kn. 1: 114-115; TESz 1: 416-417; EtSz 1: 630). М.б., прямо из гр. *σεύκλα* (Pl.), с *eu* > *é* (!) и *s* > *c*, как в нек. др. возм. {= некоторых других возможных} грецизмах.

csatorna (1261 ? Chaturna hn.; 1374 chaturna) 'канал' < схрв. (*čătrnja*, кайк. *četrnja* 'цистерна') < ит. *citerna* (> {!; о: <} *cisterna*).

deszpot (1467) 'князь Сербии' < схрв. *despot* < гр. *δεσπότης*.

gabanica (с ок. 1405 kabaricha вм. -*n*-) 'вид верх. одежды' < схрв. *kabanica*, слн. *gabanica* < ит. *gabbano* 'плащ'.

hajdina (1495) 'pohánka Fagopyrum sagiltatum' < кайк.-хорв. *hajdina* id., схрв. *хȁjдина*, слн. *hâjdina* < нем. (бав.-австр. *haidn*, ср.-в.-н. *heidenkorn*).

harisnya (1470 harÿsnat, [только] 1664 haliosniat) 'чулки' < укр. *холóшнí* [детали явно неясны], см. **xolča* ЭССЯ 8: 56.

hofnica *altung.* (1462 hofnyczas) 'вид оружия' < чеш. *houfnica* (откуда и нем. *Haubitze*).

kólya (ок. 1430 cola; 1576 kóllyának) 'телега' < схрв. **kólьja*.

lepény (1319/1342 hn.; 1500 lepenhal) 'рыба Thymallus' < слав. *lipanъ, lipenь* (видимо, под влиянием *lepény* 'лепешка').

mozsár (ок. 1405) 'ступка' < слн. *môžar*, кайк.-хорв. *možar* (< нем. *Mörser*?).

orbonász (1447) 'албанец' < схрв. *ȁрбанас*.

oszpora (1468) 'турецкая сер. {= серебряная} монета' < схрв. *ȁspra* < гр. *ἄσπρος* 'белый'.

patkány (с 1138/1329) 'крыса': скорее > чеш., слвц. *potkan*.

pepelce (только ок. 1405): RMGl. иначе, чем Kn. – *pempôlce*.

pilis (ок. 1405 plis, piles) 'тонзура' < чак. *plîš* < *plěšь*.

pogácsa (ок. 1395) 'коржик, пышка' < схрв. *pòгača*, болг. *погáча* < ит. *fogaccia*.

pohánka (1494) 'гречиха' < чеш. *pohanka*, слвц. *pohánka*.

*pokronta (ок. 1405) 'вид печенья' < слав. *pokrǫta*? Скорее < польск.

polyák (1408) 'поляк' < польск. *Polak*, слвц. *Poliak*.

pribék (1484) 'беженец' < схрв. *прибjéг*, *прèбjег* (термин эпохи тур. войн).

ráró (1273) 'сокол Cherrug cherrug' < зап.-слав. [скорее вместе с **rarog* из некоего иного источника].

tarhó (ок. 1395) 'творог' ≮ *tvaroh*.

túr (ок. 1395) 'рана, шрам' ≮ *tvorъ* (скорее слн. *túr* (~ *tvór*) < венг.).

verpec: все неясно.

viasz 'воск' ≮ *voskъ*.

(e)

{Ung. Vornamen:}

Adorján : Adrianus	Donát : Donatus
Ágoston : Augistin(us)	Dömötör, Demeter : Dimitrij (слав.)
András : гр. Andreias	Emil : Aemilius
Balázs : Blasius	Etele : Attila
Bálint : Valentinus	Fábián : Fabianus
Bence : Vincentius	Ferenc : Franciscus
Bendek : Benedictus	Fülöp : Philippos
Bertalan : Bartholomeus	Gergely : Gregorius
Boldizsár : Balthasar	Gyárfás : Gervasius
Damján : Damianus	György : Georgius
Demeter → Dömötör	Ignác : Ignatius
Dénes → Dienes	Illés : ‹Elias›
Dienes, Dénes : Dionysius	István : Stephanos
Domonkos : Dominicus	Izsák : Isaac

(f)

Группы **tort*, **tolt*, **tert*, **telt* в субстратных славянских диалектах (во всяком случае, в основной их части) совпали соответственно с **trat*, **tlat*, **trět*, **tlět*, ср. венг. *barázda* 'борозда' < **brazda* < **borzda* и *barát* 'друг' < **bratъ*; *kalász* 'колос' < **klasъ* < **kolsъ* и *palást* 'плащ' < **plaščь*; *szěrda* 'среда' < **srěda* < **serda* и диал. *ĕsztĕrha* 'стреха' < **strěxa*; ст.-венг. *bĕlĕn* (> *bĕlĕndĕk* 'белена') < **blěnъ* < **belnъ* и ст.-венг. *pelĕszn* (→ *penész* 'плесень') < **plěsnь*.

Наиболее очевидным образом рефлексы типа **trat* прослеживаются в непервых слогах, ср. *póráz* 'поводок собаки' < **povrazъ* < **povorzъ*, ст.-

венг. *páprát* (→ *páprágy, páfrány* 'папоротник') < *papratь < *paportь,
Nógrád < *Novъgradъ* < *novъ gordъ, *Zábrány* < *Zabrany* < *za borny,
pondró 'червячок, личинка' < *pondravъ < *ponorvъ, *toklász* 'колосковые
чешуи' < *stoklasъ < *stokolsъ*. В первом слоге первичная рефлексация
сильно затемнена двумя процессами, происшедшими уже на собственно
венгерской почве. Первый из них – устранение инициального сочетания
согласных путем вставки краткого гласного, качественно тождественного
первичному гласному (*barázda, bëlën* и т.д.). Второй процесс, протекавший
в нескольких вариантах в зависимости от фонетических условий и от диалекта (венгерского) – редукция гласного во втором открытом слоге до нуля,
если при этом не создавалось "трудного" консонантного сочетания (*szërda*
< др.-венг. *szërëda*; ср. аналогичный процесс в *zabla* 'удила, узда' < *zo-
balo* < *zobadlo* и т.д.), или до "нейтрального" гласного *o/ë* (реже *i, a*), если
полная редукция могла привести к "трудному" сочетанию согласных (диал.
malogya 'вид ивы' < др.-венг. *malágya* < *mladja* < *moldja*, аналогично
palota 'дворец' < др.-венг. *paláta* < *polata*), причем венгерские диалекты
расходятся в трактовке некоторых сочетаний как "трудных" и "легких"
(ср. *gabona*, диал. *gabna* 'хлебные злаки, зерно' < *gobino*), а в значитель-
ной части диалектов (особенно в западной части Венгрии) при угрозе
"трудного" сочетания долгий гласный вообще не редуцировался (ср. *szalonna*, диал. *szalánna* 'сало' < др.-венг. *szalán(i)na* < *slanina* < *solnina*).
См. Moór 1964: 48-51 (автор рассматривает эти процессы в контексте своей
гипотезы о переходе венгерского языка в конце эпохи Арпадов с моросчи-
тающей на слогосчитающую систему).

Третий процесс – сокращение долгого гласного, находящегося в не-
первом слоге перед сочетанием согласных. Поскольку точные условия его
протекания в венгерском языке ввиду недостатка примеров остаются неяс-
ными, приводим перечень форм с сокращением:

csërësznye 'черешня' < *crëšьńa* < *čeršьna*
csoroszlya 'лемех плуга' < *crëslo* < *čerslo*
Garadna МН < *Gradьna* (или *Gradina*) < *gordьna* (или *gordina*)
haraszt 'сухая листва' < *xvrastъ < *xvorstъ*
Poroszló МН < *Prëslavъ* < *perslavъ*
Zalatna МН < *Zlatьna* (или *Zlatina*) < *zoltьna* (или *zoltina*)

Аналогично: *kalangya* 'скирда, копна' < др.-венг. *kaladnya* < *kladьńa*.

В следующих словах с *tort сокращения не наблюдаются:
barázda 'борозда' < *brazda < *borzda*
Daráska МН < *dražьka < *doržьka*
parázna 'развратный' < *prazdьna/o < *porzdьna/o*
zarándok 'паломник' < др.-венг. *szaránnok* < *stranьnikъ < *stornьnikъ*

Аналогично: *garázda* 'сварливый' < *gorazda/o*.

Мы сочли необходимым бегло коснуться здесь этих процессов интонаций, накладывавшихся на еще сохранявшиеся долготно-краткостные различия. Не вдаваясь в обсуждение возможных импликаций и интерпретацию этого факта (проблема осложнена чрезвычайным разнобоем новодолготных соответствий в славянских языках, что, кстати, само по себе свидетельствует против архаичности данного явления), автор ограничивается констатацией того, что венгерский язык, по-видимому, никак не отражает различие между удлинявшимися и неудлинявшимися гласными в ранних славянских заимствованиях, ср. *bab* 'боб' (схрв. *bȍb*, слн. *bòb*, чеш. *bob*, слвц. *bôb*, польск. *bób*, укр. *біб*), *ganaj* 'гной' (схрв. *gnȏj*, слн. *gnój*, чеш. *hnůj*, слвц. *hnoj*, польск. *gnój*, укр. *гній*) и *lapát* 'лопата' (схрв. *lòpata*, слн. *lopáta*, чеш. слвц. *lopata*, польск. *łopata*, укр. *лопáта*); ср., с другой стороны, диал. *bór-fa* 'сосна' < слвц. *bôr* – позднее заимствование с отражением вторичной долготы.

В буквально считанных ранних заимствованиях отмечается отсутствие ожидаемой долготы гласного первого или закрытого последнего слога (в срединных слогах такой феномен гораздо более част, но он объясняется процессами происходившими на венгерской почве): *jegёnye* 'пирамидальный тополь' < *jagnědъ, *meděnce* 'таз' < *mědьnica, *Kamon* МН < *kamenь, *lɛngyɛl* 'поляк' < др.-венг. *lɛngyɛn* < *lędjanъ (или *lędjěnъ), *zanót* 'ракитник' < *zanovětъ, *nadrág* 'брюки, штаны' < *nadragy, *naszád* 'катер' < *nasadъ, *gatya* 'подштанники' < *gatja (по крайней мере последние два слова, судя по датам первой фиксации [первая половина XVI в.], совершенно не обязательно относятся к древнему слою славянских заимствований). Ограниченность материала позволяет лишь предположить, что перед нами отражение начавшегося сокращения долгот, в особенности в ударном, акутированном слоге (ср. *mědь, kǎmenь, ǎgnę*).

Более проблематичным остается вопрос о причинах двойственной рефлексации славянских узких долгих гласных *ū, *ý, *ī, для которых наряду с более частыми, долготными рефлексами (др.-венг. *ū, *ī, совр. *u/ú, i/í*) находим более редкие краткостные (др.-венг. *u, i, ü*, совр. *o, ё, ö*). Видимо, здесь сыграл роль комплекс факторов, среди которых определяющее место играла позиция в слове: краткостные рефлексы решительно преобладают в непервых закрытых слогах (*pásztor* 'пастух' < *pastyrъ, *karácsony* 'рождество' < *korčunъ) и в первом слоге, открывавшемся в славянском стечении двух согласных (*bëlëzna* 'дефект в ткани' < *blizna/o, *szolga* 'слуга' < *sluga); краткостные рефлексы обычно представлены в первом открытом слоге (*ruha* 'одежда' < *ruxo, *hiba* 'ошибка, изъян' < *xyba). Распределение рефлексов в других фонетических типах слов и их возможная связь со славянскими интонациями требует дополнительного изучения.

Для характеристики субстратных славянских диалектов существенно, возможно, лишь то обстоятельство, что при нередких случаях расхождения между венгерскими диалектами в трактовке слав. *i, *y, *u "долготные" формы более типичны для областей к востоку от Дуная, а "краткостные" – для Задунавья, ср. MNyA (для *villa/vëlla* 'вилка' < др.-венг. *vīlla/villa* < *vidla*).

Кроме того, сами колебания в рефлексации узких долгих гласных, при чрезвычайной редкости колебаний в рефлексации *a, *ě, говорят о том, что их фонетическая продленность (всегда или в части позиций) была сравнительно меньшей.

(g)

Группы *ort, *olt. Несмотря на ограниченность имеющегося материала, он свидетельствует о том, что метатеза плавных в этих группах обычно вела не к rat-, lat-, а к rot-, lot-, ср.:

rab 'раб, пленник' < *robъ* < *orbъ*

rabota (диал.) 'работа' < *robota* < *orbota*

rɛkëttyɛ ~ диал. *rakottya* 'дрок Genista; пепельная ива Salix cinerea' < *roky-tьje* < *orkytьje*

ladik 'плоскодонка' < *lod-* (суффиксальное оформление неясно) < *old-*

lakma (откуда производный глагол *lakmározik* 'пировать') < *lokoma/o* < *olkoma/o*.

Как и во всех славянских диалектах, дающих особую рефлексацию групп *ort, *olt, не обходится без исключений:

- ст.-венг. *rászt* 'опухоль селезенки' < *rast (не *rost!) < *orst. – Семантика, однако, заставляет видеть в *rászt* (вслед за Kn. 727, TESz 3: 349) не наследие древних контактов, а заимствование из схрв. *râst* 'болезнь селезенки';

- диал. *rásza* 'рассада' (< ст.-венг. *rászád* < *razsadъ [не *rozsadъ!] < *orzsadъ). Этот пример также, впрочем, нельзя считать безупречно чистым, т.к. аномальный рефлекс слав. *o присутствует еще в одном-двух словах со сходной структурой и судьбой:

- *pászta* 'полоса поля, постать' < др.-венг. *pasztát* < *postatъ
  и, видимо,

- *ábra* 'рисунок' < др.-венг. *abráz* < *obrazъ.

Index der slawischen Etyma

ě steht nach *e*

ь, ъ, *V* (= ein Vokal) stehen am Ende des Alphabets

→ siehe

črěda → csorda
črěslo → Anhang 26 (f)
črěšьna → csërësznye
črěšńa → csërësznye
čuma → Csoma
čьbVl(j)a → csobolyó
čьmerъ → csömör
čьmьrъ → csömör
čьrda → csorda
čьrpakъ → csorpák
čьrtovъ → Csertő
degъtь → deget
dereza → Darza
dernovica → Darnóca
dernovъ → Darnó
dobryni → Dabrony
dolica → Dalocsa
Domašь → Damás(d)
domъkъ → Damak
dorgovьсь → Dargóc
dоržьka → Anhang 26 (f)
dǫbrava → Dombró
dǫbrova → Dombró
dǫbrovъ → Dombró
dragovьсь → Dargóc
Drava → daróc
dravьсь → daróc
dražьka → Anhang 26 (f)
drěkъ → dërěk
drěnovica → Darnóca
drěnovъ → Darnó
drěstьnъ → Dercen
drisina → Dercen
drisinъ → Dercen
dristьna → Dercen
dristьnъ → Dercen
Drza → Darza
dušьnikъ → dusnok
duxъ → doh
dux(ъ)na → donha
dux(ъ)ńa → donha

dynja → dinnye
dьranь → Darány
dьrtьca → derce
dьržь → Dërzs
dьska → dëszka
dъbra → dobra
dъbrinъ → Dobrony
dъbrь → Döbör
dъbrьca → Döbör
dъska → dëszka
dъxъ → doh
edla → Gyalla
edlovьсь → Jalóc
edlovьka → Gyalóka
elьšava → Jósva
elьševa → Jósva
eretьnikъ → eretnëk
ǫtrocělъ → atracél
ědsli → jászol
gatja → gatya
gatьje → Gétye
Gdańsk → Gadány
gduľa → godolya
glavica → galóca
glěnъ → Gelén
glinica → Gelence
gljïwa → golyva
glogova → Galgó
Glogovьсь → Galgó
gobino → gabona
goljь → gally
golvica → galóca
gorazda → garázda
gorazdьna → garázna
*gordina → Anhang 26 (f)
gordja → garággya
gospoda → gazda
gostinъ → Gasztony
gǫdьсь → Gondoc
gǫsina → Gonszna
grabja → garáblya

grabľa → garáblya

Grabovnica → Garabonc

grabrъ → Halábor

gradja → garággya

Grebenьcь → Garabonc

grebja → gereblye

grebľa → gereblye

greby → gerebën

grěb- → geréb

grobьnica → Garabonc

groš → garas

gъpanъ → ispán

gъrdla → gërle

gъrla → gërle

gъrdlica → gërlice

gъrlica → gërlice

gъrča → gërcsa

jagnędь → jegënye

jaręba → iromba

jarica → jérce

jarьtъ → jerke

jarъka → jerke

jasli → jászol, jerke

javorъ → jerke

jazь → jerke

jedla → Gyalla

jelovьcь → Jalóc

jelovьka → Gyalóka

junota → Inota

jьbranъ → Ibrány

jьgrьcь → igrëc

jьgъlovъ → Igló

jьmela → imola

jьmelъ → imely

jьva → Iva

jьzgaga → izgága

jьzgъnęcь → Ignéc

jьzkazy → Iszkáz

jьzsъpъ → iszap

jьztyka → ösztöke

kača → kácsa

kadarjь → kádár

kamenь → Anhang 26 (f)

kamorъ → Kámor

kapa → kápa

kapusta → káposzta

kladьńa → kalangya

klepьca → kelepce

klětъka → kalitka

kobyla → kabala

kobylica → kabóca

kolęda → kelengye

kolьnica → kelence

kominica → kemënce

komora → kamra

kopьje → kopja

korъmanъ → karmány

košeľa → kasolya

kotъka → katka

kovьnъ → Kóny

kǫželjь → guzsaly

krasъ → Karász

krečetъ → Kerecseny

krěkъ → Kerecseny

krošьńa → karosnya

kruxъ → korhad

krъčidlo → korcsolya

krъxa → korhad

kuma → koma

kumъ → kom

kuxynja → konyha

kuželjь → guzsaly

kvarъ → kár

kvasovъ → Kovászó

kъdulja → godolya

kъlbasa → kolbász

kъlčinъ → Kölcsény

kъrčidlo → korcsolya

kъrma → kormány

lancux → lánc

lebeda → laboda

leboda → laboda

lepěnъ → lepěny

lędjanъ → lengyel

lędьnikъ → lëdnëk

loboda → laboda

lod- → ladik

lokoma → lakma

lopatьka → lapocka

lovьčjь → Lócs

lovVnja → Lónya

lętja → Csencs(e)

lьvovъ → Lövő

Markъ → Márok

matьka → mátka

metyljь → métely

męčь → mancs, Mencshely

męsarjь → mёszáros

mědьnica → Anhang 26 (f)

měra → Méra

měrica → Mёrce

měrьky → Mérk

močidlo → mocsolya

močilo → mocsolya

mogyla → máglya

mogylovica → Maglóca

mogylovьcь → Maglód

moljь → moly

myšьka → Miske

Myšьkovьcь → Miskolc

myšina → Misina

mъlynъ → halom, malom

mъrěna → márna

mъrkъvica → merkőce

mъšьka → muska

mVrkъvьcь → Markóc

mVzga → mezge

nadragy → nadrág

nasadь → naszád

nemyja → nyomja

nevolja → nyavalya

nosidlo → nyoszolya

nosilo → nyoszolya

obari → abál

obojьnьсь → abajdoc

obrazъ → ábráz

obrusъ → abrosz

obvari → abál

obьlanicy → ablánc

ogarь → agár

oko → Aka

okolь → akol

okъno → akna

old- → ladik

olějь → olaj

olkoma → lakma

oplěnъ → eplёny

orbota → rabota

orbъ → rab

orkytьje → rekёttye

orstъ → rászt

orv- → róna I

orzsadь → rásza

ostrvъ → ösztörű

ostьnъ → ösztön

Qpejь → Ompoly

paǫkъ → pók

paukъ → pók

perina → párna

perslavъ → Anhang 26 (f)

pica, piča → picsa

plakVnja → Palkonya

pluta → póta

plьxъ → pele

polica → polc

polkVnja → Palkonya

porzdьna/o → Anhang 26 (f)

postatь → pászta

posъmetъ → poszmat

povijadlo → pólya

povijalo → pólya

povilъka → póka

prazdьna/o → Anhang 26 (f)

prěčьnъ → Perecsen

Prĕslavъ → Anhang 26 (f)

pręslenъ → përëszlen

pritorъ → pitar

pritvorъ → pitvar

prusa- → poroszkál

pruska- → poroszkál

prъži- → përzsël

puxъ →puha

pьlxъ → pele

pьsarica → peszérce

pьsarь → pëcér

pьsika → piszke

pьsota → poszáta

pьstra → piszra

pьstrǫgъ → pisztráng

pьstrica → pësztërce

raca → réce

râst → rászt

robota → rabota

robъ → rab

Rodimьcь → Regmec

rokunica → rakonca

rokytьje → rekëttye

rovina → róna I, II

rovьna → róna I

rovьnina → róna I

rozsadъ → rásza

rǫbi- → rombol

ruga → ruga

rъdja → ragya, rozsda

rъžda → rozsda

sapa → szápa

sĕno → szĕna

sivъ → szőke

skoba → ëszkába

skorьnja → szekërnye

slanina → szalonna

smrĕkъ → szëmërëk

smьrkъ → szëmërëk

soldъ → szalad

solnina → szalonna

sǫsĕdъ → szomszĕd

stegъlь → tengelic

stergomъ → Esztergom

stĕrxa → ësztërha

steza → eszteze

stornьnikъ → Anhang 26 (f)

stranьnikъ → Anhang 26 (f)

strĕgomъ → Esztergom

strĕxa → ësztërha

strigunъ → Esztergom

styka → ösztöke

stьrkъ → ësztërág

stьrokъ → ësztërág

sudlica → cúca

sušьnjakъ → susnya

svĕtьnikъ → szövĕtnek

sъčetь → ecset

sъrętja → Csencs(e)

šatьrъ ~ šatъrъ → sátor

ščava → csáva

ščegъlь → tengelic

ščigъlь → tengelic

šipovьcь → sipőc

šišьka → siska

špan → ispán

taljugъ → tályog

termъ → terëm

tęžalo → tézsla

trĕmъ → terëm

truxa → torha

tъlmačь → tolmács

ug-jakъ → uzsák

užakъ → uzsák

užina → uzsonna

užinьna → uzsonna

Velimĕrъ → Velemér

verbъ → veréb

vĕtridlo → vitorla

vĕtrilo → vitorla

vĕžьnikъ → vézsnek

vidla → Anhang 26 (f)

vinjaga → venyige

vortica → verőce

vratica → verőce

vrěbъ → veréb

vrьvica → verőce

vyžьla → vizsla

vьdrъ → vödör

vьrč... → verecsen

vьršokъ → vörsök

vьrvica → verőce

vъxodъ → Ohat

xlęba → Helemba

xmurъ → komor

xolmъ → halom

xomǫtъ → hamút

xomutъ → hamút

xorbrъ → Halábor

xotьjinъ → Hetyen

xrabrъ → Halábor

xrakъ → harák

xrěnъ → Herény

xrěščany → Herencsény

xripъ → Hirip

xusarъ → huszár

xvorstъ → haraszt

xvrastъ → haraszt

xъlmьсь → Helmec

xъrtъ → hort

zanovětъ → zanót

Zlatina → Anhang 26 (f)

zobadlo → zabla

zobalo → zabla

zoltina → Anhang 26 (f)

žalьje → zséllye

želbъ → zsëlép

žena → Zsana

žeratьnikъ → zsarátnok

žlěbъ → zsëlép

žьlna → zsolna

žьltina → zsoltina

žьpanъ → ispán

Abkürzungen

acc. = accusativus

Adj. = Adjektiv

ahd. = althochdeutsch

aks. = altkirchenslawisch

alttürk. = alttürkisch

altung. = altungarisch

arab. = arabisch

arch. = archaisch

d.i. = das ist

dial. = dialektal

Dim. = Diminutiv

dt. = deutsch

e.g. = zum Beispiel

eml. = emlékkönyv 'Festschrift'

estn. = estnisch

Fem. = Femininum

gr. = griechisch

Hel. = Eugen Helimski

heut. = heutig

hn = helynév 'Ortsname'

ibid. = ibidem

id. = idem

ill. = Illativ

kirg. = kirgisisch

krimtat. = krimtatarisch

lat. = lateinisch

lit. = litauisch

liter. = literarisch

NB = nota bene

op.cit. = opus citatum

osman. = osmanisch

poln. = polnisch

Pl. = Pluralis

Px = Possessivsuffix

s. = siehe
Sg. = Singularis
slaw. = slawisch
slowak. = slowakisch
s.o. = siehe oben
s.u. = siehe unten
s.v. = sub voce
szn. = személynév 'Personenname'

авар. = аварский
австр. = австрийский
адм. = администрационный
алб. = албанский
бав. = баварский
балк. = балкарский
белор. = белорусский
болг. = болгарский
булг. = булгарский (тюркский)
бывш. = бывший
в. = век, столетие
вер. = вероятно
в.-луж. = верхнелужицкий
возм. = возможно
вост. = восточный
в-т = вариант
глаг. = (1) глагол; (2) глагольный
гр. = греческий
дет. = деталь
диал. = диалект(ный)
др. = (1) древний; древне-; (2) другой
др.-в.-н. = древневерхненемецкий
ж.р. = женский род
задун. = задунайский
заим. = заимст. = заимствование
зап. = западный
инстр. = инструмент
ит. = итальянский
кайк. = кайкавский
кн. = книга
книжн. = книжный

tat. = tatarisch
tschag. = tschagataisch
türk. = türkisch
ukr. = ukrainisch
ung. = ungarisch
vgl. = vergleiche
vs. = versus

к-рый = который
кыпч. = кыпчакский
лат. = латинский
ЛИ - личное имя
лит. = (1) литовский; (2) литературный
луж. = лужицкий
м. = (1) может; (2) ung. megye 'Komitat'
мак. = македонский
м.б. = может быть
миш. = мишерский
МН = местное название
мор. = моравский
м.р. = мужской род
напр. = например
нар. = народный
нем. = немецкий
н.-луж. = нижнелужицкий
о-в = остров
огуз. = огузский
ок = около
особ. = особенно
панн. = паннонский славянский
полаб. = полабский
польск. = польский
происх. = происхождение
р. = (1) русский; (2) река
рус. = русский
р.-ц.-слав. = русско-церковнославянский
роман. = романский

румын. = румынский
рус. = русский
с.-в. = северо-восточный
секельск. = секельский
серб. = сербский
слав. = славянский
слвц. = словацкий
след. = следующий
слн. = словенский
словин. = словинский
см. = смотри
совр. = современный
спец. = специально
ср. = сравни
ср.-в.-н. = средневерхненемецкий
ст.- = старый; старо-
с.-хорв.-словен. = сербско-хорватско-словенский
схрв. = сербско-хорватский
тат. = татарский
т.е. = то есть
тж. = тоже, также

т.к. = так как
т.о. = таким образом
трансильв. = трансильванский
тур. = турецкий
т.ч. = (в) том числе
тюрк. = тюркский
удар. = ударение
укр. = украинский
уст. = устарелый
ф. = форма
фин. = финский
фр. = французский
ф.-у. = финно-угорский
хар-р = характер
хрв. = хорватский
ю. = южный
ю.-з. = юго-западный
чак. = чакавский
чеш. = чешский
этим. = этимология; этимологический
яз. = язык

{???} = unleserlich
{???, = происхождение} = unleserliches Wort, semantisch etwa 'происхождение'
ɔ: = lies, sprich, soll sein

Marek Stachowski
ul. Barska 1/4
PL – 30-307 Kraków
[stachowski.marek@gmail.com]

Bibliographie

AECO = *Archivum Europae Centro-Orientalis.*
ÁÚO = *Árpádkori új okmánytár*, Bd. 1-12, Pest, Budapest 1860-1874.
BárcziHtört. = Bárczi G.: Hangtörténet. – Bárczi G. / Benkö L. / Berrár J.: *A magyar nyelv története*, Budapest 1967: 95-180.

Bern. = Berneker E.: *Slavisches etymologisches Wörterbuch*, Bd. 1, Heidelberg 1908-1913.

EtSz = Gombocz Z. / Melich I.: *Magyar etymologiai szótár*, Bd. 1-2, Budapest 1914-1944.

EWU = Benkő L. (ed.): *Etymologisches Wörterbuch des Ungarischen*, Budapest 1993-1994.

Györffy = Györffy Gy.: *Az Árpád-kori Magyarország történeti földrajza*, Bd. 1-, Budapest 1963-.

Kiss = Kiss L.: *Földrajzi nevek etimológiai szótára*, Budapest [1]1983.

Kiss[2] = Kiss L.: *Földrajzi nevek etimológiai szótára*, Bd. 1-2, Budapest [2]1988.

Kn. = Kniezsa I.: *A magyar nyelv szláv jövevénszavai*, Bd. 1-2, Budapest 1955.

Linde = Linde, S. B.: *Słownik języka polskiego*, Warszawa 1807-1814.

MagyRom. = Deér J. / Gáldi L. (ed.): *Magyarok és románok*, Bd. 1-2, Budapest 1943-1944.

Mikl. = Miklosich F.: *Etymologisches Wörterbuch der slavischen Sprachen*, Wien 1886.

Mikl.SlGr. = Miklosich F.: *Vergleichende Grammatik der slavischen Sprachen*, Bd. 1-4, Wien 1852-75.

MNNy = *Magyar Népnyelv.*

MNy = *Magyar Nyelv.*

MNyA = *A magyar nyelvjárasok atlasza*, Bd. 1-6, Budapest 1968-1977.

MNyTK = *A Magyar Nyelvtudományi Társaság Kiadványai.*

MTSz = Szinnyei J.: *Magyar tájszótár*, Bd. 1-2, Budapest 1893-1901.

NyK = *Nyelvtudományi Kozlemények.*

Nyr = *Magyar Nyelvőr.*

NytudÉrt = *Nyelvtudományi Értekezések.*

OklS = Szamota I. / Zolnai Gy.: *Magyar oklevél-szótár*, Budapest 1902-1906.

RMGl. = Berrár J. / Károly S. (ed.): *Régi magyar glosszárium*, Budapest 1984.

RS = *Rocznik Slawistyczny.*

SEC = *Studia Etymologica Cracoviensia.*

SP = Sławski F. et al.: *Słownik prasłowiański*, Bd. 1-, Kraków – Wrocław, etc. 1974-.

Stan. = Stanislav J.: *Slovenský juh v stredoveku*, Bd. 1-2, Turčiansky Sv. Martin 1948.

StSl. = *Studia Slavica.*

SzegSz = Bálint Sz.: *Szegedi szótár*, Bd. 1-2, Budapest 1957.

TESz = Benkő L. (főszerk.): *A magyar nyelv történeti-etimológiai szótára*, Bd. 1-3, Budapest 1967-1976.

UJb = *Ungarische Jahrbücher.*

ÚMTSz = Lőrinczy É. (ed.): *Új magyar tájszótár*, Bd. 1-4, Budapest 1979-2002.

Ашбот = Ашбот О.: Рефлекс слов вида *трът ~ трьт* и *тлът ~ тльт* в мадьарских заимствованиях из славянского языка. – *Статьи по славяноведению*, вып. 2, Санкт-Петербург 1908: 227-269.

БЕР = Георгиев Вл. И. / Анастасов, В. (ред.): *Български етимологичен речник*, т. 1-, София 1971.

ЕСУМ = Мельничук О. С. (ред.): *Етимологічний словник української мови*, т. 1-, Київ 1982-.

Топ. = Топоров В. Н.: *Прусский язык: Словарь*, т. 1-, Москва 1975-.

Фасм. = Фасмер М. (= M. Vasmer): *Этимологический словарь русского языка*, пер. и дополн. О. Н. Трубачев, т. 1-4, Москва 1964-1973.

Фасм. ГрСлЭт = Фасмер, М. (= M. Vasmer): Греко-славянские этюды. – *Сборник Отделения русского языка и словесности Имп. Академии Наук*, Санкт-Петербург 1867-.

ЭССЯ = Трубачев О. Н. (ред.): *Этимологический словарь славянских языков: Праславянский лексический фонд*, т. 1-, Москва 1974-.

Этим. = *Этимология.*

Asbóth O. 1907: *Szláv jövevényszavaink*. I: *Bevezetés és a különböző rétegek kérdése*, Budapest.

Babik Z. 2001: *Najstarsza warstwa nazewnicza na ziemiach polskich w granicach wczesnośredniowiecznej Słowiańszczyzny*, Kraków.

Eren H. 1999: *Türk dilinin etimolojik sözlüğü*, [2]Ankara.

Fehértói K. 1983: *Árpád-kori kis személynévtár*, Budapest.

Hadrovics L. 1960: Die slavischen Elemente im Ungarischen. – *Zeitschrift für slavische Philologie* 29: 1-28.

Helimski E. 1997: *Два шиша*: Turkic *šiš(ik)* and Fennic *hīsi* in Russian. – *SEC* 2: 151-157 [nachgedruckt in Хелимский 2000: 358-362].

———— 2008: Ladoga and Perm revisited. – *SEC* 13: 75-88.

Jankowski H. 2006: *A historical-etymological dictionary of pre-Russian habitation names of the Crimea*, Leiden – Boston.

Kniezsa I. 1942a: *Erdély víznevei*, Kolozsvár.

———— 1942b: Az Ecsedi-láp környékének szláv eredetű helynevei. – *MNNy* 4: 196-232.

———— 1943: Kélet-Magyarország helynevei. – *MagyRom* 1: 111-313.

Ladó J. 1978: *Magyar utónévkönyv*, 4. kiadás, Budapest.

Machek V. ²1968: *Etymologický slovník jazyka českého*, Praha.

Majtán M. 1972: *Názvy obcí na Slovensku za ostatných dvesto rokov*, Bratislava.

Melich J. 1903: *Szláv jövevényszavaink.* I: *Az óbolgár nyelvemlékek szókészlete és magyar nyelv szláv jövevényszavai*, Budapest.

Mollay K. 1982: *Német-magyar nyelvi érintkezések a XVI. század végéig*, Budapest.

Μοór E. 1936: *Westungarn im Mittelalter im Spiegel der Ortsnamen*, Szeged.

———— 1964: Szláv jövevényszavaink kvantitási anomáliái. – *NyK* 66/1: 43-57.

Munkácsi B. 1897: A magyar-szláv etnikai érintkezés kezdetei. – *Ethnographia* 8: 1-30.

Róna-Tas A. 1996: An "Avar" word: *terem.* – Berta Á. et al. (ed.): *Symbolae Turcologicae. Studies in honour of Lars Johanson [...]*, Istanbul: 181-188.

Stachowski M. 1995: Problem orientalnych etymologii polskiego *ogar* i węgierskiego *agár.* – *Studia z Filologii Polskiej i Słowiańskiej* 32: 103-120 [nachgedruckt auf engl.: On the problem of Oriental etymologies of Polish *ogar* and Hungarian *agár* 'hound'. – *SEC* 8 (2003): 169-182].

Šmilauer V. 1932: *Vodopis starého Slovenska*, Praha, Bratislava.

Zett R. 1977: Über das Verhältnis von slavisch und ungarisch *župan ~ špan ~ ispán* im Lichte der Wortgeographie. – Décsy Gy. / Dimov-Bogoev Ch. D. (ed.): *Eurasia Nostratica* (Festschrift für Karl Heinrich Menges), Wiesbaden, Bd. 1: 207-217.

Трубачев О. Н. 1960: *Происхождение названий домашних животных в славянских языках (этимологические исследования)*, Москва.

Хелимский Е. А. 1988: Венгерский язык как источник для праславянской реконструкции и реконструкции славянского языка Паннонии. – *X Международный съезд славистов: Доклады советской делегации. Славянское языкознание*, Москва: 347-368 [nachgedruckt in Хелимский 2000: 416-432].

———— 2000: *Компаративистика, уралистика. Лекции и статьи*, Москва.

Studia Etymologica Cracoviensia
vol. 14   Kraków 2009

José Andrés ALONSO DE LA FUENTE (Madrid/Vitoria)

HALICZ KARAIM *sajan* 'WAISTCOAT; SKIRT'

1. How ironic and frustrating, but at the same time beautiful and curious, the realm of etymology can be is something everyone working in the field is aware of.[1] The case under consideration is, in this respect, a jewel. That is why in my humble opinion such a case might be offered to the memory of Eugene Helimski, who discovered so many etymological treasures and confronted the Janus's double-face of etymology so many times.

In 1932 Ananiasz Zajączkowski published a very important monograph on the nominal and verbal suffixes used in West Karaim, i.e. in the Karaim dialects spoken in Troki (Lith. *Trakai*) and Halicz (Ukr. *Галич*). There one can read that *sajan* 'skirt (Pol. *spódnica*)'[2] is derived from the root *saj-* by means of the deverbal suffix *-an* (Zajączkowski 1932: 77 [16] *saịan*).[3] The definition provided by Zajączkowski with regard to the suffix *-an* (variant *-ań*) runs as follows: "[...] występuje w karaimskim rzadko. Tworzy imiona, przeważnie rzeczowniki, oznaczające podmiot lub przedmiot czynności." (Zajączkowski 1932: 76 §10).[4]

So far so good. A close look at this word reveals that its Turkic nature is just an illusion. Moreover, the ultimate origin of *sajan* is "nearer" to Zajączkowski in a way he could have never managed to think about.

2. To begin with, the root **saj-* is attested nowhere in Karaim, apart from the very word *sajan*. Given the non-self-evident meaning of such root (it seems

---

[1] I would like to express my most deep and sincere acknowledgement to Michał Németh (Uniwersytet Jagielloński) for offering me this etymological challenge. He also provided materials and discussed with me previous versions of this paper. Thanks also to Professor Ralph Penny (University of London) for his help in proofreading the paper.

[2] Baskakov, Zajončkovskij and Šapšal (1974: 459b s.v. *сайан* th [saịan K, sajan M] юбка | spódnica).

[3] Kowalski quoted the word too (1929: 247 s.v. *saịan* 'spódnica'), but he offered no morphological segmentation. It is worth noting that Kowalski, like Zajączkowski, was a Polish Turkolog.

[4] '[...] is rarely used in Karaim. It forms nominals, mainly substantives, denoting the agent or the patient of the action.'

that neither Kowalski nor Zajączkowski considered it to be worth mentioning), it is necessary to look for possible candidates throughout the Turkic lexicon. But before starting the external search, what about internal evidence? Would it be reasonable to think that the original meaning of the Karaim word *sajan* is not 'skirt', but another unattested primary meaning, and that 'skirt' is therefore secondary? In order to support the real value of the Karaim *sajan* – of course without doubting the reliability of Kowalski's and Zajączkowski's information – we can see the word in a more philological context. Sergiusz Rudkowski (1873-1944), a Karaim poet from Luck (Łuck), used this word with the meaning of 'waistcoat (pol. *kamizelka*)' in one of his verses:

> *Bunar ełcedim men ezimni erkienbe,*
> *Kim* <u>*sajan*</u> *dzamanba bołmahaj ma kienbe,*
> *Da dahy kyskaba, hanuz kiep uzunba*
> *Sawahat kyłasen inno ez usunba!...*[5]

'Dlatego zmierzyłem ja siebie liną,
Aby <u>ubranie</u> [= kamizelka?] czasem [= przypadkiem] nie było na mnie
    {zbyt} szerokim,
A zarazem krótkim, [czy] jeszcze bardzo długim,
Wzbudzisz przychylność {Bożą} tylko swoją mądrością...'[6]

In a previous passage the kind of clothing they are talking about is clearly stated:

> *Jakowusiu kari, karyndas barasen?...*
> *Erkinni nehe bu kołunda tutasen?...*
> *Saharha baramen, ajtty ma Rachelka,*
> *Ki kierek ma hali janhy* <u>*kamizelka*</u>*...*

> *Bu bary jachsydy, da nehe erkiendi?...*
> *Anłama awurdy, janhyłyk bu neńdi?...*
> *Umuzumba kienmen, belimde inćkiemen...*
> *Ełcewsiz necik men kumasny izdemen?...*

---

[5]   Németh (2006: 20 [Polish philological transl.] ft. 26 [references], 66 [facsimile]). The nature of Németh's work (critical edition) prevented him from going deeper into the etymological analysis of this word, though he already notes the oddity of Kowalski's and Zajączkowski's statements.

[6]   'That is why I measured myself with a rope, / so that the <u>clothes</u> (= waistcoat?) would not by chance be too big for me, / or too small, [or] even too long, / you ask benevolence ⟨to God⟩ only with your own wisdom...'.

Jakowusiu dokąd, bracie, podążasz?...
Czemu to trzymasz w swojej ręce linę?...
Idę do miasta, powiedziała mi Rachelka,
Że potrzebna mi teraz nowa <u>kamizelka</u>...[7]

To wszystko dobrze, lecz dlaczego ta lina?...
Zrozumieć ciężko, co to za nowina?...
W ramionach jestem szeroki, w talii jestem cienki...
Jak ja materiał wyszukam bez miarki?...[8]

The meaning, as is obvious from the above quoted text, remains in the semantic field of clothing. It is impossible to find other contexts where Karaim *sajan* means something else, for there are no other written records. Therefore, the original meaning of the word in question is likely to be 'skirt' or 'waistcoat'.[9]

3. Now, from the external viewpoint, the first obvious candidate, based on criteria of shape, is the well-known root *saj+*, that Clauson (1972: 858a s.v. 1 *sa:y*) defines as "[...] originally 'an area of (level) ground covered with stones; stone desert'". Semantics alone should lead us to refrain from comparing this root with the Karaim word under consideration. Unless an extraordinarily complicated semantic shift (not recoverable by any means) had taken place, *saj+* 'area covered with stones' is likely to have nothing to do with the Karaim term. Other roots with the same shape also fail to fit the semantics of the Karaim word. I quote them just for the sake of argument: **saja-* 'to be rare', e.g. in Tatar *sajaq* 'rare' (Räsänen 1969: 395) or **saj-* 'to slander, lie', e.g. in Uzbek *sajɨɣ* 'delirium' (ibid.), Uyghur *saj-* 'to pierce' (Räsänen 1969: 400). The well-known root **sā(j)-* 'to count, to consider' (Clauson 1972: 781-2 s.v. *sa:[y]*) must be also rejected on both semantic and phonological grounds.

---

[7] 'My dear brother Jacob, where are you going? / Why are you holding a rope in your hands? / I am going to the town, Rachel has told me / that now I need a new <u>waistcoat</u>...'.

[8] Németh (2006: 19-20). 'Everything is fine, but why that rope?... / I hardly understand what news is that?... / My shoulders are broad, my waist is thin... / How will I be looking for material without a measure?...'.

[9] We have to keep in mind that Zajączkowski used in his works materials mainly from the Troki dialect, whereas Rudkowski was a speaker of the dialect of Łuck. As a matter of fact, Rudkowski's utterance appears inserted in a poetic context. Therefore, it is legitimate to wonder whether either dialectal or non-linguistic motivations could have altered the original meaning of *sajan*.

All this rather suggests that there is no Turkic material that can be related to Karaim *sajan*.[10]

4. If there is no Turkic evidence for this word, it is necessary to consider the borrowing option. Where does a linguist have to look for it? Given the geographical location of the Western Karaim dialects, the Slavic family of languages appears to be the first good place to check. Many loanwords from Polish, Ukrainian and Russian are extensively documented in the Karaim lexicon, as Dubiński (1987) or Németh (2004) have already noticed in a number of publications. Unsurprisingly, the solution to the riddle can easily be found on the pages of Vasmer's and Brückner's etymological dictionaries. Thus, Vasmer (1955: 584) says about *саян saján* 'Sarafan aus farbiger Glanzleinwand, offener Sarafan', a loanword from Old Polish *sajan*. Brückner (1989[5] [1927]: 479a-b s.v. *sajan*) tells us that "Rej wymienia między włoskiemi i hiszpańskiemi wymysłami »ony dziwne płaszcze, *sajany*, kolety, obercuchy«".[11] Classical authors of Polish literature like Mikołaj Rej or Jan Kochanowski quoted this word, but rather as an old fashioned item. It is not surprising therefore to find that it was lost at the beginning of the 18th century. Reczek (1968: 437b s.v. *sajan*) just confirms what was said by Brückner. Therefore, we can conclude that the reason why Zajączkowski and Kowalski did not recognize Karaim *sajan* is because, though they were native speakers of Polish and philologists, for them *sajan* was already a forgotten word in Polish.[12] They were victims of the historical changes that the lexicon of their own language underwent a couple of centuries ago.

5. The ultimate origin of Old Polish *sajan* is from the far west. Already in Republican times, soldiers from Rome used to be dressed in *saga*, plural form of the noun *sagum, -ī* 'kurzer Mantel' with the variant *sagus*. This word has continued in a number of Romance languages (for a general overview cf. Meyer-Lübke 1935: 621b s.v. [7515] *sagum*), one of them being necessarily the original source of the Slavic forms. The earliest of all such continuations is documented

---

[10] Why Zajączkowski was silent about this fact goes beyond the goal of this paper. Let us say, however, that in theory there is no reason to doubt the Turkic nature of the word. The root and suffix structures fit completely what one expects from a Turkic word and many examples confirm this, e.g. Karaim *soɣan* 'onion' vs. Turkish *soğan* 'id.', or Karaim *saban* 'plough' vs. Turkmen *saban* 'id.', both quoted by Zajączkowski and Kowalski.

[11] For the complete quotation, *vide* Linde (1859: 208a): "Ony dziwne płaszcze, sajany, kolety, obercuchy, aż straszno o nich mówić", transl. 'those strange coats, short coats, [k. of] jackets, [k. of] dresses, that it is simply awful to talk about them'.

[12] The most recent etymological dictionaries of the Polish language (Długosz-Kurczabowa 2003, Boryś 2005) do not contain it, of course. Bańkowski (2000) has yet to reach the letter *s*.

in Spanish, a language in which in fact one can find two different results: *sago* (elevated style, already old fashioned) < Latin *sagum*, and *saya* (and its derivate *sayal*) < Vulgar Latin *sagĭa*, documented for the first time as early as 935.[13] Corominas (1967[2] [1961]: 527a s.v. *saya*) already notes that the Latin word could be the Greek diminutive σαγίον (sic!) or from the adjective **sagĕa*, with later semantic shift. Contrary to Corominas's assumption, the Greek diminutive is traditionally considered to be a secondary formation from σάγος 'wollener Mantel, Soldatenmantel' ← Latin *sagus*, variant of *sagum* itself (Frisk 1970: 670). The fact that σάγιον appears only in Modern Greek (pl. σάγια) provides further validation for this analysis. On the other hand, the (unattested) adjective **sagĕa* is unnecessary, since it is *communis opinio* that the usage of the plural *sagĭa* instead of the singular *sagum* / *sagus* was the result of analogical influences of *toga, -æ* 'a particular outer garment' (Walde and Hoffman 1954: 464).

However, given chronological and geographical difficulties, neither the Spanish forms nor the Latin variants could be the source of the Slavic words. It will be necessary to go a bit deeper to try to figure out which language served as donor for the Slavic word. As far as French *saie* (feminine, direct descendant of Vulgar Latin *sagĭa*, ca. 1212) is concerned, Bloch and von Wartburg (1975: 569b) explain that it was used "[…] notamment en parlant du manteau des acteurs jouant le rôle d'anciens Romains […]". As such, the French term is useless in trying to trace the origin of Slavic *sajan*. However, it turns out that *saie* (but masculine!, 1510), a paradigmatic analogical form taken from Spanish *sayo* (1400), was borrowed by Italians, yielding first the naturalized noun *saio* (Cortelazzo and Zolli 1990-1991: V.1119a s.v. *sàio*, 1531-1535) and, after derivation, *saione* (Battisti and Alessio 1951: V.3312 s.v. *saio → saione*, not glossed in Cortelazzo and Zolli).[14] Italian *saione* is probably the original source of Old Polish and Russian *sajan*. This is also the opinion of Borejszo (1990: 77, 85-6, 176).[15] Moreover, she goes further in developing her position and adds no fewer than 16 additional Italian loanwords in Old Polish, all of them referring to different kinds of clothes documented during the 16th century, e.g. *żupan* 'traditional dress of noblemen' < *giuppone, giubbone* 'a k. of shirt of coat' (cf. Spanish *jubón* 'a k. of bag') or *pontal* 'a k. of trousers' < *puntale* 'id' (cf. Spanish *panta-*

---

[13] Corominas says 941, despite the fact that two earlier sources exist: the first of 935 and the second of 937. For further details, see Menéndez Pidal, Lapesa and García (2003: 566a-b s.v. *saia, saga, sagia, saja, saya*).

[14] Italian *sàia* (1264) is the direct descendant of Vulgar Latin *sagĭa*.

[15] Borejszo (1990: 85 s.v. *sajan*) states that the Italian word was directly inherited from Latin, despite the fact that phonology does not support this view. In any case this misunderstanding may be due to Borejszo's sources. In addition, the author says nothing about Russian *saján*. On the other hand, Polonists should be aware of the misprint "sajony" in Karłowicz, Kryński and Niedźwiedzki's Polish dictionary (1902: 451a-b s.v. *obercuch* [~ *obertuch*], emended in 1912: 7a s.v. *sajan*).

lón 'id'). These examples also confirm the fact that as a rule the final vowel of the Italian words is lost in the process of naturalization.[16] The most curious thing is, therefore, that the word which has been borrowed in Old Polish and/or Russian is not the inherited one, but the masculine variant developed originally in Spanish and later spread first into French and finally into Italian.

To close the circle, a few words about Latin *sagum*. Polybius already tells us that σάγος is of Gaulish (= Celtic) origin. Walde and Hoffman (ibid.) consider that Irish *sachilli* is from *sagellum*, the diminutive of *sagum* in Vulgar Latin, whereas Irish *sái* or Welsh *sae* are said to be from Middle Latin *saia*.[17] However, these Celtic words are obviously not the origin of Latin *sagum*. Pokorny (1959: II.887 s.v. *seg-* 2) derives the Latin word from the Proto-Indo-European root with nasal infix **se(n)g-* 'heften, anhängen', to which also belong Old Persian *frā-hajam* 'hängte auf', Old Indian *(ā-)sájati* 'heftet an', Welsh *hoenyn* (*hwynyn*) < **sog-no-* and Middle Irish *sēn* < **seg-no-* 'Fangnetz', Old Church Slavonic *sęgnǫti* 'ergreifen', and also Old Prussian *sagis* and Lithuanian *sagà* 'Klammer, Schnalle' (Fraenkel 1965: 754a). Inherited forms in Celtic and Slavic makes even more ironic the external etymology of Old Polish and Russian *sajan*.

Therefore, Karaim *sajan* has probably completed the following lexical route (I prefer not to quote every word cited above in order to avoid confusions; in the chart ">" stands for "genealogical" or "derivative process", and "→" for "loanword relation" or "under the influence of"):

---

[16] Leeming (2001) comments on some Italian loanwords from this time. However, *sajan* is not among the selected items, maybe because Leeming correctly considered that it does not deserve any observation.

[17] Though not indicated by Walde and Hoffman, *saia* is the regular outcome of the Vulgar Latin adjectival form *sagĭa*, also attested in early Spanish, see above fn. 13.

Finally, taking into consideration geographical and sociological issues, the rest of the Turkic languages in which this word can be identified, certainly received it through Russian.

6. Ockham's Razor asks that *Entia non sunt multiplicanda præter necessitatem*. Without a Turkic background, but with many loanwords from Polish and Russian, the origin of Karaim *sajan* 'skirt' turns out to be in fact a perfect example for Ockham's Razor. The issue of whether the borrowing was from Polish or Russian is something that has the same degree of uncertainty as whether Russian took the word from Polish or Italian. In any case, it is irrelevant to determine the origin of the Karaim word (and of the Russian too!).

José Andrés Alonso de la Fuente
C/Miguel Ángel 2, 6°B
Móstoles, C. P. 28931
E – Madrid

References

Bańkowski, A. (2000): *Etymologiczny słownik języka polskiego*, 2 vols. Warszawa.

Baskakov, N. A., Šapšal, S. M., Zajončkovskij, A. (1974): *Karaimsko-russko-poľskij slovaŕ*. Moskva.

Battisti, C., Giovanni, A. (1951): *Dizionario etimologico italiano*, 5 vols. Firenze.

Bloch, O., von Wartburg, W. (1975[6]): *Dictionnaire étymologique de la langue française*. Paris [1st ed. 1932].

Borejszo, M. (1990): *Nazwy ubiorów w języku polskim, do roku 1600*. Poznań.

Boryś, W. (2005): *Słownik etymologiczny języka polskiego*. Kraków.

Brückner, A. (1989[5]): *Słownik etymologiczny języka polskiego*. Warszawa [1st ed. 1927].

Clauson, G. (1972): *An etymological dictionary of pre-thirteenth-century Turkish*. Oxford.

Corominas, J. (1967[2]): *Breve diccionario etimológico de la lengua castellana*. Madrid [1st ed. 1961].

Cortelazzo, M., Zolli, Z. (1990-1991): *Dizionario etimologico della lingua italiana*, 5 vols. Bologna.

Długosz-Kurczabowa, K. (2003): *Nowy słownik etymologiczny języka polskiego*. Warszawa.

Dubiński, A. (1987): "Slavjanskie èlementy v tjurkskix jazykax na territorii Pol'-ši, Litvy i Ukrainy". In: S. Piłaszewicz, J. Tulisow (eds.), *Problemy języ-ków Azji i Afryki*. Warszawa, pp. 175-85.

Fraenkel, E. (1965): *Lituaisches etymologisches Wörterbuch*, vol. 2. Heidelberg.

Frisk, H. (1970): *Griechisches etymologisches Wörterbuch*, vol. 2. Heidelberg.

Karłowicz, J., Kryński, A., Niedźwiedzki, W. (1902-1912): *Słownik języka pol-skiego*, vols. 3&7. Warszawa.

Kowalski, T. (1929): *Karaimische Texte im Dialekt von Troki*. Kraków.

Leeming, H. (2001): "Italian loanwords in sixteenth-century Polish. Some ob-servations". In: H. Leeming, *Historical and Comparative Lexicology of the Slavonic Languages*. Kraków, pp. 249-57.

Linde, S. (1859): *Słownik języka polskiego*, vol. 5. Lwów.

Menendez Pidal, R., Lapesa, R., García, C. (2003): *Léxico hispánico primitivo (siglos VIII al XII)*. Madrid.

Meyer-Lübke, W. (1935): *Romanisches etymologisches Wörterbuch*. Heidelberg.

Németh, M. (2004): "Some disputable Slavic etymologies in Crimean-Karaim", *Studia Etymologica Cracoviensia* 9, pp. 111-8.

— (2006): *Nieznane wiersze karaimskie Sergiusza Rudkowskiego (dialekt łucko-halicki). Edycja krytyczna*. Unpublished M.A. Kraków.

Pokorny, J. (1959): *Indogermanisches etymologisches Wörterbuch*, 2 vols. Bern.

Räsänen, M. (1969): *Versuch eines etymologischen Wörterbuchs der Türkspra-chen*. Helsinki.

Reczek, S. (1968): *Podręczny słownik dawnej polszczyzny*. Wrocław.

Vasmer, M. (1955): *Russiches etymologisches Wörterbuch*, vol. 2. Heidelberg.

Walde, A., Hoffman, J. B. (1954): *Lateinisches etymologisches Wörterbuch*, vol. 2. Heidelberg.

Zajączkowski, A. (1932): *Sufiksy imienne i czasownikowe w języku zachodnio-karaimskim (przyczynek do morfologji języków tureckich)*. Kraków.

Studia Etymologica Cracoviensia
vol. 14   Kraków 2009

Alfred BAMMESBERGER (Eichstätt)

ZUR ETYMOLOGIE VON ALTENGLISCH *wōgian*

1. Das altenglische Verb *wōgian* 'freien, heiraten', das bei lautgesetzlicher Weiterentwicklung zu mittelenglisch *wowen* führt, ist der Vorläufer von heutigem *woo* gleicher Bedeutung. Das schwache Verb des Altenglischen ist zuverlässig überliefert. Völlig regelmäßig gehört zu einem schwachen Verb der 2. Klasse eine Abstraktbildung auf *-ung*, nämlich *wōgung* 'das Freien'. Das nomen agentis *wōgere* glossiert lat. *sponsus* und *procus*. Der Formenbestand wird bei Fischer (1986: 121-123) dargestellt. Eine allgemein akzeptierte Etymologie für das erst im späteren Schrifttum des Altenglischen auftretende Verb liegt nicht vor. Überhaupt wurden im Laufe der Zeit nur wenige Vorschläge zur historischen Erklärung von ae. *wōgian* vorgelegt.

2. Roeder (1899: 22) behandelt die Glossierungen von *procus* durch *wōgere/fōgere* und meint, dass *fōgere* die ursprüngliche Form sei, die er mit ae. *fēgan* 'fügen' verknüpfen will. Diese Deutung ist aus mehreren Gründen nicht vertretbar. In erster Linie ist zu betonen, dass *fōgere* aller Wahrscheinlichkeit nach eine Fehlschreibung für *wōgere* ist, wie Napier unter Hinweis auf einige weitere Schreibungen von ⟨f⟩ für ⟨w⟩ eingehend ausgeführt hat: "I believe that in all these cases we have merely a graphical error of the copyists, *f* and *w* being much alike in the cramped handwriting of the gll. This is borne out by the converse mistake of *w* for *f*" (Napier 1900: 104). Insbesondere ist zu beachten, dass das zugrunde liegende Verb durchweg mit *w-* geschrieben wird, so dass dessen Ausgangsform auf jeden Fall als *wōg-* angesetzt werden muß. Ferner sollte hervorgehoben werden, dass das *nomen agentis* zu *fēgan* als **fēgere* zu erwarten wäre. Gegen Roeders Vorschlag hat bereits Pogatscher (1901: 196) entscheidende Einwände erhoben.

3. Holthausen erkennt "in *wōgian* eine Ablautsform zu *wæg*, got. *wegs*, an. *vág-r*, as. ahd. *wāg* 'Woge'" und nimmt "als Grundbedeutung des Verbums 'sich bewegen' an" (Holthausen 1910: 212-213). Lautlich und wohl auch semantisch ist die Deutung möglich. Man wird aber bedenken müssen, dass die sonst sehr gut bezeugte Wurzel urg. *weg- (< idg. *weg^h-) eine Ablautstufe $\bar{o}$ nicht aufweist.

4. Eine Verbindung von ae. *wōgian* mit lat. *vovēre* 'geloben, versprechen' wird bei Walde (1954: 837) und Anttila (1969: 129) erwähnt. Eine ausführlichere Begründung dieser Etymologie findet sich bei Petersson (1913: 322). Die in lat. *vovēre* < *wog^{wh}-éye- vorliegende Wurzel kann als idg. *h$_1$weg^{wh}- (Rix 1998: 225) angesetzt werden. Pokorny (1959: 348) notiert die Wurzel als *eweg^{wh}. Die Vorformen für ae. *wōgian* sind dann als urg. *wōgw-ōja- < idg. *h$_1$wōg^{wh}-āye- zu postulieren. Die lautliche Entwicklung einer urgermanischen Form *wōgw-ōja- zu ae. *wōgian* wird in 10. erörtert. Die Verknüpfung ist denkbar, man darf aber hervorheben, dass auch bei der Wurzel *h$_1$weg^{wh}- ebenso wie bei *weg^h- eine Ablautstufe $\bar{o}$ des Wurzelvokals nicht sicher nachweisbar ist. Das Substantiv ai. *vāgh-at-* 'Beter' kann zwar auf idg. *h$_1$wōg^{wh}- zurückdeuten, aber *h$_1$wēg^{wh}- ist freilich auch denkbar, so dass ai. *vāgh-at-* also kein zuverlässiges Zeugnis für die Vokalstufe $\bar{o}$ im Paradigma der Wurzel idg. *h$_1$weg^{wh}- bietet. Die Wurzel idg. *h$_1$weg^{wh}- scheint jedoch sonst im Germanischen keine Spuren hinterlassen zu haben.

5. Es ist unter diesen Umständen nicht überraschend, dass etymologische Werke meist davon Abstand nehmen, die Herkunft von ae. *wōgian* näher zu bestimmen. So schreibt etwa Holthausen (1934: 404) im Eintrag *wōgian* lediglich: "unbek. Herk." (= unbekannter Herkunft). Ebenso sagt das *OED* s.v. *woo* knapp "of unknown origin". Entsprechend notiert Skeat (1911: 615): "of obscure origin". Fischer (1986: 123) bemerkt: "The etymology of *wōg-* is not known, but none of the words in the list above seem to be old." Wenn sich eine brauchbare Etymologie finden läßt, dann kann freilich *wōgian* sehr wohl beträchtliches Alter haben.

6. Hinderlich für jede Einordnung ist das Faktum, dass ae. *wōgian* in den verwandten germanischen Sprachen keine direkte Entsprechung findet. Da andererseits aber auch die Annahme, dass ae. *wōgian* auf Entlehnung beruhen könnte, jeder Grundlage entbehrt, sollten wir wohl doch versuchen, dieses altenglische Verb auf der Basis des germanischen Wortmaterials zu erklären. Versuchsweise können noch folgende zusätzlichen Überlegungen vorgetragen werden.

7. Als unmittelbare Vorform für ae. *wōgian* ist urg. *wōg-ōjan- anzusetzen. Eine Verbindung zwischen *wōg-ōjan- und der bekannten Wurzel urg. *weg- (< idg. *weg^h- [3.]) dürfte unwahrscheinlich sein, da im Paradigma von *weg- die gedehnte $\bar{o}$-Stufe sonst nicht vorkommt. In ähnlicher Weise muss die Verbindung von *wōg-ōjan- mit der Wurzel idg. *h$_1$weg^{wh}- zumindest als unsicher gelten, auszuschließen ist sie freilich nicht, da ai. *vāgh-at-* möglicherweise auf idg. *h_1wōg^{wh}*- zurückgeht. Dass die Wurzel *$h_1$weg^{wh}*- sonst im Germanischen nicht nachweisbar ist, macht aber schon einen gravierenden Einwand aus (4.).

8. Primär aus morphologischen Gründen ist dagegen für eine Ausgangsform urg. **wōg-ōjan-* eine Verknüpfung mit dem althochdeutschen Präteritum *giwuog* 'erwähnte, nannte, ersann' in Betracht zu ziehen. Dem Präteritum *giwuog* steht ein Nasalpräsens *giwahinen* 'erwähnen' zur Seite. Der Formenbestand des Althochdeutschen wird eingehend bei Seebold (1970: 531) und Riecke (1996: 521) analysiert. Eine Wurzel **wah-* (mit gedehnter *o*-Stufe **wōg*) kommt als Ausgangspunkt für die germanischen Formen in Frage. Einige weitere Einzelheiten dieser Etymologie sollen kurz erörtert werden.

9. Die Wurzel urg. **wah-* kann etymologisch "an *wek^w*- 'sprechen' angeschlossen" (Seebold 1970: 531) werden. Die Wurzel idg. **wek^w*- ist in zahlreichen Bildungen erkennbar. Ein Wurzelnomen (Nom.) **wōk^w-s* ist in altindisch *vāk*, avestisch *vāxš* und lat. *vōx, vōcis* f. 'Stimme' (mit durchgeführter Dehnstufe *ō*) erkennbar. Zum abgeleiteten Verb *vocāre* 'heißen, nennen, hervorrufen' ist Steinbauer (1989: 24) zu vergleichen. Das Vergleichsmaterial für die Wurzel idg. **wek^w*- ist bei Pokorny (1959: 1135) und Rix (1998: 614) gesammelt. Die paradigmatischen Verhältnisse werden bei Sihler (1995: 118) geschildert.

10. Da Reflexe von urg. **wah-/wōg-* deutlich erkennbar sind, ist die Verknüpfung von ae. *wōgian* mit der *ō*-Stufe dieser Wurzel durchaus denkbar. Freilich kann man weder idg. **wōgh-āye-* > urg. **wōg-ōja-* noch idg. **h_1wōg^{wh}-āye-* > urg. **wōgw-ōja-* als Vorform für ae. *wōgian* mit absolut stichhaltigen Argumenten ausschließen. Da aber bei der Wurzel **wek^w*- die Ablautstufe *ō* im Wurzelnomen **wōk^w-* > urg. **wōgw-* > **wōg-* bestens beglaubigt ist, besteht guter Grund für den Ansatz eines abgeleiteten Verbs **wōk^w-āye-*: Urg. **wōg-ōjan-* (< **wōk^w-āye-*) ist von der Ablautstufe des Wurzelvokals abgesehen direkt mit lat. *vocare* (< **wok^w-āye-*) vergleichbar. Der wurzelschließende Labiovelar **k^w*- in **wek^w*- führt zu urg. **h^w-/g^w*-, und vor einem velaren Vokal erscheint *g^w*- tatsächlich als *-g-* wie aus dem Plural des Präteritums ae. *segon* < urg. **sēg^w-un-* (Präteritum zu **seh^w*- 'sehen') ersichtlich ist.[1] Somit bestehen auch in lautlicher Hinsicht gegen die Herleitung von urg. **wōg^w-ōjan-* > **wōg-ōjan-* von idg.

---

[1] Seebold (1970: 531) akzeptiert die Herleitung von urg. **wah^w-/wah-* aus idg. **wok^w-*, bemerkt aber, dass man vielleicht auch *-f-* als Reflex von *-k^w-* wie bei **wulfa-* (idg. **wl̥k^w-o-*) erwarten sollte. Möglicherweise ist aber eine derartige Lautentwicklung tatsächlich bei ae. *woffian* 'schreien, toben, lästern' zu erkennen; freilich bleiben Einzelheiten dieses schwachen Verbs unklar.

wōkʷ-āye- keine Bedenken.[2] Die Herleitung von ae. *wōgian* aus idg. *wōkʷ-āye-* wurde bereits von Pogatscher (1901: 196) in knapper Form vorgeschlagenen, in der Folgezeit ist aber Pogatschers Idee nicht mehr aufgegriffen worden.[3]

Alfred Bammesberger
Richard-Strauss-Strasse 48
D – 85072 Eichstaett
[Alfred.Bammesberger@ku-eichstaett.de]

Literaturhinweise

Anttila, Raimo. 1969. *Proto-Indo-European Schwebeablaut*. Berkeley: University of California Press.

Fischer, Andreas. 1986. *Engagement, Wedding and Marriage in Old English*. Heidelberg: Winter.

Holthausen, Ferdinand. 1910. Worterklärungen. *Wörter und Sachen* 2: 211-213.

Holthausen, Ferdinand. 1934. *Altenglisches etymologisches Wörterbuch*. Heidelberg: Winter.

Napier, Arthur S. 1900. *Old English Glosses Chiefly Unpublished*. Oxford: Clarendon Press.

OED = Oxford English Dictionary. Oxford: University Press.

Petersson, Herbert. 1912-13. Beiträge zur germanischen Wortforschung. *Paul und Braunes Beiträge zur Geschichte der deutschen Sprache und Literatur* 38: 314-324.

Pogatscher, Alois. 1901. Rezension von Roeder 1899. *Beiblatt zur Anglia* 12, 193-199.

Pokorny, Julius. 1959. *Indogermanisches etymologisches Wörterbuch*. Bern und München: Francke.

Riecke, Jörg. 1996. *Die schwachen jan-Verben des Althochdeutschen. Ein Gliederungsversuch*. Göttingen: Vandenhoeck & Ruprecht.

Rix, Helmut. 1998. *LIV. Lexikon der indogermanischen Verben. Die Wurzeln und ihre Primärstammbildungen*. Wiesbaden: Reichert.

Roeder, Fritz. 1899. *Die Familie bei den Angelsachsen: Eine kultur- und litterarhistorische Studie aufgrund gleichzeitiger Quellen*. Halle an der Saale: Niemeyer.

---

[2] Als ō-Verb mit dehnstufigem ō in der Wurzelsilbe kann gotisch *holon* 'durch Betrug schädigen' (zur Wurzel urg. *hel-* in ae. *helan* 'verbergen') zum Vergleich herangezogen werden (Wissmann 1932: 125).

[3] Die Ablautstufe ō ist wohl auch in ae. *wōma* 'Lärm' (< idg. *wōkʷ-mo-*) zu erkennen.

Seebold, Elmar. 1970. *Vergleichendes und etymologisches Wörterbuch der germanischen starken Verben*. The Hague: Mouton.

Sihler, Andrew L. 1995. *New Comparative Grammar of Greek and Latin*. Oxford: University Press.

Skeat, W. W. 1911. *A Concise Etymological Dictionary of the English Language*. Oxford: Clarendon Press.

Steinbauer, Dieter Hubertus. 1989. *Etymologische Untersuchungen zu den bei Plautus belegten Verben der lateinischen ersten Konjugation. Unter besonderer Berücksichtigung der Denominative*. Bamberg: Gräbner.

Walde, Alois; Hofmann, J. B. 1954. *Lateinisches etymologisches Wörterbuch*, 2. Band. Heidelberg: Winter.

Wissmann, Wilhelm. 1932. *Nomina postverbalia in den altgermanischen Sprachen. Nebst einer Voruntersuchung über deverbative ō-Verba*. Göttingen: Vandenhoeck & Ruprecht.

Studia Etymologica Cracoviensia
vol. 14   Kraków 2009

John CONSIDINE (Edmonton)

STEPHEN SKINNER'S *ETYMOLOGICON*
AND OTHER ENGLISH ETYMOLOGICAL DICTIONARIES
1650-1700

1. Etymology in English dictionaries before 1700

The hard-word dictionaries of early seventeenth-century England sometimes marked the languages from which the words they registered had been borrowed. So, for instance, Cawdrey's *Table alphabeticall* identifies its subject-matter on its title page as "hard vsuall English wordes, borrowed from the Hebrew, Greeke, Latine, or French," and indicates headwords from the French by placing a section sign § before them and headwords from the Greek by placing a (g) after them. This consciousness of etymology was expressed at a more or less basic level in other monolingual English dictionaries of the seventeenth century: Blount's *Glossographia*, for instance, provides etyma or identifies source languages quite consistently, and includes more extended etymological discussions in entries such as *gospel* and *scot and lot*. The closest approach to an etymological dictionary of English to be completed before 1650 was John Minsheu's *Ductor in linguas*, identified in its royal licence of 1611 as "the 'Glosson Etimologicon,' or dictionary etymological of 12 languages" (qtd. Williams 1948, 758). Despite the etymological material it included, however, Minsheu's work was in the end a polyglot dictionary with etymology in second place, as the title under which it was eventually published admitted: "The guide into the tongues with their agreement and consent one with another, as also their etymologies, that is, the reasons and deriuations of all or the most part of wordes." Meric Casaubon's *De quatuor linguis commentationes* of 1650, a discursive account of Hebrew and Old English (his treatments of Latin and Greek, the two further languages implied by the title, were not published) offered etymological speculations, coloured by his belief that English was descended from Greek, but was not a dictionary.

Casaubon was a patron of William Somner, whose Old English dictionary of 1659, the first to be printed after a century of manuscript wordlists and dictionaries of the language, made the basic materials for the study of English etymology readily available for the first time. Three significant attempts to construct etymological dictionaries of English were made between its publication and the end of the century.[1] These were undertaken by the Lincoln physician Stephen Skinner (d. 1667), the German-born philologist Franciscus Junius the younger (d. 1677), and the Oxford polymath Edward Bernard FRS (d. 1697); of these, only the last-named lived to see his work in print, as the 34-page "Etymologicon britannicum" appended to George Hickes's *Institutiones grammaticae* of 1689. Skinner's work was published under the title of *Etymologicon linguae anglicanae* in 1671 (an abridged translation appeared in 1689 as *Gazophylacium anglicanum*), and Junius' remained in manuscript until 1743. The following account will attend more closely to Skinner's and Bernard's works than to Junius' since they were much more widely available in the seventeenth century.

2. Stephen Skinner's *Etymologicon linguae anglicanae* (1671)

Skinner had begun his studies at Oxford before spending some time in continental Europe after the outbreak of the English civil war. He entered as a medical student at Leiden on 22 April 1649 and at Heidelberg on 6 May 1653 and graduated MD at the latter in 1654 (Porter and Bevan 2004). This continental residence must have given him some exposure to Dutch and German. From then on, he practised medicine in Lincoln, where he "practised his faculty there and in the neighbourhood with good success, and [was] therefore much resorted to by persons of all quality, and beloved of the Gentry." Being "a person well vers'd in most parts of learning" (Wood 1692, col. 287), he naturally made contact with other educated men in the city in which he lived – and at Lincoln, that meant the cathedral clergy, notably the book collector Michael Honywood, who had also been in exile in the Low Countries in the 1640s, and the virtuoso Thomas Henshaw FRS. On his death at the age of 45 on 5 September 1667, he left a collection of etymological wordlists in manuscript.

He had already made plans for the publication of these materials; the papers which he left were indeed fair copies made by an amanuensis (Henshaw in Skinner 1671, sig. a2r). In 1666, two title pages were printed by way of advertisement, one in English and one in Latin, identifying Skinner's forthcoming work as *An etymologicon of the English tongue* and *Etymologicon linguae anglicanae* respectively (Alston 1965-, 5:357). "After his death," Wood continues, "his before mention'd Works, which had been by him left imperfect, came into the hands of *Thomas Henshaw* of *Kensington* near *London* Esq. who correcting

---

[1] I exclude White Kennett's wordlist "Etymologia anglicana," at least part of which dates from the 1690s, since it is a dialect dictionary with etymological material rather than an etymological dictionary as such (see Fox 2000, 66-67, and Harris 1992, 48-50).

and digesting them, and adding many words to them of his own, were published
... with an Epistle before them to the Reader of Mr. *Henshaw's* writing." This
took a little time, but in 1668 the book was given its imprimatur, and in 1669 a
two-leaf proposal with a specimen page appeared (Alston 1965-, 5:358). The
Etymologicon linguae anglicanae was finally published in 1671 as a folio of 804
pages (Alston 1965-, 5:353). It is not clear how much of it really was of Henshaw's writing. Wood wrote that entries marked with the letter H were his, but
these are simply the entries in which Skinner acknowledges Henshaw's advice;
this error of Wood's has misled a fine historian of lexicography (Read 1934,
269n21). In the autobiographical sketch which he prepared for Wood twenty-
two years later (Pasmore 1982, 177-180), Henshaw appears not to have thought
his part in the publication of the *Etymologicon* worth mentioning at all.

The published dictionary began, after Henshaw's foreword, with a nineteen-
page preface. Here, Skinner set out the history of human language from the confusion of tongues at Babel onwards. He recognized seven European *linguae
matrices*, i.e. unrelated protolanguages, a concept which had been articulated by
Joseph Justus Scaliger in the sixteenth century and transmitted by the English
polymath Edward Brerewood in the early seventeenth (see Droixhe 1978, 64,
and Metcalf 1974, 239). These *linguae matrices* were Greek, Latin, Germanic,
Slavonic, the ancestor of Welsh and Breton, the ancestor of Basque, and Irish
(the idea that Irish and Welsh might be related belongs to the decades after
Skinner's death: see Poppe 1986, 67-72). Skinner then explained that linguistic
change happens because of migration and warfare, trade, and the cultural pres-
tige of languages. This last, he added, accounted for the case of Chaucer, who
had damaged English by importing "whole cartloads of words from France into
our language."[2] Seriously as he took the Germanic origins of English, he an-
nounced his strong disapproval of the "inanely subtle and laboriously useless"
Goropius Becanus, "who made the whole world and indeed God himself speak
Germanic" when arguing that the language spoken in Eden had closer affinities
with modern Dutch than with any other language.[3] He was not even prepared to
accept the more moderate arguments of the writers who believed that the Germanic languages and Persian were related, perhaps as descendants of a "Scythian"
or "Celto-Scythian" protolanguage, and animadversions on this argument occupy
the next few pages of the introduction (sigs. B3r-C3r). "But that's more than

---

[2]   Skinner 1671, sig. B3r, "*Chaucerus* poeta, pessimo exemplo, integris vocum plaus-
       tris ex ... Gallia in nostram Linguam invectis, eam ... omni fere nativa gratia & ni-
       tore spoliavit." Chaucer is more reverently treated at his place in the onomasticon
       (sig. Mmmmm2v).

[3]   Skinner 1671, sig. B3r, "Ut enim sileam illum inaniter subtilem & operose ineptum
       Jo. Goropium Becanum, qui totum ... terrarum orbem, imo Deum ipsum Teutonice
       loqui cogit"; for Goropius see Van Hal 2008, 83-125.

enough of that," he concluded, and turned to the point that English words could chiefly be traced back to Old English or Anglo-Norman, followed by a discussion of the other languages from which English had borrowed words, in which he paid sustained attention to the reasons for language contact.[4] Since, he continued, a great deal of Old English had been lost, he would supplement the insular record with continental Germanic cognates (sig. C4r). He concluded by pointing out that although he did not know as many languages as he might, that was not necessarily a bad thing: "if I were versed in as many languages as Goropius Becanus, I might place Paradise in the Gothic or Germanic snowfields."[5] Nor, he reflected, was etymology an unsuitable occupation for a physician: in both, diagnostic conjecture must often stand in the stead of hard proof (sig. D2r).

Immediately after these faintly rueful words, Skinner showed how far his etymological conjectures were from wild guesswork, setting out the sorts of sound-change which he believed to be possible, with examples, in 66 pages of "Prolegomena etymologica." These were of two kinds. First, he listed processes such as aphaeresis, the loss of initial sounds, as in the derivation of *skirmish* from French *escarmouche* or of *lady* from Old English *hlæfdig*.[6] Second, he identified particular cases of the apparent interchangeability of sounds, as in the tendency for the sound represented by *b* in Latin to become the different sound represented by *v* in Romance languages, so that Latin *probare* gives Italian *provare*, and Latin *mirabilia* gives Italian *meraviglie* and French *merveilles*. There is a great gulf between the etymological practice of the seventeenth century and that established in the nineteenth, and many of Skinner's rules and examples have not stood the test of time. His achievement was to see that language change is rule-governed, and to try to set out some of the rules. He was not alone in this: since the Spanish grammar of Antonio de Nebrija in 1492, students of the European vernaculars had investigated the possibility that features of their languages might be the products of regular phonetic development from earlier languages (see Droixhe 1978, 67-75 and 99f). His procedure was comparable to that of an eminent Continental contemporary such as Hiob Ludolf, the pioneering maker of an Ethiopic grammar and dictionary, who wrote that in certain difficult cases "my method is that I ignore the vowels, then transpose the letters which are similarly articulated."[7]

---

4   Skinner 1671, sig. C3r-v, "Sed de his satis superque. Nostra Lingua praecipue ex *Anglo-Saxonica* vetere & *Gallo-Normannica* conflata est."

5   Skinner 1671, sig. D1r, "si tot Linguas quot *Goropius Becanus* calluissem, fortean *Paradisum* inter *Gothiae* vel *Germaniae* nives statuissem."

6   Here and throughout this paper, forms given in seventeenth-century dictionaries are reproduced without comment on their accuracy or, in the case of those from living languages, their continued currency.

7   Ludolf, letter to Leibniz of 12 December 1695 in Leibniz 1923-, 1.12:235, "Mea methodus ... est, ut vocales non curem, deinde literas ejusdem Organi inter se permutem."

The main wordlist ran to 411 pages, in double columns with English head-words and Latin text. It registered about 7900 headwords. Early dictionaries tend to give more space to entries at the beginning of the alphabetical sequence than to entries at the end (see Osselton 2007). An English dictionary which does not do this will have reached the latter part of L or the beginning of M at its physical halfway mark (so, the wordlist of the second edition of the *Canadian Oxford Dictionary* extends over 1815 pages, and page 907 ends with the word *long-range*); a dictionary which gives disproportionate space to entries early in the alphabet will not have got as far (so, the wordlist of the first edition of Cawdrey's *Table alphabeticall* extends over 122 pages, and the 61st, sig. E7r, ends with the word *incorporate*). The midpoint word of the *Etymologicon* is *knap*, showing that Skinner was giving a fairly balanced treatment of material across the alphabetical range. Two further conclusions follow. First, Skinner was a more sophisticated lexicographer than some of his contemporaries (cf. Osselton 2007, 82). Second, although his dictionary was published posthumous-ly, he did probably live to complete its alphabetical sequence: had Henshaw, for instance, been preparing entries from T onwards from rough notes, one might expect these entries to be sparser than those earlier in the alphabet, in which case the midpoint of the *Etymologicon* would have been earlier.

The main wordlist was followed by four shorter ones. The first, "Etymolo-gicon botanicum," an inventory of English plant-names which appears to draw heavily on earlier works such as John Parkinson's *Theatrum botanicum* of 1640, ran to 33 pages, registering about 1000 headwords, many of them being given Latin equivalents but no etymologies. The second, "Etymologica expositio vo-cum forensium," which also drew on a strong printed tradition, citing the work of Cowell, Skene, and Spelman particularly frequently, treated about 1300 items of legal vocabulary in 67 pages. The third, "Etymologicon vocum omnium anti-quarum anglicarum," registered about 3200 obsolete words from the post-con-quest era, i.e. what we would call Middle English, in 101 pages. Many of these are from Chaucer, whom Skinner read with the assistance of the glossary in Speght's edition of 1602, but other writers are cited: Gower, Langland, Lydgate, Gavin Douglas's translation of the *Aeneid*, some chronicles, and the *Book of Saint Albans* (Kerling 141-149). The last of Skinner's shorter wordlists, "Etymolo-gicon onomasticon," dealt with about 2000 English and other proper names (with particular attention to those of the Low Countries) over 85 pages. These shorter wordlists include a considerable number of cross-references to the main one.

One characteristic of the main list is Skinner's evident interest in making sense of the words he encountered in speech or current writing. So, for instance, he appears to have been the first person to commit *poop* 'to fart quietly' to paper, remarking that although there is a Dutch *poepen* with the same sense, both words may be independent onomatopoeic formations, as may Greek ποππύζω 'blow a raspberry.'[8] Likewise he appears to have been the first to write down the phrase *to a cow's thumb* 'exactly' (s.v. *cow's thumb*) and to insert an entry for *fuck* in the alphabetical sequence of an English dictionary (see Read 1934, 268-269). His work and dictionaries deriving from it are our only sources for *gulchin* 'little glutton' and *knubble* 'knuckle'; these may be Lincolnshire words, of which he identifies a number such as *adle* 'earn,' *elsin* (s.v. *awl*), *blink beer*, *chattle* 'chat,' *chark* 'expose beer to the air during its fermentation,' *grove* 'trench,' *hack* 'rack for fodder,' *shan* 'disgrace,' and *siss* (s.v. *hiss*). He contrasted *alegar* 'malt vinegar,' which he regarded as a northern expression, with the London equivalent *ale vinegar*. *Amours* (in the sense 'illicit love affairs') he observed as a very new word in London usage. *Amper* 'swelling' he identified as Essex usage, *barken* 'farmyard' as Wiltshire, and *nesh* 'somewhat delicate' as Worcestershire. No previous survey of current English vocabulary had dealt this thoroughly with dialect words (see Wakelin 1987, 157-158 and 160-161). In his observation that Scandinavian words were more common in northern and eastern dialects of English than in others, and that this corresponded to the distribution of Danish settlements in Anglo-Saxon England, he was opening up the field of historical dialect geography (sig. C3v).

Henshaw is acknowledged at a number of places in the dictionary, for instance as having suggested that *abandon* is from Old English *abannan* 'summon, proclaim,' which he thought might have a force 'exile or ostracize by proclamation.'[9] *Mole* as the name of an animal is said to have been derived by Henshaw from *moldwarp*, itself from Old English *mold* 'earth' and *weorpan* 'throw,' but by the physician George Rogers (like Henshaw, a friend of John Evelyn's) from a form of Greek μωλύω, which refers in one passage of Hippocrates to the progress of ulcers, and was taken by Rogers to mean 'make a tunnel.' Skinner evidently talked about particular questions to a number of friends. He was not uncritical in his assessment of the suggestions they offered, remarking that Rogers's "certainly looks like an extremely neat comparison, but scarcely an etymon" (in fact, Skinner's Greek was clearly not good enough for him to know that μωλύω does not mean what Rogers thought).[10] Likewise,

---

[8] Skinner 1671, sig. Ooo1v (s.v. *poop*), "a Belg. *Poepen*, submisse Paedere, nisi malis utr[um] a sono fictum, ut & Gr. Ποππύζω, quod exponitur compressis labris acutiorem quendam sonum edo."

[9] Skinner 1671, sig. Aa1r-v (s.v. *abandon*), "ut ingeniose, pro solito, divinat *Vir Amicissimus* & hujus operis praecipuus fautor [sidenote: 'Th. J. Henshaw Arm. SRM. ab Ep. Gall.,' i.e. Armiger, Secretarius Regiae Maiestatis ab epistolis gallicis] *ab* AS. Abannan, Promulgare, Denunciare, q. d. publico edicto, seu programmate Abdicare & Ejurare."

[10] Skinner 1671, sig. Iii3r (s.v. *mole*), "Doct. autem *Th. H.* nostrum *Moldwarp* ingeniose pro solito deducit *ab* AS. *Molde*, Terra, & *Weorpan*, Jacere, Projicere. ... Doct. quidam Amicus noster [sidenote: '*G. Rogers* M. D. C. M. L. S.' i.e. Medicinae

though he paid Honywood the compliment of recording his speculative derivation of *abate* from privative *a* (as in *amoral*) and Middle Dutch *baet* 'reward, contribution,' *baeten* 'to help,' on the grounds that when something has been abated, it is less helpful, he noted tactfully that there are other possible explanations of the word, and that the learned must judge between them.[11]

Skinner's work has a general quality of shrewdness and rationality. He argues, for instance, that Scots *anent* is unlikely to be from Greek ἐναντὶ 'against, opposite,' since despite the agreement of the forms in sound and sense, there is no evidence that speakers of Scots and Greek were in contact with each other, and he wonders with at least a hint of satire why "our Hellenists" have never derived *ash* (the tree) from Greek Ἄυω 'ignite' since its wood burns so well.[12] Even when he is wrong, he is wrong thoughtfully: he decides on a Germanic derivation for *admiral* after rejecting what he thinks to be the only alternative, a hybrid form from Arabic *emir* and Greek ἅλιος 'of the sea,' on the grounds that the historical enmity of the Arabs and the Greeks makes it unlikely that such a hybrid would have arisen and that the distance between their languages and English makes the borrowing implausible.[13] On the other hand, he reflects that *amell* 'enamel' may well ultimately be from a Germanic form such as *schmalzen* 'melt,' since German expertise in metallurgy and related arts makes it likely that the terminology of these arts will be Germanic.[14]

Doctor, Collegii Medici Londinensis Socius] *Mole*, deflectit *a* Gr. μολοῦσθαι, apud *Hipp.* Cuniculos agere, quae sane felicissima videtur Allusio, vix Etymon." In fact Rogers had misunderstood the passage in question, in which the ulcer is not making a tunnel but fading away: see Estienne 1831-1865 s.v. μωλύνω.

[11] Skinner 1671, sig. Aa1v (s.v. *abate*), "Vir Reverendus, & non minus literis, quam Dignitate Ecclesiastica illustris [sidenote: 'Rev. Dom. Mich. Honywood SS. Th. Dr. & Eccl. Cath. Linc. Decanus'], libentius deflectit ab *A* priv. & Belg. *Baete*, Commodum, Fructus, Utilitas, Emolumentum, verb. *Baeten*, Prodesse, quia sc. unde aliquid detractum est, illud minus prodest; Judicent docti." Honywood is also cited ibid. sig. Hh4r (s.v. *to cant*) and Kk2r (s.v. *to choke*) and in the "Etymologica expositio vocum forensium" at sig. Mmmm3v (s.v. *broch*).

[12] Skinner 1671, sig. Bb2v (s.v. *anent*), "Sunt qui deflectunt a Gr. ἐναντὶ, ἐναντίον, Oppositum, nec male sane, si vel soni vel sensus convenientiam respicias; sed quo commercio Graeci, Scotis totius Europae longitudine dissitis, vocabula impertiri potuerunt?" Ibid. sig. Cc1r (s.v. *ash*), "Miror Hellenistas nostros nondum deflexisse *a* Gr. Ἄυω. Accendo ... est enim prae reliquis lignis Accensu facillimum."

[13] Skinner 1671, sig. Aa3r (s.v. *admirall*), "secundum alios, est vox hybrida, a dicto Arab. Emir, & Gr. Ἅλιος, Marinus ... cum *Minsevo* declinare possem *a* Belg. *Aen*, *Meer*, *Al* (i.e.) Super, Totum, Mare. Quidvis horum longe facilius & simplicius videtur quam Etymon cum aliis, a duabus gentium tam a se invicem, quam a nobis dissitarum linguis, Arabica sc. & Graeca, emendicare."

[14] Skinner 1671, sig. Bb2r (s.v. *amell*), "Nec mirum est Germanos, cum Chymiae & Metallurgiae in primis semper studiosi & periti fuerint, reliquis Europae gentibus ex sua lingua hujus artis terminos suppeditasse."

Henshaw wrote in his preface to the *Etymologicon* that Skinner was steeped through with every kind of learning, being a man who not only devoured all the best books but also digested them thoroughly, and remembered what he had read.[15] Some of this reading is reflected in his lexicographical work. He naturally used a number of the standard dictionaries. He noted that Minsheu makes ill-judged and far-fetched etymologies, and that he even makes words up to fill gaps in the evidence, but counting the named sources in the range A-AZ suggests that the *Ductor in linguas* was the source which he cited most frequently.[16] He admired and emulated Gilles Ménage's *Origines de la langue françoise* (see sig. D1r). He also used Cotgrave for French, Florio for Italian, and Sebastián de Covarrubias Orozco's *Tesoro de la lengua castellana* for Spanish, the *Etymologicum magnum* and the Byzantine encyclopedia called the *Suda* for classical Greek, Joannes Meursius' *Glossarium graeco-barbarum* and Simon Portius' *Dictionarium latinum [et] greco-barbarum* for post-classical Greek, G. J. Vossius' *Etymologicon linguae latinae* for classical Latin, and Spelman's *Archaeologus* for post-classical Latin. For English, he used the newest and biggest dictionary, Phillips's *New world of words*, which he often criticized (see extracts at Blount 1673, sigs. C2r-v), and of course Somner's dictionary. He referred to a notably wide selection of other texts. Some were the natural raw material of an etymological dictionary, for instance Meric Casaubon's *De quatuor linguis commentationes* (on which there are courteous remarks in his preface, sig. B1v) and Abraham Mylius' *Lingua belgica*. Others suggest his leisure reading. He turned on a number of occasions to the notes of Isaac Casaubon and Claudius Salmasius in the latter's edition of the entertaining and unreliable history of the later Roman emperors called the *Historia augusta*, and used other classical texts such as Oppian's *Halieutica* and Pliny's *Historia naturalis* with the commentary of Jacques Dalechamps. At one point he cited a familiar line of Virgil together with what appears to be his own translation of Virgil's Latin into Greek – but if so, it is a mistranslation.[17] He read more modern Latin texts, particularly in the

---

[15] Henshaw, preface in Skinner 1671, sig. a1r, "Virum omnigenae doctrinae non levi tinctura imbutum! nempe qui omnium aetatum optimae notae libros non solum devoraverat, sed concoxerat; & tam validi, foelici, & praesenti memoria, ut Bibliotheca loquens & vivens merito videri possit" (lightly adapted without acknowledgement in Wood 1674, 2:280).

[16] E.g. Skinner 1671, sigs. C4v-D1r, "Industriam ejus probo, Judicium & Fidem non probo. Multa absurde, multa violenter, tanquam rudentibus, detorquet; imo, quod minime omnium ipsi ignoscendum est, saepe, ne Etyma desint, vocabula ex proprio cerebro comminiscitur."

[17] Skinner 1671, sig. Aa1v (s.v. *abide*), "*Abide* etiam satis facili sensus flexu significat Sustinere, Durare contra mala, Mala non refugere, οὐκ ἀναδύεσθαι, ἀλλὰ προσκαρτερεῖν τοῖς κακοῖς, prorsus eodem sensu, quo Poeta dicit, *Tu ne cede malis, sed, contra, audentior ito*," quoting Virgil, *Aeneid* 6:95. The Greek is not to be found in

natural sciences, where he quotes Conrad Gessner's *Historia animalium*, one of the alchemical works of Andreas Libavius, and the *Thaumatographia naturalis* of the Polish-born Scottish naturalist John Johnstone. In English, he read John Evelyn's *French gardiner*, Gervase Markham on the ailments of horses, and Sylvanus Morgan on heraldry. Some of the books he used were from Honywood's remarkable library and Henshaw's very good one (Skinner 1671, sig. D1r; Kerling 1979, 149). Although I have found no evidence that he used any of Honywood's Middle English manuscripts, which included copies of the *Chronicle of Brut* and the *Medulla grammatice*, and the *Thornton romances* (Thomson 1989, 51, 62-64, 65-69), there does seem to be some correlation between Honywood's printed books and Skinner's sources, and he could for instance have read Cotgrave, Covarrubias, Florio, Meursius, Minsheu, Portius, Somner, Spelman, the *Suda*, and Vossius in Honywood's copies.[18]

His manner is at times pleasantly conversational: having suggested that *admiral* may come from Germanic words including *Meer*, he imagines the reader who counters "hey, my dear fellow, *Meer* is not part of the original vocabulary of German," and on the verb *to air*, he begins "foreign reader, this will surprise you: for us, *to air* does not simply mean to expose to the air but to expose to the heat of a fire."[19] The same geniality is perhaps evident in his treatment of *mobby*, 'alcoholic drink made from sweet potatoes,' of which, although he suspected that the etymon must really be a Caribbean word, he noted that the derivation from Spanish *muo bueno* 'very good' was recommended by the fact that "it is a cheering drink enough, and extremely healthful."[20] Henshaw admitted that although Skinner gave his spare time up to etymology rather than to sleep, dice, the pleasures of the table, or wine, he was not averse to merry meetings (*symposia*) of a philosophical and erudite kind.[21] Etymology and pleasure were, after

---

the *Thesaurus linguae graecae* database or in major dictionaries or commentaries on Virgil, and προσκαρτερεῖν τοῖς κακοῖς means the opposite of what seems to be intended: 'to persist in bad things,' not to endure or rise above them. I am grateful to Andrew Wilson for discussing this point with me.

[18] These are all preserved in the Wren Library of Lincoln Cathedral: see Hurst 1982, items C881, C911, F144, M281, M317, P421, S416, S463, S606, V141.

[19] Skinner 1671, sig. Aa3r (s.v. *admirall*), "Sed heus bone vir, inquies, *Meer* non est priscum & vere Germanicum"; ibid. sig. Aa4r (s.v. *to air*), "*to Air* nobis, quod mireris, peregrine lector, non Aeri simpliciter sed igni exponere designat."

[20] Skinner 1671, sig. Iii2v (s.v. *mobby*), "nisi, quod valde suspicor, vox haec Barbarae Americanae sit originis; fort. contracta est ab Hisp. *Muo Bueno* (i.e.) Valde Bonum; est enim potus satis jucundus & valde salubris." Cf. also the knowledgeable entries for *mulled sack* and *muscadine* at sigs. Kkk1v and Kkk2r.

[21] Henshaw, preface in Skinner 1671, sig. a1v, "solebat horis subsecivis (quas aliqui somno, aleae, ventri, vino, impendere amant; quamvis non ipse, ut omnia scias, a Philosophicis & eruditis symposiis abhorrebat) magnum voluptatem capere in venandis nostrorum verborum Originibus."

all, not distinct in his experience: "what music," he asked, "is more pleasant than that concord and harmony of languages?"[22]

Starnes and Noyes concluded in *The English dictionary from Cawdrey to Johnson* that "the *Etymologicon* of Skinner represents not something new under the sun of lexicography, but rather a convergence of influences from Latin-English dictionaries, from the accounts of the native language, and from his predecessors in compiling English dictionaries" (65). There is something mean-spirited about this, and the claim a few lines below that "It is noteworthy that Skinner puts his definitions in Latin, so that his borrowings [from Phillips] are not so readily detected" is perhaps the nadir of their book. Wiser and more just is Johan Kerling's observation that Skinner's work "shows a breadth of learning and a scholarly attitude which is not unique in the seventeenth century, but which does make him one of the most prominent scholars of his day" (136). Skinner's dictionary was a serious attempt to explain the affinities and origins of a wide variety of English words, based on interesting reading and good listening, considerably more judicious than the work of predecessors such as Minsheu and Meric Casaubon, and hardly superseded in print for two centuries after its publication. It was appreciated by discerning readers as soon as it was published (see e.g. Ray 1674, sig. A6v). Having recommended Vossius' *Etymologicum* as one of the books which a gentleman should own, John Locke added that "Skinner's ... is an excellent one of that kinde for the English Tongue" (in Locke 1693/1989, 326). Samuel Johnson's positive assessment of the *Etymologicon linguae anglicanae* will be quoted below.

2.1. Richard Hogarth's *Gazophylacium anglicanum* (1689)

The *Gazophylacium anglicanum, containing the derivation of English words* of 1689, the first English etymologicon to be published in English (Alston 1965-, 5:75), was an abridged translation of the main part and the onomastical appendix of Skinner's *Etymologicon*. It was published anonymously, and historians of lexicography have not hitherto identified its author. He was in fact Richard Hogarth, father of the artist William Hogarth. His first publication had been a teachers' handbook, the *Thesaurarium trilingue publicum, being an introduction to English, Latin, and Greek*, published in May 1689: this gives rules for spelling, syllabification, and punctuation, followed by exercises in syllabification, an English wordlist with syllable-divisions marked, and rules for the accentuation and vowel quantity of Greek, also with a wordlist. Hogarth refers at one point to "a Book intituled, *The Etymology of the English Tongue*" (Hogarth 1689a, 25), and this was his next work, appearing in November as *Gazophylacium anglicanum*. The title may have puzzled prospective readers (the word *gazophylacium*

---

[22] Skinner 1671, sig. C4v, "quid Musica illa Linguarum consonantia & harmonia jucundius?"

means 'treasury,' and had not been used before as the title of an English book), and the work was reissued as *A new English dictionary* in 1691 (Alston 1965-, 5:76). Hogarth produced other schoolbooks, opened a coffeehouse at which Latin could be spoken, and died with a big Latin dictionary unfinished (Paulson 1991, 14-15, 33-36).

The ascription of the *Gazophylacium* to Richard Hogarth was first made in a biography of his son, on the basis of an annotation on one of Richard's letters to his friend Thomas Noble, "Mr Hogarth writ of the Greek accents in English [i.e. the *Thesaurarium*] ... and an abridgemt of Dr Skinner's *Etimologicon*" (Paulson 1991, 4 and 341n5). It seems entirely plausible: apart from the reference to the *Gazophylacium* in the *Thesaurarium*, the affinity of the two books' titles, and the fact that they were both printed for sale by the same bookseller, a series of rules by which the form of the Latin etyma of English words may be calculated, beginning "Most Words in *English* ending in *nce*, or *cy*, are derived from the *Latin*, ending in *tia*" is repeated verbatim from the *Thesaurarium* in the *Gazophylacium* (Hogarth 1689a, 25-26; idem 1689b, sigs. A7r-v), and there are verbal echoes from one preface to another. One last sign of Hogarth's authorship, a compelling one, is that at one point (and I believe only one), the *Gazophylacium* adds a new entry to those translated from the *Etymologicon*: this is in the onomastical section, and it is for the name *Hogarth*.

The *Gazophylacium* was a much smaller book than its original, an octavo of 558 pages, of which the main dictionary, comprising about 6300 headwords, took up 380 and the onomasticon 162. As Hogarth worked through the main part of the *Etymologicon*, he started to abridge more drastically: whereas the midpoint word of the *Etymologicon* is *knap*, that of the *Gazophylacium* is *hostage*, earlier than that of any other monolingual dictionary. He was evidently finding it difficult to keep in control of his work. His treatment of Skinner's onomasticon was more leisurely: he omitted a handful of entries, but in fact whereas Skinner's midpoint word is *Huldericus*, Hogarth's is *Ivel*: he was abridging some of the long entries early in Skinner's alphabetical sequence judiciously. He added an eight-page appendix to the onomasticon, "Proper Names of *Men* and *Women* now commonly used, coming from the *Hebrew, Greek*, and *Latin*, truly derived," which may have been of his own composition.

In the main dictionary, he did try to improve on his original in some small ways. For instance, Skinner's treatment of *abstain* had commented that this verb, like *retain, detain*, and others, was evidently of Latin origin, all of them being from *tenere* plus a preposition, but Skinner did not say expressly that the etymon in this case was *abstinere*, and Hogarth did so. Sometimes his use of English was to his advantage: after reporting the derivation of *lask* 'diarrhoea' from Latin *laxus* 'loose' he had a natural opportunity to point out that "a looseness in the guts" is a common analogous expression. He corrected the occasional mistake, for instance emending the form *nelde* given as Danish by Skinner s.v. *nettle* to the correct *nedle*.

However, he introduced more errors than he corrected. Most pervasively, where Skinner presents etymon and cognates in a single list, Hogarth regularly treats all the forms as possible etyma. For instance, Skinner's "*Shrine, ab* AS. *Scrin*, Fr. Gr. [sc. "Fr. G." i.e. Franco-Gallica] *Escrin*, It. *Scrigno*, Teut. *Schrein*, Lat. *Scrinium*" means that the English word *shrine* is from Old English *scrin*, to which may be compared French *escrin*, Italian *scrigno*, German *Schrein*, and Latin *scrinium*. Hogarth's version is "*A Shrine*, from the AS. *Scrin*, the Fr. G. *Escrin*, the Ital. *Scrigno*, or the Lat. *Scrinium*," and this is wrong: as Skinner could have told him, since Old English has a form *scrin* and Old English *sc* corresponds very regularly with modern English *sh* (Skinner 1671, sig. R1r illustrates this rule with the example of *scrin* and *shrine*), there is no need to go hunting in French, let alone Italian, for an etymon. There are local mistranslations too: for instance, *fillip* is defined in the *Etymologicon* as "a flick with the knuckles: a word formed from the sound (*vox a sono ficta*)," and Hogarth has misunderstood *vox ... ficta* to come up with "*fillip*, a feigned word."[23] Likewise Henshaw's suggestion that *hab-nab* 'rashly' might be from a form *hap n'hap* 'with or without success' is translated nonsensically "whether it happen or no": a rash action may or may not succeed, but it does by definition happen.[24] Judging the respective merits of deriving the first syllable of Old English *wiman, wimman* 'woman' from *wif* 'female' or from *womb*, Skinner prefers the former, "because the Anglo-Saxons never wrote [the sound represented by] *o* with the letter *i*," and Hogarth translates this "the Saxons generally us'd *i*, instead of *o*."[25] A few entries are conflated, not always to good effect, for instance *crump* 'curved' and *crumple*; a number are excised, e.g. *to lase, lavolta, nescock, nesh, nice*, and *niches* (since c6300 of Skinner's c7900 headwords are retained, about one in five must have been excised or conflated with others overall). Typographical errors might be taken over slavishly, such as the entry for *Berwent-fels* in the onomasticon: since Skinner went on to say that the fells in question took their name from the river Derwent, Hogarth should have realized that the headword should be *Derwent-fels*, but he did not. Hogarth or his typesetter had problems with Old English spelling: *clæfra* becomes *chefer* s.v. *clover*, *hæca* becomes *hacca* s.v. *hack*; *hlihan* becomes *hlian* s.v. *laugh*.

---

[23] Skinner 1671, sig. Rr4v, "*Fillip*, talitrum vox a sono ficta."

[24] Skinner 1671, sig. Aaa1r, "ut ingeniose divinat Doct. *Th. H.* q[uasi] d[icens] *Hap N'hap*, (i.e.) sive Succedat, sive non."

[25] Skinner 1671, sig. Ffff2r-v (s.v. *woman*), "*Woman, ab* AS *Wiman, Wimman*, Mulier, hoc Doct. *Th. H.* εὐστόχως, ut solet, deflectit *ab* AS *Wif*, Mulier & Man, Homo, q[uasi] d[icens] Homo Femina. Possit & non absurde deduci a *Womb* & *Man*, q[uasi] d[icens] Homo Uteratus seu Utero praeditus. Sed prius Etymon longe praefero, ... quod Anglo-Saxones per *i* non *o* olim scripserunt."

In conclusion, the *Gazophylacium anglicanum* is fundamentally a piece of hack-work: it is an inaccurate abridged translation of Skinner's *Etymologicon*, with no significant additions apart from the eight-page onomastical appendix.[26] It did make English etymology newly accessible to people who knew little or no Latin, and (with the exception of G. W. Lemon's crankish *English etymology* of 1783), it was the only cheap etymological dictionary of English published before the nineteenth century. So it is not to be sneered at, but it it was not an original contribution to scholarship.

3. Franciscus Junius' "Etymologicum anglicanum" (1650s-1670s)

Franciscus Junius, the son of a Protestant theologian and classical scholar, was born in 1591 and educated at the University of Leiden.[27] After a period as a minister in the Low Countries, he moved to England and spent twenty years in the service of the collector of art and antiquities Thomas Howard, Earl of Arundel. This was followed by a period in Friesland, by the end of which Junius was fluent in Dutch and English, had some knowledge of Frisian, and had started thinking seriously about the relationship of these three languages. He had begun working on the historical records of the English language by the late 1640s, when he had helped Sir Simonds D'Ewes with his dictionary of Old English. At this stage, he was inclined to see the Germanic languages as descended from Greek, and a Scots wordlist which he appears to have prepared at the end of the 1640s, now Bodleian MS Junius 74, fos. 18-36, cites a number of supposed etyma from Greek. During the 1650s, he worked with the earliest substantial Germanic text, the translation of the New Testament into Gothic which had been made in late antiquity and preserved in a manuscript now known as the Codex Argenteus, of which he published the editio princeps, in parallel with an edition of the Gospels in Old English by the churchman and philologist Thomas Marshall. At this stage in his researches, he abandoned the idea of derivation from Greek and settled down to investigate the internal relationships of the Germanic language group.

His etymological dictionary of English, the "Etymologicum anglicanum," belongs to this last period in Junius' work on the Germanic languages. He appears to have begun work on it in the late 1650s, when he showed the book collector Sir Christopher Hatton "an alphabeticall collection of English words,

---

[26] The points at which Wakelin (1987, 161) sees him going beyond the content of particular entries in Skinner are simply cases where Hogarth has conflated two of Skinner's entries.

[27] For him, see Considine 2008, 216-235, on which the following account of Junius' etymological work is based.

whose proper signification and originall I had traced out and set downe as well
as I could"; in 1661, he asked the herald and antiquary Sir William Dugdale if
any Englishman would be interested in completing the work and publishing it
"for the credit and honour of his owne countrie and language" (letter of 1661 in
Junius 2004, 980 and 982). His manuscript of the dictionary comprises two
volumes, Bodleian MSS Junius 4 and 5, amounting to just under five hundred
folio leaves in total, written on one side only.

Some of the entries are for words which had only entered English recently,
as in the case of *artichoke*, a vegetable which was said to have been introduced
in the reign of Henry VIII, for which Junius gives two forms, *artechoke* and
hartechoke, then a Latin gloss, "Carduus altilis, cinara, strobilus," then five
cognates – French *artichaut*, Italian *articiocco*, *arciocco*, Spanish *artichosa*,
Danish *artiskock* and Dutch *artischock* – before a reference to a discussion of
the artichoke family in Claudius Salmasius' encyclopaedic *Plinianae exercita-
tiones* (MS Junius 4, fo. 28v). This is actually a noteworthy entry, since Skinner
had treated the same word, with a more limited set of cognates but with the
same reference to Salmasius. Perhaps Junius drew on Skinner's work here.

Other entries are naturally much closer to his long-standing Germanic interests: *asunder* is glossed and then compared to Gothic *sundro*, Old English *on
sundran*, *on sundron*, Old High German *suntrigo* and Dutch *in 't bÿsonder* before
Old English *syndrian* 'to separate' is adduced as a parallel and the entry *seorsum*
in an Old High German glossary in Junius' possession is cited (MS Junius 4, fo.
29r). The Germanic material is sometimes presented in digressions from headwords of Romance origin, as s.v. *assist*, where a reference to the Dutch equivalent *bij-staen* leads Junius to reflect that Satan says in an Old English poem that
"bigstandað me strange geneatas. ða ne willað me at ðam striðe geswican"
[strong companions stand by me, who will not desert me in the battle] and to
discuss this passage for five lines.

The author to whom Junius refers most often in the "Etymologicum" is
Chaucer. He also uses Gavin Douglas, to whose translation of the *Aeneid* he had
made a manuscript wordlist, and a range of Old English texts from manuscripts
which he transcribed or owned, including the Old English translation of Orosius,
the glossed gospel-book called the Rushworth Gospels, and a set of glosses on
the Psalms. There are likewise references to ancient primary sources such as Old
High German glosses and the Codex Argenteus, and perhaps to personal observation. This last, however, is difficult to judge: he mentions the English idiom *a
paire of bellowes* and the English word *blisterflie* without quoting authorities,
but both had been registered in dictionaries (MS Junius 4, fos. 43v and 50r; cf.
Somner 1659 s.v. *bilig* and H. Junius 1585, 72). Among his numerous secondary
sources are his own work on Willeram and on Gothic, and the standard English
and Continental authorities: Laurence Nowell, Spelman, and Somner; his brother-

in-law G. J. Vossius, the lexicographer of Dutch Cornelis Kiel, and the Danish antiquary Ole Worm.

Junius had undertaken the "Etymologicum anglicanum" in his sixties, and he had not prepared it for publication upon his death. The manuscript passed with others to the Bodleian Library in Oxford, where it remained until the next century. It was finally published in 1743, edited with additions by Edward Lye. It is not Junius' most dramatic work, and it was vulnerable to criticism even before the advances of nineteenth-century Germanic studies, as in the comparison with Skinner's *Etymologicon* made by Samuel Johnson, who was able, thanks to Lye's edition, to use both in his own dictionary:

> *Junius* appears to have excelled in extent of learning, and *Skinner* in rectitude of understanding. *Junius* was accurately skilled in all the northern languages, *Skinner* probably examined the ancient and re-moter dialects only by occasional inspection into dictionaries; but the learning of *Junius* is often of no other use than to show him a track by which he may deviate from his purpose ... *Skinner* is often ignorant, but never ridiculous: *Junius* is always full of knowledge; but his variety distracts his judgment, and his learning is very frequently disgraced by his absurdities. (Johnson 1755, sig. B1r; cf. DeMaria and Kolb 1998, 24-26).

Some of Junius' etymologies in which derivations from Greek occur follow in a footnote, and they are indeed most implausible. Nor was it always Greek which led Junius astray, since, as George Hickes noticed in a letter of 1694, he had been willing to derive *girl* from Latin *garrula*, 'talkative' (Harris 1992, 152). This derivation actually went back to Minsheu, and was characteristically rejected by Skinner, who postulated that Old English *ceorl* might have had an unrecorded feminine form *ceorla* and that this might be the etymon. But as Johnson acknowledged, he had used Junius and Skinner extensively in his own work because no other attempt at a comprehensive etymological dictionary of English was available to him. More than a century later, W. W. Skeat could still observe that the etymological dictionaries of his day suffered from a tradition of uncritical borrowing from the same two sources (Skeat 1881, xi). Only after work such as Skeat's had superseded Junius' *Etymologicum* could the latter be seen in historical perspective and appraised with detachment as "the first syste-matic etymology of the English Language" with the additional reflection that "from it stems the modern historical approach to lexicography" (Barker 1978, 27).

4. Edward Bernard's "Etymologicon britannicum" (1689)

Skinner was a provincial physician, Hogarth a Grub Street man, Junius an independent scholar who spent much of his time in the Netherlands. Edward Bernard, in contrast to these three, had a privileged position in English intellectual life: a Fellow of the Royal Society, who held the professorship of astronomy at Oxford and might have had that of Hebrew, best known now for his part in the production of a union catalogue of manuscripts in the libraries of the British Isles, though his other work ranged from the study of the Arabic text which preserves part of the *Conics* of Apollonius to the printing of one of the first examples of the ancient Palmyrene language to be published (Madan et al. 1895-1953, 1:xxv-xxxv; Molland 1994, 218-221; Daniels 1988, 424-425). He owned a considerable library, 170 manuscripts from which, including his unpublished recasting of a Coptic-Latin dictionary by Athanasius Kircher, are now in the Bodleian.[28] His printed books were sold after his death in an auction of 1454 lots; the only dictionary of English among them, by the way, was that of Elisha Coles (*Bibliotheca Bernardina* 1697, 30 lot 85). Edmund Castell asked him to collaborate on the *Lexicon heptaglotton* in 1661, and although he declined this invitation, he nursed other lexicographical plans, not least for a revision of Henri Estienne's enormous *Thesaurus graecae linguae* (Toomer 1996, 236; Smith 1704, 69-70). He was urged by J. G. Graevius of Leiden to effect the publication of Junius' "Etymologicum," but nothing came of this project (Carter 1975, 310).

One of his acquaintances was George Hickes, who became a fellow of Lincoln College in 1664, six years after Bernard had become a fellow of St John's. They were both members of a circle of Oxford men interested in philology, in which John Fell, Dean of Christ Church and vice-chancellor of the university, and Junius' collaborator Thomas Marshall (fellow of Lincoln from 1668 and rector, i.e. head of the college, from 1672) were important figures. Hickes eventually resigned his fellowship to become successively chaplain to Charles II and Dean of Worcester, but he did not give up his academic interests, and in 1689 he published grammars of Gothic and Old English, together with Runólfur Jónsson's pioneering Icelandic grammar (reprinted from the Copenhagen edition of 1651), a lexical index to it based on that made by Junius (see Bennett 1937, 37), and a catalogue of printed books and manuscripts bearing on Germanic philology, all under the general title *Institutiones grammaticae anglo-saxonicae et moeso-gothicae*. The final item in the volume was Bernard's "Etymologicon britannicum." On the face of it, this looks like a coherent collection: grammars

---

[28] Madan et al. 1895-1953, 3:1-24; for the Coptic dictionary, now Bodleian MS Bodl. Or. 346, see also Carter 1975, 293. Thomas Marshall likewise worked on the lexicography of Coptic, making a wordlist to the Gospels, now Bodleian MS Marshall Or. 112 (Madan et al. 1895-1953, 2.2:1208).

of two ancient Germanic languages and one very conservative one; a wordlist of the only one of those languages for which no printed wordlist was readily available; a bibliography permitting further work, either with published tools such as Somner's dictionary or with inedita; an etymologicon capable of demonstrating the connection between the ancient Germanic languages and modern English.

In fact, Bernard's contribution was not fully consistent with the rest of the volume. It began with a short preface (text and full translation are presented as an appendix below). This rehearsed the etymological theories about the origins of English which Bernard had encountered before presenting his own. He proposed that the Germanic languages originated in an early form of the language of "the Russians and Slavs," an ill-defined entity which I shall call "Russian / Slavonic" below, and which itself originated in the languages spoken by the descendants of Japhet who lived around the Black Sea and the Caspian Sea. Of these peoples, he named the Cappadocians, Colchians, Iberians (i.e. Georgians), Armenians, and Scythians; the only one of their languages of which Bernard owned specimens was Armenian.[29] He believed that the language of the Japhetides had also been adopted by the Medes and Persians. By way of an afterthought, he added that there was an evident affinity between Welsh, Hungarian, and Armenian.

Bernard offered proofs of his argument in dictionary form as a partial abstract of a monograph in progress, the only other part of which to appear was an elaborate single-sheet table showing the descent of the Greek, Roman, Gothic, Runic, Coptic, Ethiopic, Cyrillic, and Armenian alphabets from the Samaritan one, itself closely related to Hebrew (Bernard 1689b). This monograph may never have got beyond rough notes.[30]

---

[29] *Bibliotheca Bernardina* 1697, page 8 lots 42-44, lists an Armenian translation of Bellarmine's *Dichiaratione piu copiosa della dottrina christiana* (1630), Teseo Ambrogio's *Introductio in chaldaicam linguam, syriacam, atque armenicam, et decem alias linguas* (1539), and Francesco Rivola's *Grammaticae armenae libri quatuor* (1624), though not Rivola's *Dictionarium armeno-latinum* (1621; new ed. 1633); ibid. page 9 lot 127 is an Armenian Bible, but since Bernard was still trying to buy such a book in 1693 (Simmons 1950, 110), he may not have owned this one as early as 1689. The languages of the ancient Cappadocians, Colchians, and Scythians were lost; a little material in Georgian was available in Hieronymus Megiser's *Thesaurus polyglottus* (1603), available to Bernard in the Bodleian (Bodleian Library 1620, 326 col. 1), and a dictionary, Stefano Paolini's *Dittionario giorgiano e italiano*, had been produced in 1629, and may likewise have been available in the Bodleian, among John Selden's books.

[30] Bernard's first biographer did not find it among his posthumous manuscripts (Smith 1704, 67), though it may be represented by Bodleian MSS Lat. misc. e. 13 and 14, both catalogued with the date c1670-80 and described respectively as "Latin vocabulary, with equivalents in English, Russian, and Polish, in irregular order" and "Etymological and miscellaneous notes" (Madan et al. 1895-1953, 3:7, 4). The printed table of alphabets was admired by Leibniz (Schulenburg 1973, 32-33).

The dictionary was, as Bernard put it, a record of "the Russian, Slavonic, Persian, and Armenian origins of English and British words."[31] This title betrays a confusion as to the difference between etyma and cognates like that which we have seen in Hogarth's work: the modern Russian, Czech, Polish, and other Slavonic forms which he cited were presumably descended from the Russian / Slavonic mother of the Germanic languages, and Bernard had said explicitly that Persian was descended from the Japhetic ancestor of English; as for Armenian, his claim that it was one of five languages from which Russian / Slavonic was descended might likewise have been more robust as a claim that it was an extant representative of the Japhetic language from which Russian / Slavonic and Persian were both descended. So, rather than having Russian, Slavonic, Persian, and Armenian origins, English really had, by the logic of his own argument, origins which could be illustrated by the citation of forms from these languages.

Once that confusion is cleared away, Bernard's argument makes sense. He believed that the languages of Europe had, like Persian, diffused from a point in southwestern Asia, north of Babylon but south of the Caucasus, and he believed that linguistic innovation had taken place during the process of diffusion. Therefore, the languages of eastern Europe were closer to the protolanguage than those of western Europe, and Armenian was still closer to it. Like other sixteenth- and seventeenth-century comparativists who rejected the concept of *linguae matrices*, he was working with a model which adumbrated the modern understanding of the Indo-European language group – though, like them, he was critically handicapped by not knowing Sanskrit (see Metcalf 1974, esp. 238-241 and 251-252, and Szemerényi 1980, 151-160). He was misled by his assumption that innovation had only taken place during diffusion and that increasingly conservative forms could therefore be found on a line from northwestern Europe back towards the Japhetic homeland: we may say that he lacked a clear enough concept of language death for the concept of an extinct protolanguage to come naturally to him. But he knew that some languages are more conservative than others, and he was impressed by the affinity between Persian and Germanic: this was, he remarked, surprising evidence of linguistic conservatism; but he was prepared to follow the evidence where it led him.

Bernard's "Etymologicon" ran to thirty pages, handsomely laid out by the Oxford compositors, and boasting Gothic set in the Junian types, modern English in black letter, some Old English in a Saxon type, and Russian and Armenian in Greek type.[32] It had 768 headwords. Not all of them were English: the first

---

[31] Bernard 1689a, sig. Qq3r, "Vocabulorum Anglicorum & Britannicorum origines Russicae, Slavonicae, Persicae & Armenicae."

[32] Both the Cyrillic and the Armenian alphabets are of Greek origin, which is why Bernard used Greek as a substitute for them, but the Greek alphabet does not provide satisfactory equivalents for all the sounds used in Russian and Armenian; Bernard

entry, for instance, is for *a* 'and,' identified as Welsh, and the last is for *znati*, *scnati* 'to know,' identified as Serbian and Croatian. Synonyms which Bernard regarded as evidently related to the headword are then cited: those in the entry for *a* 'and' are *a* in Czech; *ē* in Russian and Armenian; *i* in Croatian; *jah* in Gothic. This brisk presentation of forms is characteristic. Slavonic forms are plentiful: English *milke* is followed by Old English *meoloc* and Icelandic *miolk*, but then by Russian *moloka* and by forms *mleko* and *mliko* which are ascribed to language varieties including Sorbian, two varieties of Croatian, Polish, and Slovenian.[33] Sometimes the evidence is forced: English *scrawles* (a new word in 1689, of which Bernard's entry appears to be the first written attestation) is defined as "the gills of fish, and letters written slantwise and awkwardly," and is followed by Polish *skrzelie* 'gills.'[34] The English word cannot in fact mean 'gills' and does not resemble any word with this meaning (nor can the Polish word mean 'scrawled letters'); Bernard must have spotted two words which looked the same, and wanted there to be a connection between them.

It is, notwithstanding this sort of bad practice, very remarkable that so many Slavonic languages should be cited by an Oxford scholar of the 1680s. There was at the time no printed grammar of any of these languages – the first would be that of Hiob Ludolf's nephew Heinrich Wilhelm Ludolf, produced with Bernard's help and encouragement, and printed in Oxford in 1696 (Simmons 1950) – and Slavonic books were hard to come by in western Europe. But anyone interested in the relationships of European languages would be aware from Scaliger and Brerewood that the Slavonic family had to be taken into account, and scattered data was available in print and manuscript: Marshall, for instance, owned a number of Slavonic books, including dictionaries.[35] At least some of Bernard's Slavonic forms come from Hieronymus Megiser's *Thesaurus polyglottus* of 1603; this dictionary is rich in Slavonic material, for which Leibniz recommended it to a correspondent in 1698 (Wieselgren 1884-1885, 31).

---

therefore obtained Cyrillic and Armenian types for the University Press in the 1690s (see Simmons 1950, 108-113). There were also problems with the transcription of Slavonic languages in the Roman alphabet, as Leibniz knew (Wieselgren 1884-1885, 27, 37-38). Persian was presented in Roman type since the Arabic font available at Oxford was incompatible with the Junian types.

[33] Bernard 1689a s.v. *milke* (sig. Ss3r), "*Milke*, lac. *meoloc*. Sax. *miolk*. Isl. μολοκο. Russ. *mleko* & *mliko*. Sclav. Lus. Dalm. Croat. Pol. Carinth."

[34] Bernard 1689a s.v. *scrawles* (sig. Tt1r), "*Scrawles*, branchiae piscium, & literae oblique & inconcinne ductae. *skrzelie*. Pol. *krelynti*. Boh."

[35] E.g. Grzegorz Knapski's *Thesaurus polonolatinograecus* of 1626 (now Bodl. Mar. 103), Danyel Adams's *Sylva quadrilinguis vocabulorum et phrasium bohemicae, latinae, graecae, et germanicae* and *Nomenclator quadrilinguis* of 1598 (now Bodl. Mar. 118 (1, 2)), and Sigismundus Gelenius' *Lexicon symphonum* of 1544 (now Bodl. Mar. 126).

The separate labelling of forms as e.g. *dalmatica* and *croatica* reflects Megiser's tendency to give separate treatment to as many dialects of a given language as he could find.[36] Bernard's use of these forms in an etymological dictionary primarily of English was intellectually adventurous: very few western scholars had tried to integrate Slavonic material into their work before him, let alone to bring it together with Persian and Armenian (see Droixhe 1978, 62).

The "Etymologicon britannicum" had other good points, as can be seen from the entry beginning with the English headword *am*. This gives *eam* and *eom* as the Old English forms and *em* as Icelandic, before expanding to cite the first, second, and third persons in Gothic as *im, is, ist*; in Armenian as *em, es, e*; in Persian as *em, i, est*; in Russian and Serbian as *esme, esē, este*. A Turkish form *im* and an Albanian *iam* follow, both with the sense 'am.' Then the entry turns to the past tense *were*, citing Icelandic and Old Norse *var*, Old English *wære*, Gothic *warst* and Armenian *er*, and also comparing Georgian *me var, shench ar, iman aris* 'I am, you are, he is.' Some of these resemblances are coincidental: the Turkish and Georgian forms are not in fact related to the English ones. But in this entry, Bernard showed that he appreciated the role of grammatical inflections in demonstrating linguistic relationships.

Having said that, his "Etymologicon" was not a success. Hickes's *Institutiones* was the forerunner of a greater work, the *Linguarum veterum septentrionalium thesaurus*, published between 1703 and 1705. In 1698, the translator and student of languages John Chamberlayne wrote to Hickes about this project, expressing his "Doubts whither it were not better to leave out both your Glossaries especially that of Dr. Bernard's as bold in his etymologies as our Friend Junius, in order to prevent the swelling both in bulk & price of your next edition" (Harris 1992, 228). Hickes retained the Icelandic glossary, and his work swelled greatly in bulk, to two folio volumes, but he evidently agreed with Chamberlayne that Bernard's work was not worth keeping.

Bernard himself was satisfied enough with it to plan a new version, which would have been substantially enlarged, and would have been further enhanced by an essay on "the Saxon people, from which we derive our origin." This would have given him an opportunity to clarify the distinction between linguistic diffusion and ethnic migration which he had made in the preface to the published "Etymologicon": the Russian language might be the key to the history of the Germanic languages, but that did not mean that the Germanic peoples were descended from Slavonic migrants. In his memoir of Bernard, the antiquary and orientalist Thomas Smith recorded the likelihood that both ill health and the

---

[36] See Stachowski 1969, 9 for Megiser's labelling of forms from the Slavonic languages, and cf. Considine 2008, 292 for his separate reporting of forms from numerous dialects of a single language.

claims of his other researches in very different fields had kept him from producing the expanded dictionary.[37]

5. Conclusion

Seventeenth-century etymologists faced two challenges whenever they worked on a word: to establish its immediate etymon, and to discuss its cognates. When identifying etyma, Skinner, Junius, and Bernard were all on the surest ground when an English word was clearly descended from an Old English form registered in Somner's dictionary. None of them thought it necessary to give a systematic account of words which were obviously learned borrowings from Latin or Greek. In other cases, Bernard regularly turned to similar forms in Slavonic and western Asian languages, and was regularly misled by coincidental resemblances; Junius was likewise often misled by coincidental resemblances, in his case with Greek forms; Skinner's preference for forms from languages such as French and Dutch which had been spoken by peoples in contact with English-speakers stood him in good stead. When discussing cognates, Skinner was again generally sound, citing plausible Romance and Germanic forms; he was on shakier ground when it came to Greek. Junius was at his best identifying cognates from the Germanic languages, which he knew better than any other seventeenth-century student of English. Bernard played, as it were, for high stakes: his pioneering identification of cognates in Slavonic languages (as at *brow*) and beyond (as at *door*, where he correctly identifies cognates in Germanic and Slavonic languages and in Welsh, Armenian, Persian, and Albanian) was not underpinned by any system, and so he often went wrong. All three had got about as far as was possible before the systematic comparative philology of the nineteenth century, which would build up a set of rules by which to distinguish, as Skinner knew the etymologist must do, between the "extremely neat comparison" and the etymon.

---

[37]   Smith 1704, 67 "Sane animo proposuit Etymologicon suum Britannicum multiplici auctario & dissertatiuncula de gentis Saxonicae, e qua nostram ducimus originem, Scriptoribus illustrasse: sed partim aegritudine, partim aliis longe diversi argumenti studiis impeditus, istud institutum, ut puto, ultra prosequi desinebat."

Appendix:
Edward Bernard's preface to his "Etymologicon britannicum"
(Bernard 1689a, sigs. Qq2r-v)

EDVARDUS BERNARDUS | GEORGIO HIXIO V. Cl. | Salutem.

Cum Viros doctos viderim Britanniae nostrae Linguae, antiquam novamque, alios quidem ad Gothiam velut sedem principem referre; Gothos vero ipsos cum loquela sua e primis molibus Babylonis, nulla media gente, arcescere: alios originibus Punicis & Hebraicis nimis sibi adblandiri: Graecanicis abuti alios, quanquam Ionis sive Iavonis dialectum fraterna regna profunde infecisse certissimum & confessum: item de paucarum vocum sonoritate Saxonici Persicique sermonum necessitudinem & cognationem conjectare alios felicius quam ostendere: caeteros vero, a Cornelio historico facile deceptos, per Germaniam, Galliam & Hispaniam, propterque Gallos in hac Insula linguam quandam Celticam jam olim excrevisse, quod nec fungi solent, sponte sua Asiaeque seminibus omnibus puram; placuit demum nobis, e dissertatione, quam de Orbis eruditi Literatura apparamus, Moesogothicis tuis apta & convenientia quaedam commodare, & amicitiae causa adjungere. Inde equidem constat, Saxonas e majoribus nostris, & Islandos & Danos & Suecos, aut nomine vetusto & peramplo Gothos, sed & plerosque omnes Germaniae populos, a Russis & Slavis sermonem quam genus in mundi Occidua acceptum propagasse. Slavis vero Russisque & vivere & loqui dederunt Cappadoces, Colchi, Iberi, Armenii & Scythae. Has denique gentes sparserunt Mosoches & Thobelus & Magoges, tot incrementa Japeti; cum a Babylone dejecta partim inter Pontos Caspium & Euxinum pergerent, partim laevum iter deflecterunt. Orbis itaque renovati quasi primordio Anglici non absimilis sermo circum mare Hyrcanum ferebat: quem Medi & Parthi eisdem temporibus ultro acceperunt. Mirandum sane in parte mundi temperata & nationum feracissima tantam linguarum adfinitatem omni aevo viguisse. Quoniam vero longum esset & meo animo grave, [sig. Qq2v] haec omnia multis exemplis persequi, ipse equidem praeclara nonnulla Lexici ordine receptiori jam exponi volo, plura multo posterorum industriae permitti. Linguarum igitur Occidentalium, excepta Latina, quae ab Hellenismi abuso Aeolico tota defluxit, initia et origines veras demonstravi, atque adeo Portas Caspeas metuenda limina aperui. Siqui tamen tot nominum congruentiam casu quodam accidisse credant, aut a regionibus nostris has merces in Asiam aliquando fuisse deportatas, gaudeant per me licet sua sagacitate. Quinetiam Britannorum veterum lingua, ne hoc sileam, Hungaricam in pluribus & Armeniacam refert: tametsi Lexicon Johannis Davisii ex quadrante Cambricum sit, semis habens a Latinis, quadrante altero Anglis dominis concedente. Ex etymis autem nostris, quae aliis non paucis dubia forte videbuntur et longinqua, tu sane ratione certiori & proxime derivata esse intelligis.

Quanquam denique ad Divini juris intima, quo salus populi principumque gloria ac felicitas omnino pendent, non ad cortices solos magnarum rerum, paratum te esse sciam & instructissimum; interim haec talia dialecto patriae utrique debuimus. Vale Vir pie, amor & lumen Vigorniae.

Oxoniae Idubus Maiis

A. D. MDCLXXXIX

EDWARD BERNARD TO THE EMINENT GEORGE HICKES, GREETINGS!

We have seen learned men deal variously with our British language, in its ancient and its modern forms. Some have referred it to the land of the Goths as if to a first seat, and have indeed derived the Goths themselves, with their language, directly from the first constructions at Babel.[38] Some have deluded themselves to excess with Punic and Hebrew origins.[39] Some have made bad use of Greek origins, as if it were most evident and acknowledged that the Ionian or Javanian language had saturated the kingdoms of the brothers of Javan.[40] Again, some, working from the sound of a few words, have made a better job of conjecturing than of demonstrating an intimacy and affinity between the Saxon and the Persian languages.[41] Others, indeed, easily deceived by the historian Cornelius Tacitus, now suppose that some Celtic language once grew up throughout Germania, Gallia, and Hispania, and, on account of the Gauls, in this island – nor are they satisfied with that, but suppose that it did so spontaneously, uncontaminated by any Asiatic seed.[42] Finally, I wished to accommodate your Moeso-Goths with something fitting and suitable from a monograph which I am preparing

---

[38] E.g. Goropius Becanus and his followers (very few as these must have been by 1689): see Borst 1957-1963, 1215-1219, and Droixhe 1978, 54-55.

[39] See Droixhe 1978, 34-50; the myth of the Phoenician ancestry of English originated in the work of John Twyne in the sixteenth century (see Ferguson 1993, 93) and had recently been aired in Aylett Sammes, *Britannia antiqua illustrata, or, The antiquities of ancient Britain, derived from the Phoenicians* (1676).

[40] Javan was one of the sons of Japheth, supposedly the progenitor of the Ionians, and of the Greeks in general: see Genesis 10.2 and cf. Milton, *Paradise Lost* 1:508. As we have seen, the myth of the Greek origins of English appealed to Meric Casaubon in the 1640s and to Franciscus Junius as late as the early 1650s, but Junius subsequently rejected it, and Stephen Skinner argued against it at several points.

[41] See Droixhe 1978, 76-85. Bernard goes on to say that he does himself believe in the affinity between English and Persian: his point here is that previous attempts to demonstrate the affinity have, compared to his, been methodologically jejune.

[42] Cf. Droixhe 1978, 128; here, inquiries into the possibility of Celtic-Phoenician affinities are recorded, but a seventeenth-century historian who identified Tacitus' Germani with the Celtic inhabitants of Britannia would have to reject this line of argument, since Tacitus argued that the Germani were autochthonous.

about the writing-systems of the literate world, and to append it to your work as a sign of friendship.

Now, for my part, it is certain that the Saxons (who are among our ancestors), together with the Icelanders, Danes, and Swedes – the Goths, to use an ancient and general name – but also nearly all the peoples of Germania, received their language from the Russians and Slavs, though they were not descended from them, and perpetuated it in the western world.[43] The Russians and Slavs, however, had their life and their speech from Cappadocians, Colchians, Iberians, Armenians, and Scythians. These people, finally, were scattered as the seed of Mesech and Tubal and Magog, so many progeny of Japhet: upon the fall of Babel, they proceeded in part between the Caspian Sea and the Black Sea, and in part they turned their way westwards.[44] And so, the language of a world renewed as if it had been newly created, which was not dissimilar to English, moved forward; moreover, in those times, the Medes and Parthians adopted it. It is truly extraordinary that in a fertile part of the world which has borne very many nations, such an affinity between languages should have flourished throughout the ages.[45]

Because it would certainly be a long business, and to my mind a burdensome one, to follow through on all these points with numerous examples, I myself wish for my part to expound some of the most striking, in the more normal dictionary order, leaving the great majority to the labour of my successors. I have showed the beginnings and true origins of the western languages, with the exception of Latin, which is entirely the product of the Aeolic corruption of Greek; and to that extent I have opened the fearful doors of the Caspian Gates.[46] If, however, any believe that so many congruences of names came about by

---

[43] Bernard is distinguishing four classes of peoples of Germania: (i) Saxons, whose language was sometimes supposed to be best represented by Old English but also to be the ancestor of Dutch and Frisian; (ii) Scandinavians, who can also be called Goths; (iii) other Germanic-speakers, i.e. speakers of High German and Alemannic language varieties; (iv) other peoples of Germania, among whom he must have had in mind the speakers of Slavonic languages such as Sorbian, Polabian, and Slovenian.

[44] Mesech or Mosoch, Tubal, and Magog are among the sons of Japhet in Genesis 10.2, variously regarded as the progenitors of the Armenians, Scythians, and other peoples located to the north of Babel, i.e. of Babylon (see Borst 1957-1963, 123). Bernard imagines them heading northwards after the confusion of tongues, and then splitting up so that one group enters the Caucasus and another turns left towards Europe.

[45] Bernard feels that linguistic conservatism can be expected in the sort of inhospitable area which may be settled by a single group who will subsequently have no rivals for their territory, such as Iceland.

[46] The Caspian Gates were a legendary barrier between the Mediterranean world and the northern barbarians: specifically, according e.g. to Josephus, the Scythians.

some chance, or that at some time these goods were brought from our lands into Asia, I am happy for them to rejoice in their own sagaciousness.

And furthermore, I should say something about the language of the ancient Britons: in many places, it recalls Hungarian and Armenian – even though the dictionary of John Davies only inherits a quarter of its contents from the language of the Cambrians, having half from the speakers of Latin, the other quarter being conceded to the English masters of Wales.

Now, from our etyma, those which will perhaps seem doubtful and far-fetched to not a few others, you certainly perceive to be derived by a surer argument, and very closely. To conclude: although I know that you are well versed and most learned in the essentials of the law of God, on which the welfare of the people and the glory and happiness of princes have all their dependence, and not on the mere externals of great matters, for the time being, I owe you these remarks, such as they are, on the language which is our shared inheritance.[47] Farewell, O man of piety, the love and the light of Worcester.

Oxford, 15 May, 1689.

John Considine
Department of English
University of Alberta
Edmonton, Alberta T6G 2E5
Canada

References

Alston, R. C. 1965-. *A bibliography of the English language from the invention of printing to the year 1800*. Leeds etc.: for the author.

Barker, Nicolas. 1978. *The Oxford university press and the spread of learning: an illustrated history 1478-1978*. Oxford: Clarendon Press.

Bennett, J. A. W. 1937. The beginnings of Norse studies in England. *Saga-book of the Viking Society* 12:35-42.

Bernard, Edward. 1689a. Etymologicon britannicum. In: Hickes 1689, sigs. Qq1r-Uu1v.

---

[47] The reference to Hickes's knowledge of the will of God on which the glory and happiness of princes depend is significant: William III and Mary II had been crowned on 11 April, and Hickes was now in grave doubt as to whether he could acknowledge them as lawful sovereigns (Harris 1992, 31-32).

————. 1689b. *Orbis eruditi literarum a charactere Samaritico hunc in modum favente Deo deduxit Eduardus Bernardus*. [Broadsheet.] Oxford: apud Theatrum.

Bibliotheca Bernardina. 1697. *Bibliotheca Bernardina, sive catalogus variorum librorum ... quos ... sibi procuravit doctissimus Edoard[us] Bernardus*. [London: for Edward Millington].

Blount, Thomas. 1673. *A world of errors discovered in The new world of words, or, General English dictionary, and in Nomothetes, or, The interpreter of law-words and terms*. London: printed by T. N. for Abel Roper, John Martin, and Henry Herringman.

Bodleian Library. 1620. *Catalogus vniuersalis librorum in Bibliotheca Bodleiana*. Oxford: excudebant Iohannes Lichfield & Iacobus Short, academiae typographi, impensis Bodleianis.

Borst, Arno. *Der Turmbau von Babel: Geschichte der Meinungen über Ursprung und Vielhalt der Sprachen und Völker*. 4 vols. in 6, continuously paginated. Stuttgart: Anton Hiersemann, 1957-1963.

Carter, Harry. 1975. *A history of the Oxford University Press, volume 1: to the year 1780*. Oxford: Clarendon Press.

Casaubon, Meric. 1650. *De quatuor linguis commentationes pars prior ... de lingua hebraica et de lingua saxonica*. London: typis J. Flesher, sumptibus Ric. Mynne.

Considine, John. 2008. *Dictionaries in early modern Europe: lexicography and the making of heritage*. Cambridge: Cambridge University Press.

Daniels, Peter T. 1999. "Shewing of hard sentences and dissolving of doubts": the first decipherment. *Journal of the American Oriental Society* 108.3:419-436.

DeMaria, Robert, and Gwin J. Kolb. 1998. Johnson's *Dictionary* and Dictionary Johnson. *Yearbook of English studies* 28:19-43.

Droixhe, Daniel. 1978. *La linguistique et l'appel de l'histoire (1600-1800): rationalisme et révolutions positivistes*. Geneva: Librairie Droz.

Estienne, Henri. 1831-1865. *Thesaurus graecae linguae, ab Henrico Stephano constructus, post editionem anglicam novis additamentis auctum, ordineque alphabetico digestum*. Ed. Charles Benoît Hase, Wilhelm Dindorf, and Ludwig August Dindorf. [First ed. 1572.] 8 vols. in 9. Paris: excudebat Ambrosius Firmin Didot.

Ferguson, Arthur B. 1993. *Utter antiquity: perceptions of prehistory in Renaissance England*. Durham, NC: Duke University Press.

Fox, Adam. 2000. *Oral and literate culture in England 1500-1700*. Oxford: Clarendon Press.

Harris, Richard L., ed. 1992. *A chorus of grammars: the correspondence of George Hickes and his collaborators on the Thesaurus linguarum septen-*

trionalium. Publications of the Dictionary of Old English 4. Toronto: Pontifical Institute of Medieval Studies.

Hickes, George. 1689. *Institutiones grammaticae anglo-saxonicae et moeso-gothicae*. Oxford: e theatro Sheldoniano.

Hogarth, Richard. 1689a. *Thesaurarium trilingue publicum*. London: printed by J. L. and are to be sold by Randal Taylor.

[————]. 1689b. *Gazophylacium anglicanum, containing the derivation of English words, proper and common*. London: printed by E. H. and W. H. and are to be sold by Randall Taylor.

Hurst, Clive. 1982. *Catalogue of the Wren Library of Lincoln Cathedral: books printed before 1801*. Cambridge: Cambridge University Press.

Johnson, Samuel. 1755. *A dictionary of the English language*. London: W. Strahan for J. and P. Knapton [et al.].

Junius, Franciscus. 2004. *"For my worthy freind Mr Franciscus Junius": an edition of the correspondence of Franciscus Junius F.F. (1591-1677)*. Ed. Sophie van Romburgh. Brill's Studies in Intellectual History 121. Leiden: Brill.

Junius, Hadrianus. 1585. *The nomenclator, or remembrancer, written in Latine, Greeke, French and other forrein tongues: and now in English*. Tr. John Higins. London: imprinted for Ralph Newberie and Henrie Denham.

Kerling, Johan. 1979. *Chaucer in early English dictionaries: the old-word tradition in English lexicography down to 1721 and Speght's Chaucer glossaries*. Leiden: Leiden University Press.

Leibniz, Gottfried Wilhelm von. 1923-. *Sämtliche Schriften und Briefe*. Darmstadt etc.: Akademie Verlag.

Locke, John. 1693/1989. *Some thoughts concerning education*. Ed. John W. Yolton. Oxford: Clarendon Press.

Madan, Falconer, et al., eds. 1895-1953. *A summary catalogue of western manuscripts in the Bodleian Library at Oxford which have not hitherto been catalogued in the Quarto series*. 7 vols. in 8. Oxford: Clarendon Press.

Metcalf, George J. 1974. The Indo-European hypothesis in the 16th and 17th centuries. In: Dell Hymes, ed. *Studies in the history of linguistics: traditions and paradigms*. Bloomington: Indiana University Press. 233-257.

Molland, George. 1994. The limited lure of Arabic mathematics. In: G. A. Russell, ed. *The "Arabick" interest of the natural philosophers in seventeenth-century England*. Brill's Studies in Intellectual History 47. Leiden: Brill. 215-223.

Osselton, Noel. 2007. Alphabet fatigue and compiling consistency in early English dictionaries. In: John Considine and Giovanni Iamartino, eds. *Words and dictionaries from the British Isles in historical perspective*. Newcastle, UK: Cambridge Scholars Publishing. 81-90.

Pasmore, Stephen. 1982. Thomas Henshaw, F.R.S. (1618-1700). *Notes and records of the Royal Society of London* 36.2:177-188.

Paulson, Ronald. 1991. *Hogarth, volume 1: the "modern moral subject" 1697-1732*. New Brunswick, NJ: Rutgers University Press.

Poppe, Erich. 1986. Leibniz and Eckhart on the Irish language. *Eighteenth-century Ireland* 1:65-84.

Porter, Bertha, revised by Michael Bevan. 2004. Skinner, Stephen (bap. 1623, d. 1667), physician and philologist. *Oxford dictionary of national biography*. Oxford: Oxford University Press.

Ray, John. 1674. *A collection of English words not generally used, with their significations and original*. London: printed by H. Bruges for Tho. Barrell.

Read, Allen Walker. 1934. An obscenity symbol. *American speech* 9.4:264-278.

Schulenburg, Sigrid von der. 1973. *Leibniz als Sprachforscher*. Veröffentlichungen des Leibniz-Archivs herausgegeben von der niedersächsischen Landesbibliothek 4. Frankfurt am Main: Vittorio Klostermann.

Simmons, John S. G. 1950. H. W. Ludolf and the printing of his Grammatica russica at Oxford in 1696. *Oxford Slavonic papers* [first ser.] 1:104-129.

Skeat, W. W. 1881. Preface to the first edition. In: *An etymological dictionary of the English language*. Ed. 4. Oxford: Clarendon Press, 1909. viii-xv.

Skinner, Stephen. 1671. *Etymologicon linguae anglicanae, seu explicatio vocum anglicarum etymologica ex propriis fontibus*. London: typis T. Roycroft, & prostant venales apud H. Brome [et al.].

Smith, Thomas. 1704. *Vita clarissimi & doctissimi viri, Edwardi Bernardi*. London: typis W. B. impensis A. & J. Churchill.

Somner, William. 1659. *Dictionarium saxonico-latino-anglicum*. Oxford: excudebat Guliel[mus] Hall, pro authore.

Stachowski, Stanisław. 1969. *Wyrazy serbsko-chorwackie w "Thesaurus polyglottus" H. Megisera (1603)*. Wrocław etc.: Zakład Narodowy imienia Ossolińskich, Wydawnictwo Polskiej Akademii Nauk.

Starnes, DeWitt T., and Gertrude E. Noyes. 1946. *The English dictionary from Cawdrey to Johnson 1604-1755*. Chapel Hill: University of North Carolina Press.

Szemerényi, Oswald. 1980. About unrewriting the history of linguistics. In: Gunter Brettschneider and Christian Lehmann, eds. *Wege zur Universalienforschung: sprachwissenschaftliche Beiträge zum 60. Geburtstag von Hansjakob Seiler*. Tübinger Beiträge zur Linguistik 145. Tübingen: Gunter Narr Verlag. 151-162.

Thomson, R. M. 1989. *Catalogue of the manuscripts of Lincoln Cathedral Chapter Library*. Cambridge: D. S. Brewer, on behalf of the Dean and Chapter of Lincoln.

Toomer, G. J. 1996. *Eastern wisedome and learning: the study of Arabic in seventeenth-century England.* Oxford: Clarendon Press.

Van Hal, Toon. 2008. *"Moedertalen & taalmoeders": Methodologie, epistemologie en ideologie van het taalvergelijkend onderzoek in de renaissance, met bijzondere aandacht voor de bijdrage van de humanisten uit de Lage Landen.* PhD thesis, Katholieke Universiteit Leuven.

Wakelin, Martyn. 1987. The treatment of dialect in English dictionaries. In: Robert Burchfield, ed. *Studies in lexicography.* Oxford: Clarendon Press. 159-177.

Wieselgren, Harald, ed. 1884-1885. Leibniz' bref till Sparfvenfelt. *Antiqvarisk tidskrift för Sverige* 7.3:1-64.

Williams, Franklin B., Jr. 1948. Scholarly publication in Shakespeare's day: a leading case. In: James G. McManaway, Giles E. Dawson, and Edwin E. Willoughby, eds. *Joseph Quincy Adams memorial studies.* Washington, DC: Folger Shakespeare Library. 755-773.

Wood, Anthony. 1674. *Historia et antiquitates universitatis Oxoniensis.* 2 vols. Oxford: e theatro Sheldoniano.

————. 1692. *Athenae Oxonienses: an exact history of all the writers and bishops who have had their education in the most ancient and famous University of Oxford ... the second volume compleating the whole work.* London: printed for Tho. Bennet.

Studia Etymologica Cracoviensia
vol. 14   Kraków 2009

Brian COOPER (Cambridge)

THE LEXICOLOGY AND ETYMOLOGY OF
RUSSIAN FAMILY RELATIONSHIPS

As soon as a person has more relatives than Adam, he or she has a problem in designating them, whether they are in a blood relationship (*rodstvo, v rodstve*) or a relationship by marriage (*svojstvó, v svojstve*), that is whether they are *rodstvenniki* or *svojstvenniki*. The terms for a blood relationship (*krovnoe rodstvo*) include, for example, *(rodnoj) otec* and *(rodnaja) mat'*, these being the parents (*roditeli*) and their children (*deti*) being *syn* 'son' or *doč* 'daughter', *brat* 'brother' or *sestra* 'sister', and in a descending line *vnuk* 'grandson' or *vnučka* 'granddaughter' and *pravnuk* 'great-grandson' or *pravnučka* 'great-granddaughter', while ancestors in an ascending line are *ded(uška)* 'grandfather' and *bab(uš)ka* 'grandmother', *djadja* 'uncle' and *tëtja* 'aunt'. Relationships by marriage include *otčim* 'stepfather', *mačexa* 'stepmother', *pasynok* 'stepson' and *padčerica* 'stepdaughter'. One or both of the parents may not be the natural ones (*nerodnoj*). They may be an adoptive or foster father (*priëmnyj otec*) and adoptive or foster mother (*priëmnaja mat'*), their adopted or foster child (*priëmnyj rebënok* or *priëmyš*) being *priëmnyj syn* or *priëmnaja doč* (adopted or foster son or daughter). A foster brother or sister, fed by the same mother as the rest of her family, will be *moločnyj brat* and *moločnaja sestra* respectively. There may equally well be a stepfather (*otčim*) or stepmother (*mačexa*) in the family. It is perhaps worth noting that in Russian, as in English, a stepmother can represent an evil or hostile force (think of all those wicked stepmothers in fairytales): «Природа была мне не злою мачехой, но доброю, нежною матерью» (V. Belinskij). The adjective *svodnyj* is commonly used in referring to the stepchildren (*svodnye deti*), the stepbrother being *svodnyj brat* and the stepsister *svodnaja sestra*, but the prefix *pá-*, a variant of *po-*, also plays a part, for stepson is either *svodnyj syn* or *pasynok* (*pá- + syn + ok*) and stepdaughter either *svodnaja doč* or *padčerica* (*pá- + dčeř + ica*, *dčeř* being a Russianized form of *dščeř*, an archaism based on the Old Church Slavonic equivalent of *doč*): «Я нисколько не удивляюсь обыкновенной вражде между падчерицами и мачехами» (A. Herzen). *Svodnyj* is also used loosely of half-relationships, which should be more correctly expressed by the adjectives *edinokrovnyj* (having the same father

but a different mother) and *edinoutrobnyj* (having the same mother but a different father), so that a half-brother and half-sister (loosely *svodnyj brat* and *svodnaja sestra*) are in the latter sense properly *edinoutrobnyj brat* (or *edinoutrob-
nik*) and *edinoutrobnaja sestra*, and in the former sense *edinokrovnyj brat* and
edinokrovnaja sestra.

Otec, otčim

Otec, from Common Slavonic **otьcь*, is related to Indo-European **ătta*
'father' and its derivative **ăttikos* 'paternal', cf. Albanian *at* 'father', Greek *átta*
'father', *Attikós* 'Attic, Athenian', Gothic *atta*, Old High German *atto* 'father',
Sanskrit *attā* 'mother', Turkish *ata* 'father' (Černyx 1994: s.v. *otec*, Miklosich
1886: s.v. *otŭ*). The Latin *atta* 'grandfather' is a children's word apparent also
in *atavus* 'ancestor' (Trubačev 1959:22). **Atta* is seen as an expressive (familiar)
formation originating in infants' babbling. Indo-European **ă-* gave Slavonic *o-*.
Proto-Slavonic **otьcь* came from **otьkъ*, a derivative of **otъ* 'father' seen in
Old Russian and Old Church Slavonic *otьnь* 'paternal' and dialectal Russian
bezotnoj 'fatherless', *otik* 'male animal' and *otëk* 'father' (Vasmer 1976-80: s.v.
otec). The change of *-k-* to *-c-* in Slavonic is apparently an example of the third
palatalization (**atta > *att-ikó-s > *otьk̂ó-s > *otьcь*). It is possible that the
adjectival sense of **att-iko-s* was maintained in Balto-Slavonic **att-ik-as* with
the suffix *-ika-* seen still in Lithuanian *brolikas* 'brother's son' : *brolis* 'brother'.

Otčim was evidently formed with the verbal suffix *-im-* seen in Russian
podxalim 'toady' (with the root *xal-* seen in *naxal* 'insolent fellow') and *pobra-
tim* 'sworn brother' (with no verbal root, like *otčim*). The stress of *ótčim* appears
to have changed from **otčím* seen still in Ukrainian *vitčím*.

Mat', mačexa

The Indo-European noun for 'mother' is **mātḗr*, common to all Indo-
European languages and without parallel in the extent of its distribution among
blood relationship terminology. Its passage into Slavonic was **mātḗr > *mátē >
mátě. This *-ě* with circumflex intonation gave *-i* (*mati*), which was subsequently
reduced to *matь*. Some have suggested that the *ma-* part of the word originated
in children's babble (Trubačev 1959:30, 33). The *-r-* is retained in the oblique
cases (genitive *materi*) and in dialect (*matьŕ*), cf. Lithuanian *motė*, genitive *mo-
ters* 'woman', Farsi *madar*, Sanskrit *mātā́* (accusative *mātáram*), Armenian
mair, Greek *mḗtēr*, Latin *māter*, Old High German *muoter* 'mother', Albanian
motrë 'sister' (Vasmer 1976-80, Preobraženskij 1958: s.v. *mat'*).

Mačexa originates in *matjexa, Common Slavonic for stepmother, formed from the word for mother with the expressive suffix *-*jex-a* giving the modern pejorative suffix -*ex-a*. It can be explained as *mat-jes-a, where -*jes-* is an Indo-European suffix of the comparative type, so that the form with the suffix means 'like a mother', cf. Latin *mater-tera* 'maternal aunt'.

Syn, pasynok

This term goes back to Indo-European *sūnus, which is common to a number of Indo-European languages. It derives from Indo-European **seu-* > **sŭ-* 'give birth to' + -*n-us*, a suffix forming deverbal nouns of the passive voice (Cyganenko 1970: s.v. *syn*), cf. Old Prussian *souns* (accusative *sunun*), Sanskrit *sūnúṣ*, Gothic *sunus*, Old High German *sunu*. With the root **sŭ-* compare Sanskrit *sūtē* 'gives birth to, produces', *sutáḥ* 'son'. *Sūnus literally means 'born by a mother' (Trubačev 1959:50).

The Common Slavonic noun *pasynъkъ is derived with the prefix *pa-* and suffix -*ъkъ*, originally only used in *u*-stems, from *synъ* < *sūnus, in much the same way as Lithuanian *pó-sūnis*, except that the Lithuanian shows a change from *u*-stem to *ja*-stem not seen in Russian *pasynok* < *pa-synъ-kъ (Trubačev 1959:53).

Doč, padčerica

The word for 'daughter' in all Slavonic languages goes back to Common Slavonic *dъkti, which originates from Indo-European *dhughǝtḗr. There are related terms in other Indo-European languages, such as Sanskrit *duhitā́*, Avestan *dugdar-*, Armenian *dustr*, Greek *thugátēr*, Gothic *daúhtar*, Old Prussian *duckti*, Lithuanian *duktė̃*, genitive *dukters*. The Slavonic lost the schwa (*ǝ*) and the ancient stem in -*r*-. Russian *doč* is a shortening of *doči* < *dъči < *dъkti. As for the meaning of *dhughǝtḗr, it has been linked with the root **dheu(gh)-* 'milk, gives milk', cf. Sanskrit *dōgdhi* 'milks' (Trubačev 1959:56, Černyx 1994, Vasmer 1976-80: s.v. *doč*). Thus *dhughǝtḗr is someone who gives milk.

Directly linked with Slavonic *dъkti (accusative *dъkterъ) is the noun *padčerica* with the prefix *pa-*. The formation *padъkti (*padъkterъ) gives rise to Russian *pa-dčer-ica*. Old Church Slavonic *dъšti* (> *dščeŕ*, an archaism in Russian) with the same prefix gives *padъšterica*, which is parallel with *padъčerica* after loss of the -*ъ*-, cf. Bulgarian *šterka* 'daughter', *pašterica* 'stepdaughter'. Cognate with these various forms are Lithuanian *pódukra* and Old Prussian *poducre* (Trubačev 1959:57).

Brat, bratan

In most Indo-European languages the word for brother goes back to Indo-European *bhrãtēr, Common Slavonic *bratrъ, Gothic brōþar, Old High German bruoder, Old English brōðor, Sanskrit bhrãtar-, Greek frātēr (member of a brotherhood), Latin frāter, Old Prussian brati. It is likely that the original meaning of the word was 'member of a brotherhood', cf. the Greek adelfós for 'brother' in the relationship sense. Slavonic bratr, bratъ go back to Indo-European *bhrãtēr, the form bratъ presumably arising by dissimilation from bratr, which survives in some languages, such as Czech bratr (Trubačev 1959:59).

Linked with brat are words such as bratan, bratanič, which in Old Russian and in dialect could be used to denote a brother's son; Ušakov lists bratan as a dialectal term meaning, among other things, a brother's son. Some of these terms are still current in standard language, as for instance Ukrainian bratanyč and Polish bratanek. They are, of course, all suffixal derivatives of the word for 'brother', cf. also bratanka 'brother's daughter'.

Sestra, sestrič

The Indo-European word for 'sister' is an ancient r-stem. It is reflected in the Indo-European languages in a contrast between the nominative singular and the oblique cases of the singular, as seen in Balto-Slavonic *sesuo, *sesers, while in Slavonic only the oblique cases are represented (*sesr- > *sestr-). Typical of Slavonic was the transition -sr- > -str-, which links the Slavonic with Germanic, cf. from Indo-European *swesr- comes German Schwester. While Slavonic changes the r-stem to an a-stem (sestra), Lithuanian keeps the archaic consonant inflexion (sesuo, genitive sesers). It is not thought that the -t- was originally part of the Indo-European root (some have supposed that it fell out). The original root was probably *swe-, cf. its survival in Slavonic svekry (see below). This can be seen in Latin soror < *swosor, while there is no trace of the ancient -w- in Lithuanian sesuo or Russian sestra. This suggests that the Indo-European root may have had two forms, one with -w- and the other simplified to s-. The etymology of the Indo-European *swésor has been convincingly thought by Pisani and Mayrhofer (see Trubačev 1959:65-66) to be *su-esor 'of one's own blood', where *esor : *esr 'blood' is seen in Sanskrit ásṛk, Hittite ešḫar.

Just as with 'brother' there are Russian dialectal derivatives of 'sister' for various relationships, e.g. sestrič, sestrinec 'sister's son' and sestrenica 'sister's daughter', cf. Ukrainian sestryč, sestrineć 'sister's son' and sestrinka, sestrinycja 'sister's daughter' and Polish siostrzeniec, siostrzenica. Most of these words follow typical Slavonic word-forming practices. One might notice especially *sestrĕnьсь, Polish *siostrzeniec*, Ukrainian *sestrineć* 'sister's son', from **sestrĕnъ*, Polish **siostrzan*.

Deti, rebënok

Dĕtę (Russian *ditja*) is the one name for a child that is undoubtedly Common Slavonic. Nearly all Indo-European words for child are neuter (German *Kind*, Greek *téknon*, Slavonic *dĕtę*) and many are deverbal substantivized adjectives, cf. *Kind* < Indo-European *ĝentóm* 'born', *téknon* (also meaning 'that which is born') < *tíktō* 'I bear', *dĕtę* < **dĕtent-* 'fed'. The plural *deti* (singular **dĕtь* alongside **dĕtę*) is still the normal word for 'children', though the singular is limited in use and has been replaced by *rebënok*. The plural form **dĕti* is a special form of **dĕtę* (the usual plural of which would be **dĕtęta*); in effect what is being avoided is the neuter form as being too inanimate for living things, although in Indo-European the neuter was used for young creatures. Slavonic *dĕtę* contains *ĕ* < *oi* < Indo-European *əi*, cf. Sanskrit *dháyati* 'he sucks the breast' and Old Church Slavonic *dojǫ* 'I feed with the breast', from Indo-European **dhēi-* : **dhoi-* 'milk, give milk'. Thus **dĕtę* goes back to **dhojtent-*, with the participial suffix *-ent-* and the suffix *-t-*, which may indicate a passive form ('fed with the breast'). Cognate are Latvian *dēls*, Latin *filius* 'son' (< *fēlius* with normal *f* < Indo-European *dh*), Latin *fēllare* 'suck', *fēmina* 'woman', Sanskrit *dhēnús* 'milch cow' (Vasmer 1976-80: s.v. *ditja*, Černyx 1994: s.v. *deti*).

Another word for child was Indo-European **orbh-*, which can be seen in some Indo-European languages as meaning 'orphan', cf. Greek *orfanós*, Latin *orbus*, Armenian *orb*. The original root meant 'young', cf. Sanskrit *árbha(ká)* 'small boy'. The derivative forms in Russian have been said by Meillet to fall into three groups: *rab*, *rabota*, *rebënok* (Trubačev 1959:39). Indo-European **orbho-* gave Proto-Slavonic **orb-* 'weak, powerless', which gave East and West Slavonic *robъ* and South Slavonic *rabъ*, cf. Old Russian *robę* 'child', Russian dialect *robja*, *robjatko*, *robёnok*, Ukrainian *párubok* 'fellow, lad' (< *párobok*), Polish *parobek*. Russian *rebenok* is a local change from *robenok* due to assimilation before the change *e* > *ё* (Trubačev 1959:40). The initial form was **orbę*, genitive **orbęte*, and Russian *robenok* came from *robja*, Old Russian *robę* (Vasmer 1976-80, Černyx 1994: s.v. *rebёnok*).

When considering members of the so-called nuclear family, one should not forget that its sociological pre-eminence, at least in some cultures, represents the modern result of a transition from earlier predominance of the extended family, expressed thus in *Literaturnaja gazeta* 9, 1971 (cited in Kotelova 1984: 426, s.v. *nuklearnyj*): «переход от так называемой объединенной семьи (де-

душка, бабушка, их дети и внуки) к семье 'нуклеарной' (отец, мать, дети)». In this broader conception of the family, aunts and uncles played a major
role and their position in the hierarchy was clearly defined. In Old Russian, for
example, there were separate words for paternal uncle, i.e. father's brother and
father's sister's husband, and maternal uncle, i.e. mother's brother and mother's
sister's husband, viz. respectively *stryj* (or *strij, stroj*) and *vuj* (or *uj*), as in
modern Polish (*stryj, wuj*) and Latin (*patruus, avunculus*). Daľ (1912-14: s.v.
vuj) gives the following early example, which records them both: «Святослав
не хотел против вуя своего Изяслава воевать, но, опасаясь стрыя Свято-
слава, не смел от него отстать» (taken from the Russian Primary Chronicle,
Povesť vremennyx let, with the orthography modernized). The feminine *stry(n)ja*
and *(v)ujka* could be used respectively for paternal and maternal aunt, i.e.
father's and mother's sister (= *tëtja rodnaja*) and father's and mother's brother's
wife (*tëtja po svojstvú*), as can the western Ukrainian *stryna* and *vujna* respectively (compare the Latin *amita* 'paternal aunt' and *matertera* 'maternal aunt').
Perhaps fortunately these subtleties did not survive in modern Russian, where
djadja and *tëtja* are now used for uncle and aunt, respectively, regardless of the
side of the family involved. It is worthy of note that outside the nuclear family
no special stress tends to be placed on relationship by marriage; separate words
are not normally used for uncle in the sense father's or mother's sister's husband (i.e. aunt's husband) as distinct from father's or mother's brother.

Stryj (stroj)

In Indo-European the paternal uncle had a name almost identical to the
word for 'father', i.e. **pətru(j)o*, derived with a suffix from **pəter-*, cf. Latin
patruus, Greek *pátrōs*, Sanskrit *pítrvyaṣ*. The form **stryjь* has survived in Slavonic languages other than East Slavonic, where it has been replaced by *djadja*,
but until the 14th century *stryj* was widely used in Old Russian and only later
became an archaism. Ukrainian still keeps the old name in south-western dialects,
e.g. *stryj, stryk, stryjko, stryko*. It is cognate with Lithuanian *strūjus* 'grandfather', Old Irish *struith* 'old, respected', Old High German *fatureo, fetiro*, German *Vetter* 'cousin' (Vasmer 1976-80: s.v. *stroj* II). Mikkola gives the correct
etymology (Trubačev 1959:80), likening it to *patruus*, especially in the Indo-
Iranian (Avestan) *tūirya-*, which contains the null grade of **pəter*, i.e. *ptr-*. Vey
has pointed out (1932:65-67) that Slavonic *st(r)-* is normally derived from Indo-
European *pt(r)-*, so that Slavonic **stryjь* is thus from **ptruwjo* (see Trubačev
1959:80, note 492).

Uj (vuj)

Old Russian *ui*, Old Church Slavonic *oui*, Ukrainian *vuj*, Old Polish *uj*, Polish *wuj* all derived from Common Slavonic **ujь*. The word has been forgotten in Russian and one must therefore be cautious about Dal' when he lists as Russian the words *uj*, *vuj*, *uec*, *ujčič*, *vuec*, *ujka* and *vujka* (1912-14: s.v. *uj*), since he is essentially listing Old Russian words. Phonetically one should notice the prothetic consonants that develop in the word, especially *v*- but also *h*- in Czech dialect *hojec*, *hojček* and Lower Sorbian *huj*, *hujk* (Trubačev 1959:80), but the oldest form is *ujь* with *u*- continuing the Indo-European diphthong *au*-. The Indo-European form is therefore **awjos* with the comparative degree suffix *-jo-*, which can be seen in a number of Indo-European languages (Vasmer 1976-80: s.v. *uj*), e.g. Latin *avia* 'grandmother' (cf. *avus* 'grandfather'), Old Prussian *awis*, Lithuanian *avýnas* 'maternal uncle', Gothic *awō* 'grandmother', Old High German *ō-heim* (modern German *Oh(ei)m*), Old Irish *aue* (**awjo*), Armenian *hav* 'grandfather'. The differences in syllable separation are notable: Latin *avia* < **a/wja* and Lithuanian *avýnas* < **a/w*- but Slavonic *ujь* < **aw/jos*. In Slavonic, Indo-European **-jos* gives *-jь*. Lithuanian *avà* 'maternal aunt' goes back to Indo-European **awos*. One should note that Lithuanian *avà* and *avýnas* are being ousted by *teta* and *dėdė*, just as *(v)uj* and *(v)ujka* have been ousted in Russian by *djadja* and *tëtja*. *Avýnas* was derived from **awos* with the suffix **-īno* forming adjectives, which is seen in Russian dialect *djad-ina* 'uncle's wife' (Trubačev 1959:83). In recent years there have been suggestions that Indo-European **awos* was simplified from an earlier version having laryngeals which survives in Hittite *ḫuḫḫaš* 'grandfather'. William Austin derives both Latin *avus* and Hittite *ḫuḫḫaš* from a common 'Indo-Hittite' form *xauxos* (Trubačev 1959:84).

Djadja

The modern East Slav languages have forgotten both ancient specialized terms for maternal and paternal uncles and use *djadja* for both. In early Old Russian and Old Church Slavonic works *djadja* does not occur at all. Its first meaning in East Slavonic dialects was not only 'uncle' but also 'father'. In Ukrainian dialects *djadja* and *djadik* still mean 'father'. In the literature Russian *djadja* is seen as related to *dědъ* 'grandfather'. It is a word derived from children's babbling (Preobraženskij 1958, Černyx 1994: s.v. *djadja*) like dialectal Russian *tjatja* 'father'. Vasmer (1976-80: s.v. *djadja*) sees it as formed by assimilation of *dědę* from *dědъ*. Old Russian *dędę* meant 'father's or mother's brother' (there was no differentiation of maternal from paternal grandfather or grandmother): «Изяславъ и Святославъ выяша дядю стрыя своего Судислава изъ поруба» (Trubačev 1959:85). In Russian dialects derivatives exist meaning 'aunt': *dédina, dédinka, dédinuška, dédna, djádina, djádinka*, cf. Ukrainian *djadina* 'aunt, uncle's wife'. Serbian (Dalmatian) *dundo* = *stric* 'father's brother' is not clear.[1] Lavrovskij sees it as reflecting a nasal as in Old Russian *dědę*, but here the *ę* is only an orthographical feature and does not mean that nasals were actually present.

Tëtja

From Common Slavonic **teta* derive Old Church Slavonic and Old Russian *teta, tetъka* 'aunt', Russian *tëtja, tëtka, tëteńka, tëtuška* and dialectal *tëta, tëtjuxa*. *Tëtja* with a soft second *t* was rare before the end of the 18th century. The Russian dialect *tjat'ka* is externally reminiscent of dialectal *tjatja* 'father'. Here belongs Lithuanian *teta* 'aunt', cf. *tėtė, tėtis* 'daddy'. The similarity to words for father is apparent also in Greek *tétta* and Latin *tata* 'father'. Generally Slavonic *teta* is seen as a reduplicated form of infants' speech, similar to *baba* and *tata, tjatja* (Trubačev 1959:86-87, Vasmer 1976-80: s.v. *tëtja*). French *tante* and German *Tante* are not connected with Russian *tëtja, tëtka* (Černyx 1994: s.v. *tëtja*).[2]

Plemjannik, plemjannica

From an aunt's and uncle's point of view, their brother's or sister's daughter and son (niece and nephew) are respectively *plemjannica* and *plemjannik*. These words developed from Old Russian *plemjanьnik*, from *plemę (plemja)* 'tribe', literally 'relative, member of the same tribe', cf. dialectal *plemjannyj* (= *plemennoj*). The modern meaning became established in the 16th to 17th century. *Plemenьnikъ* with the suffix *-ikъ* came from the Common Slavonic adjective **plemenьnъjь*, derived from *plemę* in the genitive *plemene* (Černyx 1994: s.v. *plemjannik*, Cyganenko 1970: s.v. *plemja*). It survives with the prefix *so-* giving *soplemennik* 'fellow tribesman'. *Plemja* itself derives from the Common Slavonic **plemę < *pled-men* 'people, progeny', formed from **pled-*, a variant of **plod-*, with the suffix *-men* (Vasmer 1976-80: s.v. *plemja*). *Pled-*, from Indo-

---

[1]   It appears to originate from Istro-Romanian *cuńåt* 'brother-in-law' from Italian *cognato (konjato)*; an analogous Romanian form could give **kunjdo, *kundo* with following assimilation to *dundo*.

[2]   The French is from Old French *ante* < Latin *amita*, where *-it-a* is a suffix and *am-* is from **amma* (as in Greek *ammá* 'mother').

European *ple- (*pel-) 'produce, engender' with the suffix -d, is related to Greek plẽthos 'multitude', Latin plebs 'common people, crowd', plēre 'fill, fulfil', cf. Russian dialect plemit́sja 'multiply, breed'. Trubačev (1959:79) notes that plemę could be directly from *ple-men.

In older Russian it was possible to distinguish between a brother's son (synovec, bratan(ok), bratanič) or daughter (synovica, bratanka) and a sister's son (sestrënok, sestrič(ič), sestrinec) or daughter (sestrenica, sestrična), as it still is to some extent in Russian dialect. For example, Ušakov records bratan as a dialectal word meaning, among other things, 'brother's son'. Some of these terms are still current, for instance, in Ukraine (bratanyč and bratanka, brata-nycja; sestrinok, sestryč, sestrineć and sestrinka, sestrinycja) and also in Poland (bratanek and bratanica, siostrzeniec and siostrzenica).

*Netij

In Old Russian, the word netii meant a nephew (son of a brother or sister) and was derived from neptii, cf. Sanskrit nápāt, náptār 'grandson', naptī 'grand-daughter' (Vasmer 1976-80: s.v. netii). The Indo-European root was *neptjo, *neptijo > Common Slavonic *netij. Indo-European *nepot- was made up of *ne- 'not' + *pot(is) 'powerful' as seen in Slavonic gos-podь = elder in a tribe; the meaning seems to have been 'under-age, dependent'. *Nepōt-, a vowel-length-ened form of *nepŏt-, is seen in many Indo-European languages, such as Latin nepōs, Sanskrit nápāt-, Lithuanian nepuotis, Old High German nevo. *Neptjo has the null-grade obtained from *nepŏt-. Slavonic netij was obtained by the simplification of -pt- to -t- (Trubačev 1959:77-78).

Ded(uška), praded

Slavonic dědъ goes back to the Indo-European root *dhē- reduplicated (as in infants' babbling) to give Slavonic dě-d-(o) < *dhēdh(ē)-, which is reflected in some Greek relationship terms, such as theîos 'uncle' (< théios), téthē 'grand-mother' (dissimilated from *thēthē) and tēthìs 'aunt' (see Vasmer 1976-80, Čer-nyx 1994: s.v. ded). All these are respectful terms for older relatives. East Sla-vonic djadja 'uncle' is related to dědъ, cf. Polish dialect dziadko 'uncle', al-ready coinciding phonetically with dziad, dědъ. From *dhēdh- stretch semantic threads to uncle and even father, cf. the phonetic closeness of tat-, tet- : dad-, ded-. There are other examples of an etymological link between father and uncle (Trubačev 1959:69, see under stryj above). Compare also Venetian deda 'aunt'.

Further ascending lines of this relationship are expressed with the prefix *pra-* from Indo-European **pro-* 'before', cf. Common Slavonic **pradědъ*, Russian *praded* 'great-grandfather' as in Latin *pro-avus* 'great-grandfather'. The prefix is added again if a further line of the relationship is required, as in *pra-praded* 'great-great-grandfather', but in practice these are rarely used (Trubačev 1959:70). No attempt to differentiate a maternal from a paternal grandfather with special nouns is found; one would just use *ded po materi* and *ded po otcu*.

Bab(uš)ka, prababuška

The root word *baba* is fairly unanimously treated as a word of infants' babble (with a long *-ā-* it would continue Indo-European **b(h)āb(h)-*), cf. Italian *babbo* 'father', Welsh *baban* 'child', English *baby*, Swedish dialect *babbe* 'child, little boy', Middle High German *bābe*, *bōbe* 'old woman, mother', *buobe* 'child, servant', Lithuanian *boba* 'woman', Albanian *bebe* 'child' (Trubačev 1959:72). This reduplication is found in words for 'father' in some non-Indo-European languages, such as Turkish *baba*, Chinese *baba*, Indonesian *bapa(k)* (Černyx 1994, Vasmer 1976-80: s.v. *baba*). The derivative *babuška* is popular in Russian.

As with *ded*, further ascending lines of relationship are shown with the prefix *pra-* (and *prapra-* if necessary), cf. *pra(pra)babuška* 'great-(great-)grandmother'. There is no differentiation of a maternal from a paternal grandmother using special words; one would simply use *babuška po otcu* and *babuška po materi*.

(Pra)vnuk, (pra)vnučka

Russian *vnuk* 'grandson' and *vnučka* 'granddaughter' are derived from Common Slavonic **vъnukъ*, which early lost the jer in its weak position. The *v-* was prothetic before *ъ-*, which could not stand alone at the start of a Slavonic word. This *ъ-* was a reduction of Indo-European **ă-*, so that Slavonic **ъn-* (without the suffix *-ukъ*) was from Indo-European **ăn-*. Polish *wnęk* shows late nasalization from *wnuk*. The Indo-European root **ăn-* is found in a number of relationship terms, such as Latin *ănus* 'old woman', Old High German *ano*, Middle High German *ane*, *an*, *ene*, German *Ahn* 'forefather', Old Prussian *ane* 'grandmother', Lithuanian *anyta* 'husband's mother', Hittite *annaš* 'mother', Greek *annís*, Armenian *han* 'woman'. The closest to the Slavonic in formation and use is German *Enkel* from Old High German *eninchilī* 'grandson' (a diminutive of *ano* with the suffix *-inklī(n)*). The root **ăn-* is perhaps an element of infants' speech like *at-* in *atta* (see under *otec* above). Černyx (1994: s.v. *vnuk*) points out, however, that Common Slavonic *ъn-* could come from Indo-European **un-* but not **ăn-* (which would give **on-*). Machek has suggested that *ъ-* instead of *o-* could have come about as a result of influence of *u-* in the following suffix, but Černyx suggests that the root may have been **nu-* (< Indo-European **new-* : **now-*, as in Russian *novyj*), giving *vъ-nu-k-ъ* with a meaning something like 'another new', i.e. a second generation. However, Trubačev (1959:74-75) points out that there was probably a laryngeal present at the start of Indo-European **(h)an-*; this may have affected the succeeding vowel qualitatively but not quantitatively.

Further descending levels of the relationship are indicated with the prefix *pra(pra)-* to give *pra(pra)vnuk* 'great-(great-)grandson' or indeed *pra(pra)vnučka* 'great-(great-)granddaughter'. Etymologically *pra-* has no meaning here and is used by analogy with *praded* and *prababuška*.

As for cousins, the Latin distinction between mother's sister's child (*consobrinus, consobrina*) and father's sister's child (*patruelis*) is not made in Russian. Though the loanwords *kuzen* and *kuzina* occur in some contexts, they are of limited currency. The usual way of expressing these relationships in Russian is with the adjectives *dvojurodnyj, trojurodnyj* and if need be *četverojurodnyj* (related in the second, third and fourth degree respectively). The adjectives *dvojurodnyj* and *trojurodnyj* thus serve to express the relationship to each other of persons descended in separate lines from a common ancestor, respectively a grandparent and a great-grandparent. Alongside *rodnye bratja* 'brothers german' (having both parents the same) there are *dvojurodnye bratja* '(male) first cousins, cousins german' (having both grandparents the same on one side) and *trojurodnye bratja* '(male) second cousins' (with two great-grandparents the same). The female equivalents are *rodnye sëstry, dvojurodnye sëstry* and *trojurodnye sëstry*. In descending lines of relationship of this type (*nisxodjaščie kolena/pokolenija*), although not ascending (*vosxodjaščie*) ones, the adjective *vnučat(n)yj* can be used instead of *trojurodnyj*; for instance, *vnučatnyj brat* is the (male) second cousin. A more distant relationship (*dal'nee rodstvo*) is usually expressed periphrastically; a third cousin, for example, would normally be *brat* (or *sestra*) *v četvërtom kolene* (or *pokolenii*), i.e. brother or sister in the fourth generation, though one occasionally finds *četverojurodnyj brat* or *četverojurodnaja sestra*.

In English the phrase 'second cousins' properly expresses the relationship of the children of first cousins to each other, but it is loosely used to express the relationship of one first cousin to the children of another first cousin, who are more correctly described as 'first cousins once removed'. In Russian this affinity (a sort of nephew/niece versus uncle/aunt relationship at one remove) is expressed with the phrases *dvojurodnyj plemjannik* / *dvojurodnaja plemjannica* for the son/daughter of the first cousin and *dvojurodnyj djadja* / *dvojurodnaja tëtja* for this son's/daughter's parent's first cousin. Each of these Russian phrases means 'first cousin once removed', but in slightly different senses according to the sex and standpoint of the people concerned (whether along the descending or the ascending line of relationship). If we move one step down the line of descent, this same relationship one generation further on (in English 'second cousin once removed') is described in Russian as *trojurodnyj* (*vnučatyj*) *plemjannik* / *trojurodnaja* (*vnučataja*) *plemjannica* for the grandson/granddaughter of the first cousin, and *trojurodnyj* (not *vnučatyj*) *djadja* / *trojurodnaja* (not *vnučataja*) *tëtja* for the grandson's/granddaughter's parent's second cousin.

The grandparents are *ded* and *babuška* and their grandchildren (*vnučata*) are *vnuk* and *vnučka*. By combining the familiar adjective *dvojurodnyj* with these terms, the concept of great (or grand) uncle/aunt and great (or grand) nephew/niece can be conveyed, since this affinity is a sort of grandfather/grandmother v. grandson/granddaughter relationship at one remove. Thus *dvojurodnyj ded* is a great-uncle (parent's uncle) and *dvojurodnaja babuška* is a great-aunt (parent's aunt), while *dvojurodnyj vnuk* is a great-nephew (nephew's or niece's son) and *dvojurodnaja vnučka* is a great-niece (nephew's or niece's daughter). When the epithet *trojurodnyj* (but not in this case *vnučat(n)yj*) is attached to the words for grandparents and grandchildren, the idea of first cousins <u>twice</u> removed can be expressed, since these are in a sort of grandfather/grandmother v. grandson/granddaughter relationship at one more step down the line of descent from the grand-uncle/grand-aunt v. grand-nephew/grand-niece kinship. Thus a (male) first cousin twice removed is *trojurodnyj vnuk* (the female equivalent being *trojurodnaja vnučka*) in the sense 'grandson or granddaughter of a first cousin' and *trojurodnyj ded* or *trojurodnaja babuška* in the sense 'grandparent's first cousin'.

As mentioned above, the great-grand relationships are expressed in Russian with the help of the prefix *pra-* and the great-great-grand ones with *prapra-*, so that *praded* and *prababuška* are respectively great-grandfather and great-grandmother, *pravnuk* and *pravnučka* great-grandson and great-granddaughter, *prapraded* and *praprababuška* great-great-grandfather and great-great-grandmother, and *prapravnuk* and *prapravnučka* great-great-grandson and great-great-granddaughter. These words combine with *dvojurodnyj* to denote great-granduncle (*dvojurodnyj praded*), great-grandaunt (*dvojurodnaja babuška*), great-grandnephew (*dvojurodnyj pravnuk*), great-grandniece (*dvojurodnaja pravnučka*) and so on. When combined with *trojurodnyj* they convey the notion of first cousins three (or more) times removed; thus a (male) first cousin three times removed is *trojurodnyj pravnuk* (great-grandson of a first cousin) or *trojurodnyj praded* (great-grandfather's first cousin).

It is also possible to use the adjective *dvojurodnyj* (and presumably *troju-rodnyj* if required) with some of the words for in-laws (for which see below) to express such ideas as cousins-in-law if need be. For example, the words *svojaki* and *nevestki* denote respectively men married to two sisters and women married to two brothers, so that *dvojurodnye svojaki* are men married to two first cousins, i.e. (male) cousins-in-law (Dal' 1912-14: s.v. *svojak*). However, relationships by marriage outside the nuclear family are not generally dignified with special terms. Notions like cousin-in-law and nephew-in-law, if required, could be expressed with the phrase *po svojstvú*, cf. *tëtja po svojstvu*. Indeed, distant relationships tend not to be described with a high degree of precision, and the more remote the relationship, the more vague may become the phrases used to express it, such as *rodstvennik do pjatogo kolena*.

Perhaps the most difficult problems in family relationships are presented by the in-laws, particularly because there are in Russian separate words for in-laws on both sides of the immediate family, that of the husband and wife.

Muž, žena

The Indo-European for 'man' underwent a change of meaning in Slavonic that brought it into the terminology of relationships. Thus Common Slavonic **mǫžь* 'man, husband' was formed. As for its etymology, it is traditionally linked with the Indo-European word for 'man': German *Mann*, Sanskrit *manu-* < **man-* 'think', which distinguishes him from animals as *Homo sapiens*. We find the same root in the Slavonic term **mǫdo* 'testicle', a derivative of Indo-European **man-* with suffix *-do*. **Mǫžь* is derived from **man-* with suffixes: **mon-g-jo-s*. Numerous scholars have seen the suffix *-g-* in this word (Trubačev 1959:96-97) but in fact more than one suffix is involved here (**mon-g-jo-*). The development of its sense into 'husband' is secondary and late (Trubačev 1959:104).

Common Slavonic **žena*, which developed *ž* from g^w, goes back to the Indo-European form **g^wenā*, cf. Old Prussian *genno* 'woman' (vocative), *gema* 'wife', Gothic *qinō* (< **g^wen-ōn*) 'woman, wife', *qēns* (< g^wēn-) 'spouse', Old High German *quena* 'woman, wife', Old English *cwene*, *cwēn*, English *quean* 'hussy', *queen* 'king's wife' (see Barnhart 2000: s.vv. *quean*, *queen*), Sanskrit *jāniṣ* 'woman, wife', *gnā* 'goddess', Armenian *kin* 'wife' (< g^wena), Albanian *zonjë* (< g^weniā) 'woman', Old Irish *ben* (< g^wenā) 'woman', Persian *zän* (Černyx 1994: s.v. *žena*). The root is g^wen- 'give birth' (Pokornyj 1959:473), i.e. a woman gives birth (Cyganenko 1970: s.v. *žena*). G^w- before the front vowel *e* gave Slavonic *ž*. The final stress of Indo-European g^wenā́ gave Slavonic *žená*.

Traditionally the music-hall comedian will joke about his mother-in-law, *tёšča* (wife's mother), while the comedienne might joke about her *svekróv* (husband's mother). The fathers-in-law are respectively *test'* (wife's father) and *svёkor* (husband's father). Although uncomplimentary references to mothers-in-law, especially by husbands, can be found in Russian literature («и он вспомнил противную свою тёщу» – M. Roščin), *tёšča* can suggest a friendly family atmosphere: «Неподалёку, на углу канала Грибоедова, был ресторан-подвальчик, в просторечьи 'под тёщей'» (Ju. German).

Svёkor, svekróv

Slavonic **svekry*, originally a *ū*-stem with genitive **svekrъve*, has undergone a complicated series of phonetic and morphological changes. Russian even has in dialect the original form *svekrý* (indeclinable), which has been eliminated from other Slavonic languages. Generally it has been changed to an *a*-stem (in dialect *svekrova, svekróvja*) or an *i*-stem (in standard Russian *svekróv*). The standard form came from the accusative singular *svekrъvь* from *svekry* (Cyganenko 1970: s.v. *svekróv*). Other dialectal forms include *svekra* and *svekruxa*. The male equivalent is more uniform. The Common Slavonic was **svekrъ* < **swekros*, cf. Old Church Slavonic *svekrъ*. The modern Russian form *svёkor* suggests an earlier *svekъr-* with epenthetic *-ъ-* via the intermediate **svekr̥*. Russian *svekróv* is cognate with Latin *socrus* (genitive *socrūs*, feminine) 'mother-in-law', Sanskrit *śvaśrūs*, Old High German *swigur* (< **svegrū-*), Welsh *chwegr* (< **svekru-*), Armenian *skesur*, Albanian *vjéhёrrë*, Greek *hekurá*, while *svёkor* is cognate with Latin *socer* 'father-in-law', Greek *hekurós*, Sanskrit *śvaśuras*, Lithuanian *šešuras*, Old High German *swehur*, Albanian *vjerr, vjehёrr* (Vasmer 1976-80: s.vv. *svёkor, svekróv*, Černyx 1994: s.v. *svekróv*). Forms in other languages suggest an Indo-European **swek̑rū-s* with palatal *-k̑-*, but Slavonic *k* could not derive from this unless there was dissimilation from *s-s* to *s-k*,[3] i.e. unless Slavonic **svekry* derived from earlier **sve-sry* (Trubačev 1959:120; Cyganenko 1970: s.v. *svekróv*), the first part of which is *sve-* : *svo-* : *svojь* 'one's own' (Trubačev 1959:122) and the second unclear part of which was changed to *kry* 'blood' by popular etymology, as if the meaning were 'of one's own blood'. The masculine *svёkor* would then follow by analogy. Pedersen argues that **svekrūs* (feminine) existed alongside **svék̑uros* (masculine) and from the former came the *-k-* in Slavonic, which was passed by analogy to the masculine **svekrъ* (Vasmer 1976-80: s.v. *svekróv*). Cyganenko (1970: s.v. *svekróv*) suggests that *svekrъ* goes back to Common Slavonic **swekros* < Indo-European **swekrūs*

---

[3]   Though, as Trubačev points out (1959:121), Slavonic does not usually dissimilate *s-s*.

with the root *swe-* > *sve-* (*svoj*) and perhaps *kr-* < *kur-* linked with Greek *kúrios* 'having strength or power'. It would seem that parallel Indo-European *u*-stems existed, one with and one without palatal *k̂*: **swekrū* : **swek̂rū*. From these were derived the parallel masculine forms **swékūros* : **swék̂ūros* (< **swekru-os*). This is analogous to what later happened in Slavonic: *svekrъ* > *svekъrъ*.

Test', tĕšča

The etymology of Slavonic *tьstь* has not been definitively established, but Lavrovskij (1867:66) has an interesting suggestion: comparison with the Greek *tíktō*, *tékō* 'give birth', i.e. *tьs-tь* signifies the parent of one's wife, cf. Frankish *tichter*, with which Hirt compared the Slavonic word (Trubačev 1959:125). The feminine *tĕšča* is a derivative (from **tьst-jā*) of the masculine, for which there are three deverbal possibilities: *tьstь* is a collective noun with an ancient *i*-stem; *tьstь* is the name of a figure of masculine gender like *gostь*; or *tьstь* is the name of a female figure. The masculine is most likely and the collective sense would fit well. The original sense was therefore not wife's father when the verb from which it derived was lost. It determined rather the relationship of a parent or parents to me myself: a son-in-law called his wife's parents his parents.

Tьstь, a collective with the sense 'having given birth', is a kind of epithet involving the ancient custom of treating a relationship by marriage as equal to a blood relationship. Besides the root **tek̂-* there is another etymology of the words: **tьstь* and **tьstja* are linked with Slavonic **teta*, Lithuanian *teta* 'aunt', cf. Greek *tétta*, Russian *tjatja* 'father'. In this etymology *tьstь* is from **tьt-stь* with suffix *-st-(h)i* and reduced vocalism of the root **tьt-*, its meaning being 'finding oneself in place of (*-st-(h)i*) a father (*tьt-*). Here, with the suffix *-io-*, belongs Old Prussian *tisties*, which may be borrowed from Slavonic (Trubačev 1959:126; Fasmer 1964-73: s.v. *test'*). Černyx (1994: s.v. *test'*) sees the word as possibly belonging to a group of relationship terms with the Indo-European root **tat-* : **tet-* : **tit-* and the suffix *-t-(ь)*. Thus Common Slavonic **tьstь* is from *tьt-t-ь* (< **tĭt-t-ĭs*) with dissimilation *tt* > *st*, a view shared by Isačenko (Trubačev 1959: 127).

Suppose the Russian mother-in-law wished to remonstrate with her son-in-law. How would she address him? As *zjat'* (daughter's husband) or one of its diminutives such as *zjatĕk* or *zjatjuška*, the same word as her husband would use in addressing his son-in-law.

Zjať

The Common Slavonic *zętъ is an old formation, as suggested by its presence in all the Slavonic languages with little or no variation in form or meaning, and derives from Indo-European *ĝenətis, the root of which is *ĝen- : *ĝenə- (: *ĝₑnə-) 'bring into the world'. Cognates include Lithuanian žentas (< Indo-European *ĝenətos) 'daughter's husband', Old High German kind (< *ĝentóm) 'child', Latin genitus (< *ĝenətos) 'birth', (g)nātus (< *ĝₑnətos) 'born', Sanskrit jātáḥ (root jan-) 'born', jnātíṣ 'relative', jánati 'gives birth', Greek gnōtós 'relative', Albanian (Tosc) dhëndër 'suitor, young married man, son-in-law'. To this root but without the suffix -t- belong Latin geno : gigno (with reduplicated stem) 'bring into the world' and genesis 'origin' (Trubačev 1959:129-130, Černyx 1994: s.v. zjať, Fasmer 1964-73: s.v. zjať). The original meaning of the word would be either someone continuing the family or conceivably someone known: the Indo-European root ĝen- 'know', giving Russian znat' from *ĝnō- (*ĝenə) with the change ĝ > z, is the same as that meaning 'give birth, be born' and probably derives from the latter (Fasmer 1964-73: s.v. zjať).

If the mother-in-law and father-in-law had a son who was married and not a daughter, mother and father would traditionally speak to their daughter-in-law using two different words. To a woman her daughter-in-law is nevestka (son's wife in relation to her mother-in-law), but to a man his daughter-in-law is properly snoxa (son's wife in relation to her father-in-law) or affectionately snošeńka, although nowadays nevestka is often used instead (see Ušakov 1935-40: s.v. nevestka). Usage in this respect has changed; snoxa can now be found used by both a father-in-law and a mother-in-law to their daughter-in-law (especially in rural areas), i.e. as a synonym of nevestka in this sense (Kuznecov 2000: s.v. snoxa).

Snoxa

Old Church Slavonic and Old Russian snъxa has cognate forms in other Indo-European languages: Sanskrit snuṣấ, Latin nurus (genitive nurūs) < *(s)nusus < *snusos, Greek nuós < *(s)nusós, Armenian nu, Old High German snur, archaic and dialectal German Schnur (see Kluge 2002: s.v. Schnur 2), Old English snoru, Old Norse snor, snør. Apart from a few reworkings after a-stems (notably Sanskrit snuṣấ and Old Church Slavonic snъxa), all these forms continue an old feminine o-stem, Indo-European *snus-ós < *sneu- 'bind, knit';[4]

---

[4]   The closeness in sound and constant association with Indo-European *sūnus 'son' (snoxa = son's wife) explains the earlier etymology *snusā from sūnu-, with the normal change s > x after u in Slavonic, but the disappearance of -ū- caused doubts and

someone 'bound' in a relation by marriage is someone 'related'. Germanic *snuzó- came from Indo-European *snus-ós if the accent falls on the syllable after the consonant z (Trubačev 1959:131, Kluge 2002: s.v. Schnur 2); Old High German snur, snura has r < z (Černyx 1994: s.v. snoxa). It is not clear whether *snus-ós goes back to cross-cousin marriages of the matriarchate, when one's wife was one's cousin, i.e. whether it meant 'niece, cross-cousin' as well as 'son's wife'; otherwise one must conclude that it arose a little later than cross-cousin marriage, already as a term for relationship by marriage (Trubačev 1959:131). Derivatives of this word exist, mainly in Russian dialect, for a father-in-law living in sin with his daughter-in-law: Dal' gives snoxar̂, snoxač and snošnik with this sense (1912-14: s.v. snoxa), while Ušakov gives only sno-xač with the note 'dialectal' (1935-40: s.v. snoxač). Being in a sexual relationship of this kind is snoxačestvo.

Nevestka

Nevestka has displaced snoxa in some Slavonic languages, such as Ukrainian. It is a derivative of nevesta 'fiancée, bride', Old Church Slavonic nevĕsta. The Common Slavonic is *nevĕsta. Miklosich gives two possible etymologies (1886: s.v. nevêsta): from the root ved- 'lead', cf. Old Russian 'vedena byst' Rostislava za Jaroslava'; and with the sense 'unknown', ne-vĕsta. Other suggestions include nevĕ-sta (locative of *newos 'new' + suffix -sta as in starosta, but such compounds do not have a locative form), *nāv-esta (connected with naṽ 'corpse' and nevod), a link with Lithuanian vaisa 'fertility' (i.e. meaning 'maiden'), a link with Sanskrit viś 'enter', niviś 'marry, take a husband', and a link with Lithuanian viešéti 'be a guest'. Trubeckoj gives a detailed study of the word (Trubačev 1959:92). He considers *ne-vĕd-ta 'unknown' pure popular etymology and also discounts nevo-vĕsta, associated with vesti. He deems it best to see the word as a whole and not view it as a compound. He views it as an Indo-European prototype *newisthā, the superlative of *newos 'new, young' meaning 'youngest'. The Slavonic underwent a phonetic transition to *newьsta. There then occurred a change of sense linked with *wistos, the past passive participle of the verb *weid- : *woid- : *wid-, i.e. *ne-vьstā 'not known (by a man)'. Then the oi-grade penetrated into all forms, giving *nevoistā. Trubačev regards this as unconvincing (1959:92) but admits that all new etymologies are equally doubtful and notes that Vasmer (1976-80: s.v. nevesta) with justification cites the old etymology nevĕsta = unknown, which came about by linguistic taboo that

---

most now accept the link with *snus-ós < *sneu-. As a result of this link, German Schnur in the sense 'string, lace' is etymologically identical with Schnur in the old sense 'daughter-in-law' (Fasmer 1964-73: s.v. snoxa).

would protect a woman entering a new household from evil spirits. Isačenko prefers to see a link with *vesti* 'lead, marry', cf. Latin *uxorem ducere* 'lead (= marry) a wife'. Černyx (1994: s.v. *nevesta*) notes that a similar usage occurs in the Novgorod birch-bark writ number 9: «*водя* новую жену». Accordingly he surmises that Common Slavonic *nevěsta* was made up of two roots, *nev-* and *ved-* with the suffix *-t-*: **nev-ved-t-a*, i.e it originally meant 'newly led (in marriage)'. This does not, however, account for the jat́ (*ě*) in the word, and Černyx suggests there was later influence of the verb **věděti* 'know'; after Christianization, when the viriginity of the bride was important, the meaning of the word could have been interpreted as 'unknown (by a man)'. Thus Černyx combines the two original etymologies advanced by Miklosich. On the whole the straightforward derivation favoured by Vasmer is probably the best; Trubačev notes (1959:93-94) that it was customary to treat the bride to be as a stranger in the house of the groom, as part of the ritual for protecting her from harm.

Unfortunately *zjat́* and *nevestka* are potentially ambiguous words, since they can denote other in-laws, namely brother-in-law and sister-in-law, though properly speaking only in limited circumstances. *Nevestka*, for example, is strictly a sister-in-law only in the sense of a brother's wife or husband's brother's wife. However, it is used for a wife's brother's wife too (like the old, now dialectal, *jatroǐ* and *jatrovka*, which could also mean a husband's brother's wife) and, loosely, as a synonym of *zolovka* 'husband's sister' and *svojačenica* 'wife's sister'. In other words *nevestka* has broadened its range of meanings to include all uses of the English word 'sister-in-law' (and indeed daughter-in-law); one dictionary defines it as 'a married woman in relation to the relatives of her husband – father, mother, brothers, sisters, sisters' husbands, brothers' wives' (Evgeńeva 1981-84: s.v. *nevestka*). This development is perhaps to be understood when it is borne in mind that Russians themselves sometimes confuse the words available and tend to seek a more straightforward way of expressing these relationships (Forbes 1964:396, fn.), often preferring less confusing phrases like *otec ženy* (= *test́*), *otec muža* (= *svëkor*), *sestra ženy* (= *svojačenica*), *sestra muža* (= *zolovka*). Similarly *zjat́* could be rendered as *muž dočeri* 'son-in-law', *muž sestry* 'brother-in-law' and *muž zolovki*, literally the husband of one's husband's sister, as required.

Jatroǐ

Common Slavonic **jętry* 'husband's brother's wife', Old Russian *jatry* (genitive *jatrъve*) are now reflected in old dialectal forms like *jatroǐ, jatrova, jatrovka, jatroǐja* and *jatrovica*. All these old names are dying out in Russian as the old terminology is forgotten and new forms appear, like *snošenicy* 'brothers' wives'. For example, Ukrainian *jatrivka* has virtually gone out of use. The related forms in Indo-European languages point to a common Indo-European form **jenəter*, which in some languages, e.g. Greek, kept its schwa (ə), while in others, e.g. Balto-Slav, it was lost; this is parallel to Indo-European **dhŭghətĕr* 'daughter' > Greek *thugátēr*, but Balto-Slav **dŭktēr*, Gothic *daúhtar*. Loss of the schwa in medial position gave **jenəter* > **jęti* (like *mati*), but this was influenced by *svekry* to give **jętry*. Baltic has retained the correct forms, Lithuanian *jentė* (genitive *jentės, jenters*), Latvian *ietere, ietaļa*. Cognates include Sanskrit *yātar-, yātā-* 'husband's brother's wife', Greek *enatéres*, Homeric plural *eináteres*, Latin *jānitrīces* 'brothers' wives, sisters-in-law', Armenian *ner, nēr* 'brothers' wives or wives of the same man', Phrygian (accusative singular) *ianátera* (Trubačev 1959:138, Vasmer 1976-80: s.v. *jatrov*). The original etymological meaning of **jenəter, *jętry* is unknown (Trubačev 1959:138).

Zolovka

The Common Slavonic form is **zъly* (genitive **zъlъve*), the Old Church Slavonic *zъlъva*, the Russian dialect *zolva* (Irkutsk), *zolvica* (Tver') and the standard Russian *zolovka* 'husband's sister'. The word has been lost to most West Slavonic languages and survives in Russian better than in Ukrainian (*zovícja*), where it is little used. **Zъly* is an old *ū*-stem that has been reshaped in Russian like *svekry* as *zъlъva > zolovka*. It therefore follows the usual path of a *ū*-stem in developing into an *ā*-stem. The Common Slavonic is related to Indo-European words going back to **ĝ*e*lōu-s*: Greek *gálōs*, Latin *glōs*, Armenian *tal, calr*, all with the preserved meaning 'husband's sister'. **Ĝ*e*lōu-s* may be linked with the Greek root *gal-, gel-* 'enjoy oneself, make merry' (Trubačev 1959:136), cf. Greek *geláō* 'laugh', *gélōs* 'laughter'.

Svojačenica, svojak

These forms are derived from the Indo-European pronominal root **swe-*, the implication of which is 'one's own', *svoj*, i.e. related by marriage (*svojstvenniki*). The masculine form *svojak* should properly be used for a wife's sister's husband, i.e. the husband of a *svojačenica* 'wife's sister'. In Slavonic there are different grades of root vocalism for these compounds: alongside **svo-, *svojo-* in Russian *svojak* there is **svъ- < *svĭ-* in Russian dialect *svesť, svëstka, svëstočka* (= *svojačenica*) < **svъstъ*, cf. Ukrainian *svisť* 'sister-in-law' (husband's sister or brother's wife). Daľ lists other dialectal variants parallel with *svesť*

(1912-14: s.v. *svest'*): *svestja, svěst', sveś, sviś* and *svjaś*. The ending of the word is unclear: is it **svьs-ti* or **svь-stь*? Il'inskij thinks the latter (Trubačev 1959: 140), with *-stь* from **st(h)ā* 'stand, be in a state', so that **svьstь* = standing in relationship by marriage. Trubačev thinks it is better to see **svьstь, *svěstь* as an ancient abstract noun with the sense 'belonging to one's own' (*svojstvo*, relationship by marriage, with *-stь* having its typical word-forming function), followed by semantic transfer to a person of the female sex, *svojačenica*. Russian *svojak, svojačenica* (dialectally *svojačina, svojka, svojakinja*) have a transparent etymological link with **svojь*, Russian *svoj*. Baltic examples are analogous: Lithuanian and Latvian *svainis* 'wife's sister's husband' (Trubačev 1959:141).

On the male side, no single word covers all senses of the English 'brother-in-law'. *Zjat'* for instance is only a brother-in-law in two senses: sister's husband or husband's sister's husband (husband of *zolovka*). For a wife's sister's husband (husband of *svojačenica*) the word *svojak* should strictly be used. Readers of Gogol's *Šinel'* will perhaps recall another word for brother-in-law in the rather amusing account of the Basmačkins' footwear: «И отец, и дед, и даже шурин, и все совершенно Басмачкины ходили в сапогах». *Šurin*, occasionally *šurak*, is a wife's brother (*svojačenica* being a wife's sister), but to a wife her husband's brother is *dever* (*zolovka* being her husband's sister). As for the parents of the spouses, they would refer to their opposite numbers as *svat* (son-in-law's or daughter-in-law's father) and *svatja* (son-in-law's or daughter-in-law's mother). The latter word, of course, is not to be confused with *svaxa*, the female equivalent of *svat* in its other sense, 'matchmaker'.

Svat, svatja

Svat can be defined as the father or male relative of one of those entering into matrimony in relation to the parents or relatives of the other. Likewise *svatja* is the mother or female relative of one of those entering into matrimony in relation to the parents or relatives of the other. In Russian dialect, *svatovstvo* is a relationship by marriage (*svojstvo*), though in the standard language it is rather 'matchmaking'. The word is connected with the pronominal stem **svo-, *sve-* 'one's own', cf. Greek *étēs* 'relative, cousin', Lithuanian *svečias, svetys* 'guest, stranger', Latvian *svešs* 'someone else's' (stem **svetjos*), Gothic *swēs* 'own', Sanskrit *svás* 'one's own', Russian *svoj* 'one's own'. *Svat* can be explained as deriving from Indo-European **swōtos*, from the Indo-European root **sewe- : *swe- : *swo-* and the suffix *-t-* (Černyx 1994: s.v. *svat*, Trubačev 1959:142). From the same root comes Russian *svad'ba* 'marriage' (= **svat'ba*). The original meaning of *svat* would therefore have been 'of one's own, a close relative' and it would have applied to relationship by marriage (when a stranger becomes one's own); compare the feminine form *svatja* in that sense with *svaxa* applied to a female matchmaker (the latter derived with the characteristic suffix for names of female professions, e.g. *portnixa*). The matchmaker sense is a relatively new development brought about by the later verbal forms like Russian *svatat'*. As a result of contamination the form *svaxa* is sometimes used in dialect in the sense 'mother of a son-in-law (*zjat'*) or of a daughter-in-law (*snoxa*)'.

Šurin

The most likely etymology of *šurin* is from Indo-European **sjəur(io)* < **sjū-* 'sew', i.e. 'bind, knit'. Here belong not only Slavonic *šurъ* but also Sanskrit *syālá-ḥ* 'wife's brother', with a different grade of root vocalism from *šurъ*. This is preferable to Berneker's linking of *šurъ* and *sve-kъrъ* and Pedersen's assumption that *šurъ* comes from **seur-*, with the same root as Russian *svojak* (see above), i.e. *svoj* 'one's own'. There are phonetic difficulties with this last etymology (Trubačev 1959:139), whereas *šurъ* presupposes not **seur-* but **sjour-* (**sjəur-*), which has the same quantitative alternation as Slavonic *šiti*, Lithuanian *siūti*, Indo-European **sju-*. Vasmer (1976-80: s.v. *šurin*) dismisses any connection with *praščur* 'forefather' (< Proto-Slavonic **praskjurъ* < Indo-European **(s)keur-*, **(s)kur-*, cf. Lithuanian *prakurėjas* 'ancestor') and with **ḱeuros*, connected by vowel alternation with Greek *hekurós* and Sanskrit *śváśuras* 'husband's father, father-in-law' (see also Trubačev 1959:72-73).

Dever

Old Church Slavonic *děverъ* and Russian *dever* are of Common Slavonic origin. Common Slavonic **děverъ* has been largely lost in West Slavonic but is still represented in East and South Slavonic. It has a large number of cognates in other languages, e.g. Latin *lēvir*, Greek *dāḗr* < *dai(w)ēr*, Sanskrit *dēvā́r*, Old High German *zeihhur*, Old English *tācor*, Armenian *taigr*, which all have a similar sense to *děverъ*, husband's brother (Vasmer 1976-80, Černyx 1994, Preobraženskij 1958: s.v. *dever*). The common form is Indo-European **dāiwēr*. Latin *lēvir* shows a local Italic replacement of Indo-European *d* with Sabine *l* and alteration of the ending *lēver* under the influence of Latin *vir* 'man'. Lithuanian and Latvian *dieveris* may be borrowed from Slavonic (Trubačev 1959:134). Owing to the closeness of meaning of Lithuanian *laiguonas* (*laigonas*, *laigūnas*) 'wife's brother' (= *šurin*), it may be etymologically related to Indo-European **dāiwēr*, if one assumes **daiguonas* as an earlier form. The change *d* > *l* may be a rare sound change in Indo-European or a desire to avoid linkage with Lithuanian *iš-daiga* 'joke, prank'. The occurrence of -g- in this Lithuanian form is interestingly like old Indo-European dialect forms such as Old High German *zeihhur* < Germanic **taikuraz* with Germanic *k* = Indo-European **g*, cf. Armenian *taigr*. The change may have happened in Indo-European as there occur instances of strengthening *w* by prefixing *g* > *g^w* in a number of Indo-European languages. If this is so, Lithuanian *laiguonas* preserves the initial form of the Indo-European name for a husband's brother. The final stress pattern in Greek *dāér* and Sanskrit *dēvár* suggests that the original stress on *děverь* was final, though it is now initial (Trubačev 1959:135).

Before concluding this study it would perhaps be useful to note a form of relationship that is neither exactly by marriage nor necessarily by blood: godparenthood. The godparents are *krëstnyj (otec)* and *krëstnaja (mat')*, i.e. godfather and godmother respectively, who are known in more formal ecclesiastical language as *vospriemnik* and *vospriemnica*, because they receive from the font the child being christened (i.e. *krestimyj* or *krestimaja*). The godfather and godmother would refer to, and be known by, each other and the parents of the godchildren (*krëstnye deti*) as *kum* and *kuma* respectively. This sort of spiritual relationship is therefore called *kumovstvo*. More than one godson (*krestnik* or *krëstnyj syn*) or goddaughter (*krestnica* or *krëstnaja doč*) of the same godparent would be known to each other as *krëstnyj brat* or *krëstnaja sestra*, corresponding to the obsolete English terms godbrother and godsister respectively.

Kum, kuma

Kum is generally seen as a reduction of *kъmotrъ* 'godfather' (in modern dialectal Russian, *kmotr*), which is a new formation from *kъmotra* 'godmother', which goes back to popular Latin *commāter* with the same sense. Probably a godfather was originally called **kъpetrъ* or **kopetrъ*, cf. Old Church Slavonic *kupetra* 'godmother' and Old Church Slavonic glagolitic *kupotrъ*, from popular Latin *compater* 'godfather', whence Albanian *kumptër*, *kundër*. Compare also the Romanian *cumetră* 'godmother' and *cumetru* 'godfather' (Fasmer 1964-73: s.vv. *kmotr*, *kum*). However, the relationship *u* : *ъ* in *kum* is hard to account for. Similarly *kuma* is seen as a shortening of *kъmotra*, but this does not explain the vocalism *u* : *ъ*. Attempts to link it to Turkic *kuma* 'young wife' are unsatisfactory owing to the difference in meaning. In that case one must assume a semantic effect of *kъmotrъ*, *kъmotra* and the new formation *kum* from *kuma* (Vasmer 1976-80: s.v. *kuma*). Černyx (1994: s.v. *kum*) plausibly surmises that Latin *commāter* was borrowed during the Christianization of the Slavs in two variants, *kъmótrъ (which later acquired the sense 'godfather' and survives in dialect as *kmotr*) and *kúmotrъ (which was reduced to *kumъ*).

Clearly the terminology that is associated with family relationships in Russian is complex (though not all the terms in this survey are equally widely used), but the relationships themselves are in some cases complex and the terminology used in English is not always straightforward either. Each language has its own peculiarities. In English, for instance, there is a convenient method of denoting relationships by marriage by appending *in-law* to the appropriate noun, but Russian has its convenient adjectives *dvojurodnyj* and *trojurodnyj*, and if necessary *četverojurodnyj* etc., which allow a number of complex and sometimes distant relationships to be concisely expressed. It is rare to reach a point where these adjectives no longer suffice to characterize a distant relative (*dal'nij rodstvennik*). Not many, after all, are inclined to take genealogical nicety to the point described here: «Родство, свойство и кумовство считается там чуть не до двенадцатого колена» (P. I. Mel'nikov-Pečerskij, *Na gorax*, cited in Evgeńeva 1981-84: s.v. *kumovstvo*).

Brian Cooper
21 Redgate Road
Girton
Cambridge CB3 0PP
Great Britain

Bibliography

Barnhart, R. K., 1988, *Chambers Dictionary of Etymology*, reprint 2000, Edinburgh: Chambers.

Černyx, P. Ja., 1994, *Istoriko-ètimologičeskij slovaŕ sovremennogo russkogo jazyka*, Moscow: Russkij jazyk.

Cyganenko, G. P., 1970, *Ètimologičeskij slovaŕ russkogo jazyka*, Kiev: Radjanśka škola.

Dal', V. I., 1912-14, *Tolkovyj slovaŕ živogo velikorusskogo jazyka*, St Petersburg /Moscow: M. O. Vol'f.

Evgeńeva A. P., 1981-84, *Slovaŕ russkogo jazyka v četyrëx tomax*, Moscow: Russkij jazyk.

Fasmer, M., 1964-73, *Ètimologičeskij slovaŕ russkogo jazyka*, perevod s nemeckogo i dopolnenija O. N. Trubačeva, Moscow: Progress.

Forbes, N., 1964, *Russian Grammar*, edn. 3, revised and enlarged by J. C. Dumbreck, Oxford: Clarendon Press.

Kluge, F., 2002, *Etymologisches Wörterbuch der deutschen Sprache*, Elmar Seebold (ed.), 24th edn., Berlin: Walter de Gruyter.

Kotelova, N. Z. (ed.), 1984, *Novye slova i značenija. Slovař-spravočnik po materialam pressy i literatury 70-x godov*, Moscow: Russkij jazyk.

Kuznecov, S. (chief ed.), 2000, *Boľšoj tolkovyj slovař russkogo jazyka*, St Petersburg: Norint.

Lavrovskij, P., 1867, 'Korennoe značenie v nazvanijax rodstva u slavjan', *Sbornik statej, čitannyx v Otdelenii Russkogo Jazyka i Slovesnosti Imperatorskoj Akademii Nauk*, 2 (3).

Machek, V., 1957, *Etymologický slovník jazyka českého a slovenského*, Prague: Akademia Věd.

Miklosich, F. von, 1886, *Etymologisches Wörterbuch der slavischen Sprachen*, Vienna (reprint 1970, Amsterdam: Philo Press).

Pokorny, J., 1959, *Indogermanisches etymologisches Wörterbuch*, vol. 1, Bern: Francke.

Preobraženskij, A. G., 1958, *Ètimologičeskij slovař russkogo jazyka*, Moscow: Gosudarstvennoe izdateľstvo inostrannyx i nacionaľnyx slovarej (first published Moscow 1910-49).

Trubačev, O. N., 1959, *Istorija slavjanskix terminov rodstva*, Moscow: Akademija nauk SSSR.

Ušakov, D. N., 1935-40, *Tolkovyj slovař russkogo jazyka*, Moscow: Ogiz.

Vasmer, M., 1976-80, *Russisches etymologisches Wörterbuch*, 2. unveränderte Auflage, Heidelberg: Carl Winter.

Vey, M., 1931, 'Slave *st*- provenant d'I.-E. *pt-', *Bulletin de la Société de Linguistique de Paris*, 32, 65-67.

Studia Etymologica Cracoviensia
vol. 14   Kraków 2009

Bernd GLIWA (Rīga)

ZU EINIGEN BALTISCH-OSTSEEFINNISCHEN KONTAKTEN*⁾

0. Leider war es mir nicht vergönnt, Professor Eugen Helimski persönlich kennenzulernen. Die Einladung, an dem Gedenkband ihm zur Erinnerung mitzuarbeiten, ist eine Ehre und Verpflichtung gleichermaßen.

Zweifellos stand die ethnische und sprachliche Entwicklung im östlichen Nordeuropa ganz im Zentrum der Aufmerksamkeit von Professor Helimski. Daher habe ich ein Thema ausgewählt, das dieser Interessenlage entspricht: Sprachkontakte zwischen Balten und Ostseefinnen. Mein gegenwärtiges Arbeitsfeld sind die baltischen Pflanzennamen, mit dem Ziel eines etymologischen Wörterbuches dieses speziellen Wortschatzes im Preussischen, Litauischen und Lettischen.[1] Die gegenseitige Entlehnung von Pflanzennamen, so etwa finn. *angervo* 'Filipendula ulmaria' aus einer baltischen Sprache und lett. *pīladze* 'Sorbus aucuparia', *madara* 'Galium spp.' aus ostseefinn. Sprachen, deuten neben anderem, da es sich hierbei sicher nicht um Kultur- oder Wanderworte handelt, sondern Namen verbreiteter einheimischer Pflanzen, auf enge Sprachkontakte, wohl mit langer Zweisprachigkeit. Eng mit den Pflanzennamen verbunden sind auch die Bezeichnungen verschiedener Biotope, da diese oft im Kontext mit Pflanzennamen genannt werden und erheblich zur Identifizierung der jeweiligen Pflanzen beitragen können. Auch diese lexikalische Gruppe ist unter den baltischen Entlehnungen in den ostseefinnischen Sprachen anzutreffen – und lässt in der etymologischen bzw. namenkundlichen Behandlung oft Sachkenntnis vermissen. Sowohl Pflanzen als auch geographische Bezeichnungen finden sich recht häufig in Ortsnamen.

Das Problem der frühesten Sprachkontakte zwischen Balten und Sprechern der Finno-Ugrischen Sprachen äußert sich insbesondere in der Onomastik. Genaues ist unbekant und unsicher und entsprechend werden auch genaue Datierungen vermieden. Dennoch scheint es, dass oft implizit davon ausgegangen

---

*⁾ Besonderer Dank gilt E. Trumpa sowie den Kollegen der onomastischen Abteilung des Institutes für Lettische Sprache in Riga für Unterstützung mit Literatur und Kartotheken.

[1] Gegenwärtig als Teil dieses Vorhabens mit einem DFG finanzierten Forschungsstipendium "Untersuchungen zur Etymologie lettischer Pflanzennamen".

wird, dass große Teile der später baltisch bewohnten Gebiete vorher von ostsee-finnischen Stämmen bewohnt waren. So wird auch explizit von finnougrischem Substrat in der Gewässernamenschicht Litauens gesprochen (Vanagas 1981b: 143). Helimski plädiert dafür, dass die Migration der Vorgänger der Ostseefin-nen von der oberen Wolga nach Norden und Westen nicht vor dem Beginn des ersten Jahrtausends vor Chr. zu datieren ist (2006: 112; 2008: 76) und räumt sehr diplomatisch ein, dass diese Sicht "not compatible with [...] the thesis of the ethnic continuity of Balto-Fennic in the Baltic area for 5000 years or more" ist (Helimski 2006: 114).

1. Lett. dial. *vañga*

Der jüngste Beitrag zu lett. dial. *vañga* (ME IV 470f.; EH II 756) findet sich bei Kagaine, die lokale Finnougrismen in den nordöstlichen lettischen Dia-lekten zusammenstellt und hierbei das Lemma *vañga²* 'Heuschlag am Gewäs-ser; niedrig gelegene, feuchte Wiese' listet (Kagaine 2004: 225f.), ebenso wie *vañga¹* 'Griff, Henkel; Schlinge' (2004: 223-226). Überraschend dabei die Un-kenntnis des aus finnistischer Sicht vorgetragenen Plädoyers für baltischen Ur-sprung von Vaba (1998).

Zunächst ist klar, dass ein direkt vererbtes baltisches Wort im Lettischen nicht *vanga* sondern **voga* [*vuoga*] lauten würde, wie lit. *lángas* : lett. *logs* [*luôgs*] 'Fenster, Öffnung', lit. *angìs*, lett. *odze* [*uôdze*] 'Kreuzotter u.a.'. Daher ergibt sich die Notwendigkeit ein Substratwort, bzw. Entlehnung, aus einer an-deren baltischen oder eben finnougrischen Sprache anzunehmen. Zinkevičius (1984: 349) nimmt **vanga* in den Ortsnamen *Alsvanga* (heute *Alsunga*) und *Ievanga²* vorbehaltlos als kurisches Wort an, wobei er den üblichen Vergleich mit apr. *wangus* bemüht. Nicht eingegangen wird dabei auf die so nicht zu er-klärenden Formen *vanga* im nördlichen Livland, kartiert bei Kagaine (2004: 225).

Den Befürwortern einer baltischen Herkunft von *vañga²* 'Heuschlag am Gewässer...' steht zumindestens eine Verbreitung des Begriffs, bzw. vermutlich zugehöriger ablautender Formen ähnlicher Bedeutung, in mehreren baltischen Sprachen zur Disposition, auch wenn einzelne Formen wie das altlitauische, nur bei Bretke belegte *vanga* 'Acker' trotz Deutungsversuchen von Mažiulis (1997: 219f.) weitgehend unklar bleibt (Smoczyński 2000: 135f.). Hingegen fehlt eine entsprechende Zusammenstellung wenigstens in den ostseefinnischen Sprachen, vom weiteren ugrofinnischen Kontext ganz zu schweigen. Hauptargument für

---

[2]   Nicht mehr genau lokalisierbar, bei Liepāja (Dambe 1990: 55), belegt als *Ewangen* 1350 und im Namen für den Fischgrund *Ievangas valgums* (Laumane 1996: 97). Wohl aus *Iev-vanga*, zu *ieva* 'Ahlkirsche – Prunus padus', ein typischer Baum der Auen.

eine Entlehnung aus dem Lybischen ist die Verbreitung des Begriffs *vañga*[2] 'Heuschlag am Gewässer' im Lettischen dort wo lybisches Substrat zu erwarten ist, nämlich in Kurland um Kuldīga und in den ON *Alsunga* und *Vandzene*, letzteres bei Talsi, und in Livland um Limbaži, auch in mehreren Flur-, Gewässer- und Hofnamen. Und die umstrittene Etymologie möglicher apr. und lit. Entsprechungen – wenn es sich denn um baltisches Erbe handelt. Der Ortsname *Vangaži*, ein Städtchen östlich von Riga, ist zudem durch -*aži* als livisch gekennzeichnet, was natürlich eine vorausgehende Entlehnung des Erstgliedes nicht ausschließt.

Eine Zusammenstellung der Belege in den ostseefinnischen Sprachen gibt Vaba (1998: 180f.), wobei die Areale des Landschaftswortes 'Wiese am Fluss' und des technischen Begriffs 'Henkel, Griff, Krampe etc.' deutlich voneinander abweichen. Ersteres ist nur in salislivisch (Salaca) *vanga* und estn. (Saarema, Helme, Põlva) *vanga*, *vangu* bezeugt. Der technische Begriff findet sich darüberhinaus auch in finn. *vanki*, *vanka*, udmurtisch *vug*, *vugy* 'Handgriff; Klammer...', komi *vug* 'ds.' (Vaba 1998: 180).

Ich halte es für angebracht, die baltistische Seite der Angelegenheit nochmal ganz von vorne zu untersuchen. Ältester Beleg ist das Apr. *wangus* (E588). Die Übersetzung lautet *dameraw* (Mažiulis 1997: 219).[3] In der Literatur findet sich nach Trautmann (1910: 457) als moderne Deutung 'schlecht bestandener Eichenwald; halb ausgerodete Waldfläche', das immer mal wieder neu formuliert und interpretiert wird, bis man schließlich mit Zinkevičius (1984: 349) sehr frei bei 'Rodung' (lit. "lydimas") ankommt. *Damerau* und *Dammerau* sind zweifellos nur Varianten (in anderen Fällen auch *Dammer*, *Dambrau*). Sie sind insbesondere als Ortsnamen bekannt und davon ausgehend als Familienname. Die Ortsnamen entsprechen poln. *Dąbrowa*,[4] und sind ohne Zweifel Entlehnungen bzw. Adaptionen. Die tatsächliche Bedeutung von *dameraw* um 1400 und damit apr. *wangus* lässt sich m.E. nicht aus späten deutschen Dialektformen erschließen, sondern eher aus dem polnischen Original. Ungeachtet ob sl. *dǫbъ* 'Eiche' und *dǫbrava* 'Wald, Hain' denn nun zusammengehören, was umstritten ist (ESSJ V 93-97) und hier nicht zur Debatte steht, so ist doch insbesondere im Polnischen die Bedeutung 'Eichenwald' für *dąbrowa* präsent. Die sehr spezifischen Bedeutungsnuancen 'schlecht bestandener Eichenwald; halb ausgerodete Waldfläche' sind hieraus nicht abzulesen, genausowenig wie aus dem Kontext im Wörterbuch (E586-E589) *Walt*, *Pusch*, *Dameraw*, *Heyde*. Eine Rodung hätte man eher bei *Acker*, *Stucke* (E237-E238) anzusiedeln. Auch Wiesen und Weiden, Feuchtwiesen inklusive, fallen aus, denn die sind zwischen E282 und

---

[3] Fraenkel (LEW 1195) und Smoczyński (2000: 136) haben abweichend – normalisiert – *Dammerau*.

[4] Eine Auswahl: [http://de.wikipedia.org/wiki/Dąbrowa].

E288 gelistet: *Wesen, Gras, Gromot, Ror, Schilf, Bruch*,[5] *Mosebruch*.[6] Wie sich nun *Walt* zu *Dameraw* verhält ist eine offene Frage; ob es sich dabei um Nadel-wald gegenüber Laubwald handelt oder ob durch Anklang von *-aw*[7] eine Asso-ziation zum *Auwald*,[8] auch Laubwald, geweckt wurde oder ob es sich original-getreu um Eichenwald handelte, wird sich schwerlich feststellen lassen.

Wenn man andererseits im altpreußischen Material den FN *Wangrapia* (1326) > *Angerapp* (Mažiulis 1997: 219) und den ON *Strowange* bei Bisztynek (Gerullis 1922: 175; LEW 888; Nepokupnyj 2000) betrachtet, so sind beide im Zusammenhang mit Flüssen zu sehen, im ersten Fall durch den Zusatz *Ape – Vlys* (E60) 'Fluss', im zweiten Fall wird *Stro(w)-* mit lett. *strava*, lit. *srava*, *sro-vė*, dial. *strovė* verglichen (LEW 888). Mit der üblichen Deutung von *wangus* als Flussbogen (Mažiulis 1997: 219), in dem entweder Wald wachsen, sich ein Heuschlag befinden oder ein Dorf, wie hier *Strowange*, liegen kann, passt das ganz gut zusammen. Abweichender Meinung ist hier nur Pėteraitis (1992: 64), der das Erstglied von *Wangrapia* mit apr. *Angurgis – Oel* (E565) vergleicht und also als einen 'Aalfluss' annimmt, sich dabei auf litauische Formen *Ungura*, *Unguriškė* stützend (lit. *ungurỹs* 'Aal') und ferner das in vielen Formen anlau-tende *w-* als prothetisch annimmt. Weiterhin erwähnenswert *Alxwangen*, worin Blažienė (1998: 35), in Anlehnung an Gerullis (1922: 9) anhand der 1514 beleg-ten Form *Alexwange* als Erstglied einen pr. Personennamen *Alex, Alxe* zu erken-nen meint. Ich stimme hingegen Blažek (2001: 31) zu, dass es sich um die Erle handelt, vgl. lit. *alksnis* mit typisch baltischem *k*-Einschub gegenüber sl. **olъxa*, wobei Erlen ja sehr häufige Uferbewohner sind. Ebenso lett. *Alkšņupe* u.a. (Balode 1993: 193). Zu erwähnen sind noch 1342 *Aysmowangen* : apr. *aysmis* 'Spieß' (Gerullis 1922: 8) und *Wangikaym* : *caymis* 'Dorf' (Gerullis 1922: 194).

Einmalig belegt ist lit. *vanga* in Bretkes Bibelübersetzung. Joel 1,10 lautet dort in moderner Orthographie folgendermaßen: *Laukai esti išpūstyti, ir vangos stov vargiai...* (LKŽ XVIII 113). Damit übersetzt wird die Stelle *Das Feld ist verwüstet, und der Acker steht jämmerlich (das Getreide ist verdorben, der Wein stehet jämmerlich und das Oel kläglich.)* in der Lutherbibel, syntaktisch weitgehend identisch, hingegen abweichend von der Vulgata: *Depopulata est regio luxit humus...* Ziemlich sicher ist also, dass Bretke hiermit Ackerland meinte. Zudem ist der Begriff später nicht mehr belegt, dürfte also bereits zu Bretkes Zeit obsolet gewesen sein. Lässt sich dies mit dem oben Gesagten ver-einbaren? Prinzipiell ist das Land am Flusslauf auch als Ackerland geeignet, ge-

---

5   Ob Bruchwiesen oder Bruchwald ist unklar, im Kontext wohl aber eher auf Bruch-wiesen, bezogen, in jedem Falle Niedermoor.

6   Hoch- und Zwischenmoor.

7   Vgl. die ON *Ilmenau, Aarau* nach FN und *Eichenau, Lindenau, Buchenau* nach Baum-bestand.

8   Die Stieleiche Quercus robur ist ein prägender Baum der Hartholzaue.

düngt durch die jährlichen Überschwemmungen. Welche Gründe sprechen dafür, dass dieses Land in historischen Zeiten überwiegend als Weide und Wiese benutzt wurde? Ausführlich erläutert dies Krünitz:

> In Feldgütern, heißt Aue oder Au=Feld, L. *Tractus vallensis*, ein Stück Land, so in einem Grunde oder Thale, oder aber an einem Strohme, Flusse oder Bache gelegen, und mit Höhen umgeben ist. Die Auen von guter Art werden als eine Weide für das Vieh genutzt; und wo fruchtbares Erdreich sich findet, werden Aecker angeleget, und zu gehöriger Zeit bestellet. Diejenigen Auen, welche bloße Gründe und angenehme Thäler sind, und in einiger Entfernung von Flüssen liegen, bestehen gemeiniglich in einem fetten und starken, doch warmen und mürben Boden, welcher sich für alle Früchte und zu aller Witterung schicket, und sind die gesegnetesten und sichersten Felder; diejenigen Auen aber, welche um die Ufer der Ströhme liegen, sind gemeiniglich sehr leimigt, vest und bindend. Leztere sind nicht nur der Gefahr der Ueberschwemmung unterworfen, und also gar selten sicher, sondern gehen auch jenen wirklich in der Güte nach... (Krünitz 1782: II 650)

Der Versuch einer Deutung: gesetzt den Fall in frühen kleinen Siedlungen befanden sich Weiden, Wiesen und Ackerland zu großen Teilen an Wasserläufen, die damals noch in natürlichen Mäandern mit zahlreichen Altarmen flossen. Das heißt, der Begriff eines Bogens am Fluss konnte auch zur Benennung von Ackerland verwendet werden. So wie lit. *lañkas, lankà* 'Bogen, Flussbiegung' eben auch 'Wiese dortselbst' und dann verallgemeinert auch 'Wiese' nennt, ebenso poln. *łąka* 'Niederung, Heuschlag am Fluss' oder *łęg* 'feuchte Wiesen, gewöhnlich im Flusstal' und 'Laubwald im Flusstal' im Altpolnischen auch weitergefasst 'las, zagajnik, pole, łąka lub pastwisko, najczęściej położone nad rzeką...' (Boryś 2005: 298f.) : lit. *lengė* 'Niederung', könnte eine solcher Begriff eben auch Ackerland in der Niederung nennen, wie im Altpolnischen für *łęg* belegt. Mit der Ausdehnung der Landwirtschaft und der nun dafür benötigten Nutzfläche wurde mehr und mehr Abstand, auch im wörtlichen Sinne, von den Flussläufen genommen. Neues Rodeland ist zunächst als Ackerland geeignet, nicht jedoch als Heuschlag, so dass die Entscheidung, welche Art der Nutzfläche vom Ufer wegzuverlagern ist, leicht fällt. Möglicherweise wurde trotz dieser räumlichen Änderung aber der Begriff auch für Acker beibehalten. Möglicherweise ergibt sich aus dieser Sicht auch ein neues Verständnis für apr. *wangan – ende* (III 51,20), *enwangen – endlich* (III 55,22), aus dem Enchiridion (Mažiulis 1970: 132, 136). Die semasiologische Zusammenstellung *wangan : enwangan*, stimmt hier sowohl mit dem Deutschen *Ende : endlich* als auch dem Litauischen überein *galas : pagaliau*. Für einen Acker, der am Flusslauf liegt, ist, unabhängig davon wie weit er sich ausdehnt, der Flusslauf eine natürliche Begrenzung, ein Ende, dass nicht so ohne weiteres durch weitere Rodung oder Umpflügen erweitert werden kann. Semasiologisch hierzu lit. *galas* 'Ende' aber auch '(kleines) Stück Land' – letzteres dürfte den vielen Ortsnamen mit -*gala* zugrunde liegen: *Baisogala*, *Dievogala*, *Tendžiogala*, *Ramygala*. Ähnlich *kraštas* das neben 'Ufer, Rand' eben auch 'Gegend, Land' bedeutet. Auch deutsch *Ende* kann für eine 'Wegstrecke' oder ein 'Stück Land' gebraucht werden, wenigstens umgangssprachlich. Smoczyński (2007: 720) plädiert ebenfalls für die Zusammengehörigkeit des litauischen Apellativs mit den ON und den o.g. Formen im Lettischen und Altpreußischen, allerdings ohne die Frage der Bedeutungsentwicklung hin zu 'Acker' zu berühren.

Wie eingangs erwähnt, sollte eine lettische Form nicht *vanga* sondern **vuog-* lauten. In dieser Konstellation ist der Ausfall des anlautenden *v-* denkbar, so wird argumentiert bzw. eher stillschweigend angenommen (Būga [1913] 1958: 513; ME IV 413). Belege für diese Annahme werden nicht gebracht. Es findet sich aber das Gegenteil, nämlich zusätzliches *v-*, so in *vodze* [*vuodze*] (BW 30796, Var. 8; ME) 'Kreuzotter o.ä.' : *odze* 'ds.', lit. *angis* 'ds.' oder im Litauischen *vuoga* neben *uoga* 'Beere' u.a. (Zinkevičius 1966: 188). Trotzdem sei die Möglichkeit eingeräumt. Als zugehörig vorgeschlagen werden einerseits *odzīte* (mit *uô*) 'eine sumpfige Stelle im Wald' und nach dem Liedtext ... *matus uodzītē izmazgāja ... kumeliņus uodzītē dzirdināja ... es iekritu* (Var.: *apmirku*) *uodzītē* (Var.: *upītē*) (BW 16520) 'ein kleiner Bach' und der FN *Odze* (mit *ùo*) (ME IV 413). Andererseits der FN *Ogre* [*Ùogre*] (Būga [1913] 1958: 512), im Oberlauf *Ogriņa* [*Ùogriņa*] genannt (Baluodė 1994: 208). Für den letztgenannten FN wurde, gerade auch wegen des fehlenden *v* im Anlaut, stattdessen ein Vergleich mit den baltischen Aalnamen vorgeschlagen (LEW 1163). Das wären *ungurỹs*, dial. *ingurys* im Litauischen, apr. *Angurgis* – *Oel* (E565), der See *Engure*[9] in Kurland, 1253 als *stagnum angere* belegt (Balode 1998: 48) und finn. *ankerias*, est. *angerjas* etc., Entlehnungen aus dem Baltischen (Būga 1959: 325), die ebenfalls auf anlautendes *an-* deuten in einem frühen Stadium der baltischen Sprachen, aus denen entlehnt wurde. Angesichts der guten Vergleichsmöglichkeiten für *ungurỹs*, sl. **ǫgorĭ* (Smoczyński 2007: 703) muss man die formal zulässige Idee, dass es sich bei *ung-* um eine Saṁprasāraṇa-Schwundstufe zu idg. **ṷeng-* 'krümmen' (vgl. LIV 682) handelt,[10] der gegenüber die verbreitete Schwundstufe mit *ving-* eine Innovation ist, fallen lassen, so schön das auch semantisch passen würden für den sich windenden und schlängelnden Fisch.

---

[9] Der Name des Fisches ist im Lettischen nicht erhalten, kann aber aus ON als bestanden habend rekonstruiert werden (Laumane 1973: 13).

[10] Lett. *jiûdze* (BW 31347, Var.1) und *vûdze* (BW 30796, Var.8) werden als **ûdze* 'Otter' (die Schlange nicht der Fischotter) gelesen (ME IV 406) und würden dann in der Ablautstufe mit lit. *ungurys* übereinstimmen.

Zudem ist lit. *vingurys* ja tatsächlich für den Aal belegt (LKŽ XIX 467) und *vingilis*, *vingiulis* nennt die Querder, die Larven des Flussneunauges, und wohl auch erwachsene Neunaugen (LKŽ XIX 457ff.). Nicht unerwähnt bleiben darf an dieser Stelle est. *vingerjas* 'Schlammbeißer – Misgurnus fossilis', ein Fisch, der ganz ähnlich den vorgenannten schlangenförmig ist und sich schlängelnd bewegt und litauisch *vijūnas* aber auch *vingilis* (LKŽ XIX 458) genannt wird gegenüber lett. *pīkste*, *spiga*, *piuka* u.a. (Laumane 1973: 155ff.) und offensichtlich aus irgendeiner baltischen Quelle **vinger-is* o.ä. entlehnt ist.

Möglicherweise ist lit. *ungurỹs* aber gar nicht schwundstufig, sondern das anlautende *u* ist durch Assimilation an das *u* des Suffixes entstanden.

Lett. *odzīte* fällt mit dem Diminutiv von *oga* 'Beere' zusammen. Und dieses Diminutiv ist auch in der Bedeutung 'eine Stelle im Walde, wo Beerenstauden wachsen' belegt (ME IV 413), als Eigenname? Für die oben genannten Belege *odzīte* 'eine sumpfige Stelle im Wald' fehlt eine genaue Angabe, was man denn mit "Sumpf" hier meint. Denkbar wäre, dass es sich um einen Typ Kiefernmoorwald handelt, dann wären hier Heidelbeere, Rauschbeere, Preiselbeere, Moosbeere, Moltebeere – sicher nicht alle gleichzeitig, je nach Bedingungen – zu erwarten. Und damit wäre der Name *odzīte* als zu *oga* gehörig zu verstehen. Auch das Bächlein, das ja nur einmal erwähnt ist kann ein Eigenname sein, schließlich gibt es auch lit. *Uogė* (FN), *Uogys* (FN), *Uoginėlis* (See), *Uogynė* (Moor) u.a., wozu Vanagas (1981a: 353) eben auch lett. *Odze* (FN; Wiese), *Odzene* (Wiese), *Odziene* (FN) stellt. Weitere ähnliche Eigennamen sind lit. *Spangė* (Moor), lett. *Spaņģupurvs*, als Wald ausgewiesen, dann dem Namen nach ein Moorwald, die ich im Gegensatz zu Vanagas (1981a: 311) zu *spanguolė* 'Moosbeere' stelle sowie der in Varianten mehrfach anzutreffende FN *Serbenta* : *serbenta* 'Johannisbeere'.

Kurz, die lettischen Belege, die als Reflexe eines *o*-stufigen *vanga* aufgefasst werden können sind sehr bescheiden.

Betrachten wir die anderen Ablaustufen. Da ist zunächst *vingis* 'Bogen, Kurve; Umweg', davon abgeleitet *vingiris*, *-as* 'Thalictrum spp., Filipendula spp.' u.v.a.m. davon wiederum *vingirykštis* 'Mädesüß – Filipendula spp.; Schlangenknöterich – Bistorta officinalis[11]', beide letztgenannte Bedeutungen bereits im 17. Jh. belegt: *Schlangen=Kraut – Wingurykßtis* (C II 439) und *Meht Kraut – Wingirykßtis* (C II 30). Die Pflanzennamen liegen im Litauischen und Lettischen in zahlreichen Varianten vor, lit. *vangarykštis*, *vangurūkščia*, *vengarūkštis*, *vendrykščia*, *vienrykštis*, *vindrykštis* (Gritėnienė 2006: 157f.), *vunguriūkštis* (LKŽ XIX 986) u.v.a.m. sowie lett. *vīgrieze*, *vedriekši*, *vīderksne*, *vīdrikste*, *vijgrieste* u.a. (EO 419ff.). Weiterhin lit. *viñgras* 'Igelkolben – Sparganium spp.' (LKŽ XIX 463).

---

[11] Wissenschaftliche Pflanzennamen sind nach Zander (2000) aktualisiert.

Der PfN *vengiarykštė*, *vingerýkštis* u.a., lett. *vīgrieze* wird in der linguisti-
schen Literatur häufig genannt, zumeist im Kontext mit *vaivorykštė* 'Regenbogen' als Evidenz dafür, dass *rykštė* 'Rute, Gerte' hier nicht als Bestandteil eines
Kompositums anzusehen ist, sondern durch Resegmentierung aus -*r(i)*- + Suffix
-*(y)kštė* entstand bzw. volksetymologisch auch so umgedeutet wurde (Būga
1959: 323, 326; Skardžius 1943: 24, 373, 404; LEW 1223; LEV 528; Kabašinskaitė 1998: 41). Für den gegenwärtigen Gebrauch der PfN ist aber oft Anlehnung an *rykštė* anzunehmen, woraus eine Umformung von *vingirýkštis* zu *vin-
giarýkštė* mit Einfügung von *a* oder *o* an der angenommenen Kompositionsstelle
folgt. Ebenso ist die Entstellung des angenommen Erstgliedes zu beobachten:
ilgarykštė, *langarykštė*, u.a. (Gritėnienė 2006: 157).

Karulis (LEV 528, 534) sieht in lett. *vīgr*- < *vingr*- das gleiche Element wie
vingrs, lit. *vingrùs* 'gewunden, verschlungen', würde dann den PfN also als
'Gewundenes' o.ä. interpretieren. Diese Sicht vertritt auch Gritėnienė (2006:
157), die *ving*- als Attribut auf den gebogenen blütenbesetzten Spross bezieht
und *rykštė* auf die Form der Blütenrispe – anscheinend sogar im etymologischen
Sinne.[12] Mit dieser Sicht schwer zu vereinbaren ist die Deutung von -*(y)kštė* als
Suffix, denn der Stamm an den dieses angefügt wird, sollte substantivisch nicht
adjektivisch sein. Zudem zeigen die litauischen Formen nicht *vingr*- wie in
vingrùs, sondern *vinger*- oder *vingir*- was als Basis den PfN *vingìris* 'Thalictrum spp.; Filipendula spp.' wahrscheinlich macht. Derartiges muss auch dem
lett. *vīderksne*, *vīdrēksnis*, *vīdrieksne* etc. (EO 420) zu Grunde gelegen haben,
über balt. *vingir*- > lett. **vindzir*-, mit lett. -*ksn*- statt lit. -*kšt*-. Ein anderer Reflex der gleichen Form dürfte *vidzirksne* sein, stattdessen in der Anfangssilbe
gekürzt. In Bezug auf die Funktion des Suffixes lit. -*kšt*- wäre dann noch zu be-
merken, dass dieser einen pejorativen Anstrich haben kann, vgl. lit. dial. *kiau-
lykštė* 'mageres Schwein' (LKG I 282), aber auch nur Zugehörigkeit ausdrücken
kann, wie in *šeiminykštis* 'Familienangehöriger, Gesinde' (LKG I 414).

Diese PfN dürften sich kaum auf gebogene Triebe beziehen, sondern auf
den Standort vorzüglich auf Wiesen im Flussbogen wie lit. *lankas*, russ. *луг*
'Bogen; Wiese'. Ein derartiger Standort ist allen bisher genannten Pflanzen gemein: Thalictrum spp., Filipendula spp., Bistorta officinalis, Sparganium spp.,
letztgenannte unmittelbar am oder im Wasser.

Liukkonen (1999: 21) rekonstruiert als Quelle für finn. *angervo* 'Filipendula
ulmaria' balt. dial. **vangar-vā* mit dissimilativem Verlust des anlautenden *v*- im

---

[12] Dazu wird auch der Gattungsname *Filipendula* als auf die langen Staubfäden (lat. *fī-
lum* 'Faden'), die hängen sollen (lat. *pendula*) bezogen (Gritėnienė 2006: 158). Dies
ist indessen unwahrscheinlich, denn der Name geht auf die Brüder Bauhin zurück
und nennt F. vulgaris nach den fädenförmigen Wurzeln an denen die Knollen "hängen" (Genaust 1996: 250), Botaniker hätten hier wohl sonst lat. *stamen* 'Staubblatt'
verwendet.

Finnischen.[13] Denkbar wäre wohl auch *vanger-vā oder gar *vangir-vā, vgl. lit. žirnis : finn. herne 'ds.' (vgl. Liukkonen 1999: 161). Beeindruckend ist die exakte Übereinstimmung in der Bedeutung. Hinzuzufügen ist est. angervaks 'Filipendula ulmaria' und angerpist 'F. vulgaris'.[14]

An den obigen Beispielen konnte bereits ersehen werden, dass die litauischen Belege in Hinblick auf Anlaut und Wurzelvokal stärker variieren als die lettischen, wo kein *vanger- als Fortsetzung der Quelle für die Entlehnung ins Finnische zu erkennen ist. Insbesondere für das Litauische erhebt sich ferner die Frage, ob die Formen mit a in der Wurzel auf vang- zurückgehen, was dann mit altlit. vanga 'Acker' zu verbinden wäre und auch als Quelle für die ostseefinn. PfN taugte. Oder ob es sich bloß um phonetische Varianten handelt. Insbesondere dann, wenn man, wie in vangurūkščia 'Filipendula ulmaria' anscheinend einen -u-Stamm statt des sonst vorhandenen -i-Stammes hat. Ein -u-Stamm *vanger-u- könnte dann ähnlich wie *ling-u- : lengvas (Smoczyński 2007: 346) zu dem gesuchten *vanger-vā- geworden sein. Natürlich sind auch andere Prozesse denkbar und es ist hier müßig auf Details wie Vokallänge oder Betonung zu setzen. Insbesondere für vingiarūkštis 'Bistorta officinalis' (Gritėnienė 2006: 127), die zeitweilig als Polygonum bistorta klassifiziert war und auch sonst große Ähnlichkeit mit den rūgtis, rūgštis genannten Pflanzen der Gattung Polygonum hat, kann das ū durch Assoziationen an rūgštis erworben sein. Die Schreibweise von vingiarūkštis mit k ist dabei irrelevant, vgl. lit. augti 'wachsen' : aukštas 'hoch, groß', wo sich die phonetische gegenüber der zeitweilig von Būga favorisierten etymologischen Schreibweise /augštas/ durchgesetzt hat.

Mit der Bedeutung als Bogen verträglich sind auch die beiden seltenen Bezeichnungen des Regenbogens lit. vangarykštė (LKŽ XVIII 113) und vingiorykštė (LKŽ XIX 458), wobei die Bedeutung 'Regenbogen' aber wohl sekundär erworben wurde, durch Anklang an übliches vaivorykštė 'ds.'.

Die Schwundstufe vingis, und hier wiederum mit dem r-Suffix als vinger-, liegt auch dem FN Wingeruppe (1557 erwähnt, Ksp. Budwethen, Kr. Ragnit, zit. Deltuvienė 2006: 265f.) zugrunde, auch wenn Deltuvienė ein *Vingrup- ansetzt. Ähnliche FN sind auch in Litauen zahlreich vorhanden: Vingis, Vingiai, Vingainis, Vingarė, Vingutis, Vingelupis, Vingra, Vingrė, Vengrė, Vingerinė, Vingerykščia, Vingirykštė, Vendrykštis (Vanagas 1981a: 372, 385f.). Vanagas (1981a: 385) sieht hierbei allerdings Vingerinė als direkte Ableitung vom PfN vingiris 'Thalictrum spp.' und entsprechend Vingerykščia etc. als Ableitung von PfN, unter Hinweis auf Flurnamen von Wiesen Vingirė, Vingerykštė, Vingerykštynė u.a., wo eine solche Ableitung vom PfN wesentlich sicherer ist. Ferner,

---

[13] Denkbar auch die Dissimilation in der Quelle, so wie ingirykštis (Gritėnienė 2006: 157) neben vingirykštis besteht, ist *angar- neben vangarykštis etc. möglich.

[14] Damit erweist sich dann Venckutės (2001: 126) Bemerkung, dass finn. angervo keine Entsprechung in den anderen ostseefinn. Sprachen habe, als hinfällig.

und das ist für die ursprüngliche Fragestellung noch relevanter, gibt es mehrere FN *Vangà*, nebst derartigen Namen für Bruchwald, Moore und Weiden in Litauen und Lettland (Vanagas 1981a: 361f.). Die vorgestellte Entlehnungsrichtung bei Vanagas (1981a: 361) "iš liet. *vanga* 'dirva, laukas'" folgt einfach dem Schema bezeugtes Apellativ → FN und kann nicht überzeugen. In der Kartothek der lettischen Ortsnamen (LVK) lassen sich weitere Gewässer-, Flur- und Ortsnamen finden, die teilweise sogar das Verbreitungsareal ergänzen, z.B. *Vañʒarîte* (Nebenfluss der Lielupe, Kalnciems),[15] *Vañga* (Wiese, Limbaža), *Vanga* (Wiese, Lāde), *Vañga* (Gut, Kazdanga) u.a. Hinzuzufügen ist *Wang=Uppe* einer der Depkin (1401) bekannten Flüsse: "sind folgende so mir in Liefland bekandt [...] Wang=Uppe. im lemsalischen".

Auffällig ist eine gewisse semantische Sonderentwicklung der *e*-Stufe, *vengti* 'ausweichen, meiden' mit hier ansetzenden Weiterbildungen wie *vangstyti* 'sich ständig verstecken, regelmäßig meiden, simulieren', *vangus, vengus* 'faul, meidend, ausweichend' gegenüber den anderen oben diskutierten Formen. Am ehesten lässt sich eine solche übertragene Verwendung – insbesondere, wenn man idg. *u̯eng-* '(sich) krümmen' ansetzt (LIV 682) – noch über Anwendung auf Bewegungen, die man macht, um beim Kampf den Waffen des Gegners auszuweichen, erklären. Belege dafür gibt es allerdings nicht. Und für Übertragungen 'drehen, winden' → 'meiden' kann vielleicht noch lit. *išsisukti* beigebracht werden, ebenso wie gleichbedeutendes d. *sich herauswinden*. Neben der Verwandtschaft mit d. *wanken, winken*, wiederum in abweichender Bedeutung, fällt noch die sachliche Entsprechung der Sippe, die auf idg. *u̯enk-* 'sich krümmen, biegen' (LIV 683, Kluge 1999: 874) beruht, auf.

Anhand des Lettischen *vēdzele* 'Quappe – Lota lota', als *wehdsele – eine Qvappe* bei Fürecker (F2 519), wäre eine baltische Form *vengelē* zu rekonstruieren. Da die Quappe auch ein langer schlanker Fisch ist, würde er sich hier neben den bereits genannten Aal, Neunauge und Schlammbeißer gut einreihen. Dagegen steht allerdings die litauische Form, die *vėgė̃lė̃, vėgėlė* lautet, bei Szyrwid *mientus / lacertus fluuialis, vulgô barbocha, wegiełe* (SD1 80). Die Etymologie des Wortes, das auch ins Livische als *vägāl* entlehnt wurde, gilt als unklar (LEW 1212; Smoczyński 2007: 727).[16] Zwar könnte man annehmen, dass das litauische Wort aus dem Lettischen entlehnt wurde; das zeitliche Fenster dafür müsste dann nach lett. *ē* < balt. **en* datieren aber vor lett. *dz(e)* < **g(e)*, wobei man aber eine teilweise Renormierung, also *g* in der Entlehnung trotz *dz* in der

---

[15] Im Mittellettischen, entfernt von den lybisch geprägten Dialekten. *Vañʒarîte* liegt wegen *ʒ = dz < *ǵ *vanger-* oder *vangir-* zugrunde mit späterer Assimilation des Suffixvokals an das *a* der Wurzel.

[16] Vielleicht kann man auch eine Kentumvariante zu lit. *vėžys* 'Krebs' annehmen, das seinerseits aber über keine gesicherte Etymologie verfügt und auch als *wähi* ins Estnische entlehnt wurde (Smoczyński 2007: 746).

Quelle, nicht ausschließen kann – zumal dieser Wechsel ja nicht statisch sondern grammatikalisiert ist, vgl. lett. *bargs* 'zornig, streng' : *bardzība* 'Zorn'. Alles in allem sehr unsicher, wozu noch kommt, dass es eigentlich keinen vernünftigen Grund gibt, den Namen des Süßwasserfisches aus dem Lettischen zu entlehnen. Anders wäre die Sache, wenn es sich um einen Meeresfisch handeln würde – denn immerhin reicht die historische Verbreitung des Litauischen nicht bis ans Meer. Hier könnte zumindest erwogen werden, ob nicht ursprünglich die Aalmutter Zoarces viviparus gemeint war – tatsächlich ein Meeresfisch, litauisch *jūrinė vėgėlė* genannt. Weiter kann vielleicht lit. *vėgis* 'Kringel; ringförmiges Gebäck', nur belegt in Joniškis und Žeimelis, also an der lettischen Grenze und offensichtlich (wegen *ģ*) daraus entlehnt lett. *veģis* (LKŽ XVIII 502), genannt werden. Hierzu ferner *vegio kunkalas*[17] 'Bachnelkenwurz – Geum rivale' (LBŽ 155). Wie aus lateinischem und deutschem Namen ersichtlich, wächst die Pflanze bevorzugt am Gewässer, auf feuchten Standorten. Es wäre also denkbar, dass sich das lit. Attribut *vegis* darauf bezieht und dahinter ein **vengis* oder **vingis* steckt. Schließlich seien noch lett. *Wehģeht – winken* (F1 301) und *Neweglis – ungestalt, ungeschaffen* (F1 166) bzw. *Neweglis – ungestalt, ungeschikt, heßlich* (F2 240) genannt. Das Verb deckt sich bestens mit der Entwicklung von **u̯eng-* '(sich) krümmen' zu d. *winken*, vorausgesetzt man zieht wiederum eine litauisch-lettische "Mischform" in Betracht, die hier aber weitaus plausibler ist als im Fall *vėgėlė*. Auch für *neweglis* gibt es im modernen Lettischen keine Belege. Aufgrund der variierenden Schreibweise kann man dies auch als **nevēglis* lesen. Semasiologisch möchte ich auf d. *unflexibel*, lit. *nelankstus* verweisen, die zwar formal 'unbeweglich' bedeuten, dies aber überwiegend übertragen verstehen; noch passender ist daher das etwas archaisch klingende *ungelenk* und aus der gleichen Wurzel aber ohne Verneinung *linkisch*.

Lett. dial. *vañga*[2] 'Heuschlag am Gewässer; niedrig gelegene, feuchte Wiese' reiht sich daher problemlos in den weiteren baltistischen Kontext ein, der da lautet mäandernde Flüsse und an diesen gelegene Wiesen.[18] Die Annahme eines

---

[17] LKŽ (XVIII 502) bietet als normierte Variante **vėgio kañkalas*, unter der Annahme, dass es sich bei dem von Matulionis gegebenen Pflanzennamen um eine aukštaitische Variante mit *un* statt *an* handelt. Möglich aber nicht sicher. Und Betonungen gibt Matulionis nun wirklich nicht. Sowohl *kankalas* 'Glocke u.a.' als auch *kunkalas* : *kukti* 'biegen, knicken', *sukukę* 'reif (Gerste), d.i. mit herabhängenden Ähren', *kunkti* 'biegen, wölben (intr.)' (Šeškauskaitė, Gliwa 2005: 73-78), lett. *kuncis* 'Lota lota' (Polanska 2002: 226), sind hier plausibel. Der Stängel ist zur Blütezeit geneigt; daran hängt die glockenähnliche Blüte.

[18] Für den geographischen Terminus ist der Vergleich mit ahd. *wang* 'Aue, Wiese, Feld', vielfach in süddeutschen und österreichischen ON enthalten, z.B. *Furtwangen*, verlockend. Die Rekonstruktion als **u̯engh-* (IEW 1149) würde dies zulassen – auf Kosten anderer Vergleiche. Semasiologisch ist der Vergleich in jedem Falle aufschlussreich.

baltischen Substrates mit anderem Verhalten bzgl. tautosyll. -an- wie dies ja mit dem Kurischen geschieht kann dann auf eine nicht näher zu bezeichnende Sprache im Norden ausgedehnt werden. Oder man nimmt eine frühzeitige Entlehnung in die finnougrischen Sprachen mit Konservierung von tautosyll. -an- und anschließender Rückentlehnung, ganz im Sinne von Kagaines "lokalen Finnougrismen", an. Zu bedenken ist dabei, dass bei vielen Entlehnungen aus den baltischen Sprachen in die finnougrischen die Quellsprache nicht sicher ist und man durchaus andere als die bis heute bezeugten Sprachen nicht ausschließen kann. Im Lettischen kommt erschwerend hinzu, dass die Reflexe, die aus *vanga* zu erwarten sind, mit anderen Lexemen zusammen gefallen sind, was den Nachweis erschwert. Dass hierzu Schwundstufe und *o*-Stufe alternierend verwendet werden, hat eine Parallele in lit. *lankas* 'Bogen, Wiese am Fluss', *įlanka* 'Bucht' neben lett. *līcis* 'Bucht, Flussbogen' im gleichen semantischen Bereich. Eine semantisch naheliegende Entlehnung aus dem Baltischen ist etwa finn. *luhta* 'Uferwiese, die im Frühjahr überschwemmt wird; feuchte Niederung; grasbewachsenes Ufer' mit Entsprechungen in den anderen ostseefinnischen Sprachen, z.B. est. *luht* 'Feuchtwiese'; die Entsprechungen lauten lit. *lukštas*, lett. *luksts* (SSA II 98).

Zu *vañga¹* 'Griff, Henkel; Schlinge' sind die Vergleichsmöglichkeiten bescheidener, aber wie man an lit. *lankas* 'Bogen am Fluss, Weide dortselbst' und *lankas* 'Henkel am Korb' sieht, kann man beide Bedeutungen recht gut miteinander verbinden. Auch hier gibt es keinen Grund, der gegen baltische Herkunft spricht.

2. Finn. *liiva*

Das etymologische Wörterbuch der finnischen Sprache (SSA II 75) unterscheidet zwei Begriffe *liiva¹* 'Sand, Schlamm' und *liiva²* 'Schleim, Seetang, etwas zu Brei gekochtes oder verfaultes'. Dabei wird für *liiva¹* 'Sand, Schlamm', est. *liiv* 'Sand', isch. & wot. *līva* 'ds.' baltische Herkunft angenommen, allerdings mit Fragezeichen, und als mögliches Kognat der Quelle auf lett. *glīve* 'Wasserblüte, grüner Schleim auf dem Wasser, Schlick, Schleim' verwiesen. Hingegen soll *liiva²* 'Schleim, Seetang, etwas zu Brei gekochtes oder verfaultes', mit Entsprechungen im Karelischen *liiva* und Lüdischen *līv* aus germ. *slīwa* stammen unter Hinweis auf an. *slý* 'schleimige Wasserpflanze' (IEW 663). Im älteren SKES (II 294) war für beide Begriffe gemeinsame Herkunft aus dem Baltischen angenommen worden. Die Trennung erscheint semantisch durchaus begründet. Unbefriedigend ist dabei jedoch, dass dem Begriff für Sand eine Quelle zugrundegelegt wird, die eher mit der zweiten Bedeutung korrespondiert, vgl. noch lit. *gleivė* 'Schleim', slow. *gliwa* 'eine Pilzart', idg. *glei̯H-*

'bestreichen, kleben bleiben' (LIV 190; Smoczyński 2003: 22f.). Das war sicher mit ein Grund warum der Vorschlag mit Fragezeichen versehen ist. Welchen Vorteil die germanische Etymologie gegenüber der baltischen hat, kann ich nicht erkennen. M.E. sind beide möglich. Angesichts der weiteren Entlehnungs-annahmen kann man derart aber dem Zirkel entkommen. Es wird nämlich finn., karelisch *liiva* 'Schlamm, Tang' als Quelle für russ. *лыва* 'Moor, Morast, Senke nach Regen, Bruchwald' angesehen (Vasmer 1967: 541; SSA II 75). Hieraus sei dann wiederum lett. *līvenis* 'Morast, sumpfiges Ufer', *līvis* 'Moor, Bruch, Sumpf' entlehnt (Vasmer 1967: 541). Dieser Argumentationskette folgend wurde sogar der apr. Flussname *Lywa* (1250 belegt, Pėteraitis 1992: 118) als finnougrischen Ursprungs deklariert (Górnowicz 1974: 234).

Einerseits trennt Vasmer (1967: 541f.) lett. *līvis* 'der Sumpf, eine moorige schwankende Stelle' (ME II 491) strikt von lett. *livens* 'moorig, schwankend' (ME II 491) und *lēvenis* 'moorige sich bewegende Stelle, ausgespülter Ufer-rand; Haufen, Menge' (ME II 463), und auch Endzelīns (ME II 491) erwägt eine Entlehnung von *līvis* aus dem Russischen *лыва*, andererseits sieht Vanagas (1981a: 195) einen Zusammenhang zwischen den FN lit. *Livinta, Lėvuo, Liuvy-nas*, und den Apellativen zur Bezeichnung von Moor und Morast lett. *līvenis, lēvenis, ļuvenis*, insbesondere in Hinblick auf thrak. **leva* 'Moor, morastige Stelle'[19] und *Leven* 'Name mehrerer Flüsse und Seen in Schottland und Eng-land[20]' kelt. Ursprungs (Duridanov 1969: 14, 89). Dabei spricht Vanagas bezüg-lich *līvenis, lēvenis, ļuvenis* von "ähnlichen Formen", ob damit auch Verwandt-schaft gemeint ist bleibt offen. Jedenfalls wird, da es zu den Eigennamen auch Apellative gibt, für Vanagas anscheinend ein wichtiges Kriterium, finnougri-sche Herkunft zurückgewiesen. Gleichfalls unklar ist, ob damit auch die Entleh-nung von lett. *līvis* aus dem Russischen zurückgewiesen wird; anscheinend wird das aber impliziert.

Zunächst ist zu prüfen, ob die Etymologie dieser Formen im Baltischen ge-klärt werden kann. So nicht, ist der Vergleich mit ähnlichen Begriffen auf dem Balkan und in Schottland ziemlich wertlos und kann auch einfach auf Zufall be-ruhen, zumal ja das thrakische Wort nur anhand der baltischen Wortbedeutung rekonstruiert wird.

Zweitens wurden bisher keine alternativen baltischen Quellen für eine mögliche Entlehnung in ostseefinnische Sprachen erörtert. Neben lett. *glīve* etc. zu idg. **gleiH-* 'bestreichen, kleben bleiben' kommen hier ggf. die genannten

---

[19] Nur belegt im Flurnamen *'Αβρολέβας* mit anhand der baltischen Wörter rekonstru-ierter Bedeutung (Duridanov 1969: 14). Die bei Theophrastos (Theophr. Chr. 470, 18 u. 20, Boor – die Quelle fehlt aber im Abkürzungsverzeichnis bei Duridanov) ge-gebene Beschreibung als 'Dickicht, Gestrüpp, Halde an der Tundža' (Durivdanov l.c.) deutet aber nicht unbedingt auf morastiges Gelände.

[20] [http://en.wikipedia.org/wiki/Leven], eingesehen am 19.5.2008.

Formen lett. *līvenis, lēvenis, ļuvenis* in Frage, wenn sich zeigen lässt, dass das *ī* nicht erst eine späte Dehnstufe ist. Formal würde auch *šlỹvas* 'krumm, schief', *šlìvas* 'ds.', *šlìvis, šlivỹs, šlỹvis* 'krummbeinige Person', *šlyvéti, šlỹvi, -ėjo* 'angelehnt stehen', *šlỹvinti, šlỹvoti* 'ds.', *Šlìvė* (FN, Veiveriai) zu idg. * k̂leį̯-* 'sich anlehnen' in Frage kommen (Gliwa 2008; Hyllested, Gliwa 2009). Die Formen mit Suffix *-u̯o-* sind zwar semantisch anders entwickelt, aber mit *-no-* liegt vor *šlỹnas* 'weißer Ton, Kaolin; Gley', auch in FN *Šlỹna* nebst benachbarter *Šlynáitė* bei Raseiniai. Hierzu möglicherweise auch die FN *Šlėna* (Jonava), *Šlėnupỹs* (Gudžiūnai) und das Moor *Šlė̃nė* (Giedraičiai), wenn man berücksichtigt, dass in vielen Dialekten neben der Form *šlieti* auch die Form *šlėti* besteht (bei Szyrwid *przystosuie /co do czego/ Accomodo, aliud ad aliud, apto, transfero. prißleiu/priliginu* SD3 367) (Gliwa 2008: 55ff.).

Das lettische Material ist recht umfangreich, wobei die Zugehörigkeit noch zu diskutieren ist. Zu dem bereits o.g. kommt lett. *līvans* 'niedrig; flach' (Varakļāni, ME II 491), *livens* 'moorig, schwankend' (Salaca, ME II 491), *līveris* 'Herumtreiber; Hafer', *līviņa* 'Kiebitz' (ME II 491), *liverêt* 'ohne bestimmte Arbeit leben, bummeln', *liverêties* 'wacklig sein, sich hin und her bewegen' (*ap meitām liverēties*) (ME II 475), *liveris* 'ein loser wackliger Teil eines Gegenstands; jemand der sich der Arbeit zu entziehen sucht', *livers* 'eine moorige sich bewegende Stelle' (ME II 476), *lèvere, -is* 'Fetzen, Lumpen; Zerlumpter; Eingeweide (Fische); Klumpen; nicht anliegendes, lose herabhängendes Gewand' (ME II 464), *lēvins* 'zum Trocknen ausgebreitetes Heu' (ME II 464). Ferner *ļuns* 'moorige sich bewegende Stelle', *ļuvenis* 'ds.', *ļuvens* 'weich, schlaff; sumpfig, moorig' (*gar ezermalu puopenis ir tik ļuvens, ka grūti pa viņu iet*). Im Litauischen haben wir hier *liūnas*[21] 'Schwingrasen' als genaue Entsprechung zu *ļuns* und sonst die FN *Livinta, Lėvuo, Liuvynas*. Aus dem Altpreußischen fehlt leider belastbares vergleichbares Material.

Etymologische Bemerkungen bei ME umfassen den bereits genannten Verdacht, dass *līvis* aus dem Russischen *льіва* stammen könnte (ME II 491), dass *livers* aus *luvers*, vgl. lett. *zivis* : lit. *žuvis* 'Fisch' u.a., stamme und mit *льіва* verwandt (ME II 476) und dass *lêsa* anscheinend mit sl. *lēsa* 'Geflecht' identisch sei (ME II 462). Ferner wird *ļuvens* mit *ļuns* und *ļūt* 'zusammenknicken' verbunden (ME II 545). Fraenkel (LEW 380f.) sieht in lit. *liūnas*, lett. *ļūns, ļuvens, ļūt* Ausdrücke onomatopoetischen Ursprungs wie *liulėti*, die sich dann auf das Schwanken, Schaukeln beziehen.

Būga (1959: 297f.) legt *Lėvuõ*, lett. *lēvens* etc. idg. *lew-, *lēw-* zugrunde, wozu ferner *paliáuti* 'abbrechen', *lavonas* 'Leichnam' (= *paliovusio gyventi žmogaus kūnas*), *lėveris* 'Trottel, Lotter', ferner stellt er hierzu *liũvis* 'Anhalten, Pause, Stop' : *lióvimas* (1959: 135).

---

[21]   Am Rande sei bemerkt, dass dieses Wort auch in Dialekten im Polnischen, Russischen und Weißrussischen als Lehnwort anzutreffen ist (Laučiutė 1982: 32).

Smoczyński (2003: 74f.; 2007: 361) stellt lit. *liūnas* 'Schwingrasen', *liūtas* 'regnerisch', *liūtis* 'heftiger, langer Regen; Regenzeit', *liūtinas*, *liùtinas* 'dreckig, schlammig', *liūtynas* 'Morast' und wohl auch *liūgas* 'Tümpel; Schlamm, Morast; Schwingrasen' zu idg. *leu̯H₃-* 'waschen'. Dazu noch lett. *ļavêt* 'wackeln (vor Fett)', *ļava* 'eine moorige sich bewegende Stelle, ein zuwachsender See'. Der FN *Liuvýnas* zeigt, wie auch lett. *ļuvens* 'sumpfig, moorig; weich schlaff' und lett. *ļuvu* in der Flexion von *ļùt*, *ļūstu*, Laryngalhiat (vgl. Smoczyński 2003: 75). Ausgangspunkt für *li-* liegt in *leu-C-* > (ost)balt. *liáuC-*, von wo aus es verallgemeinert in andere Stufen wurde.

Somit stellt sich die Frage ob in der Konstellation vor Vokal *leu̯H-V-* *lēv-V-* oder *lev-V-* zu erwarten ist, während vor Konsonant *leu-C-* folgt > (ost)balt. *liáuC-*. Dabei wird der Wechsel *a : o* wie in *liáuti : lióvė*, *kráuti : króvė* durch Dehnstufe zur *o*-Stufe erklärt (Smoczyński 2007: 310, 349), sicher plausibel angesichts der Tendenz gerade im Präteritum Dehnstufe einzusetzen. Aber wäre es nicht sinnvoller hier Laryngaldehnung anzunehmen? Das würde mit dem Akut besser passen und in struktureller Übereinstimmung mit der Formulierung, z.B. lit. *árti*, lett. *aȓt* 'pflügen' < *ārC- < p-idg. *H₂erH₃-C- (Smoczyński 2006: 189) oder *lāu̯V- > lit. *lóva* 'Bett, Liege' (Smoczyński 2003: 74). Wenn man der Zwischenstufe *ārC- oder *lāu̯V- tatsächlich Berechtigung einräumt und dies nicht nur als ganz formellen Marker und darin Vorgänger des Akuts ansieht, dann ist ganz analog *-āvC-, bzw. *-ēvC- nicht abwegig – schließlich haben wir ja auch in lit. *lóva* den Akut. Somit ließe sich, wie das ja auch Būga schon ähnlich vorgeschlagen hatte, zu einer Wurzel der Struktur *leu̯H- sowohl *lēv-* als auch *lev-* als zugehörig ansehen. Lit. *Lévuõ*, acc. *Léveni̯*, lett. *lēvens* sind also mit *liūnas* zu verbinden. Formen mit *i* sind durch die lettische Besonderheit *-uvi-/-ubi-* zu *-ivi-/-ibi-* werden zu lassen (Rudzīte 1993: 126) zu erklären, die teilweise auch im Litauischen anzutreffen ist, etwa *živis* neben *žuvis* 'Fisch'. Für den FN *Livinta* (bei Kaišiadorys) muss man aber die Zugehörigkeit nicht aufrecht erhalten, abenso für den FN apr. *Lywa*, denn hier ist Ursprung aus *-uv-* weniger annehmbar, passend ist vielleicht Anschluss an *lieti* 'regnen, gießen', *lietus* 'Regen' zu idg. *lei̯H₂-* 'gießen'. Wobei dann aber eher *y* (*ī*) statt *i* zu erwarten ist und *liH-u̯o-* 'gießend; d.i. überschwemmend' als Ausgangsform anzusehen ist.

Neben *leu̯H₃-* 'waschen' steht *leu̯H-* 'abschneiden, lösen', woraus *lavonas*, *liautis* (Smoczyński 2003: 72-74; 2007: 349). Smoczyński (2003: 72-74) stellt hierher ferner lett. *ļuvens* 'weich schlaff', *ļiverîgs* 'schlaff, lose, nachlässig', lit. *liáunas*, *liaũnas* 'beweglich, flexibel; schlank; schwach',[22] *lóva* 'Bett, Liege'.

---

[22] Und wohl auch *liauzgas*, *liauznas* ähnlicher Bedeutung mit unklarem *z*.

Die Trennung beider Wurzel ist in der Tat schwierig, worauf auch Smoczyński (2003: 72) hinweist. An vielen Stellen wohl gar unmöglich und vermutlich haben sich beide Bedeutungsgruppen auch gegenseitig beeinflusst. Zu der
Bedeutungsgruppe 'Morast, Schwingrasen' bedarf es eines sachlichen Kom-
mentars, hier wurden in ME allerlei Zitate gesammelt ohne aber offensichtlich
den Landschaftstyp in natura zu kennen. Moorige Gewässer, die durchaus auch
langsam fließend seien können neigen unter bestimmten Bedingungen zum Zuwachsen mit Torfmoosen. Auf dieser Torfmoosschicht siedeln sich dann Seg-
gen, Binsen u.a. an, bei hinreichender Dicke auch Kiefern und Moorbirken. Das
besondere am Schwingrasen ist, dass er nicht mit dem Grund verbunden ist, sondern auf dem Wasser schwimmt. Daraus resultiert erstens das schwingende Verhalten der lose verbundenen Schicht bei Belastung und auch die Gefahr einzu-
sinken und ggf. im tiefen Wasser darunter zu ertrinken. Stücke solcher Schwingrasen können sich vom Ufer ablösen und auf dem Gewässer treiben, sogar mit
Baumbestand. Gewässer können auch komplett zuwachsen und sind dann
besonders trügerisch, da kein Wasser sichtbar ist. Mehr oder weniger deutlich
weisen alle o.g. lettischen Begriffe wie auch lit. *liũnas* auf diesen Biotop, wobei
der Bewuchs sich natürlich von Fall zu Fall unterscheiden kann. Die Verbindung mit *$leuH_3$*- 'waschen' ist plausibel, denn der Biotop ist untrennbar mit
Wasser verbunden und bei Trittbelastung sinkt man unweigerlich ins Nasse. Genauso gut passt aber auch *leuH*- 'abschneiden, lösen', wenn man die baltische
Entwicklung hin zu lit. *liaũnas* 'beweglich, flexibel; schlank; schwach', lett. *ļuvens* 'weich, schlaff; moorig', *ļverîgs* 'schlaff, lose, nachlässig' betrachtet – in
dieser Sicht gäbe es nicht mal einen Grund *ļuvens* 'weich, schlaff' und 'moorig,
sumpfig' voneinander zu trennen. Lett. *līviņa* 'Kiebitz' ist am ehesten als Zuge-
hörigkeitsbildung zum Biotop anzusehen, oder onomatopoetisch.

Damit ist es extrem unwahrscheinlich, dass lett. *līvis* aus dem Russischen
льива stammt. Russ. *льива* könnte theoretisch auch als *luH-ueH_2*- ein Erbwort
sein. Aber die begrenzte Verbreitung spricht für die allgemein angenommene
Entlehnung.

Damit besteht sogar die Möglichkeit, dass lett. *līvis* o.ä. die Quelle für finn.
liiva[1] 'Sand, Schlamm', mit Einschränkungen wegen unsicherer Datierung von
-*uvi*-/-*ubi*- zu -*ivi*-/-*ibi*- und damit nicht übereinstimmendem Stamm von finn.
liiva. Die Bedeutungsentwicklung hin zu Sand hat man ähnlich auch in lett. *lêsa*
'Lagerung des Getreides, Flachses; ein loses schwimmendes Rasenstück am Ufer;
auf dem Wasser ineinander verwachsenen Pflanzen; eine moorige, sich unter
dem Fuße bewegende Stelle; eine Moosschicht auf einem Gewässer; ein zähes
Rasenstück; eine Sandbank' (ME II 464). Trotzdem halte ich lit. *šlỹvas* 'krumm,
schief' für eine bessere Quelle, unter der Annahme, dass in der Gebersprache
die Bedeutung eher denen entsprach, die im Litauischen mit Suffix *-no-* anzutreffen sind: *šlýnas* 'weißer Ton, Kaolin; Gley'. Lett. *glīve* 'Wasserblüte, grüner

Schleim auf dem Wasser, Schlick, Schleim' ist meines Erachtens keine geeignete Quelle für finn. *liiva¹* 'Sand, Schlamm'.

Hingegen ist lett. *glīve* 'Wasserblüte, grüner Schleim auf dem Wasser, Schlick, Schleim' sachlich sehr gut als Quelle für *liiva²* 'Schleim, Seetang, etwas zu Brei gekochtes oder verfaultes' annehmbar, nicht schlechter als das favorisierte germ. *slīwa*.

3. Finn. *hauki* 'Hecht', est. *haug* 'ds.'

Liukkonen (1999: 40-42) schlägt für finn. *hauki* 'Hecht' eine baltische Etymologie vor, die an dem Problem leidet, dass die angenommene baltische Form *šaukē* nirgends belegt ist. Die im Ursprung etwas ältere und konkurrierende Etymologie setzt ein urslawisches *ščaukā* 'Hecht' an (Koivulehto 2006: 180). Koivulehto (2006: 181) billigt dieser Etymologie auch eine hohe Beweiskraft zu: "Es sollte nunmehr unstrittig sein, dass die Berührungen zwischen den Urfinnen und Urslaven bereits vor der sogenannten späturfinnischen[23] Zeit begonnen haben. Und natürlich können nicht nur die (bisher) zwei Wörter, die dies explizit beweisen, die einzigen Lehnwörter dieser Zeit sein." Das andere beweiskräftige Wort ist finn. *hirsi* 'Balken, Bohle', estn. *hirs* 'Zaunstange', das aus ursl. *(d)žirdi-* stamme, woher russ. жердь 'Stange' (Koivulehto 2006: 180). Koivulehto lässt dabei die Deutung Liukkonens für *hauki* außen vor, ebenso wie die Erörterung von Nieminen (1949), wonach *hirsi* baltischen Ursprungs sein könnte und mit lit. *žardas, žardis* 'Stecken, Stange, Bock' zu vergleichen ist. Dies ist insofern auffällig, als die Beweiskraft einer Etymologie nicht mit einem Beweis im mathematischen Sinne verglichen werden kann, sondern bestenfalls ein Argument darstellt, das zudem schwächer wird, wenn es auch alternative Erklärungsmöglichkeiten gibt.

Kallio (2006) hat im gleichen Band ein ähnliches Thema wie Koivulehto und vielfach identisches Material. Er erwähnt beide Alternativen zu der slawischen Deutung, vermerkt zu *hirsi* aber "… because the crucial zero-grade is unattested from Baltic. Therefore, the Baltic loan etymology must indeed be considered inferior to the Slavic one." (2006: 159). Zu Liukkonens Deutung gibt es folgenden Kommentar: "Once again, the Slavic loan etymology seems not to be convincing enough for Liukkonen (1999: 40-42), who would like to replace the Early Middle Slavic source *ščaukā* (< *škeukā*) with its Baltic pseudo-cognate *šaukē* (< *skoukē*) although no such word is attested from Baltic. At least I remain unconvinced as to what grounds we have to reject the phonologically and semantically faultless Slavic source in favour of his fabricated Baltic source,

---

[23] Traditionell und nach Koivulehto (2006: 181) beginnt diese Periode um 500 BC.

whose previous existence he circularly bases on Early Proto-Finnic *šavki alone." (2006: 159f.). Dabei wird das Hauptargument von Liukkonen doch sehr deutlich – der enorme geographische Abstand zwischen Urslaven und Ostseefinnen zu der fraglichen Zeit, bzw. phonetische Unmöglichkeit für diese Entlehnung zur Zeit als die Slawen Nachbarn der Finnen wurden (Liukkonen 1999: 40). Was daran nicht zu verstehen ist? Immerhin versucht Kallio (2006: 162) dies zu umgehen, indem er argumentiert: "As loanwords are indeed borrowed from people instead of peoples, all we basically really need is only one Early (Middle) Slavic speaking trader who just happened to wander far enough to the north." Handel passiert und Handel führt zu Lehnwörtern, sicher. Aber 'Hecht' gehört nicht zu der dazu prädestinierten Gruppe. Daran ändert auch Koivulehtos (2006: 181) Bemerkung, "dass der Name eines großen und als Nahrung wichtigen Fisches übernommen wurde, ist nicht verwunderlich: ist doch auch finn. *lohi* 'Lachs' aus dem Baltischen übernommen worden" nichts, denn die Situation lässt sich nicht vergleichen, da die Ostseefinnen mit den Balten in unmittelbarer Nachbarschaft und wohl auch teils vermischt mit Zweisprachigkeit wohnten.

Die Diskussion ist geprägt von verschiedenen Interpretationen zum Thema Balto-Slawisch. Wenn man diese Gemeinschaft anerkennt, ist es ziemlich egal ob man das Ur-Baltisch, Balto-Slawisch, Slawo-Baltisch oder gar Ur-Slawisch nennt und mit allerlei Proto-, Vor-, Früh- versieht, genauso wie es egal ist, ob man das nun als Sprache, Dialektgemeinschaft oder Isoglossengemeinschaft bezeichnet (vgl. Hock 2006). Das Deutsche wird gewöhnlich als Sprache bezeichnet, doch wird es keinem in den Kram kommen, zu bestreiten, dass es gleichzeitig eine Dialekt- und Isoglossengemeinschaft ist. Während Koivulehto (2006) seinen Aufsatz "Wie alt sind die Kontakte zwischen finnisch-ugrisch und balto-slawisch?" nennt, fällt das Baltische bei Kallio (2006) im Titel weg "On the Earliest Slavic Loanwords in Finnic". Während Liukkonen (1999: 13) in bestimmten Fällen "die Termini Baltisch und Balto-Slavisch praktisch synonym" verwendet,[24] scheint dies Kallio ganz analog für Slawisch und Balto-Slawisch zu machen. Darauf deutet seine Aussage: "On the other hand, as Early (Middle) Slavic was still a Balto-Slavic dialect rather than a Balto-Slavic language, many of the loanwords traditionally regarded as Baltic could similarly be taken for Early (Middle) Slavic" (Kallio 2006: 163). Schön. Wenn man also deutsche Entlehnungen im, sagen wir mal, Kaschubischen, hat, dann werden die am ehesten niederdeutsche Quellen haben – da nun aber das Bairische wie auch das Niederdeutsche ein deutscher Dialekt ist, so können wir diese Entlehnungen mit Kallio jetzt auch als Bairisch klassifizieren. Boah.

---

[24] Was angesichts dessen, dass Entlehnungen dem Dialektbereich des Balto-Slawischen entstammten, aus dem sich die baltischen Sprachen entwickelten, durchaus plausibel ist.

"Es erscheint mir als ein gesundes Prinzip in der Wissenschaft, sich mit einfachen und durchschaubaren Erklärungsprinzipien zu begnügen, solange die Hoffnung auf ihren Erfolg nicht in einsichtiger Weise falsifiziert, also wenigstens als höchst unwahrscheinlich erkannt ist" (von Weizsäcker 1993: 41). Einfacher ist die Entlehnung aus der benachbarten Sprache als aus der entfernten – jedenfalls angesichts der damaligen Kommunikationsmöglichkeiten. Und wenn man das Konzept des Wanderworts ins Spiel bringt, so sollte dies auch sachlich mit dem Weiterreichen eines neuen Gegenstandes oder Prozesses verbunden sein – und die Transitsprachen nicht unbedingt aussparen.[25]

Ich halte es ist in diesem Falle für leichter eine nicht belegte Schwundstufe zu *žardis* anzunehmen[26] als die Entlehnung aus entfernten Sprachen. Apophonie ist in den baltischen Sprachen in begrenztem Maße immer noch produktiv und war zweifellos früher verbreiteter; die Annahme von *žird-* neben *žard-* ist daher hinreichend trivial – ganz im Gegensatz zur Vorverlagerung der slawisch-finnischen Kontakte um unbescheidene 1000 Jahre. Auch die Annahme von balt. *šaukē* ist im Vergleich dazu eine schwache Annahme. Der Hecht ist hinreichend weit verbreitet, so dass er den Finnen bekannt gewesen ist, kein Gegenstand des Kulturtransfers. Grundnahrungsmittel waren sicher keine Handelsware für den Fernhandel.[27] Wenn sich nun dennoch eine Entlehnung durchsetzt, dann ist dies am Ehesten mit Zweisprachigkeit zu begründen.

Lässt sich ein baltisches *šauk-*[28] nachweisen oder wenigstens plausibel mit anderen Daten verbinden? Liukkonen (1999: 42) überlegt ganz am Rande ob hier lit. *Šaūkupis* (Fluss; Sėda, Plungė) hergehören könnte. Die favorisierte Etymologie verbindet diesen FN mit lit. *šaūkti* 'schreien' (Vanagas 1981a: 327, Smoczyński 2007: 626). Dazu dann weiter *Šaūkbalė* (Tümpel, Niedermoor), *Šaukės* und *Šaukančioji* (Wiesen), *Šaukys* (Bruch).

---

[25] Von den 11 Etymologien die Koivulehto (2006) gibt, werden, abgesehen von *hauki* und *hirsi* nur noch saam. *multi* 'Seife' und der Name der Düna, finn. *Väinä-joki*, als urslawischen Ursprungs gehandelt – für alle anderen werden alternativ auch balto-slawische Quellen zugelassen. Dabei scheint die Seife die Krierien für Wanderwörter zu erfüllen, auch wenn das Konzept der Seifenherstellung archäologisch schwer fassbar ist. Die Quelle *dveinā* ist viel zu indifferent, als dass man sie sicher als ursl. bezeichnen könnte. Verdächtig, u.a., sind hier eher die ferneren Ostbalten, zu denen man aber auch nicht viel weiß...

[26] Ähnlich wie z.B. Koivulehto (2006: 181) auch keine Probleme hat balt. *virda-* für finn. *virsi* anzunehmen, obwohl diese Stufe nur in apr. *wirds* 'Wort' belegt ist, gewissermaßen nur zufällig in einer Kleinkorpussprache, die sicher nicht die Gebersprache war.

[27] Im Gegensatz zu Seife, wo mindestens die Rezeptur als Kulturgut zu werten ist, und das auch in den baltischen Sprachen als slawische Entlehnung vorliegt, lit. *muilas*.

[28] Die Rekonstruktion des Stammvokals halte ich nicht für sonderlich zwingend, angesichts von Wechsel und alternativer Verwendung mehrerer Varianten.

Ferner ist hier der lett. See *Saukas ezers* zu nennen, der am gleichnamigen Ort *Sauka* liegt. Man kann also argumentieren, dass der See den Namen vom Ort hat. Andererseits ist es nichts ungewöhnliches, wenn der Ort nach dem Gewässer benannt wird, so wird i.A. *Alytus* und auch *Vilnius* gedeutet (Vanagas 1996), bestes Beispiel in Lettland ist *Ogre* am gleichnamigen Fluss. Für den mit fast 8 km^2 recht großen See und den Ort ist die Möglichkeit der Herkunft aus dem Personennamen lit. und lett. *Sauka* kaum wahrscheinlich. Dabei ist dieser PN ebenfalls in der Herkunft nicht gesichert. Vanagas (1989: 682) schreibt zwar, dass man den Verdacht einer Verbindung mit lit. *šaukti* 'schreien, rufen', lett. *saukt* 'rufen, nennen'[29] haben kann, dass aber slawische Herkunft wahrscheinlicher ist, vgl. wruss. *Саўка, Савка* u.a.[30] Bei Ursprung aus lit. *šaukti* sollte man auch oder sogar überwiegend **Šauka* finden. Dies ist indessen nicht der Fall, man hat nur *Šauklys* u.ä. (Vanagas 1989: 895). Damit entfällt der Weg über den PN. Wenn man die Gewässernamen mit lit. *šaukti*, lett. *saukt* verbindet, so kommt man in der Deutung schwerlich an der Folklore vorbei, da kein unmittelbarer Bezug besteht. Selbst Smoczyński (2007: 626) bringt hier eine Redensart *Baloje nešūkalok, o tai velnią prisišauksi* 'im Sumpf schrei nicht, sonst kommt der Teufel herbei' – ein häufiges Thema, dass man den Teufel in Mooren und Sümpfen antreffen und hier leicht herbeirufen kann. Ein anderes Thema, m.E. hier besser passend, ist der Sagenkomplex über Seen, dass nämlich diese wandern – in Form von Wolken – und erst sesshaft werden oder aber überhaupt aus Wolken entstanden sind, wenn man diesen einen Namen gibt. Nun heißt im Lettischen *saukt* eben auch 'nennen' und oft existieren Sagen, dass der See nach dieser Erstbenennung auch seinen Namen hat (vgl. Gliwa 2005: 190f.).

An der Stelle des Moores *Saukas purvs* (Meirāni) befand sich, der Sage nach, früher der See *Saukas ezers* (Rezakova 2007: 21). Dort wo sich heute das Moor *Strupbrencis* befindet, war früher der See *Saukas* oder *Strupbrencis*, der sich wegen seines schlechten Namens empörte und einen neuen Platz suchte. Und da wo der See *Vecsaukes* 'Altsauka' *ezers* ist, war früher eine Weide, wo ein kleines Flüsschen floss. Drei Mädchen die am See *Jaunsauka* 'Neusauka' wuschen, sahen die Gewitterwolke und sangen *Rūci, kauci, ezariņi, sev vietiņas meklēdams, ja tev tika, meties še, būs mums Saukas ezariņš* 'Du wüteste und

---

[29] Diese sind nur baltisch und haben keine Vergleichsmöglichkeiten (Smoczyński 2007: 626), als Kentumvariante kann man lit. *kaukti* 'heulen (Wolf, Wind), schreien' auffassen, nach Smoczyński (2007: 266) "dźwiękonaśladowcze, ... jak np. stpol. *kukać*". Onomatopoetisch wohl auch lit. *staugti* und gleicher Bedeutung d. *heulen, jaulen*. Semasiologisch darf lett. *saukt* 'nennen' dann mit d. *Rufname* verglichen werden.

[30] Nicht abwegig erscheint auch Kontraktion aus *Savukas*, das man als Diminutiv zu *savas* 'eigen', *sau* 'sich (Dat.)' auffassen kann. Ähnlich werden ja auch einige PN mit *Sau-* den zweistämmigen altererbten Namen zugerechnet, etwa *Saudargas, Saukantas, Saugintas, Saunora*, wo *Sau-* ebenfalls mit *savo, sau* verbunden wird (Vanagas 1989: 681f.).

tobst, Dir einen Platz suchend; wenn es Dir passt, lass Dich hier nieder, und uns wird der Saukas See sein', womit der See dann auch herabfällt (Rezakova 2007: 37). Die zweite Ortssage lässt etwas an Logik vermissen aber die Alternativnennung zweier Namen lässt die Möglichkeit zu, dass *Sauka* sich auf den Charakter des Sees bezieht, dass er nämlich durch Menschen benannt und damit kultiviert wurde und in gewisser Weise ein Appellativ darstellt, das vereinzelt zum Eigennamen wurde.

Damit könnte man leben. Der Vorschlag von Liukkonen, ein baltisches **šaukē* 'Hecht' anzunehmen würde die Seenamen allerdings weit besser erklären, ganz ohne Ausflug ins Mythologische. Dass das Moor, das aus dem verlandeten See *Saukas ezers* entstanden ist, diesen Namen weiterführt ist nicht weiter verwunderlich – insbesondere, wenn man bedenkt, dass der Hechtname, so es ihn denn gab, irgendwann obsolet geworden sein muss. Vergleichbar wäre das *Hechtmoor* in Schleswig-Holstein. Selbst Namen von Wiesen lassen sich mit dem Hecht in Verbindung bringen. Lagen Mähwiesen doch einst an mäandernden Flüssen, die im Frühjahr Hochwasser hatten und dann in Senken Wasserlachen bis in den Sommer hinein hatten. In diesen Senken, das wird oft akzentuiert wenn man nach Flurnamen und vor-melioriertem Flussverlauf fragt, wimmelte es insbesondere von Hechten. Der Wiesenname *Šaukančioji* 'wörtl.: die Rufende' deutet schon auf Bildung von *šaukti* 'schreien, rufen', wobei die Motivation allerdings völlig unklar ist.

Vereinzelt ist es auch möglich, den PN *Sauka* mit **šaukē* 'Hecht' zu identifizieren, wobei allerdings fehlendes lit. †*Šauka* stört. Immerhin sind Familiennamen, die da Hecht lauten weit verbreitet, im Litauischen als *Lydeka* oder in der entlehnten Form *Ščiuka*, wruss., ukr., russ., pol. *Szczuka*, unter *Hecht* gibt es immerhin über 10.000 Telefoneinträge in Deutschland.[31]

Zur Wortbildung von **šaukē* o.ä. 'Hecht' bringt Liukkonen (1999: 41) das Standardbeispiel lit. *spėkas* 'Kraft, Vermögen'. In ähnlich abstrakter Bedeutung wäre lit. *stoka* 'Mangel' < **steH2-keH2-* : *stoti* '(auf)stehen, anhalten' (Smoczyński 2007: 605) zu nennen. Ähnlich konkret wie der vorgeschlagene Hechtname wäre apr. *slayx*, lit. *sliekas, sliēkas, slieka* 'Regenwurm' (Smoczyński 2007: 572), wozu mit *sliekễ* 'dünn gesponnener Faden' auch ein passender *ē*-Stamm vorliegt, in diesem Fall aber wohl sekundärer Natur.

Damit ist naürlich kein Beweis angetreten, dass ein balt. **šaukē* o.ä. 'Hecht' bestanden hat. Trotzdem ist diese Annahme weniger stark, als die der extremen Vorverlagerung einer slawischen Entlehnung. Da der sl. Hechtname gemeinslawisch ist, wäre es denkbar, diesen noch weiter vorzudatieren und als baltoslavisch anzusehen.

---

[31] [http://www.verwandt.de/karten/absolut/hecht.html], eingesehen am 30.4.2008.

Bernd Gliwa
Latvijas Universitāte
Baltu valodniecības katedra
Visvalža iela 4a
LV – 1050 Rīga
[berndgliwa@yahoo.de]

Literatur

Balode, L. 1993: Latvian hydronyms derived from botanical names. *Linguistica Baltica* 2: 189-210.

Balode, L. 1998: Hidronīmi 16.-17. gs. Latvijas kartēs. *Baltistica* V priedas: 47-52.

Baluodė, L. 1994: Dauguvos intakų hidroniminė analizė potamonimų stratifika-cijos aspektų. *Baltistica* XXIX(2): 207-214.

Blažek, V. 2001: Old Prussian arboreal terminology. *Linguistica Baltica* 9: 29-61.

Blažienė, G. 1998: Die altpreußischen Ortsnamen anthroponymischer Herkunft. *Colloquium Pruthenicum Secundum*. Kraków: Universitas, 25-37.

Boryś, W. 2005: *Słownik etymologiczny języka polskiego*. Kraków: Wyd. Lite-rackie.

Būga, K. 1958: *Rinktiniai raštai* I. Vilnius: Valstybinė politinės ir mokslinės literatūros leidykla.

Būga, K. 1959: *Rinktiniai raštai* II. Vilnius: Valstybinė politinės ir mokslinės literatūros leidykla.

BW = Barons, K., Wissendorffs, H. 1894-1915: *Latwju dainas*, 1-6. Jelgawa / Peterburga. [Faksimile-Reprint 1989-1994, Rīga: Zinātne, zitiert wird je-weils die Nr. des Liedes.]

C = Anonymus o.J. (ca. 1680) *Clavis Germanico-Lithvana*, Manuskript. Faksi-mile in Ivaškevičius, A. et al. (Hrsg.) 1995: *Clavis Germanico-Lithvana. Rankraštinis XVII amžiaus vokiečių lietuvių kalbų žodynas* 1-4. Vilnius: Mokslo ir enciklopedijų leidykla. (Paginierung nach dem Faksimile des zweibändigen Originals.)

Dambe, V. 1970: *Latvijas apdzīvotu vietu un to iedzīvotāju nosaukumi*. Rīga: Zinātne.

Deltuvienė, D. 2006: *Baltiški Mažosios Lietuvos XIV-XVIII a. oikonimai*. Vil-nius: VUL.

Depkin = Depkin, L. ms. o.J. *Lettisches Wörterbuch*. The original manuscript transcribed and annotated by Trevor G. Fennell. Vol. 3. 2007. Rīga: LAB. (Seitenangaben nach dem Manuskript.)

Duridanov, I. 1969: *Thrakisch-dakische Studien* I – *Die thrakisch- und dakisch-baltischen Sprachbeziehungen*. Sofia: BAN.

E = Elbinger Vokabular. Zitiert nach Mažiulis 1981: 14-46.

EH = Endzelīns, J., Hauzenberga, E. 1934-1946: *Papildinājumi un labojumi K. Mülenbacha Latviešu valodas vārdnīcai*. Rīga.

Endzelīns, J. 1951: *Latviešu valodas gramatika*. Rīga: Latvijas valsts izdevniecība.

EO = Ēdelmane, I., Ozola, A. 2003: *Latviešu valodas augu nosaukumi*. Rīga: Augsburgas institūts.

ESSJ =Trubačev, O. N. et al. 1978, 1987: *Ėtimologičeskij slovaŕ slavjanskich jazykov* V, XIV. Moskva: Nauka.

F1 = Fennell, T. G. 1997: *Fürecker's dictionary: the first manuscript*. Rīga: LAB.

F2 = Fennell, T. G. 1998: *Fürecker's dictionary: the second manuscript*. Rīga: LAB.

Fennell, T. G. 2000: *Fürecker's dictionary: a concordance* II – N-Ž. Rīga: LAB.

Genaust, H. 1996: *Etymologisches Wörterbuch der botanischen Pflanzennamen*. Basel, Boston, Berlin: Birkhäuser.

Gerullis, G. 1922: *Die altpreußischen Ortsnamen*. Berlin, Leipzig: W. de Gruyter.

Gliwa, B. 2005: Einige litauische Ortssagen, bodenlose Gewässer und Frau Holle (KHM 24, AaTh 480). *Studia Mythologica Slavica* 8: 187-223.

Gliwa, B. 2006: *Studien zu litauischen Pflanzennamen im indogermanischen Kontext*. Dissertation. Uniwersytet Jagielloński w Krakowie.

Gliwa, B. 2008: Litauische toponomastische Miszellen. *SEC* 13: 55-66.

Górnowicz, H. 1974: Das altpreußische Suffix *-īt-* und das polnische Suffix *-ic-* in Ortsnamen des preußischen Pomesaniens. *Zeitschrift für Slawistik* 19(2): 234-240.

Gritėnienė, A. 2006: *Augalų pavadinimų motyvacija šiaurės panevėžiškių patarmėje*. Vilnius: LKI.

Helimski, E. 2006: The "northwestern" group of Finno-Ugric languages in the place names and substratum vocabulary of the Russian north. *Slavica Helsingiensia* 27: 109-127.

Helimski, E. 2008: Ladoga and Perm revisited. *SEC* 13: 75-88.

Hock, W. 2006: Baltoslavisch III. Teil: Die baltoslavische Sprachgemeinschaft, Nachträge. *Kratylos* 51: 1-24.

Hyllested, A., Gliwa, B. 2009: Metatony in Lithuanian internal derivation. Olander, T. & Larsson, J. H. (eds.) *Stressing the past. Papers on Baltic and Slavic accentology*. Amsterdam / New York: Rodopi, 51-56.

IEW = Pokorny, J. 1994: *Indogermanisches etymologisches Wörterbuch* I (3. Aufl.). Tübingen, Basel: Francke.

III = 3. altpreußischer Katechismus 1561. Text in Mažiulis 1981: 91-240.

Kabašinskaitė, B. 1998: *Lietuvių kalbos liaudies etimologija ir artimi reiškiniai*. Vilnius: Mokslo ir enciklopedijų leidybos institutas.

Kagaine, E. 2004: *Lokālie somugrismi latviešu valodas Ziemeļrietumvidzemes izloksnēs*. Rīga: LU Latviešu valodas institūts.

Kallio, P. 2006: On the earliest Slavic loanwords in Finnic. *Slavica Helsingiensia* 27: 154-166.

Kluge, F. 1999: *Etymologisches Wörterbuch der deutschen Sprache*. Bearbeitet von Elmar Seebold. Berlin, New York: de Gruyter.

Koivulehto, J. 2006: Wie alt sind die Kontakte zwischen finnisch-ugrisch und balto-slavisch? *Slavica Helsingiensia* 27: 179-196.

Krünitz, J. G. 1773-1858: *Oekonomische Encyklopaedie, oder allgemeines System der Staats= Stadt= Haus= und Landwirthschaft*. (Online unter [www.kruenitz.uni-trier.de].)

Laučiūtė, J. [Laučjute, Ju.] 1982: *Slovař baltizmov v slavjanskich jazykach*. Leningrad: Nauka.

Laumane, B. 1973: *Zivju nosaukumi latviešu valodā*. Rīga: Zinātne.

Laumane, B. 1996: *Zeme, jūra, zvejvietas*. Rīga: Zinātne.

LBŽ = Dagys, Jonas. 1938: *Lietuviškas botanikos žodynas*. Kaunas: L. Vailionis.

LEV = Karulis, K. 1992: *Latviešu etimoloģijas vārdnīca* I-II. Rīga: Avots.

LEW = Fraenkel, E., 1962, 1965: *Litauisches etymologisches Wörterbuch* I-II. Heidelberg / Göttingen: Winter / Vandenhoeck & Ruprecht.

Liukkonen, K. 1999: *Baltisches im Finnischen*. Helsinki: Finnisch-Ugrische Gesellschaft.

LIV = Rix, H. et al. 2001: *Lexikon der indogermanischen Verben. Die Wurzeln und ihre Primärstammbildungen* (2. Aufl.). Wiesbaden: Dr. Reichert.

LKG = Ulvydas, K. et al. 1965: *Lietuvių kalbos gramatika* I. Vilnius: Mintis.

LKŽ = *Lietuvių kalbos žodynas* I-XX (1956-2002). Vilnius: Mintis, Mokslo ir enciklopedijos leidybos institutas, LKI.

Mažiulis, V. 1981: *Prūsų kalbos paminklai*. Vilnius: Mokslas.

Mažiulis, V. 1997: *Prūsų kalbos etimologijos žodynas* IV – R-Z. Vilnius: Mokslo ir enciklopedijų leidybos institutas.

ME = Mühlenbachs, K. 1923-1932: *Lettisch-Deutsches Wörterbuch*. Redigiert und fortgesetzt von J. Endzelīns, I-IV. Riga.

Nepokupnyj, A. 2000: Ukr. *Str'jash-Strivigor, Strivjash* i prus. *Strowange*. Range, J. D. (Hrsg.) *Aspekte baltistischer Forschung*. Essen: Die Blaue Eule, 226-238.

Nieminen, E. 1949: Fińskie *hirsi* 'belka'. *Lingua Posnanienis* 1: 99-120.

Pėteraitis, V. 1992: *Mažoji Lietuva ir Tvanksta*. Vilnius: Mažosios Lietuvos fondas, Mokslo ir enciklopedijų leidykla.

Polanska, I. 2002: *Zum Einfluss des Lettischen auf das Deutsche im Baltikum.* Inauguraldissertation Universität Bamberg. [http://elib.uni-bamberg.de/volltexte/2003/3/polanska.pdf].

Rezakova, L. 2007: *Zemgale – novadu teikas.* Rīga: J. Roze.

Rudzīte, M. 1993: *Latviešu valodas vēsturiskā fonētika.* Rīga: Zvaigsne.

SD1 = Szyrwid, C. 1621: *Dictionarium trium linguarum.* Vilnius: Soc. Jesu. Faksimile in Pakalka, K. 1997: *Senasis Konstantino Sirvydo žodynas.* Vilnius: Mokslo ir enciklopedijos leidybos institutas.

SD3 = Szyrwid, Constantin 1642. *Dictionarium trium linguarum.* Vilnae. Faksimile in: Lyberis, A. et al. (Hrsg.) 1979. *Pirmasis lietuvių kalbos žodynas.* Vilnius: Mokslas.

Skardžius, P. 1943: *Lietuvių kalbos žodžių daryba.* Zitiert nach der identisch paginierten Fassung in: Skardžius, P. 1996: *Rinktiniai raštai* 1. Vilnius: Mokslo ir enciklopedijų leidykla.

SKES = Toivonen, Y. H., Itkonen, E., Joki, A. J., Peltola, R. 1958-1981: *Suomen kielen etymologinen sanakirja* I-VII. Helsinki.

Smoczyński, W. 2000: *Untersuchungen zum deutschen Lehngut im Altpreußischen.* Kraków: Wydawnictwo Uniwersytetu Jagiellońskiego.

Smoczyński, W. 2003: *Hiat laryngalny w językach bałto-słowiańskich.* Kraków: Wydawnictwo Uniwersytetu Jagiellońskiego.

Smoczyński, W. 2006: *Laringalų teorija ir lietuvių kalba* [Bibliotheca Salensis II]. Vilnius: LKI.

Smoczyński, W. 2007: *Słownik etymologiczny języka litewskiego.* Vilnius: VUL.

SSA = Itkonen, E. et al. 1992-1995: *Suomen sanojen alkuperä. Etymologinen sanakirja* 1-2. Helsinki: SKS.

Šeškauskaite, D., Gliwa, B. 2005: Lit. *kūkalis* – Pflanze, Korndämon und Kobold. *Res Balticae* 10: 69-111.

Trautmann, R. 1910: *Die altpreußischen Sprachdenkmäler.* Göttingen: Vandenhoeck & Ruprecht.

Vaba, L. 1998: Die Rolle des altpreussischen Sprachmaterials in etymologischen Untersuchungen ostseefinnischer Baltismen. *Colloquium Pruthenicum Secundum.* Kraków: Universitas, 177-185.

Vanagas, A. 1981a: *Lietuvių hidronimų etimologinis žodynas.* Vilnius: Mokslas.

Vanagas, A. 1981b: Lietuvių hidronimų semantika. *Lietuvių kalbotyros klausimai* XXI: 4-153.

Vanagas, A. 1989: *Lietuvių pavardžių žodynas* II – L-Ž. Vilnius: Mokslas.

Vanagas, A. 1996: *Lietuvos miestų vardai.* Vilnius: Mokslo ir enciklopedijų leidykla.

Vasmer, M. 1964-1973: *Этимологический словарь русского языка* 1-4, перевод с немецкого и дополнения О. Н. Трубачева, Москва: Прогресс.

Venckutė, R. 2001: [Rez.] Kari Liukkonen, Baltisches im Finnischen, Suoma-
    lais-Ugrilaisen Seuran toimituksia… *Baltistica* XXXVI(1): 125-131.
von Weizsäcker, C. F. 1993: *Der Mensch in seiner Geschichte*. München: dtv.
Zander, R. 2000: *Handwörterbuch der Pflanzennamen*, 16. Auflage bearbeitet
    von W. Erhardt, E. Götz, N. Bödeker, S. Seybold. Stuttgart: Ulmer.
Zinkevičius, Z. 1966: *Lietuvių dialektologija*. Vilnius: Mintis.
Zinkevičius, Z. 1984: *Lietuvių kalbos kilmė* [*Lietuvių kalbos istorija* I]. Vilnius:
    Mokslas.

Studia Etymologica Cracoviensia
vol. 14   Kraków 2009

Juha JANHUNEN (Helsinki)

SOME ADDITIONAL NOTES
ON THE MACROHYDRONYMS OF THE LADOGA REGION

In one of his last but not least ingenious papers, published posthumously in *Studia Etymologica Cracoviensia* 13, Eugene Helimski (2008) deals with the etymologies of the names *Ladoga* and *Neva*. Following V. S. Kuleshov (2003), he assumes that the river Neva, which was formed only slightly over three thousand years ago as a result of postglacial isostatic uplift, got its name from an Indo-European-speaking population who observed the birth of the 'New' river. The semantic identification of *Neva* with 'new' is synchronically supported by the homonymy of this hydronym with the Scandinavian words for 'new', as still in modern Swedish *Nyen* 'Neva' vs. *ny* 'new'. Helimski concludes that the Neva region must have been within the range of the linguistic expansion routes which brought Germanic from the Indo-European homeland to northern Central Europe and Scandinavia. He also implies that the Neva has since its formation remained within the sphere of the geographic consciousness of Germanic speakers, especially the Scandinavians. In fact, the Swedish fort of *Nyenskans* was replaced by the Russian city of St. Petersburg only 300 years ago.

The etymology of *Neva* is potentially important in that it shows that the historical presence of the Finnic branch of Uralic on both sides of the Gulf of Finland is secondary to an earlier Indo-European expansion to the region. In addition to Germanic, Indo-European was represented by Baltic (Balto-Slavonic). This conclusion, also obvious from the modern distribution of the Germanic and Baltic languages, is confirmed by the well-known fact that the entire marine terminology of the Finnic languages is of an Indo-European origin. In some cases, as in that of the very word for 'sea', Finnic **meri* : **mere-* : **mer-*, the exact identification of the Indo-European source language is controversial (cf. SSA s.v. *meri*), and it cannot be ruled out that the borrowing took place from some earlier stage of Indo-European (Pre-Balto-Germanic), or also from some subsequently extinct branch (Para-Germanic, Para-Baltic). Even so, it is clear that both Germanic and Baltic were spoken at the Baltic Sea already in the second millennium BZ, while Finnic can have spread to the region from the east only a millennium later.

It may be added that the chronological anteriority of Germanic and Baltic at the Baltic Sea, as compared to Finnic, is also suggested by the notoriously large general corpora of early Germanic and Baltic loanwords in Finnic, as well as by the overall typological 'Europeanization' of the Finnic languages, apparently under Indo-European influence. The fact that the loanwords include even basic vocabulary items such as body part terms of the type 'tooth' and 'neck' (cf. SSA s.vv. *hammas, kaula*) and kinship terms of the type 'daughter' and 'mother' (ibid. s.vv. *tytär, äiti*) further suggests that the contacts took place in a situation in which local communities of Germanic and, especially, Baltic speakers changed their language in favour of Finnic (Pre-Proto-Finnic). While it is possible that this process of language replacement continued during the expansion of Finnic on both sides of the Gulf of Finland, the interaction is likely to have begun somewhat further to the east and south. The Germanic and Baltic influence also reached Saamic, and, to a lesser extent, Mordvinic, whose homelands must have been located immediately to the north and east of the Finnic centre of expansion.

The general conclusion from these considerations is that the territorial history of the Finnic and Saamic languages in the Baltic region and Fennoscandia is very shallow, extending back no more than three millennia, at most. In the Uralic context, this shallow dating is confirmed by the conspicuously close relationship of Finnic and Saamic with Mordvinic. In fact, Finnic and Mordvinic were until the Middle Ages geographically linked with each other by the language of the Muroma of the Russian chronicles (Para-Mordvinic or Para-Finnic?). The dispersal and differentiation of the Finnic languages on both sides of the Gulf of Finland, on the other hand, should primarily be seen as a consequence of the Slavonic expansion in the first millennium AZ. Moreover, as was pointed out by Helimski in another paper (2006), the Finnic languages also spread towards the Arctic coast of Northern Russia, where traces of their recent presence are still preserved in the local toponymy. In general, it may be said that Helimski's views concerning the chronology and territorial history of the western branches of Uralic represented a bold deviation from the conventional paradigm of Finnish and Estonian historiography, which still continues to date the local roots of the 'national' languages as far back as the Neolithic. As a sign of change, however, researchers of the younger generation, such as Petri Kallio (2006) and Janne Saarikivi (2006), are now revising the conventional paradigm in favour of a more critical approach.

A minor problem with the Indo-European etymology of *Neva* is that the word **newa* also appears in Finnic as a topographic term denoting 'broad river, river system, open marshland'. Traditionally, it has been assumed that the appellative meaning is primary (SSA s.v. *neva*), but Helimski is probably correct in assuming (with Kuleshov) the opposite. In fact, since the Neva basin must have been the very region from where the modern Finnic languages started their expansion during the first millennium AZ, the local landscape can well have left traces in their topographic terminology. It is therefore entirely possible that the appellative *newa, which, moreover, has a diagnostically late phonotactic structure (the vowel combination *e-a) represents a secondary development of the more original usage of the word as a proper noun. In the territory of today's Finland, toponyms ending in -neva are particularly common in the Finnish-speaking parts of Ostrobothnia along the northwestern coast of the country, where the landscape is dominated by broad and seasonally flooding rivers of the Neva type (though smaller), with adjoining plains and marshlands (SPNK s.v. neva).

Helimski's proposal of a Scandinavian etymology for Ladoga is more problematic. Although it is clear that the modern Finnic (Finnish-Karelian) shape Laatokka is based on Russian, it is far less obvious whether the Russian name can really be derived from Scandinavian *Ald-aug-ja 'Old Eye(d)'. According to Helimski, this would originally have been the Scandinavian name of Lake Ladoga, from which the fort name Aldeigju-borg would have been derived. However, as Helimski himself points out, for the Russians, at least, the fort name Ladoga is more basic than the name of the lake (Ladozhskoe ozero), and there is also a river with a related name (Ladozhka). One would rather see a parallel with the name Onega, which for the Russians primarily denotes the river Onega, according to which the corresponding (though hydrographically unconnected) lake (Onezhskoe ozero) was named. Since both the Russian and the Scandinavian sources on Ladoga (with any reference) date only from the Middle Ages, it is difficult to see definitive evidence of the linguistic priority of any particular data. Even if the fort of Ladoga was operated by Scandinavian speakers at the time of the chronicles, its name may well have had a non-Scandinavian origin.

In this connection, it is impossible to ignore the traditional observation that Ladoga (Ládoga) also formally (except for the location of the accent) parallels Onega (Onéga) as well as several other Northern Russian hydronyms ending in -ga, notably Pinega (Pínega). In spite of occasional doubts, Onega and Pinega (cf. ESRIa s.vv.) are probably best explained as deriving from the Finnic composite names *enä-yoki 'large river' and *peen(i)-yoki 'narrow river', respectively, with *-yoki 'river' as the final component. It is natural to view Ladoga as a member of the same hydronymic series, in which case it might derive either by dissimilation from *Lagoga << *laaka-yoki 'wide river' or by simplification from *Lagdoga << *laketa-yoki id., with either (*)laaka or *laketa 'flat, low, wide' as the first component. Both (*)laaka and *laketa are Germanic loanwords, at least partly from the same original(s) (cf. SSA svv. laaja, laaka, laakea, lakea, lavea), but the hydronym itself would have to have been formed in a Finnic context. The element (*)laaka- (> laa-), in particular, is attested in several hydronyms in eastern Finland (cf. SPNK s.v. Laakajärvi), but *laketa also has the topographic meaning of 'treeless, open'. In modern Finnish, the derivative lakeus 'width' is used in reference to the flood plains of Ostrobothnia.

It appears, consequently, likely that the name Ladoga originally refers to a river. Some of the earlier etymologies of this hydronym, as listed by Helimski (2008: 78-79) also start from this assumption, but they are either semantically or phonetically unacceptable. At first glance, the derivation of Ladoga from the meaning 'wide river' is also problematic, since there is no actual wide river synchronically bearing the name. The location of the fort of Ladoga on the lower course of the river Volkhov, running between the lakes Il'men (from Finnic *Ilma-yärwi) and Ladoga, suggests, however, that Ladoga originally was the Finnic name of the Volkhov. Although the origin of the Russian (Slavonic) name of the Volkhov is controversial (cf. ESRIa s.v.), there is no reason to regard the Russian data as secondary to Finnic Olhava and Swedish Ålhava. In this case, none of the languages seems to provide a formally and semantically credible explanation of the hydronym. However, in Finnic, at least, Olhava may be seen as a borrowing from Russian, rather than vice versa. Most probably, Olhava replaced the original Finnic name of the river, which must have been the source item of Ladoga.

It is fairly safe to assume that the river names Ladoga and Onega were borrowed by the early Russians of the Novgorod region directly from the local Finnic speakers, who represented the 'aborigines' of the region at the time of the Russian expansion.. This lexical contact may be dated to the last centuries of the first millennium AZ, a period when also many other items of regional and cultural vocabulary were exchanged in both directions. Soon after this, the name Ladoga was transferred from Russian to the Scandinavians, who at this time may be regarded as a 'foreign' element in the region, and who probably also initially used the item as a river name with reference to the Volkhov (or the lower course of the latter). The Scandinavian shape *Aldauga is, of course, not in a regular relationship to the Russian data, and it may, in fact, represent a folk-etymological reinterpretation along the lines proposed by Helimski. In any case, with the decline of the Viking trade, and with the growth of Russia, toponyms also underwent changes, and the Russian names Volkhov and Ladoga were introduced into local Finnic in the shapes Olhava and Laatokka, respectively.

To be exact, the linguistic situation behind the toponyms in question may also have been more complicated, in that the Western Uralic source language of hydronyms of the Ladoga and Onega type need not have been Finnic in the strict sense of the term. At least in the northern parts of the region it may also have been a language more closely connected with Saamic (Para-Saamic). It is therefore not immediately possible to tell what the exact shape of the end component underlying Russian -*ga* was. The word for 'river' shows in Finnic and Saamic an irregular variation between two different shapes: **yoki* (Finnic) vs. **yuki* (Saamic), and there is also the apparently more original (Proto-Uralic) shape **yuka*, which is attested in Finnic in the meaning 'rapids' (cf. SSA s.vv. *joki, juka*). The presence of a Saamic type of language in the region is suggested by the modern Finnic (Finnish-Karelian) shape of the name of Lake Onega, which is *Ääninen* (or *Äänisjärvi*). Although synchronically associated with the noun (**)ääni* 'sound', the lake name actually reflects Saamic **äänV-* 'large', the cognate of Finnic **enä(-)* id. Of a similar origin is the hydronym *Äänekoski* (with -*koski* 'rapids') in Central Finland (SPNK s.v.). In the Middle Ages, the Finnic-Saamic language boundary still seems to have been located in the Onega region, as is pointed out by Saarikivi (2004a: 174 map 1).

The fact that the modern Russian hydronyms of the Ladoga region are of a Finnic and/or Saamic origin does in no way interfere with the general ethno-historical picture sketched by Helimski. Finnic and Saamic were certainly the principal languages of the region at the time when the Russian expansion started, that is, towards the end of the first millennium AZ. The Russian language gradually pushed the southern boundary of Finnic towards the north, while the resulting Finnic expansion had a similar impact on the southern boundary of Saamic. In this context, the mediaeval Scandinavians, whose Finnic name (Finnish *ruotsalaiset*) even became the name of Russia (Russian *Ruś*), represented a secondary intrusion from the coastal parts of Sweden, and it is only natural that they borrowed most of their local toponyms from, or via, Russian. Even so, as Helimski proposed, it is possible that the name of the Neva represents a more ancient stratum of Indo-European (Pre-Germanic) toponyms, which had been preserved in Scandinavian since earlier times. It is quite likely that the Scandinavians, even prior to the Vikings, never completely lost an understanding of the geography of the Baltic Sea and its eastern extremity, including the mouth of the Neva.

An important circumstance to be considered here is that there must also have been other languages that were spoken in the Baltic region and Fennoscandia until, at least, mediaeval times. These other languages need not have been either Uralic or Indo-European, rather, they belonged to entirely different language families that can only generically be labelled as 'Palaeo-European'. Most importantly, traces of these languages are preserved in the local toponyms, especially in the macrohydronyms, as well as in other substratal features in the modern languages, as has also been pointed out by Saarikivi (2004b). In large parts of Finland, for instance, the current Finnish toponyms are layered upon an earlier toponymic stratum of a Saamic type, as has been demonstrated most recently by Ante Aikio (2003), but several macrohydronyms in different parts of the country cannot be explained from any known language. In the Ladoga region an example of such a hydronym is the name of Lake Saimaa (Finnish *Saimaa*, Swedish *Saima* or *Saimen*), the largest lake of today's Finland (cf. UVF s.v. *Saimen*). Extant etymologies of the lake name (possibly from **Saimas* : *Saimaa-*) are based on vague Saamic comparisons (cf. SPNK s.v. *Saimaa*), but more probably it is a question of a Palaeo-European substratal hydronym.

It is, however, relevant to note that the river draining Saimaa into Ladoga has the name *Vuoksi* (Swedish *Vuoksen*, earlier also written as *Woxen*), which at least formally is of a Finnic origin. This is particularly interesting since the Vuoksi is a river that was formed in the same way as, and apparently only slightly earlier than, the Neva, that is, as a result of isostatic uplift about four millennia ago. Like the Neva, the Vuoksi is a short but broad and rapid river (cf. UVF s.v. *Vuoksen*), whose birth involved a significant change in the local environment. The river must have had a name already prior to the expansion of Saamic and Finnic to the region, but its current name is rather transparently identical with the Finnic appellative noun **wooksi* > Finnish *vuoksi* '(rapid) stream, tide', based on the noun-verb **(w)oxi(-)* > **(w)oo(-)* 'flow; to flow' (SSA s.vv. *uoma, vuo, vuoksi, vuotaa*). It is true that the derivational type *vuo-ksi* (: *vuo-kse-*) is rather unique due to the monosyllabic structure of the root, but there is no formal problem to derive the word especially from the verbal base **(w)oo-* > *vuo-* 'to flow' (as in Finnish *kuto-* 'to weave' : *kudo-s* : *kudokse-* 'weft', cf. also SPNK s.v. *Vuoksi*).

Even so, it is impossible not to notice that the hydronym *Vuoksi* bears a distant resemblance to the name of the Central European river Waag (*Vág*, *Vah*), a tributary of the Danube, as most recently discussed by Albrecht Greule (2008: 73-74). According to Greule, the river name *Waag* is connected with Germanic words meaning 'wave, flow, flood' (English *wave*), ultimately based on **weg-a-* 'to move' (German *bewegen*). It happens that a similar hydronym with the shape *Vaga* is attested from the Northern Dvina basin, though the similarity may, of course, be accidental. Of more immediate interest is the passage in the *Getica* of Jordanes (mid 6th century AZ) to which both Greule (l.c.) and Helimski (2008: 75 note 1) refer. Jordanes mentions a river by the name *Vagus*. According to Aalto & Pekkanen (1980: 161 s.v. *Scythia*) the passage goes as follows: *haec ergo habet ab oriente vastissimum lacum in orbis terrae gremio, unde Vagi fluvius velut quodam ventrae generatus in Oceanum undosus evolvitur*, which in Mierow's (1915) translation is: "This [= the island of Scandza] has in its eastern part a vast lake in the bosom of the earth, whence the Vagus river springs from the bowels of the earth and flows surging into the Ocean."

From the context of the passage it is fairly obvious that the large lake mentioned by Jordanes is, indeed, Ladoga, while the Ocean must refer to the Baltic Sea. The river Vagus, on the other hand, could well refer to the Neva, as Helimski (l.c.) proposes. Helimski assumes that *Vagus* "must be another name of the Neva river [...] not attested from other sources". This may be so, but the similarity with *Vuoksi* < *Wooksi* might also mean that Jordanes, or his sources, have somehow confused the two rivers, or their names. Another possibility is that, since *wooksi* seems to have been an appellative for '(rapid) stream', it can have been used by Finnic speakers also of other rivers than *Vuoksi* proper. In that case, it could possibly also have referred to the Neva. In any case, the formal similarity of *wooksi* and *Vagus* suggests that Jordanes may have had knowledge of the Finnic name, though its exact shape has been distorted in the surviving version(s) of the text, possibly due to the influence of hydronyms of the *Waag* type.

It is also theoretically possible, though difficult to verify, that the Finnic hydronym *Vuoksi* represents a folk-etymological adaptation based on an originally non-Finnic item. In this respect, the possibility of a parallelism with *Neva* is obvious, though in the latter case it is not certain whether the language had a homonymous appellative (*newa*) before the introduction of the hydronym, while in the former case the appellative association is beyond doubt. It is interesting to note that the Vuoksi basin contains the exceptionally spectacular rapids of Imatra (UVF s.v.), which must have attracted the attention of local people since the formation of the river. The name *Imatra* has been subject to many speculations (cf. SPNK s.v.), including, most commonly, a comparison with the name of Lake Imandra on the Kola Peninsula. Obviously, both *Imatra* and *Imandra*, which may or may not have a common origin, belong to the general corpus of Northern European substratal hydronyms, which Peter Schrijver (following Krahe) prefers to derive from a single language of 'Old European Hydronymy' (Schrijver 2001: 418-419), but which are more likely to derive from a variety of different languages.

The difficulty of making a distinction between appellatives and proper names, and between semantically motivated native items and loanwords in hydronyms is also illustrated by the name of the river Kymi, flowing into the northeastern section of the Gulf of Finland from Lake Päijänne in Central Finland. The name *Päijänne* (: *Päijäntee-*) is itself a substratal hydronym (cf. SPNK s.v.), and so may *Kymi* (or *Kymijoki*) be, although the word is also attested in restricted appellative usage as Finnish dialectal *kymi* : *kyme-* 'large river' (SSA s.v.). Jorma Koivulehto (1987: 36-37) has, however, proposed that *Kymi* could also be derived from a Germanic original of the type *kwem-* 'easy to approach' (German *bequem*), which seems to be attested as a hydronym in the shape *Kymmen* also in Värmland, Sweden. It is perhaps relevant to note that the Swedish name of the Kymi is *Kymmene*, which is conventionally thought to be based on the Finnish genitive *Kyme-n-*, but which in actual fact could also be a native Scandinavian form preserved since ancient times, like Swedish *Nyen* for the

Neva. Possibly, the shape *Kymmene* has also been influenced by the Swedish name of Päijänne, which has the form *Päjäne*, though the latter is certainly a borrowing from Finnish.

Koivulehto (op. cit.) also correctly looks for Germanic (including Pre-Germanic and Para-Germanic) explanations for other hydronyms along the Finnish coast. The most promising example is formed by the two river names *Aura* and *Eura*, which both seem to belong to the context of the widespread hydrographic term represented in German as *Ader* 'vein, stream' (as in *Wasserader*), and also in the hydronym *Oder*. The presence of such hydronyms in Finland can hardly mean anything else but that the coastal parts of the country were once inhabited by Germanic and/or other Indo-European-speaking populations. These populations were at least partly assimilated by the expanding Finnish speakers towards the end of the first millennium AZ, but it is also possible that in some parts of the coastal belt the non-Finnic-speaking population has persisted until modern times, being now represented by the so-called 'coastal Swedes'. It goes without saying that the origin of the toponyms in the Finnish coastal regions has been a topic of much dispute between Finnish and Scandinavian scholars. The widely-held nationalist doctrine of many Finnish linguists and archaeologists according to which there are no 'old' (pre-mediaeval) Germanic toponyms in Finland seems, in any case, to be mistaken. On the other hand, it is always necessary to reckon with the possibility of substratal toponyms which are originally neither Finnic (Uralic) nor Germanic (Indo-European).

Accepting the probable presence of Indo-European toponyms, especially hydronyms, in the coastal belt extending from the Neva to, at least, the rivers Aura and Eura in southwestern Finland, we may summarize the ethnohistorical situation as follows: The original (pre-Bronze-Age) population(s) of the region spoke a variety of unspecifiable Palaeo-European languages whose traces are still preserved in the names of several large rivers, lakes, and rapids. Subsequently, but not necessarily before the second millennium BZ, the coasts of the Gulf of Finland were occupied by Indo-European speakers, who represented the northern margins of the waves of linguistic expansion that have brought the Germanic and Baltic languages to their historical and modern territories. The speakers of the languages belonging to the western branches of Uralic interacted with these Indo-Europeans already in the region between Ladoga and the Volga, from where Finnic and Saamic gradually moved towards the Gulf of Finland. While the coastal parts of Finland continued to be occupied by Germanic and/or Baltic speakers, the inner parts of the country became a target of a Saamic expansion, possibly already in the first millennium BZ. Later, in the first millennium AZ, Finnic started its expansion from the Ladoga-Neva region and pushed Saamic both in Finland and in Karelia towards the north, where Saamic, in turn, absorbed the last Palaeo-European languages.

Final note. The author remembers with gratitude the many discussions he had with Eugene Helimski concerning the linguistic history of Northern and Eastern Europe. The author's impression was that our understanding of the chronology and territorial history of the Uralic and Indo-European languages concerned was gradually approaching a mutual consensus. Recent developments among younger scholars in Finland and elsewhere suggest that this consensus, or some parts of it, may also be gaining a wider support against other, as it would seem, methodically antiquated paradigms, which often serve hidden nationalist interests.

Juha Janhunen
Institute for Asian and African Studies
Box 59
FIN – 00014 University of Helsinki

Literature

Aalto, Pentti & Tuomo Pekkanen (1975-1980). *Latin Sources on North-Eastern Eurasia.* Asiatische Forschungen 44 & 57. Wiesbaden: Otto Harrassowitz.

Aikio, Ante (2003: 99-106). 'Suomen saamelaisperäisistä paikannimistä.' *Virittäjä* 107. Helsinki.

Greule, Albrecht (2008: 67-74). 'Exonyme im etymologischen Wörterbuch der deutschen Gewässernamen.' *Studia Etymologica Cracoviensia* 13. Kraków.

Helimski, Eugene (2006: 109-127). 'The "Northwestern" group of Finno-Ugric languages and its heritage in the place names and substratum vocabulary of the Russian North.' [In:] Juhani Nuorluoto (ed.). *The Slavicization of the Russian North*. Slavica Helsingiensia 27. Helsinki.

Helimski, Eugene (2008: 75-88). 'Ladoga and Perm revisited.' *Studia Etymologica Cracoviensia* 13. Kraków.

Kallio, Petri (2006: 2-25). 'Suomen kantakielten absoluuttista kronologiaa.' *Virittäjä* 110. Helsinki.

Koivulehto, Jorma (1987: 27-42). 'Namn som kan tolkas urgermanskt.' [In:] Lars Huldén (ed.). *Klassiska problem inom finlandssvensk ortnamnsforskning*. Skrifter utgivna av Svenska Litteratursällskapet i Finland 539. Studier i Nordisk filologi 67. Helsingfors.

Kuleshov, V. S. (2003: 27-36). 'Neva'. [In:] *Ladoga: Pervaia stolica Rusi. 1250 let nepreryvnoi zhizni*. Sedʹmye chteniia pamiati Anny Machinskoi. St. Peterburg.

Mierow, Charles C. (1915). *The Gothic History of Jordanes*. Princeton: Prince-
    ton University Press. (Revised internet version: [http://www.ucalgary.ca/~
    vandersp/Courses/texts/jordgeti.html#geograph].)

Saarikivi, Janne (2004a: 162-234). 'Über das saamische Substratnamengut in
    Nordrußland und Finnland.' *Finnisch-Ugrische Forschungen* 58. Helsinki.
    (Also included in Saarikivi 2006.)

Saarikivi, Janne (2004b: 187-214). 'Is there Palaeo-European substratum interfer-
    ence in western branches of Uralic?' *Journal de la Société Finno-Ougrienne*
    90. Helsinki. (Also included in Saarikivi 2006.)

Saarikivi, Janne (2006). *Substrata Uralica: Studies on Finno-Ugrian Substrate
    in Northern Russian Dialects*. [Tartu & Helsinki:] Tartu University Press.

Schrijver, Peter (2001: 417-425). 'Lost languages in Northern Europe.' [In:]
    Christian Carpelan & Asko Parpola & Petteri Koskikallio (eds.). *Early
    Contacts between Uralic and Indo-European: Linguistic and Archaeological
    Considerations*. Mémoires de la Société Finno-Ougrienne 242. Helsinki.

ESRIa = Maks Fasmer. *Etimologicheskii slovar' russkogo iazyka* 1-4. Perevod s
    nemeckogo s dopolneniiami O. B. Trubacheva. Moskva: Izdateľstvo
    "Progress", 1964-1973.

SPNK = *Suomalainen paikannimikirja*. Kotimaisten kielten tutkimuskeskuksen
    julkaisuja 146. [Helsinki:] Karttakeskus, 2007.

SSA   = *Suomen sanojen alkuperä: Etymologinen sanakirja* 1-3. Suomalaisen
    Kirjallisuuden Seuran Toimituksia 556. Kotimaisten kielten tutkimus-
    keskuksen julkaisuja 62. Helsinki, 1992-2000.

UVF   = *Uppslagsverket Finland* 1-5. Esbo & Helsingfors: Schildts Förlags Ab,
    2003-2007.

Studia Etymologica Cracoviensia
vol. 14   Kraków 2009

Simas KARALIŪNAS (Vilnius)

POLNISCH *Warszawa* UND LITAUISCH *Ãpvaršuva*

Der Ortsname *Ãpvaršuva* (Laukuva, Kreis Šilalė) (*Vietovardžių žodynas*, 26) ist strukturell ohne Zweifel aus dem Präfix *ap-* und dem Stamm *-varšuva* zusammengesetzt. *Varšuva* fällt formell mit der Benennung der Hauptstadt Polens – litauisch *Varšuva*, polnisch *Warszawa* (*Lietuviški tradiciniai vietovardžiai*, 144) zusammen. Das Präfix *ap-* tritt auch in manchen Gewässernamen auf, z.B. *Apvardaĩ* (See; bei Rimšė, Kreis Ignalina) (*Lietuvos TSR upių ir ežerų vardynas*, 7; *Vietovardžių žodynas*, 25), dialektal *Apardaĩ* (mit weggefallenem *-v-*). Früher wurde dieser Name *Api-vardaĩ* ausgesprochen, wie in historischen Quellen bezeugt: so in russischen – *Opivarda* (*Опиварда*), in polnischen – *Opiwarda* (Būga 1958: 525). Nicht zu vergessen ist ferner, dass es auf dem Gebiet Litauens auch mehrere Oikonyme gibt, die mit der Bennenung der Hauptstadt Polens formell zusammenfallen, bzw. Ableitungen einer solchen Form sind: *Varšauka* (Einsitze; Troškūnai, Kr. Anykščiai, Velykiai, Kr. Panevėžys), *Varšuvėlė* (Einsitz; Rūdiškės, Kr. Trakai) (*Lietuvos TSR administracinio-teritorinio suskirstymo žinynas*, 338). Deren Stamm ist möglicherweise mit dem des Oikonyms *Ãpvaršuva* (s. unten) identisch. Bekannt ist auch der Familienname *Varša* (Betonung unbekannt; Panevėžys, Vilnius), falls er nicht aus dem Polnischen kommt, vgl. die polnischen Familiennamen *Warsz, Warszo* [*Lietuvių pavardžių žodynas* (L – Ž), 1167].

Bei der Suche nach Appellativen mit Wurzeln wie im Toponym *Ãpvaršuva*, fällt das Adjektiv lit. *apvaržùs* 'verwelkt (von Birken)' (Šatės, Kr. Skuodas – LKŽ I 281) auf, das von der ebendort gebrauchten Zusammensetzung *apvìrž-beržis* 'warzige Birke' (← *apvìržęs béržas*) und wahrscheinlich von *apviržėlis* (Betonung unbekannt) nicht zu trennen ist, vgl. den von Juška gegebenen Beispielsatz: *Vaikas, kurs neauga, tas apviržėlis* (LKŽ I 283) 'Ein Kind, das nicht wächst, ist ein *apviržėlis*'. Daraus kann man Zugehörigkeit zum Verbum *viřžti* (*-ta*, *-žo*) intr. 'sich mit einer Kruste überziehen, an der Oberfläche steif werden; schlechter werden, nicht wachsen' (LKŽ XIX 678) folgern, häufig auch mit dem Präfix *ap-* gebraucht, vgl. den Beispielsatz *epušė nulupta, bet nepjauta, suviřžta savė(je)* (Tryškiai, Kr. Telšiai – LKŽ XIX 679) 'die Espe abgeschält, aber nicht gesägt, verhärtet sich'.

Wie ersichtlich, bestehen für die Erklärung von *Ãpvaršuva* andere Mög-
lichkeiten als die Annahme einer Herleitung vom Namen der Hauptstadt Polens,
trotz formaler Entsprechung. Andererseits wurde die Frage der eventuellen baltischen Herkunft des Namens der Hauptstadt Polens *Varšuva* erörtert, so verband man z.B. den Namen *Warszawa* mit dem Gewässernamen *Warszyn* (< balt.
**virš-ĭn-* adj. 'oberer') im Flussgebiet von Weichsel und Oder, den man für bal-
tisch hielt und zu einigen Hydronymen im Gebiet Litauens: *Viršýtis*, *Viršupis*
und *Viršupis* (← lit. *viršùs* 'Höhe; Spitze; Gipfel' und *ùpė* 'Fluss; Strom') (Oriol
1991: 84; Oriol 1997: 353) stellte.

In seinem etymologischen Wörterbuch verknüpfte A. Brückner *Warszawa*
mit Personennamen. Zu *Warszawa* und auch zu der in den Dokumenten des
15.-16. Jh. belegten Form *Warszewa* meinte er: "przezwana od *Warsza*, czes.
Wrsz (*Wrszowce*)" (Brückner 1993: 603), d.h. 'benannt nach *Warsz*, tschechisch
Wrsz (*Wrszowce*)'. Angenommen wurde auch, dass der Name *Warszawa* früher
die Benennung eines Grundbesitzes ("osada lub wieś Warsza") war und der Personenname *Warsz* oder *Warch* selbst von derselben Wurzel wie poln. *warchoł*
'Krakeeler, Lärmer; Schläger; Meuterer' kam oder aus der Kürzung des Perso-
nennamens *Warcisław* resultierte (Staszewski 1969: 466).

In historischen Quellen ist der Name Warschaus zum ersten Mal im Jahre
1241 bezeugt, wo von der Schenkung des Dorfes Służew bei Warschau an einen
gewissen Gotald für einen Sieg gegen die Jotwinger die Rede ist: *actum et da-
tum Varschevie* 'verfügt und ausgegeben in Warschau'. Die Form mit dem Suffix *-ev-* ist durch den Beleg von 1386: *in districtu Warszeuiensi* bestätigt, doch
mit der Zeit wurde dieses Suffix in der polnischen Sprache geändert, indem es an
das allgemein übliche Suffix *-ow*, *-owa*, *-owo* (vgl. *Varsouiam* im Jahre 1355)
angepasst wurde, so dass endlich Formen mit dem Suffix *-awa* aufkamen, die
vom 15. Jh. an immer öfter verwendet wurden.

J. Staszewski nahm an, dass sich das Suffix *-ev-* im Bewusstsein der Spre-
cher zu *-ow-* infolge der Anpassung des Namens *Warszewa* an Gewässernamen
in Masuren ändern konnte, wie der Seename *Warszawskie*, der 1365 als *Warssen*
bezeugt wurde neben späterem *Warschaw*. J. Gerullis (1922: 197) hatte die Gewässernamen *Warssen* und *Warschaw* mit dem Flussnamen *Varžė* (Betonung
unbekannt) in Litauen und dem litauischen Appellativ *varžas* 'Fischreuse' verbunden. Die Frage ist auch, welcher Natur die Beziehung des Namens der polnischen Hauptstadt zur ähnlich lautenden Benennung der Vorstadt von Prag *Vršo-
vice* ist, zumal es mehrere phonetisch ähnliche Benennungen von Bezirken von
Warschau und Prag gibt, so z.B. Solec, Ujazdów, Sielce, Rakowiec in Warschau
und Solnice, Ujezd, Sedlec, Rakovice in Prag und um Prag herum. Warum und
wie diese Ähnlichkeiten entstanden sind, etwa als Ergebnis einer Kolonisation,
von Einwanderung aus Pommern oder aus dem Gebiet um die Flüsse Narwa
und Pilica, – all das bleibt unklar (Staszewski 1969: 466-467).

Sollte die Benennung von *Warszawa* tatsächlich von einem Personennamen gekommen sein, würde es sich lohnen, auch an litauische Familiennamen zu denken, wie *Viršauskas* (Kaunas), *Viršelis* (Kr. Molėtai), *Viršickas* (Kr. Pakruojis, Panevėžys), *Viršinskas* (Kr. Zarasai), *Viršulas* (Kr. Panevėžys, Kr. Ukmergė), *Viršulas* (Kr. Šilutė), *Viršulis* (Kr. Ukmergė), *Viršulys* (Kr. Širvintai) und *Viršutis* (Kr. Prienai, Kaunas) [*Lietuvių pavardžių žodynas* (L – Ž), 1230-1231]. Die letzteren Familiennamen mit den Suffixen -*ul*- und -*ut*- kommen von lit. *viršus* 'Höhe, Spitze, Gipfel' [*Lietuvių pavardžių žodynas* (L – Ž), 1231]. Von diesem Appellativ können auch alle übrigen Familiennamen hergeleitet werden, da sie verhältnismäßig spät erschienen sind, und der Vokal *i* phonetisch kaum aus *e* entstanden sein kann.

Aber die Benennung der Hauptstadt Polens ist möglicherweise einer anderen Herkunft (falls überhaupt baltisch). Weil der Sonorlaut *ar* der polnischen Sprache auch aus idg. *$\dot{r}$ entstanden ist (Mańczak 1983: 32), vgl. polnisch *gardło* 'Kehle; Kehlkopf' < idg. *$g\dot{r}dlo$, – kann *Warszawa*, in Dokumenten *Warszewa* (< nom. coll. *$V\dot{r}šev\bar{a}$) etymologisch mit den ersten Gliedern solcher Eigennamen im Territorium Litauens verknüpft werden wie *Viršu-prūdė* (Kardokai, Kazlų Rūda [*Lietuvos TSR upių ir ežerų vardynas*, 199]), wo an zweiter Stelle ein *prūdas* 'Teich' (LKŽ X 820) steht, und *Viršu-žiglis* (Taurakiemis, Kr. Kaunas) – wegen seines zweiten Gliedes vgl. *žiglus* und *žyglus* 'schnell, geschick' (LKŽ XX 572), – sowie mit *Viršu-rodukis* (Marcinkonys, Kr. Varėna), ursprünglich wahrscheinlich *Viršurodis* mit dem Suffix -*uk*-. Die ersten Glieder dieser Gewässernamen waren *u*-Stämme wie dies auch beim Appellativ *viršus* 'oberer, höherer Teil; Überfluss…' (LKŽ XIX 628-637) der Fall ist. Den Gewässernamen *Viržuva* (Nebenfluss der Virvyčia, Viržuvėnai, Kr. Varniai) sowie den Flussnamen *Viržuona* (Nebenfluss der Šaltuona, Kr. Eržvilkas) verglich K. Būga mit den Flussnamen *Veiviržas* und *Viviržė* (Betonung unbekannt) und verknüpfte sie mit lit. *viržės* 'Heidekraut' (Būga 1958, 337; 1961, 545). Aber man kann diesen Gewässernamen auch zur Verbalwurzel *veržtis* (-*iasi*, -*ėsi*) 'schnell strömen; sich ergießen, anschwellen, steigen' (LKŽ XVIII 916), besonders *persi-viršti* (-*ia*, -*ė*) 'sich zur Oberfläche durchschlagen, umfassen' (LKŽ XIX 617). In diesem Fall wäre die Benennung der Hauptstadt Polens dem Gewässernamen oder eher einem Oikonym entsprungen. Aber eine Ableitung vom Substantiv *viršus* ist auch das Verb *viršiuoti* (-*iuoja*, -*iavo*) 'an Höhe gewinnen, besiegen; z u - s ä t z l i c h   b e w i r t e n' (LKŽ XIX 614). Der Infinitiv des lettischen Verbs im Satz *viņš virsās uz zirgu* 'er springt mit aller Kraft auf das Pferd' kann auch *virsoties* (nicht unbedingt *virzoties*) (ME IV 614) gewesen, also von derselben Wurzel wie lett. *virsus*, lit. *viršus* gebildet worden sein. In diesem Kontext erscheint ein möglicher Zusammenhang von *Warszawa*, in historischen Dokumenten *Warszewa* (< nom. coll. *$V\dot{r}šev\bar{a}$) mit lit. *viršus* möglich. In der litauischen Sprache können die ursprünglichen Stammauslaute -*u*- und -*ū*- der Substantive mit -eu- und -ou- in Wechselbeziehungen stehen, deshalb gab es früher ohne Zweifel Suffixe *-eu-ā und *-ou-ā (Endzelynas 1957, 70-71; Skardžius 1943, 381 [= 1996]).

Aber das alles wäre nur die etymologische Bedeutung der Benennung der Hauptstadt Polens. Die echte, s o z i a l e Bedeutung könnte daraus enstanden sein, dass mit diesem Wort der Ort (ein Gut oder königliches Dorf) bezeichnet wurde, wo der visitierende König (oder sein Beauftragter) sich aufhielt sowie aufgenommen und bewirtet wurde. Solche Orte sind in den folgenden Beispielen ersichtlich: *Opvoišovo 1) korolev. selo vъ Pojur. v., vozle im. Laukova, ležaščago vъ Mostaitjach; 2) oselychъ volokъ 7, a pustych 16 vъ Lovkov. voitovstve* [*Опвойшово 1) королев. село въ Поюр. в., возле им. Лаукова, лежащаго въ Мостайтях; 2) оселыхъ волокъ 7, а пустыхъ 16 въ Ловков. войтовстве*] (Sprogis 1888: 213) 'Opvoišovo 1) königliches Dorf im Amtsbezirk Pajūris, neben dem Gut Laukuva, das in Mosteiten liegt; 2) bewohnte Walache 7, verlassen 16 im Amt Laukuva'.

Wie ersichtlich, gibt es in der Gegenwartssprache – anstatt des in historischen Quellen belegten *Opvoišovo* (*Опвойшово*) – die Benennung *Apvaišava*, die die primäre Bedeutung 'Ort (Gut), dessen Pflicht Annahme und Bewirtung des visitierenden Königs (oder seines Statthalters) war' hatte. Diese Benennung ist mit dem Suffix -ava von *ap(i)vaišas oder *ap(i)vaišys 'Bewirtung, Bewirten' gebildet, und etymologisch gehört sie der Wurzel solcher Verben der litauischen Sprache wie *apvaišinti* (-ina, -ino) 'alle bewirten' (LKŽ XVII 957), gebraucht in den žemaitischen Mundarten, auch *ap-viešėti* (-vieši/-ia/-ėja, -ėjo) 'zu Gast bleiben, besuchen; refl.: länger zu Gast bleiben' (in Daukantas Schriften, im Wörterbuch von Juška und in Mundarten, z.B. Barstyčiai, Šatės [LKŽ XIX 273]) und daraus gebildetem Substantiv *vaišės* 'die Bewirtung, ihre Feierlichkeit, das Trinkgelage', vgl. *[Linarovio] pabaigtuvėms būdavo daromos vaišės – patalkys su alumi ir šokiais* (LKŽ XVII 954) 'Zum Ende der Flachsernte wurde Bewirtung – eine Gesselligkeit mit Bier und Tanzen veranstaltet'.

Dass *Warszawa*, in historischen Quellen *Warszewa* (< nom. coll. *Vr̥ševā*), die primäre Bedeutung 'Ort, dessen Pflicht die Aufnahme und Bewirtung des visitierenden Königs war' haben konnte, bestätigt das Verb *viršiuoti* (-iuoja, -iavo) mit seiner Bedeutung 'besiegen, überwinden; z u s ä t z l i c h b e w i r t e n'.

Simas Karaliūnas
Žadeikos 13-46
LT – 06324 Vilnius

Literatur

LKŽ = *Lietuvių kalbos žodynas*, I[1] (A – B). Redagavo J. Balčikonis, Vilnius, 1941; I[2] (A – B), II[2] (C – F). Antras leidimas. Atsak. redaktorius J. Kruopas, Vilnius, 1968-1969; III (G – H) – V (K – Klausinys). Atsak. redaktorius K. Ulvydas, Vilnius, 1956-1959; VI (Klausyti – Kvunkinti) – X (Pirm – Pūžuoti). Atsak. redaktorius J. Kruopas, Vilnius, 1962-1976; XI (R) – XVI (Tema – Tulė). Vyr. redaktorius K. Ulvydas, Vilnius, 1978-1995; XVII (Tūlė – Valgus) – XIX (Veša – Zvumterėti). Vyr. redaktorius V. Vitkauskas, Vilnius, 1996-1999; XX (Ž). Vyr. redaktorius V. Vitkauskas, Vilnius, 2002.

Lietuviški tradiciniai vietovardžiai, Vilnius, 2002.

Lietuvių pavardžių žodynas (L – Ž), Vilnius, 1989.

Lietuvos TSR administracinio-teritorinio suskirstymo žinynas, II dalis, Vilnius, 1976.

Lietuvos TSR upių ir ežerų vardynas, Vilnius, 1963.

Vietovardžių žodynas, Vilnius, 2002.

Brückner 1993 = Brückner A. *Słownik etymologiczny języka polskiego*. Przedruk z pierwszego wydania, Warszawa, 1993.

Būga 1958 = Būga K. *Rinktiniai raštai*, I, Vilnius, 1958.

———— 1961 = Būga K. *Rinktiniai raštai*, III, Vilnius, 1961.

Gerullis 1922 = Gerullis G. *Die altpreußischen Ortsnamen*, Berlin und Leipzig, 1922.

Mańczak 1983 = Mańczak W. *Polska fonetyka i morfologia historyczna*, Warszawa, [3]1983.

Oriol 1991 = Орел В. Э. Балтийская гидронимия и проблемы балтийского и славянского этногенеза – *Советское славяноведение*, 2, Москва, 1991.

Oriol 1997 = Орел В. Э. Неславянская гидронимия бассейнов Вислы и Одера – *Балто-славянские исследования 1988-1996*, Москва, 1997.

Sprogis 1888 = Спрогис И. Я. *Географическій словарь древней Жомойтской земли XVI столѣтія*, Вильна, 1888.

Staszewski 1968 = Staszewski J. *Mały słownik. Pochodzenie i znaczenie nazw geograficznych*, Warszawa, [3]1968.

Studia Etymologica Cracoviensia
vol. 14   Kraków 2009

Michael KNÜPPEL (Göttingen)

NOCH EINMAL ZUR MÖGLICHEN HERKUNFT
VON OSM. *tambur(a)* ~ *dambur(a)* ~ *damur(a)* ETC.

Wenngleich es an Versuchen der Ermittlung der Herkunft von Osm. *tambur(a)* ~ *dambur(a)* ~ *damur(a)* etc. 'Saiteninstrument, Mandoline, etc.' (mit recht verschiedenen Ergebnissen) nicht mangelt, so müssen diese Herleitungen doch immer noch als "unsicher" gelten. Es ist dies ein Zustand, der – wie nachstehend aufgezeigt – längst hätte behoben sein können, würden die Vertreter verschiedener Forschungsfelder die (nicht nur jüngsten) Ergebnisse aus "benachbarten" Disziplinen bloß häufiger zur Kenntnis nehmen – aber für welche Etymologisierungsversuche gilt dies nicht?

Bekanntlich gelangte die Bez. *tambur(a)* ~ *dambur(a)* ~ *damur(a)* für diverse Saiteninstrumente besonders durch das Osm.,[1] in dem es bereits in einer Vielzahl von Varianten belegt ist,[2] in zahlreiche Idiome, die im Zuge der osm. Expansion mit diesem in Kontakt gerieten: Alb. *tambura* ~ *tamura* ~ *tamar* 'kleine Gitarre mit drei Saiten', *tamburan* ... 'Bogen': *tambura, tambúra, tambur* 'Langhalslaute' (Boretzki [1976], p. 127), Dial. v. Çamëria *tambúra* ~ *tambura* 'id.' (ibid., p. 206), Bulg. *tamburá* 'mandolin-like folk instrument', 'Народден струнен музикален инструмент, на който се свири чрез дърпане на струните' (Grannes / Hauge / Süleymanoğlu [2002], p. 242[3]), Griech. *ταμπουρας*;[4] Rum. *tambŭră* 'Lăută – ... *tambur* ... *tămbără*, ... *tambură*';[5] Ung. *tambura* 'théorbe, pandore, guitare' (Kakuk [1973], p. 386), 'Tanbur', 'Art Zither' (Benkő [1994], p. 1476).[6] An Versuchen, den Ursprung der Bez. zu ergründen hat es daher aus naheliegenden Gründen – wie erwähnt – nicht gefehlt. Diese griffen zumeist recht kurz. Entweder wurde eine Arab. oder aber – und dies weitaus

---

[1] Eine recht gute Zusammenstellung der Osm. Formen findet sich bei Kakuk (1973), p. 386.
[2] Zu verschiedenen Ableitungen (nach Meninski) cf. Stachowski (1981), p. 120 f.
[3] Nach dem "Bǎlgarski tǎlkoven rečnik" (Popov [1996]).
[4] Benkő (1994), p. 1476; Ciorǎnescu (2001), Nr. 8492.
[5] Ciorǎnescu (2001), Nr. 8492.
[6] Nach dem "Etymologischen Wörterbuch des Ungarischen" ein Lehnwort aus dem Serb.-Kr. (Benkő [1994], p. 1476).

häufiger – eine Pers. Herkunft angenommen,[7] womit der Frage grundsätzlich beantwortet schien. Tatsächlich verbreitete sich die Bez. auch über das Pers. in "nördlicher Richtung" in zahlreiche Sprachen Zentralasiens und diesem benachbarter Regionen (Kasan-Tat. *dumbra*, Krim-Tat. *dambura*, Kirg. *dombra*, Mong. *dombura*, Kalm. *dombı̣* [Vasmer (1953), p. 362[8]]) – ja bis ins Russ. (*domrá*, *dombrá* 'Art Balalaika mit Drahtsaiten'[9]) und ins Mari (*tombɘra* 'balalaika')[10] und Čuv. (*tu̦mra* ~ *tɘmra* 'viersaitige Zither')[11] hinein und im Raum des Ind. Ozeans bis ins Swahili.[12]

Der Vf. dieser Zeilen, der bereits bei einer Durchsicht des Türk., Pers. und Ind. Lehnguts im Swahili auf das Problem der Herkunft von Osm. *tambur(a)* ~ *dambur(a)* ~ *damur(a)* etc. gestoßen ist, ist bei der Bearbeitung des von K. H. Menges nachgelassenen "Wörterbuchs der türkischen und anderen orientalischen Elemente im Serbokroatischen"[13] einmal mehr mit der scheinbar längst geklärten Herkunft dieser Bez. konfrontiert worden. So schrieb Menges in der Einleitung zum Ms. des erwähnten Wb.s, p. 22 (die weitgehend identisch ist mit seinem Besprechungsaufsatz[14] zu A. Kneževics "Die Turzismen in der Sprache der Kroaten und Serben"[15]): "... [ist] unter *tālim* 'Militärübung' (ᶜAr. *taᶜlīm*) angeführt, wobei auf *dambulhana* verwiesen wird; dies Letztere findet sich aber nicht an seiner alfabetischen Stelle, p. 97, sondern schon p. 95 unter *dabulhàna*. Die Varianten dieses Wortes zeigen eine Kontamination der Wörter Osm. *davul* (< ᶜAr. *ṭabl*) 'Trommel', Osm. *tulumbaz* 'Paukenspieler' > Sb.-Kr. *talàmbas* 'Pauke' und Osm. *tambur* 'ein Saiteninstrument', die etwas erläutert hätten wer-

---

[7]   So auch K. Lokotsch: "Ar. *ṭanbūr*: 'Zither, Mandoline oder ein anderes Saiteninstrument', vulg. *tambūr*; hieraus sp. *tambor*, it. *tamburo*, frz. *tambour* 'Trommel'. Mit Metathesis wurde mlat. *pandura*, it. (alt) *pandura*, *pandora* > (neu) *mandola*, frz. *pandore* > *mandore*, *mandole*, dtsch. *Mandoline*. Das ar. Wort kommt selbst aus einem pers., aus dem u.a. afrz. *tabouret* 'Trommel', prov. 'kleiner Sessel', frz. *tabouret* 'dass.', prov. *taborel*, *taborin* 'Tamburin' und viele Ableitungen geflossen sind" (Lokotsch [1927], p. 159, Nr. 2015), S. Kakuk: "Mot d'origine arabo-persane; cf. pers. *ṭaṃbūra* 'a kind of mandoline'; *ṭuṃbūr* 'A kind of lute or guitar with a long neck' (Steing.) < ar. *ṭambūr* (Wahrm.), *ṭunbūr* (Wehr): 'id.'" (Kakuk [1973], p. 386) oder das "Etymologische Wörterbuch des Ungarischen" (Benkő [1994], p. 1476).

[8]   Nach Ramstedt (1953), p. 95, Radloff (1905), pp. 1008, 1653, 1727, Räsänen (1923), p. 70, Preobraženskij (1910), p. 190.

[9]   Vasmer (1953), p. 362; dort noch der Hinweis "Südrußl. (D.). Zuerst δοmpa Avvakum [dies = Gudzij (1934)] 77 (s. auch Duvernoy Aruss. Wb. [dies = Duvernoy (1894)] 35). Turkotat. Lehnwort".

[10] Räsänen (1923), p. 70.

[11] Paasonen (1974), p. 173.

[12] Knappert (1983), p. 136.

[13] Dieses wird vom Vf. gerade für den Druck aufbereitet und wird voraussichtlich 2008/2009 erscheinen.

[14] Menges (1968).

[15] Knežević (1962).

den sollen".[16] Im Ms. selbst findet sich dann schließlich ein Eintrag zu Serb.-Kr. *tàmbura*, in dem Menges die Herleitungen von Knežević[17] und A. Škaljić in dessen Wb. der Turzismen im Serbo-Kroatischen,[18] zurückweist und sich – mit Räsänen – für einen Aram. Ursprung des Wortes ausspricht:[19] "*tàmbur, -a*, 'Musikinstrument (ähnlich der Mandoline)'; Šk. auch *tânbura*, wird von beiden auf Osm. *tambur* 'id.' und dies von Kn. auf ᶜAr. *ṭanbur*, von Šk. auf ᶜAr. *ṭunbur* und weiter auf Pers. *dūnbäri bärä* 'Lammschwanz' zurückgeführt. Das Osm. hat *ṭunbur* (< ᶜAr., pl. *ṭanābur*), vulgär *tambur*, 'a larger six stringed lute' (Redh., p. 1246), Pers. *tunbūr* (< ᶜAr.) 'a kind of lute or guitar with a long neck' (Steingass, p. 820 mit der Bemerkung: < Pers. *dumba-barra* 'lamb's tail', das oft zu *dumbara* 'guitar' kontrahiert wird; p. 820, 537 f.), dieselbe Volksetymologie, wie bei Šk. Der Prototyp ist Aram. *ṭanbūrā* (Räs., p. 459). (Kn., p. 317; Ms., p. 434; Šk., p. 599)".[20] Von der Aram. Herkunft des Wortes scheint Menges selbst später allerdings abgerückt zu sein. Auf den letzten Seiten seines Ms.s finden sich nachträgliche Anmerkungen, die dies nahe legen. So notiert er auf p. 493 (311 A): "*tambur, dombra* etc. etc. < Ar., Pers. *ṭbbūr* etc. << Ind.: Skr., Bengālī *ḍamaru* 'kleine Trommel, dgl. Attribut von Gottheiten', Hindī *ḍamrū*, Marāṭᶜī *ḍámru* 'id., <u>kürbisartig</u>'; Marāṭᶜī *ṭamburā* 'ein vīṇā-artiges Instr.', Hindī *ṭamburā* 'eine Art Laute' – viell. alle Austro-Asiat. Herkunft" und verweist hier auf Lévi / Przyluski / Bloch (1929), p. 158 ff. Auf ausführlichere Angaben sowie sich hier ergebende Probleme geht Menges in dem telegrammartigen Stil, in dem sein Wb. bisweilen abgefaßt ist, nicht weiter ein. Es stellt sich also die Frage, ob und inwieweit einer möglichen "Austro-Asiat. Herkunft" vor der Aram. oder Pers. der Vorzug zu geben ist – dies umso mehr, als Menges zum einen ja bekanntlich eine Schwäche für "weitgewanderte" Lehnwörter hatte und an der betreffenden Stelle zum anderen keine ausführlicheren Angaben macht.

Bei der von Menges angeführten Arbeit handelt es sich um einen in dem Band von S. Lévi, J. Przyluski und J. Bloch enthaltenen Aufsatz von J. Przyluski (pp. 149-160 "Non-Aryan loans in Indo-Aryan"), der seinerseits auf einen Beitrag desselben im "Journal Asiatique" zurückgeht.[21] In diesem Beitrag, in dem Przyluski im Zuge der Herleitung des skr. *udumbara* aus dem Austro-Asiat. resp. der Zuordnung desselben zu einer Austro-Asiat. Schicht im Indo-Arischen vorschlägt, wird von diesem auch die Herkunft von Skr. und Bengālī *ḍamaru*, Hindī *ḍamrū* sowie Marāṭᶜī *ḍámru* und *tamburā* erörtert:

---

[16] Menges (1968), p. 138.
[17] Knežević (1962), p. 317.
[18] Škaljić (1965), p. 599.
[19] Eine Auffassung, der sich auch S. Stachowski (1981), p. 120 anschließt.
[20] Im vom Vf. des vorliegenden Beitrags herausgegebenen Wb. Nr. 1296.
[21] Przyluski (1926).

Ḍamaru is the Sanskrit and the Bengali name of a small drum
which plays an important role in Indian iconography as the attribute of
several divinities ... The instrument called in Marathi *ḍamru*, in Hindi
ḍamrū, etc., resembles a gourd, with two swellings, cut in such a way
as to have only the two hemispheric ends. The analogy of the names
of this drum with those of the *udumbara* fruit in the Indian languages
can be therefore explained by their common resemblance to some cu-
curbits. Tamburā is the Marathi word for a kind of *vīṇā*. It does not
appear doubtful at all that the instrument owes its name to that of the
two hollow appendices which are suspended from the tube like the
gourds from their stalk.[22]

Wie bereits angedeutet, ergeben sich bei der Zusammenführung resp. gemeinsamen Herleitung von Skr. und Bengālī *ḍamaru*, Hindī *ḍamrū*, Marāṭᶜī
ḍamru und *tamburā* etc. mit Pers. *ṭanbur ~ tunbūr*, Arab., pl. *tanābur*, Osm.
tunbur ~ tambur (vulg.) etc. einige Schwierigkeiten, welche J. Przyluski sehr
wohl bewußt waren, die Menges jedoch "unterschlägt" (was die "Inner-Ind."
resp. Austro-Asiat. Verhältnisse betrifft, so mögen sich hier die dazu berufene-
ren Fachkollegen aus den betreffenden Disziplinen äußern). Zum einen haben
die Ind. Sprachen eine ganze Reihe von Instrumentenbezeichnungen aus dem
Persischen empfangen[23] (warum also nicht auch pers. *ṭanbur ~ tunbūr?*) und
zum anderen bezeichnen die im vorderasiat. Raum und durch das Osm. auf dem
Balkan resp. das Pers. in Zentralasien verbreiteten Termini ein Saiteninstrument,
während sich die sich auf dem Ind. Sub-Kontinent findenden Bezeichnungen
auf ein Membranophon beziehen.

Hierzu wäre zunächst anzumerken, daß nahezu allen Instrumentenbezeichnungen, die sich in Ind. Sprachen finden und Pers. Parallelen haben, gemein ist,
daß hier nur Belege aus "jüngeren" ind. Sprachen vorliegen (von Skr. *ḍhōlak*,
eine Faßtrommel < Pers. *duhul* [Sachs (1923), p. 73] einmal abgesehen). D.h.,
sich diese Formen gewöhnlich allenfalls in M.-Ind. Sprachen finden, nicht aber
aus dem Skr. belegt sind. Ausgerechnet aber *ḍamaru* bildet in dieser Hinsicht
eine Ausnahme. Nicht etwa, daß das Skr. in Bezug auf musik. Termini keine
Lehnwörter aus dem Pers. empfangen hätte oder der Beleg aus dem Skr. bereits
als ein zweifelsfreies Indiz für eine Ind. Herkunft der Bez. zu werten wäre –
wenngleich der Umstand, daß die sog. "Sanduhrtrommel" (Skr. *ḍamaru*) als Attribut hinduist. Gottheiten wohl verbreitet ist,[24] bereits einen Ind. Ursprung na-

---

[22] Lévi / Przyluski / Bloch (1929), p. 159.

[23] Vgl. Pañj. *daf* 'Rahmentrommel', Hindī *daf ~ ḍaf ~ ḍhaplā* etc. 'id.' < Pers. *daff*
      (Sachs [1923], p. 64), Beng. *dārā* 'Rahmentrommel', Marāṭᶜī *ḍair* 'id.', Hindī *dāe-*
      rah 'id.' < Pers. *daīre* 'Kreis' (ibid., p. 63).

[24] Sachs (1923), p. 75 f. "Die Sanduhrtrommel (...) spielt in der indischen Mythologie
      eine bedeutsame Rolle als Attribut zahlreicher Persönlichkeiten des Pantheon. Brah-

helegt. In Verbindung jedoch mit der Bedeutung 'Trommel' in den Ind. Sprachen kommen berechtigte Zweifel auf an der Pers. Herkunft des Terminus. Dies zum einen aufgrund des Umstandes, daß die Herleitung aus einem Austro-Asiat. *udumbara* – in der Bedeutung der Bezeichnung einer kürbisartigen Frucht – sowohl lautlich als auch semantisch aufgeht. Zum anderen aber auch im Hinblick darauf, daß auch Pers. *ṭanbur* ~ *tunbūr*, Arab., pl. *tanābur* (vielleicht sogar Osm. *tunbur* ~ *tambur* [vulg.] etc.) einmal zur Bezeichnung eines Membranophons gedient haben muß – schließlich hat es diese in seiner ursprüngl. Gestalt in den Roman. Sprachen bis heute (Span. *tambor*, Ital. *tamburo*, Franz. *tambour* 'Trommel' [Lokotsch (1927), p. 159, Nr. 2015]). Interessant ist in diesem Kontext auch, daß im Amhar. *tambur* 'eine Art Trommel' bezeichnet. Es handelt sich hier sicher nicht um ein Lehnwort aus dem Ital. – wie von Amsalu Aklilu gelegentlich angenommen[25] –, da ein direkter ital. Einfluß erst im Zuge der kolonialen Präsenz Italiens am Horn von Afrika anzunehmen ist,[26] die Bez. aber zu dieser Zeit bereits in Äthio-Semit. Sprachen nachweisbar ist.[27] Da diese vor der Mitte des 19. Jh.s keinen unmittelbaren Kontakt zur Sprachenwelt Indiens hatten, kommen als Vermittlersprachen – wenn das Amhar. *tambur* nicht auf Portug. *tambor* 'Trommel' zurückgehen sollte – hier nur Arab. Dialekte oder das Osm. in Frage. Die Bedeutungserweiterung auf Saiteninstrumente mag bereits früh im Arab. oder Pers. erfolgt sein und dürfte sich aus dem Umstand erklären, daß verschiedene der zahllosen Ind. Instrumente (wie Zupftrommeln oder verschiedene *vīṇā*-artige Instrumente) für die mit den Kulturen Süd-Asiens nicht vertrauten, westl. Nachbarn bei einem nur losen Kontakt kaum eindeutig als "Saiteninstrumente" oder "Membranophone" bestimmt werden konnten.

Michael Knüppel
Seminar für Turkologie und Zentralasienkunde
Waldweg 26
D – 37073 Göttingen

---

mā's gelehrtes Weib Sarasvatī, die Todesgöttin Bhadra-Kālī, der vierzehnhändige Zornesgott Aghōra, die Schutzgöttin Piḍāri, Īśvara in der Form des Īśāna, Śiva, die Gaṇa's und Ḍākinī's (Hexen), sie alle tragen in der Hand die Trommel Ḍamaru, umwunden mit der Schlange, dem Symbol des Heils wie des Todes".

[25] Amsalu Aklilu (1986), p. 133.

[26] Eine dauerhafte ital. Präsenz am Roten Meer war erst infolge des Erwerbs Assabs durch die *Società di Navigazione Rubattino* am 15.11.1869 gegeben.

[27] *Tambur* bezeichnet in Äthiopien – vor allem in Gondar und N-Godscham – die Trommeln, die von den Debtära für die Kirchenmusik benutzt werden. Von jüngeren Sprechern des Amhar. wird die Bez. geradezu als lokale Besonderheit und bereits als ungebräuchlich betrachtet.

Abkürzungen des Verfassers

Alb. = Albanisch; Amhar. = Amharisch; Arab. = Arabisch; Aram. = Aramäisch; Bulg. = Bulgarisch; Čuv. = Čuvašisch; Franz. = Französisch; Griech. = Griechisch; Ital. = Italienisch; Kalm. = Kalmückisch; Kasan-Tat. = Kasan-Tatarisch; Kirg. = Kirgisisch; Krim-Tat. = Krim-Tatarisch; M.-Ind. = Mittel-Indisch; Mong. = Mongolisch; Osm. = Osmanisch; Pañj. = Pañjābī; Rom. = Romanisch; Rum. = Rumänisch; Russ. = Russisch; Serb.-Kr. = Serbo-Kroatisch; Skr. = Sanskrit; Span. = Spanisch; Türk. = Türkisch; Ung. = Ungarisch

Abkürzungen anderer Verfasser

Afrz. = Alt-Französisch; ᶜAr. = Arabisch; Aruss. = Alt-Russisch; Dtsch. = Deutsch; Frz. = Französisch; It. = Italienisch; Kn. = Knežević; Mlat. = Mittel-Lateinisch; Prov. = Provençalisch; Räs. = Räsänen; Redh. = Redhouse; Sb.-Kr. = Serbokroatisch; Šk. = Škaljić; Sp. = Spanisch; Steing. = Steingass; Wahrm. = Wahrmund

Literatur

Amsalu Aklilu:
  (1986) *Amharic-English dictionary*. Addis Ababa 1986.
Benkő, Loránd:
  (1994) *Etymologisches Wörterbuch des Ungarischen*. Bd. II. Budapest 1994.
Boretzky, Norbert:
  (1976) *Der türkische Einfluss auf das Albanische*. Teil 2: *Wörterbuch der albanischen Turzismen*. Wiesbaden 1976 (Albanische Forschungen 12).
Ciorănescu, Alexandru:
  (2001) *Dicţionarul etimologic al limbii Române*. Bucureşti 2001.
Duvernoy, A.:
  (1894) *Matĕrjaly dlja slovarja drevne-russkogo jazyka*. Moskva 1894.
Grannes, Alf / Hauge, Kjetil Rå / Süleymanoğlu, Hayriye:
  (2002) *A dictionary of turkisms in Bulgarian*. Oslo 2002.
Gudzij, Nikolaj Kallinikovič:
  (1934) *Žitie protopoa Avvakuma: im samim napisannoe I drugie ego sočinenija*. Moskva 1934 (Russkie memuary, drevniki, piśma i materialy).
Kakuk, Suzanne:
  (1973) *Recherches sur l'histoire de la langue Osmanlie des XVIᵉ et XVIIᵉ siècles. Les éléments Osmanlis de la langue Hongroise*. The Hague, Paris 1973.

Knappert, Jan:
(1983) Persian and Turkish loanwords in Swahili. In: *SGA* 5. 1983, pp. 111-143.
Knežević, Anton:
(1962) *Die Turzismen in der Sprache der Kroaten und Serben.* Meisenheim am Glan 1962 (Slavisch-Baltisches Seminar der Westfälischen Wilhelms-Universität, Münster, Veröffentlichung, Nr. 3).
Lévi, Sylvain / Przyluski, Jean / Bloch, Jules:
(1929) *Pre-Aryan and Pre-Dravidian in India.* Calcutta 1929 [2. Aufl. Calcutta 1975, Neudruck: New Delhi 2001].
Lokotsch, Karl:
(1927) *Etymologisches Wörterbuch der europäischen (germanischen, romanischen und slavischen) Wörter orientalischen Ursprungs.* Heidelberg 1927 (Indogermanische Bibliothek. 1. Abt.: Sammlung indogermanischer Lehr- und Handbücher, 2. Reihe: Wörterbücher, 3. Bd.).
Menges, Karl Heinrich:
(1968) Türkisches Sprachgut im Serbo-Kroatischen. In: *UAJb* 40. 1968, pp. 135-154 [Bespr. v. Knežević, Anton: *Die Turzismen in der Sprache der Kroaten und Serben.* Meisenheim am Glan 1962].
Paasonen, Heikki:
(1974) *Tschuwaschisches Wörterverzeichnis.* Szeged 1974 (Studia Uralo-Altaica IV).
Popov, Dimităr:
(1996) *Bălgarski tălkoven rečnik. Četvărto izdanie. Dopălneno i preraboteno ot Dimităr Popov.* Sofia 1996.
Preobraženskij, Aleksandr G.:
(1910) *Ètimologičeskij slovaŕ russkogo jazyka.* Bd. I. Moskva 1910.
Przyluski, Jean:
(1926) Un ancien peuple du Penjab: Les Udumbara. In: *JA.* 1926, pp. 25-36.
Radloff, Wilhelm:
(1905) *Versuch eines Wörterbuchs der Türk-Dialecte.* Bd. III. St.-Pétersbourg 1905.
Räsänen, Martti:
(1923) *Die tatarischen Lehnwörter im Tscheremissischen.* Helsingfors 1923 (MSFOu 50).
(1969) *Versuch eines etymologischen Wörterbuchs der Türksprachen.* Helsinki 1969 (Lexica Societatis Fenno-Ugricae 17: 1).
Ramstedt, Gustav John:
(1953) *Kalmückisches Wörterbuch.* Helsinki 1953 (Lexica Societatis Fenno-Ugricae 3).

Redhouse, James William:

(1890) *A Turkish and English lexicon. Shewing in English the significations of the Turkish terms.* Constantinople 1890.

Sachs, Curt:

(1923) *Die Musikinstrumente Indiens und Indonesiens. Zugleich eine Einführung in die Instrumentenkunde.* 2. Aufl. Berlin, Leipzig 1923 (Handbücher der Staatlichen Museen zu Berlin).

Škaljić, Abdulah:

(1965) *Turcizmi u srpskohrvatskom jeziku.* Sarajevo 1965 (Bibliotheka Kulturno Nasljeđe).

Stachowski, Stanisław:

(1981) *Studien über die arabischen Lehnwörter im Osmanisch-Türkischen.* Teil III. Wrocław, Warszawa, Kraków, Gdańsk, Łódź 1981 (Polska Akademia Nauk – Oddział w Krakowie, Prace Komisji Orientalistycznej 17).

Steingass, Francis Joseph:

(1947) *A comprehensive Persian-English dictionary. Including the Arabic words and phrases to be met with in Persian literature being Johnson and Richardson's Persian, Arabic, and English dictionary.* 3. Aufl. London 1947.

Vasmer, Max:

(1953) *Russisches etymologisches Wörterbuch.* Bd. I. Heidelberg 1953 (Indogermanische Bibliothek. 2. Reihe: Wörterbücher).

Wahrmund, Adolf:

(1877) *Handwörterbuch der arabischen und deutschen Sprache.* Giessen 1877.

Wehr, Hans:

(1956) *Arabisches Wörterbuch für die Schriftsprache der Gegenwart.* 2. Aufl. Leipzig 1956.

Studia Etymologica Cracoviensia
vol. 14   Kraków 2009

Ivan KOTLIAROV (St. Petersburg)

LAWS OF NON-INDO-EUROPEAN LANGUAGES

Two existing catalogues of linguistic laws (Collinge 1985, Collinge 1995) are entirely dedicated to Indo-European languages, which is hardly surprising – this branch of linguistics is by far the most developed one. To the best of my knowledge, there are no catalogues of laws in non-Indo-European languages (descriptions of these laws are generally more or less chaotically given in encyclopedic sources on general linguistics (LES 1990), (Trask 2001)).

The aim of the present article is to fill in this gap and to compile a catalogue of laws in non-Indo-European languages.

First of all, it is important to highlight that there are two types of regularities studied in the historical linguistics – linguistic laws and linguistic rules. The difference between them, while being obvious, is somewhat difficult to define. We might say that a law is a formal description of a typologically important regularity with no exceptions at all or with small number of exceptions that can be plausibly explained (preferably by effects of other laws, not on a case-by-case basis). A rule may be defined as a trend, not as a completely regular process in the strict meaning of this word. That is, a rule is respected in most cases, but has numerous exceptions and/or is (or, better, is *considered* to be) less important for this language and/or for linguistics in general.

I include in this catalogue sound laws and rules that meet the following requirements:

1. They apply to non-Indo-European languages – even if these laws have parallels in Indo-European languages, they were initially formulated for non-Indo-European ones.

2. This issue is dedicated to the memory of Evgeny Helimski, an outstanding scholar who achieved excellent results in many fields of linguistics. I believe that it would be logical to choose for this catalogue the laws that lie within the field of interests of Evgeny Helimski (Altaic and Uralic languages, comparative linguistics, phonology). Therefore laws related to other language families (like Afrasiatic or Amerindian) were excluded from this catalogue.

3. They are eponymous (and have been referred to as such in the literature[1]) –
this is a very important requirement. According to the existing tradition, if a
sound change did not deserve to bear a name, it normally does not deserve
the status of law either. In other words, scholars do not consider this sound
change important enough to assign it a special name.

The list of laws is broken down by (macro)families. Within each specific
(macro)family the laws are listed in alphabetic order. The laws (according to the
notation proposed by Neville Edgar Collinge (1995: 28)) are cited by the inven-
tor's name in small capital letters.

1. Altaic

This family (supposed to include Turkic, Mongolic, Tungusic, Korean and
Japonic languages) is not recognized by most linguists; however, the aim of the
present article is not to repeat all the arguments *pro et contra*. We will simply
admit the existence of the Altaic hypothesis and list relevant eponymous sound
laws (as well as different points of view within this hypothesis).

HELIMSKI (I)

This law describes "regular phonetic developments that accompanied the
voicing of word-medial obstruents and affricates in Monguor" (Helimski 1984:
27). While HELIMSKI (I) should be considered as a restriction on RAMSTEDT-
PELLIOT (see below), it deals with one specific language within Mongolic family and is therefore recognized by all scholars working in this field – both by pro-
and anti-Altaicists.

According to (Helimski 1984), Monguor word-medial consonants splitted
into their voiced counterparts and the distinctive feature of voicelessness. The
latter moved to the beginning of the word, where it produced one of the following effects:
1. Development of this feature into **h-* (> *x, f, s, ṣ, ś*) before word-initial vowels (the latter have often disappeared later): Monguor *xarDan* 'gold', Written
   Mongolian (WM) *altan* 'id.'; Monguor *sDōGu* 'old', WM *ötegü* 'id.'.
2. Devoicing of word-initial voiced consonants: Monguor *p'ierGeDi-* 'to be
   difficult', WM *berged-* 'id.'.
3. Word-initial consonants preserved their voicelessness: Monguor *k'uGuo*
   'blue', WM *köke* 'id.'.

---

[1] There is one exception to this requirement where I dared to propose a name for a
law.

4. Intermediate voiced consonants in words with word-initial resonants underwent devoicing: Monguor *k'irDŹiaG* 'pack saddle, pack load', WM *yanggirčay* 'id.'.

5. *s*, *ṣ*, *ś* were added to intermediate clusters (**rT*, **bt*, **dT*, **gT*) in words with word initial resonants: Monguor *mu(r)ṣDā-* 'to forget', WM *marta-* 'id.'.

6. Voicing did not occur in word-medial position, if the first position in the word is occupied (or separated) by a resonant and there are no intermediate voiced consonants or clusters (as in pts. 4-5 above): Monguor *nik'i* 'to weave', WM *neke* 'id.'.

7. Effect similar to pts. 5-6 above occurred if the (original) voiceless consonant belonged to a productive suffix: Monguor *tś'igiśDŹi* 'ear-flap', WM *čikibči* 'id.'; Monguor *Dūtś'i* 'singer', WM *dayuči* 'id.'.

HELIMSKI (I) is the point 1 in the list above, that is: in Monguor, the distinctive feature of voicelessness (that appeared after the split of word-medial voiced consonants into their voiced counterparts and this feature) moved to the beginning of the word with word-initial vowel and became a phoneme (**h-* > *x*, *f*, *s*, *ṣ*, *ś*). This law is very important both for historical phonology of Mongolic languages and for historical phonology in general as it provides an example of a distinctive feature that became a phoneme.

The main consequence of this law for the Altaic hypothesis is that word-initial *x-*, *f-*, *s-*, *ṣ-*, *ś-* in Monguor may come not only from proto-Mongolic **h* (according to RAMSTEDT-PELLIOT), but also from the distinctive feature of voicelessness. However, HELIMSKI (I) is not mentioned by name in EDAL.

It should also be noted that the scientific value of Helimski article (1984) goes far beyond this law as he succeeded in explaining several phonetic phenomena (pts. 1-7 above) by one reason – the transfer of the distinctive feature of voicelessness to the beginning of the word.

RAMSTEDT-PELLIOT

This law is one of the main pillars of the Altaic hypothesis (Kormushin 1990: 28) and establishes the following series of sound correspondences in word-initial position: Mongolic **φ-* or **p-* > Middle Mongolian **h-* > Mongolian *Ø-* – Turkic **Ø-* – Tungusic **φ-* or **p-* (Tungus *p*, Manchu *f*): Mongolic *φulagan* or *pulagan* 'red' – Manchu *fulgiyan* 'id.' (Poppe 1951: 319). This law was proposed by Gustav John Ramstedt in his article (1916) and discussed at great length by Paul Pelliot (1925). The law is mentioned by name in (Kormushin 1990: 28).

The authors of EDAL extended RAMSTEDT-PELLIOT (but did not mention it by name) to include Korean and Japonic (EDAL 2003: 24, 25-28) – so maybe RAMSTEDT-PELLIOT in Starostin-Mudrak-Dybo's formulation? (see below):

Table 1.

Proto-Altaic	Mongolic	Turkic	Tungusic	Korean	Japonic
*p'-	*h-, *j-	*∅-, *j-	*p-	*p-	*p-

According to EDAL (2003: 26), the most frequent reflex of Proto-Altaic (PA) *p'- in Turkic is *∅-; however, it may also yield *j- before original diphthongs *ia, *io (but never before *iu). PA *p'- regularly yields *h- in Mongolic, but sometimes it produces *j- (normally before *e and diphthongs) – however, this development is much less frequent than the regular one (EDAL 2003: 26).

In one of the Turkic languages, Khalaj (spoken in Central Iran), PA initial *p'- > h- (instead of expected ∅-): Khalaj (Khal.) *hadaq* 'foot' < Proto-Turkic (PT) *(h)adak* 'id.' < PA p'ágdi 'id.' (EDAL 2003: 26). However, in some words Khal. initial *h- represents an innovation (a prosthetic consonant): Khal. *hil-* 'to die' < PT *öl-* 'id.' < PA *oli-* 'id.' (EDAL 2003: 27). Rules for appearance of this prosthetic consonant are not proposed in EDAL (2003: 27-28).

Of course, it is not necessary to indicate that RAMSTEDT-PELLIOT is not recognized by anti-Altaicists.

An important restriction of RAMSTEDT-PELLIOT is HELIMSKI (I) – see above.

WHITMAN

This law was published in (Whitman 1990)[2] – but proposed for the first time in John B. Whitman's doctoral thesis (Whitman 1985) – and referred to as "Whitman's law" in (Vovin 2001: 96). This law is based on possible Koreo-Japonic cognates within the Altaic hypothesis and states the following: medial *-m- and *-r- were lost in pre-Proto-Japonic (PJ) if they followed a short vowel (Whitman 1990: 528) – Old Japanese (OJ) *kwo* 'child', Middle Korean (MK) *kwòma* 'concubine' (Korean *kkoma* 'child, little one'); OJ *kwo* 'flour' < PJ *kaCu*, MK *kòlò* 'id.'; OJ *pari* 'needle' < pre-PJ *parari* < *panari*, MK *pànól* 'id.' (Vovin 2001: 96). The most frequent phenomenon is the medial *-r-loss (Vovin 2001: 96), (EDAL: 44). The medial *-m-loss is less frequent, but covered by WHITMAN (Whitman 1990: 524) and analyzed in EDAL (44). Interestingly enough, EDAL does not mention WHITMAN.

However, in EDAL we find the following: "any resonant preceding the weakened *-γ- in the third syllable was also weakened and dropped, together with the following vowel, viz.: *CVRVγV > *CVRγV > *CVγV. On the other hand, *CVCVγV > *CVCV", this weakened γ being due to suffixation *CVCV-γV < *CVCV-gV, because all voiced consonants in the third syllable in pre-Proto-

---

[2]   I am happy to express my sincere gratitude to Prof. John B. Whitman, who kindly sent me a copy of his publication (Whitman 1990).

Japonic were fricativized (EDAL 2003: 44). Hence PJ *kua (in EDAL reconstruction (53); but kuà in (EDAL 2003: 572)) 'flour' < Altaic *gure-gV 'id.',
with suffixation (EDAL 2003: 53), while MK word comes from a form without
suffix – MK kằrằ (in EDAL reconstruction) 'id.' < Altaic *gure 'id.' (EDAL
2003: 202); PJ sua 'hemp' < Altaic *súme-ga (EDAL 2003: 44, 1317-1318) 'a
kind of weed, hemp'. It is interesting to note that the authors of EDAL mention
loss of other medial resonants in pre-Proto-Japonic (in addition to *-r- and *-m-)
– namely loss of *-l- and *-ŋ- (EDAL 2003: 44), but they do not elaborate this
subject any further in the part of EDAL dedicated to the historical phonology of
Altaic languages.

So, while accepting the phenomenon of *-r-loss in pre-Proto-Japonic, the
authors of EDAL give it a different explanation and therefore reject WHITMAN.
It means that this law is not yet universally accepted by Altaicists and its future
depends on additional research in this field.[3] However, it is referred to as eponymous law even by opponents of the Altaic theory (Vovin 2008: 112)[4] so the title
is fully justified.

2. Uralic

HELIMSKI (II)

This law was proposed by Evgeny Helimski (2007: 124-133). As Helimski
put it:

> Proto-Samoyed (PS) high-rise and middle-rise vowels in the first
> syllable followed by a syllable with a PS Schwa undergo lengthening
> (partly accompanied by narrowing of middle-rise vowels) in (Common
> – I.K.) Selkup. No lengthening occurs when the next syllable contained
> a PS non-Schwa (full) vowel; under certain conditions lengthening is
> blocked by the closeness of the first syllable. (Helimski 2007: 133)

As Helimski indicated, this lengthening was triggered by the PS Schwa,
not by the Selkup one. Selkup ə reflects PS *ə as well as PS *a, *ä and *e, but
only the vowels that were followed by PS *ə underwent lengthening: Common
Selkup (CSelk.) *īlə 'to rise' < PS *īlə 'id.', but CSelk. *ilə 'to live' < PS *īlä
'id.' (Helimski 2007: 125).

---

[3] Obviously, the same is true for the explanation of the medial resonant loss formulated in EDAL.

[4] I am grateful to Prof. Alexander Vovin (University of Hawai'i, Manoa), who kindly
allowed me to read an electronic version of his book (Vovin 2008) before publication.

The law has different realizations depending on the quality of the length-ened vowel and the type of the syllable (open or closed). Some examples (the list is not exhaustive):

1. PS high rise vowels underwent lengthening in CSelk.: CSelk. *īlə 'to rise' < PS *īlə 'id.' (Helimski 2007: 126). The lengthening does not occur in a pri-marily closed syllable: CSelk. *šümtə- 'to whistle' < PS *kümtə- 'id.' (He-limski 2007: 127-128).

2. PS middle rise vowels underwent lengthening and rising: PS sejə 'heart' > CSelk. sīćə 'id.' (Helimski 2007: 128-129).

3. PS *e underwent lengthening and preserves its quality in closed syllables ending on an occlusive: PS mektə 'heart' > CSelk. mēktə 'id.' (Helimski 2007: 129). The lengthening does not occur if the closed syllable ends on a resonant: PS (?) *ńerkə 'to fight; to swing' > CSelk. ńerkə 'id.' (Helimski 2007: 130).

The importance of this law should not be underestimated as it helps to solve two important problems in Samoyedic studies:

1. It gives one more source of vocalic length in Selkup (this length being an in-novation in comparison with PS) (Helimski 2007: 124). Other sources are PS *a, ä, monophthongisation of diphthongs and vocalic combinations and par-tial lengthening of vowels in open monosyllabic roots (which was often ex-tended on derivates of these words) (Helimski 2007: 132).

2. Paradigmatic ablaut in Selkup is explained as a synchronic parallel of this diachronic sound law: CSelk. *nir 'staff' (Taz Selkup nir 'id.', Gen. nīrən) < PS *nir 'id.', Gen. nirən.

This law has not been assigned a name yet. However, this law is important for the historical phonetics of Selkup, and, taking into account the attention He-limski paid to this language and his deep involvement into the destiny of small Samoyedic languages of the Russian North, I think it would be justified to name this law in Helimski's honor.

HONTI[5]

Normally Proto-Finno-Ugric (PFU) *s yields ∅ in Hungarian (Hung.): PFU *säppä 'bile' > Finnish (Fin.) sappi 'id.', Hung. epe 'id.'; PFU *sōne 'vein; sinew' > Fin. suoni 'id.', Hung. ín 'id.'; PFU *sükśe 'autumn' > Fin. syksy 'id.', Hung. ősz 'id.' The way of sound evolution is PFU *s > Proto-Hung. *h > Hung. ∅.

However, there is one notable exception from this regular development: Hung. fészek 'nest' – cf. Fin. pesä 'id.', Udmurt puz 'id.', Komi poz 'id.' – where PFU *s > Hung. s (spelt sz). An explanation of this exception was pro-

---

[5]   This sound development has been assigned the status of a rule, not a law.

posed by László Honti (1983) and is known now as Honti's rule (HONTI). According to HONTI, PFU *s > Hung. s (spelt sz) after *pV and disappears in other positions. This specific development is explained by the partial assimilation between proto-Hung. *f (< PFU *p) and proto-Hung. *θ (< PFU *s): in this case *θ yielded *s (that is, came back to the starting point of the phonetic change) instead of *h under the influence of the preceding *f.

Unfortunately, this rule is valid for only one word (no other words containing the PFU sequence *pVs survived in Hungarian), therefore, its legal status was unclear. However, Helimski in his article (1987: 57-60) provided additional typological evidence that can be used to support HONTI.

According to Helimski, the sequence *pVs had a special status in the other branch of Uralic – namely, in the historical phonetics of Mator (Mator-Taigish-Karagassic, Mat.), an extinct Samoyedic language. Normally, Proto-Samoyedic (PS) *p- > Mat. h-: PS *$p\mathring{a}rk\mathring{a}$ 'cloth; fur-coat' > Mat. $harga$ 'fur-coat'; PS *$pä$ 'tree; forest' > Mat. $hä$ 'forest'. But PS *p in the word-initial sequence *pVs yielded b in Mator: PS *$pisin$- 'to laugh' > Mat. $bisin$- 'id.'; PS *$pos\mathring{a}$ 'to get rotten' > Mat. $bosomo$ 'rotten'.

One can easily see that the evolution of the sequence *pVs is different in Hungarian and Mator. However, as Helimski indicated, they have one thing in common: the final result of the development of the consonants from this sequence in Mator and Hungarian is phonetically more similar to the initial sequence (Hung. s ~ *PFU s, Mat. b ~ PS *p) than the sounds that should have appeared if the evolution of this sequence followed the regular way (*h instead of s in Hungarian, *h instead of b in Mator). Maybe this law should be referred to as HONTI in Helimski's formulation or even HONTI-HELIMSKI?

The fact that HONTI in both Hungarian and Mator blocked the evolution of one of the consonants of the sequence *pVs into (or via) *h (that is, it affected only the consonant that should have normally yielded *h (Mat.) or passed through *h-stage (Hung.), whatever its position within the sequence *pVs was) may be worth additional study.

MEINHOF

This law was initially proposed by the famous German linguist Carl Meinhof for Ganda (Bantu family) and states the following:

> Wenn auf die Verbindung eines Nasals mit einem stimmhaften Konsonanten in zweiter Silbe wieder eine Nasalverbindung oder rein Nasal folgt, so bleibt von der ersten Nasalverbindung nur der Nasal übrig. (Meinhof 1913: 274)

An example of the action of this law (Ganda): *en* + *bondeevu* 'shy' > *emmondeevu* 'shy (Pl.)' (Gusev 2002: 477).

This effect does not occur in Bantu languages if it is followed by an unvoiced consonant, a fricative, *j* [ʤ] and *f*. In many Bantu languages MEINHOF is marginal (affects just a few words). At last, the nasal and the alternating occlusive must be homorganic. Due to these limitations MEINHOF is often referred to as rule, not a law.

Effects similar to this law were later found in other language families (for example, in Austronesian (Gusev 2002: 477)). It is interesting to mention that MEINHOF is also present in Selkup (Gusev 2002: 479-481).

In Selkup MEINHOF has no exceptions and affects all groups "nasal + occlusive" (Gusev 2002: 480) and can therefore be considered a law in the strict meaning of the word. It can be formulated as follows: if in a Selkup word there is a sequence of combinations "nasal + occlusive", separated by vowels, only the last combination is preserved. In all preceding combinations the occlusive is replaced by a homorganic nasal. There is no requirement for the alternating occlusive to be homorganic with the preceding nasal (Gusev 2002: 479-481).

Example: *ōmty-* 'to be sitting' + *-mpy* 'Dur.' + *-nty-* 'Fut.' + *-nty* 'Latent' + *-nty-* '2 pers. Sg.' > *ōmnymtmynnynnanty* 'see, you will be sitting for a while'.

Ivan Kotliarov
Do vostrebovaniya
RU – 197101 St. Petersburg

References

Collinge, N. E. 1985. *The Laws of Indo-European*. Amsterdam – Philadelphia: Benjamins.

Collinge, N. E. 1995. Further laws of Indo-European. // *On Languages and Language. The Presidential Addresses of the 1991 Meeting of the Societas Linguistica Europea*. Ed. by Werner Winter. Berlin – New York: Mouton de Gruyter, 27-52.

EDAL. 2003. – Starostin, S. A., Dybo, A. V., Mudrak, O. A. *An Etymological Dictionary of Altaic Languages*. Leiden: Brill.

Gusev, V. Yu. 2002. – Гусев, В. Ю. Закон Майнхофа в селькупском. // *Языки мира. Типология. Уралистика. Памяти Т. Ждановой. Статьи и воспоминания*. Сост. В. А. Плунгян, А. Ю. Урманчиева. М.: «Индрик», 476-482.

Helimski, E. 1984. A distinctive feature that became a phoneme: the case of Monguor. // *5th International Phonology Meeting. Abstracts.* Wien, 27. Reprinted in: Хелимский, Е. А. *Компаративистика, уралистика. Лекции и статьи.* Москва: Языки русской культуры, 2000, 267.

Helimski, E. 1987. – Хелимский, Е. А. Правило Хонти для венг. *fészek* и его аналог в маторском языке. // *Советское финно-угроведение* XXIII:1, 57-60. Reprinted in: Хелимский, Е. А. *Компаративистика, уралистика. Лекции и статьи.* Москва: Языки русской культуры, 2000, 218-220.

Helimski, E. 2007. – Хелимский, Е. А. Продление гласных перед шва в селькупском языке как фонетический закон. // *Linguistica Uralica* XLIII:2, 124-133.

Honti, L. 1983. Zur ugrischen Lautgeschichte (Beiträge zur relativen Chronologie einiger Lautwandel in den ugrischen Sprachen). // *Acta Linguistica Hungarica* 33, 113-122.

Kormushin, I. V. 1990. – Кормушин, И. В. Алтайские языки. // *Лингвистический энциклопедический словарь.* Москва: «Советская энциклопедия», 28.

LES. 1990. – *Лингвистический энциклопедический словарь.* Гл. ред. В. Н. Ярцева. Москва: «Советская энциклопедия».

Meinhof, C. 1913. Dissimilation der Nasalverbindungen im Bantu. // *Zeitschrift für Kolonialsprachen,* III:4.

Pelliot, P. 1925. Les mots à *H* initiale aujourd'hui amuie dans le Mongol des XIIIe et XIVe siècles. // *Journal Asiatique,* 193-263.

Poppe, N. 1951. Obituary: Gustav John Ramstedt 1873-1950. // *Harvard Journal of Asiatic Studies* 14:1/2, 315-322.

Ramstedt, G. J. 1916. Ein anlautender stimmloser Labial in der mongolisch-türkischen Ursprache. // *Journal de la Société Finno-Ougrienne* 32:2.

Toporova, I. N. 1990. – Топорова, И. Н. Майнхофа закон. // *Лингвистический энциклопедический словарь.* Москва: «Советская энциклопедия», 277-278.

Trask, R. L. (ed.). 2001. *The Dictionary of Historical and Comparative Linguistics.* Fitzroy Dearborn.

Vovin, A. 2001. North East Asian historical-comparative linguistics on the threshold of the new millennium. // *Diachronica* XVIII:1, 93-137.

Vovin, A. 2008. *Koreo-Japonica. A Critical Study in Language Relationship* (forthcoming).

Whitman, John B. 1985. *The Phonological Basis for the Comparison of Japanese and Korean.* Harvard University Ph.D. dissertation.

Whitman, John B. 1990. A rule of medial *-r-* loss in pre-Old Japanese. // *Linguistic Change and Reconstruction Methodology.* Ed. by Philip Baldi. Berlin – New York: Mouton de Gruyter, 511-545.

Studia Etymologica Cracoviensia
vol. 14   Kraków 2009

Guus KROONEN / Alexander LUBOTSKY (Leiden)

PROTO-INDO-EUROPEAN *tsel- 'TO SNEAK'
AND GERMANIC *stelan- 'TO STEAL, APPROACH STEALTHILY'

1. The Proto-Indo-European root for 'to creep, sneak' is traditionally reconstructed as *sel- (Pokorny's 5. sel- 'schleichen, kriechen'), while Skt. tsar- is taken as a compound with an abnormal zero-grade of the PIE preverb *h_2ed, i.e. *h_2d-sel-. This reconstruction is unsatisfactory for a number of reasons: (1) the zero-grade *h_2d is practically unknown elsewhere and is totally *ad hoc*; (2) since the preverb *h_2ed- is unattested in Indo-Iranian, we have to assume that the *Univerbierung* took place in PIE already, but at that early stage there were no preverbs, only loose adverbs, and it is difficult to explain how such a syntagm could have arisen; (3) the form *tsel- is not restricted to Sanskrit and must be reconstructed for other IE cognates as well. Let us first discuss the evidence presented in Pokorny's dictionary.

2. Skt. *tsar-* 'to approach stealthily, sneak, creep up on somebody' is a relatively rare verb, attested since the RV. Its paradigm includes *tsárati* pres., *atsār* aor. (ŚB *atsāriṣam* nonce), *tatsāra* pf., *upa-tsárya* abs. (ŚB). Further derivatives are *tsarā́-* f. 'creeping up to' (MS), *tsáru-* m. 'a crawling animal (snake)' (RV 7.50.1), 'handle' (AVP 3.39.5+); *tsārín-* adj. 'sneaking' (RV+).

3. Bartholomae (1904: 1643, 1649f) connected two Avestan forms with Skt. *tsar-*, viz. YAv. *vəhrkā̊ŋhō srauuaŋhauuō* nom.pl. (3V 18.65) and *zəmō ... upa.sr(a)uuatō* gen.sg. (3V 7.27). The meaning of these forms is unclear, but a connection with the root for 'to sneak' seems out of the question, since wolves and a harsh winter are in no way sneaking (see Gershevitch 1959: 183 and Klingenschmitt 1968: 157f. for a discussion).

A very likely Iranian cognate is the verb attested in the Pamir languages (cf. Morgenstierne 1974: 75): Sh. *sā̆rd*, Yazgh. *sard* 'to creep, steal, sneak up to, lie in ambush, spy upon', Ishk. *surd* 'to creep, slink'.[1] Iranian *s-* then shows the reflex of *ts-.

---

[1]   Morgenstierne himself has proposed a different etymology, comparing Skt. *śaraṇá-* 'shelter', Lat. *cēlāre* 'to conceal', which seems much less attractive.

4. Arm. *solim* 'to crawl, creep; to move on smoothly, steal, glide' (Bible+), *solam* 'id.' (John Chrysostomos+); *solun* 'reptile' (Bible+); *sol* 'creeping' (nom. act.) in Łazar Pʻarpecʻi (5th cent.), 'creeping' (adj.) in the Alexander Romance. Since Petersson (1916: 256), these Armenian words are connected with Skt. *tsárati*, under the assumption of the development *tsV- > Arm. *sV-, which seems uncontroversial.

5. The situation in Irish is rather complicated. Pokorny mentions *selige* (later *seilche*) m. 'turtle or tortoise; snail' and a more recent *seilide* 'snail' and two verbal nouns: OIr. *sle(i)th* f. (< *sl̥tā-) 'act of surprising a sleeping woman, having intercourse with her', the meaning of which incidentally has a close parallel in Sanskrit (AVŚ 8.6.8 *yás tvā svapántīṃ tsárati* 'he (a demon), who surprises you (fem.) sleeping...'), and *intled* (= *ind-sleth*) f. 'snare, ambush; act of lying in wait, ambushing'.

These two verbal nouns were separated from *selige* by Loth (1907: 40), who rather connected them with MW *flet* 'deceit, trick' thus reconstructing initial *spl-*. This etymology was accepted by Vendryes (1974: 130) and Schrijver (1995: 436ff.). Loth further connected σπλεκόω 'futuere', Skt. *spr̥śáti* 'to touch', but Schrijver has shown that this etymology is unlikely and proposed OHG and OS *spil* 'game, play' (which themselves have no etymology) as possible cognates. This controversy can hardly be resolved, as both reconstructions of OIr. *sle(i)th* (with *s- and *sp-) seem formally and semantically cogent. OIr. *selige* must at any rate be related to our root. Its anlaut is totally ambiguous though: it can reflect *s-, *ts- and even *st-.

6. Lith. *selė́ti* 'to lurk, sneak, prowl' (3sg. *sė̃la / sė́li / selė́ja*), *sė̃linti* 'to steal, slink, sneak, prowl; to waylay', *pasalà* 'deceit, deceitfulness', etc. The Lithuanian *s-* is ambiguous: it can represent both PIE *s- and *ts-, although there are no exact parallels for the latter development.

7. The other cognates, mentioned by Pokorny, are uncertain or improbable. The meaning of Gr. εἰλί- in εἰλίποδας βοῦς (Hom.) acc.pl. and in εἰλιτενής (said of ἄγρωστις 'dog's-tooth grass') is unclear, and the interpretation of εἰλίποδας as 'schleichfüßig' and εἰλιτενής as 'die sich schleichweise ausdehnende' has little to recommend itself. Alb. *shlligë* 'viper' is a variant of *sheligë* and does not belong here, see Demiraj 1997: 359.

8. It seems attractive to add PGm. *stelan- 'to steal, approach stealthily' (Goth. *stilan*, ON, OFri. *stela*, OE, OS, OHG *stelan*) to the dossier of our root. In the oldest sources, the verb primarily has the meaning 'to steal', but on fur-

ther consideration the evidence seems to suggest that the notion 'to steal' may
have developed from older 'to sneak'.

The meaning 'to sneak' is particularly prominent in reflexive use of the verb,
viz. ON *stela-sk*, Dan. *stjæle sig (ind)*, MHG *sich steln*, G *sich stehlen*, MLG *sik
(weg) stelen*, MDu. *hem stelen* 'to sneak'. The wide distribution of this reflexive
indicates that its use must be of an early date.

The same sense is furthermore retrieved from some active forms, cf. MDu.
stelen, MoE *to steal (into)*, and in view of the lexicalized participles MHG *ver-
stoln*, MDu. *verstolen* 'secretly', cf. also MoDu. *steels* 'sneakingly', this is likely to be an archaism. Additional proof of the seniority of the meaning 'to sneak'
over 'to steal' comes from the Anglo-Frisian formation *stal-k-ōjan-*: OE *bi-
stealcian* 'to stalk', OFri. *stolkens* 'hidden' (for the formation cf. *to talk* < *tal-
kōjan-*), as it must be derived from the active verb.

PGm. *stelan-* has no generally accepted etymology, all extant etymological
proposals being fraught with formal difficulties. A frequently mentioned idea is
that *stelan-* is a conflation of Gr. στερέω 'to steal' and *helan-* 'to conceal'
(Osthoff 1888: 460-1; Hellquist 1922: 872; Pokorny 1959-69: 1028), but this
etymology is no more cogent than other suggestions such as Skt. *stená-* 'thieve'
(Seebold 1970: 468-9), Lat. *stellio* 'villain', *stolō* m. 'shoot, runner', MoIr. *slat*
'robbing' < *stlatto-* (Falk – Torp 1170; Franck – Van Wijk 1912: 663), Av.
star- 'to sin', Gr. ἀτάσθαλος 'sinful' (Franck – Van Wijk). It has also been suggested that the word originates from a Pre-Germanic substrate language (De Vries
– Tollenaere 1997: 695). Finally, *stelan-* has been tied to OIr. *tlenaid* 'to steal'
by assuming an *s* movable for Germanic (Pedersen 1913: 649, also mentioned
by Kluge – Seebold 2002: 879). This suggestion raises the question whether *tlenaid* must not be rather reconstructed as *tsl-neh₂-. Since, however, the meaning
'to steal' originally was alien to the root *tsel-* and, consequently, must be assumed to have independently arisen in both Celtic and Germanic, it still seems
preferable to maintain the generally accepted link of OIr. *tlenaid* with Lat. *tollō*
'to lift' < *tl-n-h₂-* (cf. Pokorny 1959-69: 1060-1), the more so as the formations
are identical.

9. Connecting PGm. *stelan-* with Skt. *tsar-* presupposes that the initial cluster of the root *tsel-* was metathesized in Germanic. Unfortunately, this development cannot be supported by parallels, as there are no other clear instances of
an initial cluster *ts-*. If Goth. *afskiuban*, OEngl. *scūfan* 'to shove' are related to
PIE *k^(w)seub^h- (Skt. *kṣubh-* 'to stagger, begin to swing, tremble', YAv. *xšufsqn*
3pl.pres.subj. 'to tremble'), it would show that PIE *k^(w)s-* develops into Germanic *sk-*, but the etymology is uncertain because of the deviating semantics.

We do encounter a metathesis in three-consonant initial clusters, cf. the
development of PIE *psten-* 'teat' (cf. Av. *fštāna-* 'breast of a woman') into ON

speni, Kil. *spene*, and possibly of *psteiHu- / *tspeiHu- 'to spit' (Skt. *ṣṭhīv*-, Gr. πτύω, Lat. *spuō*) into Goth. *speiwan*. This process shows that a sibilant always emerges word-initially in Germanic. The principle can even be maintained if one wishes to think that the triple clusters survived until the Proto-Germanic stage, so far as can be judged from the doublet *špewwu* ~ *štewwu* 'to spit' (< *spīwan- ~ *stīwan-) in the Swiss dialect of Visperterminen (Wipf 1910: §50, II).[2]

10. It seems plausible to assume that the PIE root *tsel- originally was a compound with a nominal first part (of which only *t- is left) and the aoristic root *sel- 'to start moving' (Gr. ἅλλομαι 'to jump', Gr. ἰάλλω 'to stretch out, send out'; Skt. *sar*-[1] 'to flow, run, hurry', *sar*-[2] 'to extend', To.AB *säl*- 'to arise, fly; throw').

Guus Kroonen / Alexander Lubotsky
Leiden University
Dept. of Comparative Indo-European Linguistics
P.O.B. 9515
NL – 2300 RA Leiden

References

Bartholomae, C. 1904. *Altiranisches Wörterbuch*. Strassburg.
Demiraj, B. 1997. *Albanische Etymologien (Untersuchungen zum albanischen Erbwortschatz)* (= Leiden Studies in Indo-European 7). Amsterdam – Atlanta.
Falk, Hj. – A. Torp. 1960. *Norwegisch-dänisches etymologisches Wörterbuch*. 2. Auflage. Oslo & Bergen – Heidelberg.
Franck, J. – N. van Wijk. 1912. *Franck's etymologisch woordenboek der Nederlandsche taal*. Tweede druk. The Hague.
Gershevitch, I. 1959. *The Avestan hymn to Mithra*. Cambridge.
Hellquist, E. 1922. *Svensk etymologisk ordbok*. Lund.
Klingenschmitt, G. 1968. *Farhang-i ōīm*. Diss. Erlangen.
Kluge, F. – E. Seebold. 2002. *Etymologisches Wörterbuch der deutschen Sprache*. Berlin.
Loth, J. 1907. Notes étymologiques. *Archiv für celtische Lexicographie* 3, 39-42.
Osthoff, H. 1888. Etymologica I. *Beiträge zur Geschichte der deutschen Sprache und Literatur* 13, 460-1.

---

[2]   It is of course also possible that *štewwu* has secondarily developed out of *spīwan-.

Pedersen, H. 1913. *Vergleichende Grammatik der keltischen Sprachen. Zweiter Band. Bedeutungslehre (Wortlehre)*. Göttingen.

Pokorny, J. 1959-69. *Indogermanisches etymologisches Wörterbuch*. Bern.

Schrijver, P. 1995. *Studies in British Celtic historical phonology* (= Leiden Studies in Indo-European 5). Amsterdam – Atlanta.

Seebold, E. 1970. *Vergleichendes und etymologisches Wörterbuch der germanischen starken Verben*. The Hague.

Vendryes, J. 1974. *Lexique étymologique de l'irlandais ancien*. Lettres R S. Dublin.

De Vries, J. – F. Tollenaere – M. Hogenhout-Mulder. 1997. *Nederlands etymologisch woordenboek*. Vierde druk. Leiden.

Wipf, E. 1910. *Die Mundart von Visperterminen im Wallis* (= Beiträge zur schweizerdeutschen Grammatik 2). Frauenfeld.

Studia Etymologica Cracoviensia
vol. 14   Kraków 2009

Michał NÉMETH (Kraków)

VARIA ETYMOLOGICA HUNGARO-SLAVICA

The present paper aims to revisit the etymologies of two Hungarian words, *gazda* and *korcsolya*, the origins of which have not yet been wholly and indubitably explained. In both cases the opinions presented in the foregoing articles are compared here with Helimski's brief remarks on these words. We have also tried to add some details to their word-history.

Hung. *gazda* 'householder'

The origin of Hung. *gazda* (after 1372 / around 1448) 'householder, master of the house' has usually been described as *uncertain* and, in the overwhelming majority of works dealing with its history, has been connected to the Slavic cognates of Proto-Slavic **gospoda* 'rulers; members of a higher social order, establishment; householders' (cf. e.g. SłPrasł VIII 137). This short explanation is the "official" commentary which can also be found in such major Hungarian etymological dictionaries as e.g. Bárczi 1941: 92, TESz II 1037-1038, EWU 450-451 and even in the most recent Zaicz 2006: 247.

As the meaning of Slavic *gospoda* (for attested forms cf. e.g. SłPrasł loc. cit.) fits in well within the semantic field of Hung. *gazda*, the above mentioned uncertainties are most prominent in the detailed description of the phonetic adaptation of the word.[1] To be more specific: these uncertainties have arisen from the fact that the structure of the Slavic word is three-syllabic, while in Hungarian only the well-known two-syllabic form *gazda* appears, *nota bene* for the first time it is attested as early as Jókai-Kódex (cf. Balázs 1981: 72, 74: ⟨gaȝda⟩; for further information concerning the use of the word see also Jakab 2002: 118). Given the fact that consulting Kniezsa 1955: 641 one can find a concise but detailed overview of the attempts made to explain the word, we would

---

[1]   The Slavic word itself is a collective form derived from Slav. **gospodь* 'sir; lord', see e.g. Sławski I 1974: 60.

like to present briefly the most important ones[2] and augment its etymology with some – in our opinion – valuable data.

Horger 1911: 324, and after him Schubert 1982: 328-329, assume a metathetical change here with a subsequent shortening of the word form due to frequent use when addressing people; in other words: Slav. *gospoda* > OHung. **gozdapa* > **gozda* > *gazda*. This scenario, however, is not convincing, as there are no clear phonetic reasons for such a metathesis. The consonant clusters like *-sp-* or, to be more precise, the consonant clusters consisting of a fricative and an occlusive consonant in an inner position are not usually reduced in Hungarian, a good illustration being e.g. the word *Veszprém* 'a town in Hungary' attested as early as the 11th century as ⟨βεσπρὲμ⟩ [besprém] in *Veszprémvölgyi apácák adománylevele* (before 1002 / 1109). This is a good example, all the more so because we know that it is – similarly to *gazda* – also a Slavic loan (FNESz II 758), its etymological equivalent being e.g. OPol. *bezbřem* (1031) 'personal name' (SSNO I 129: ⟨Bezbriem⟩, today known as Pol. *Bezprzem ~ Bezprzym*). For other, similar examples of such preserved segments cf. e.g. OHung. *našpoľa* (around 1395) 'medlar' (EWU 1016: ⟨naʃpolẙa⟩, s.v. *naspolya*), OHung. *jášpiš* (after 1372 / around 1448) 'a kind of venomous snake' (EWU 53: ⟨yaʃpiʃ[...]⟩, s.v. *áspis*).

Melich in EtSz II 1134 proposes an explanation based upon haplology, according to which Slav. *gospoda* > OHung. **gosda* > *gazda*. It is doubtful, however, whether the syllables *-po-* and *-da* are auditively similar enough to each other to fulfil the essential phonetic conditions for such a change. Consequently, such an interpretation must remain merely speculative – as is generally the case for those etymologies that are tied to irregular phonetic changes.

In the present paper we would like to revisit the so called *tendency of two open syllables* (known also as Horger's Law), which has been rejected as an explanation in the majority of articles dealing with Hung. *gazda* written by Hungarian etymologists. The tendency has usually been considered as a possible solution since it is the only more or less regular process which changes the syllabic structure of Slavic (as well as other) loanwords in Hungarian by reducing their number. The crux of the tendency is that in words with three or more syllables, where two or more consecutive open syllables are to be found (not counting the final one), the vowel of the second (or, respectively, the third and so on) open syllable may be dropped, e.g. Slav. **sluga* 'the one who serves, servant' (see e.g. Miklosich 1886: 308) > OHung. *suluga* (1222) id. ~ *sulga*

---

[2]   Other attempts, not discussed here, on etymologising the word from Russ. *государь* 'ruler', Slav. *gospodar* id. or Slav. *gospodъ* 'lord, ruler' (for these three word forms cf. e.g. SłPrasł VIII 138-140) face insurmountable phonetic problems, mainly concerning the word-final segments, which has already been pointed out in Kniezsa 1955: 641.

(1223) id. > Hung. *szolga* id. (see e.g. EWU 1446: ⟨Zuluga⟩, ⟨Sculga⟩ respectively).

There might, at first glance, be certain difficulties in justifying this assumption in the case of *gazda*. Namely, as we can see, the Slavic word **gos.po.da* with the first syllable being closed does not have the syllabic structure the tendency, in the vast majority of cases, covers. Nevertheless, the answer may be quite simple: we can also find several words showing that the open syllable vowel could have been dropped in a syllable following a *closed* one as well, there being a few undisputed examples like: Slav. **lędava* 'name of a river, a right side tributary of Kerka' > OHung. **lendava* > Hung. *Lendva* id. (cf. FNESz II 26), Lat. *Stephanus* 'Stephen' > OHung. *estefän* (1350) > *eštfán* (1331) ~ *ištván* (1415) id. (see. e.g. OklSz 418: ⟨Estephan[...]⟩, ⟨Estfan[...]⟩, ⟨istwan⟩ respectively, Kázmér 1993: 500). We do not agree with Kniezsa (1955) saying that the Hungarian word cannot be explained by Slav. *gospoda* since we have no examples for vowel loss in a *closed syllable*.[3] We cannot agree for the simple reason that the syllable in question (*-po-*) is *open*! This has also been pointed out by Helimski: "< slaw. *gospoda* [...]. Kn. [= Kniezsa 1955] сомневается, не замечая, что в *gospoda* 2-й слог открытый" (cf. Stachowski 2009: 57 [in the present volume]).

A similar explanation has been proposed by Skok (1971: 594), however the examples he provides are not relevant and therefore the etymology itself is not free from certain inaccuracies. Namely, Skok assumes that Slav. *gospoda* has been adopted by Hungarian as *gazda* after a vowel loss "according to the *vojvoda* > *vajda*, *pojata* > *pajta* pattern", whereas in the case of both words the Slavic etymons and the first Hungarian attested forms have purely open syllables. On the one hand this can be seen at first glance on SSlav. *pojata* 'hut; shed, barn' > OHung. *pajata* (1363) attested in the place name ⟨Payatasfeye⟩ [pajatášfeje] (EWU 1097), which was later developed into (M)Hung. *pajta* 'shed, barn'; and on the other hand, we can see it in the case of Hung. *vajda* 'voivod' as well, as the etymon of the word is rather Slav. *vojevoda* id. (see e.g. Boryś 2005: 706) than SSlav. *vojvoda* id. The latter statement can be corroborated by the first certain attestation in Hungarian as ⟨voieuoda⟩ [vojeβodå] (1199) 'prince; war lord; the highest office-holder of a province' (cf. EWU 1597 for further similar examples).

In the final analysis, we believe that Slav. *gospoda* has been loaned into Hungarian as **gospoda* and this has yielded **gozda* after the syncope of *-o-* argued above, reducing the consonant cluster *-spd-* > *-sd-* and regular progressive assimilative voicing of *-s-* > *-z-*. Finally, the *o* > *å* opening process is widely attested in the 11th-14th century Old Hungarian. As such, we believe that the

---

[3] See Kniezsa 1955: 641: "[...] egy gospodá-ból a **gozda* > *gazda* nem magyarázható, mert a szóbelseji magánhangzók elliziója [...] csak nyílt szótagban történhetett [...]".

lack of OHung. *gospoda* – as TESz II 1038 argues – does not fundamentally weaken this explanation.

Hung. *korcsolya* 'skate'

It was Bárczi (1941: 171) who – to the best of our knowledge – first pointed out that Hung. *korcsolya* might be connected to Slk. "*krčula* (?) ~ *krčuľa* ~ *korčuľa*". In the same place, however, Bárczi also remarked that the relation of the Slovak words to the Hungarian one remains uncertain. Later on, TESz II 571-572 qualified Hung. *korcsolya*, which was already considered to be a word of unknown provenance, definitely rejecting the Slavic explanation and argued that the Italian origin proposed before had not yet been convincingly proved (for further reading see TESz loc. cit.). This Italian origin has been positively revised and richly supported by linguistic data in Hadrovics 1975: 82-86. Consequently, the following etymological dictionaries, EWU 797 and Zaicz 2006: 433-434, treated the Italian etymology as being probable and refuted the Slavic etymology. The last authority who dealt with the word was Helimski (2000a: 427 [= 1988, cf. references] and 2000b: 454) making an attempt, once again, to explain the word on Slavic grounds. Considering that some additional Slavic linguistic data has come to light since Hadrovics's article appeared, let us compare below the enumerated etymologies and add, where it is possible, further details to the discussion.

First of all let us present the semantic field of the discussed Hungarian word. In present-day literary language *korcsolya* means 'skate', but when set against the meanings recorded in Old Hungarian sources, one can see that the semantic development of the word is far from being simple. Although the first reliable record to confirm the primeval meaning 'a wooden construction used for rolling barrels' appears around 1510 (see OklSz 520: ⟨Ad celarium pro korcyola⟩), the history of the word can be traced back to 1339 as we have its -*s* derivative attested, namely Hung. *korcsolyás* 'a person dealing with loading and unloading barrels and other weights', see Hadrovics 1975: 83: ⟨Korcholyas⟩. In the 18th-19th centuries the word has been attested as 'sledge' (1758) and, finally, in the modern meaning: 'blade attached to the sole, used for skating on ice' (before 1781). It is also worth mentioning that the verb *korcsolyázik* 'to skate' (a verbal derivative from *korcsolya*), attested as early as 1708 (see TESz loc. cit.), shows that the latter meaning had developed far before 1781. The first and second meanings are still present in Hungarian dialects (see ÚMTsz II 486).

What makes Hadrovics's article indispensable here is the detailed description of *korcsolya*'s usage, which is based upon Old and Middle Hungarian written sources (Hadrovics 1975: 82-85). In the light of these we can say that *korcsolya* used to be a ladder-like instrument consisting of two rods and cross-bars used for transporting barrels and other weights. With this construction and a special rope the workers loaded and uploaded barrels onto and off carts, delivering them to cellars and pulling them out from there. Additionally we know that the barrels and weights were lowered and pulled up by means of a pulley. A good source of information for this is, among others, a 18th century Latin-Hungarian dictionary where Lat. *vectiārius* 'porter; the one who operates a lever to move loads' (cf. LLP II 928) has been explained as (1767) ⟨Kortsolyás, tsigán valamit tekerő⟩ [= *Korcsolyás*: the one who is winding something on a pulley] (see Hadrovics 1975: 85 for further references).

Based on the latter, namely that the primeval *korcsolya* consisted of pulley as well, Hadrovics and after him the authors of the latter two etymological dictionaries *una voce* claimed that the etymon of the Hungarian word is in all probability Ital. (arch.) *chiocciola* 'shell; snail' (or such dialectal forms as *còcciula ~ cociola* id.) as it has a whole range of other, technical-related meanings – examples being: (12th cent.) 'female screw'; (14th-15th cent.) 'screw-stairs'; (16th cent.) 'water-wheel' (see Hadrovics 1975: 86, EWU loc. cit. and also: DEI II 903, 905, DELI I 233). The *tertium comparationis* of such etymology is – as they argue – the similarity of a snail shell to a pulley as a part of the primeval *korcsolya*. Let us add that Hung. *csiga* – recorded in the entry of the Latin-Hungarian dictionary we mentioned above – has exactly these two meanings, namely 1. (around 1395) 'snail' (RMG 145: ⟨chÿga⟩) and 2. (1493) 'pulley' (OklSz 127: ⟨chyga⟩). This is a good example which demonstrates that the visual similarity between a snail shell and a pulley could have led to such a semantic shift. Consequently, Hadrovics concludes that Hung. *korcsolya* originally has been used to denote 'pulley' and the 'ladder-like instrument' *as a whole* and only later started to mean solely the ladder-like construction. The latter meaning is displayed by the modern Hungarian and Slovak dialectal forms, namely 'an instrument consisting of two rods and a bottom used for loading and unloading barrels, e.g. on and from carts' (see ÚMTsz II 486, SSN I 827 respectively), but we will take a more detailed look at the Hungarian dialectal data a bit later.

The question remains how the development of the meaning 'sledge', 'skate' should be explained. As we can see, the Italian forms themselves fail to explain the semantic field of the word which has been used from the 18th century onwards. EWU argues that it has been developed as a result of back-formation from *korcsolyázik* 'to skate', but this cannot be treated as a serious explanation – how then can we explain the occurrence of the verb *korcsolyázik*? We have to reject for a similar reason Zaicz's interpretation that "the secondary meaning 'to slide on ice' [...] has been developed from 'to roll barrels' [...]" (Zaicz 2006 loc. cit.). Such semantic shift seems to be rather implausible or, at least, not clear enough.

We believe that Hadrovics 1975: 84 already mentioned a possible explanation, albeit not as an answer to our question, but on the margin of his argumentation. Namely, while describing how the barrels have been pulled he assumes that on the ladder-like construction a sledge kind of instrument had been (or could have been) moved carrying the transported weights. This, and the similarity of *korcsolya*'s two rods to the skids of a sledge could have been the basis for such a semantic shift. Additionally, the fact that both constructions have been used for transporting weights could have reinforced this change. Finally, we believe that the 'sledge' → 'skate' shift is highly plausible and needs no detailed explanation.

The only point of this etymology which seems to contain some uncertainties is the phonetic development of the word as presented in these works; Hadrovics assumes a -*čč*- > -*rč*- dissimilative change for which we do not have similar examples, and he provides examples only for -*šš*- > -*rš*-. This, along with the supportive examples, has been repeated in EWU. Moreover, we do not have OHung. **koččola* recorded.

By contrast with the Italian etymology, Helimski's proposition mentioned above is based on the adaptation process of a small group of Slavic words in Hungarian, having the same word-final segment as Hung. *korcsolya*, namely: Slav. **močidlo* 'a place where something is soaked' (ÈSSJa XIX 78-80) > Hung. (dial.) *mocsolya* (1138 / 1329) 'puddle; a place where flax or hemp is soaked' (OklSz 662, TESz II 939: ⟨Machala⟩), Slav. **nosidlo* 'strecher, an instrument used for transporting people, goods &c.' (ÈSSJa XXV 202-204) > Hung. *nyoszolya* (1452) 1. 'stretcher'; 2. 'bed' (OklSz 701, TESz II 1053; first attested probably as a proper name (-*s* suffix form) in 1215, see EWU 1046: ⟨Nazalas⟩), see Helimski 2000: 427, 2000b: 454.[4] Basing his proposition on this philological evidence Helimski reconstructs Slav. **kъrčidlo* 'sledge; skid' (ÈSSJa does not note such a form), a derivative from **kъrčiti* 1. 'to bend; to bow'; 2. 'to stump, to grub' (see ÈSSJa XIII 209-210), as an etymon of the OHung. *korčola*. This form, due to the regular -*l*- > -*l'*- > -*ly*- [-j-] palatalisation process, could have yielded *korčol'a* and finally *korcsolya*.[5]

---

[4]   For cognates corroborating the reconstructed Slavic forms cf. (1) for **močidlo* e.g. SCr. *močilo* 'a deep part of a stream used for soaking flax', OCz. *močidlo* 'puddle', ORuss. *мочило* 'a flooded dip, pond'; (2) for **nosidlo* e.g. SCr. *nosila* 'strecher', Cz. *nosidlo* 'a vessel, a basket (or the like) used for transporting goods', ORuss. *носило* 'strecher'. For further materials, concerning nearly all Slavic languages, see ÈSSJa XIX 78-80 and ÈSSJa XXV 202-204 respectively.

[5]   This *l* > *l'* > *j* change demonstrates that the Slk. *korčuľa* is in all probability a borrowing from Hungarian. The word, *nota bene*, means 'skate' in Slovak as well, see SSJ I 745, SSN I 827. We could not find the rest of the Slovak forms enumerated by Bárczi 1941: 171, namely "*krčula* (?) and *krčuľa*". They are missing from all the major dictionaries of Slovak and its dialects, see SSJ, HSSJ, SSN, SV, GN. What the

The notion Helimski presents is attractive; however, trying to explain the original meaning of *korcsolya* by the reconstructed Slav. **kъrčidlo* 'sledge; skid' is problematic. Moreover, the semantic shift 'to bend; to bow' → 'sledge; skid', as a result of the derivation process, is not completely clear to us as well. A few corrections, however, added to Helimski's idea would make it more probable and would allow us to explain the whole semantic field of the Hungarian word. These *addenda* are as follows:

As mentioned above, the meaning 'sledge', 'skate' appeared in Hungarian around 17th-18th century, so we cannot claim that Slav. **kъrčidlo* has been loaned into Hungarian when it comes to that particular meaning. If we assume, however, that the Slavic verbal stem (**kъrčiti*) had a secondary meaning 'to twist; to roll' – besides the semantically similar 'to bend; to bow' – then we could accordingly reconstruct the meaning of **kъrčidlo* as *'a construction on which something is rolled' – analogically to **nosidlo* 'an instrument on which something is carried' and **močidlo* 'a place where something is soaked'. Such a meaning corresponds with the first attested one in Hungarian.

The following question needs to be answered: in which language and in what way has the meaning 'sledge, skate' developed? Let us start with two dialectal forms used in the neighbouring Slavic languages: Ukr. dial. (Hutsul) *korčjuhy ~ korčuha ~ korčuhy* 'short but robust sledge used for transporting long pieces of wood or logs out of the forest' (Janów 2001: 102) and Pol. dial. *korczuha* 'a sledge used for transporting wood from the forest' (KarSGP II 432). At first glance, in the light of the semantic field and the phonetic shape of the words, they seem to be obvious derivatives from Slav. **kъrčь* 'stump with roots, left after cutting down a tree' (ÈSSJa XIII 210-211) – to be more precise from Ukr. *korč* 'trunk, stump; shrub; *dial.* log' (SUM IV 302). The Polish dialectal word – in the light of the *-o-* in the first and *-h-* in the third syllable – is a borrowing from Ukrainian. This allows us to treat Ukr. dial. *korčuha* as an *-uha* augmentative derivative and, in this case, to assume that analogically an *-ula* diminutive derivative could have existed in the Eastern Slavic dialects. The latter, loaned into Hungarian, could have yielded MHung. **korčula* '(a small) sledge', cf. Hung. dial. *korcsula* (ÚMTsz II 485). This borrowing should have been – obviously – unrelated to the first one, i.e. we have to assume on the one hand (1) Slav. **kъrčidlo* > OHung. **korčola* and, on the other hand (2) ESlav.[6] **korčula* > MHung. **korčula* (reconstructed but highly probable, cf. the Hungarian dia-

---

question mark stands for in Bárczi's entry must remain speculative. Moreover, another important detail to be mentioned here is the article of Polák, who claims that Hung. *korcsolya* has been borrowed from Slk. *korčuľa* (Polák 1951: 188) but, again, this assumption fails to explain the palatal *ľ* in the Slovak form.

[6] We use the term "Eastern Slavic" here in the geographic sense, not as a period in the history of Slavic languages.

lectal form). The 'sledge' → 'skate' semantic shift, as mentioned above, could have taken place on Hungarian ground and eventually only this meaning entered the literary language.

We are, however, aware of the weakness of such an etymology in respect of the lack of attested *korčula in any of the Eastern Slavic languages and the hypothetic meaning of Slav. *kъrčiti. What is more, Hungarian dialectal data cast doubt on such a scenario as well. Namely, in the meaning 'a small sledge used for carrying loads or as a toy' ÚMTsz II 486 notes the word in the overwhelming majority for Székely dialects spoken in the South-Eastern part of Transylvania (cf. also EMSzT VII 238-239) with the sole exception of two occurrences in Andrásfalva (Bukovina region) and Felsővisó (Maramureş region). If the word in this meaning was of Eastern Slavic origin we would expect this kind of attestations to be found within the Ukrainian-Hungarian borderland, but the word in the above mentioned meaning appears in an area where Hungarian-Eastern Slavic contacts did not take place on a large scale. Even the data collected in Bukovina fail to be representative since we know that Andrásfalva was founded in 1785/1786 by Székely settlers (see e.g. Szádeczky 1927: 343-344).

In the light of what we have said above it seems to be highly probable that Ukr. korčuha should be explained rather as a derivative based on such Hungarian forms as e.g. korcsula (cf. ÚMTsz loc. cit.), in which the morphological boundaries have been reinterpreted as korč + ula. Consequently, the word ending, matching the diminutive suffix -ula, could have been replaced by the augmentative -uha. If so, we have failed to give a possible explanation for the *ʻa construction on which something is rolled' → 'sledge' semantic shift.

One is forced to conclude that Helimski's parallels for a similar phonetic evolution of the word – nyoszolya and mocsolya – do not have enough support in order to allow us to discard the Italian provenience of Hung. korcsolya and prove the Slavic one. The Italian origin, nota bene, seems to be more probable, not least because the word attested in Hungarian in 1594 as korchiolina 'an instrument used for transporting barrels of wine' (see Hadrovics 1975: 83, 86) exhibits an Italian diminutive form, cf. Ital. chiocciolino 'a small shell' (Prati 1969: 270).

Michał Németh
Uniwersytet Jagielloński
Katedra Filologii Węgierskiej
ul. Piłsudskiego 13
PL – 31-110 Kraków

Abbreviations

arch. = archaic; **Cz.** = Czech; **dial.** = dialectal; **ESlav.** = Eastern Slavic; **Hung.** = Hungarian; **Ital.** = Italian; **Lat.** = Latin; **MHung.** = Middle Hungarian; **OCz.** = Old Czech; **OHung.** = Old Hungarian; **OPol.** = Old Polish; **ORuss.** = Old Russian; **Pol.** = Polish; **Russ.** = Russian; **SCr.** = Serbo-Croatian; **Slav.** = Slavic; **Slk.** = Slovak; **Slv.** = Slovene; **SSlav.** = South Slavic; **Ukr.** = Ukrainian

Symbols

> < borrowing
* reconstructed form; not existing form

Abbreviated references

DEI = de Felice, E. (ed.), 1951, *Dizionario etimologico italiano*, vol. 2, Firenze.

DELI = Cortelazzo, M. / Zolli, P., 1979, *Dizionario etimologico della lingua italiana*, vol. 1, Bologna [reprinted in 1991].

EMSzT = Szabó T., A. (ed.), 1995, *Erdélyi magyar szótörtneiti tár*, vol. 7, Budapest.

ÈSSJa = Trubačev, O.N. (ed.), 1987, *Ètimologičeskij slovaŕ slavjanskich jazykov*, vol. 13, Moskva.

EtSz = Gombocz, Z. / Melich, J., 1934-1944, *Magyar etymologiai szótár*, vol. 2, Budapest.

EWU = Benkő, L. et al. (eds.), 1993-1994, *Etymologisches Wörterbuch des Ungarischen*, Budapest.

FNESz = Kiss, L., 1988, *Földrajzi nevek etimológiai szótára*, vol. 1-2, Budapest [reprinted in 1997].

GN = [Joint work], 2003, *Goralské nárečie. Slovník*, Námestovo.

HSSJ = Majtán, M. et al. (eds.), 1992, *Historický slovník slovenského jazyka*, vol. 2, Bratislava.

KarSGP= Karłowicz, J., 1901, *Słownik gwar polskich*, vol. 2, Kraków.

LLP = Bobrowski, X.F., 1844, *Lexicon latino-polonicum. Słownik łacińsko-polski, z dodaniem wyrazów, w naukach medycznych używanych przez D^{ra} Felixa Rymkiewicza*, vol. 2, Wilno.

OklSz = Szamota, I., 1902-1906, *Magyar Oklevél-Szótár. Régi oklevelekben és egyéb iratokban előforduló magyar szók gyűjteménye*, Budapest [edited by Zolnai, Gy.].

RMG   = Berrár, J. / Károly, S., 1984, *Régi magyar glosszárium*, Budapest.
SłPrasł = Sławski, F. (ed.), 2001, *Słownik prasłowiański*, vol. 8, Wrocław –
          Warszawa – Kraków.
SSJ   = Peciar, Š. (ed.), 1959, *Slovník slovenského jazyka*, vol. 1, Bratislava.
SSN   = Ripka, I. (ed.), 1994, *Slovník slovenských nárečí*, vol. 1, Trenčín –
          Bratislava.
SSNO   = Taszycki, W. (ed.), 1965, *Słownik staropolskich nazw osobowych*,
          vol. 1, Wrocław – Warszawa – Kraków.
SUM   = Bilodid, I.K. et al. (ed.), 1973, *Slovnyk ukrajinśkoji movy*, vol. 4,
          Kyjiv.
SV   = Halaga, O.R. (ed.), 2002, *Východoslovenský slovník*, vol. 1-2, Košice
          – Prešov.
TESz   = Benkő, L. et al. (eds.), 1964-1984, *A magyar nyelv történeti-etimoló-
          giai szótára*, vol. 1-4, Budapest.

Further references

Balázs see P. Balázs
Bárczi, G., 1941, *Magyar szófejtő szótár*, Budapest [reprinted in 1994].
Boryś, W., 2005, *Słownik etymologiczny języka polskiego*, Kraków.
Hadrovics, L., 1975, *Szavak és szólások* (= *Nyelvtudományi Értekezések* 88),
     Budapest.
Helimski, E., 2000a, Vengerskij jazyk kak istočnik dlja praslavjanskoj rekon-
     strukcii i rekonstrukcii slavjanskogo jazyka Pannonnii. – Helimski, E.:
     Komparativistika, uralistika. Lekcii i statʼi, Moskva: 416-432 [first pub-
     lished in: *Slavjanskoe jazykoznanie. X Meždunarodnyj sъezd slavistov. Do-
     klady sovetskoj delegacii*, Moskva 1988: 347-368].
Helimski, E., 2000b, Leksiko-semantičeskie raritety v rannich slavjanskich
     zaimstvovanijach vengerskogo jazyka. – Helimski, E.: *Komparativistika,
     uralistika. Lekcii i statʼi*, Moskva: 452-455.
Jakab, L., 2002, *A Jókai-kódex mint nyelvi emlék szótárszerű feldolgozásban*,
     Debrecen.
Janów, J., 2001, *Słownik huculski*, Kraków [prepared for printing by Janusz
     Rieger].
Kázmér, M., 1993, *Régi magyar családnevek szótára. XIV-XVII század*, Buda-
     pest.
Kniezsa, I., 1955, *A magyar nyelv szláv jövevényszavai*, vol. 1/1-2, Budapest.
Miklosich, F., 1886, *Etymologisches Wörterbuch der slawischen Sprachen*, Wien.
P. Balázs, J., 1981, *Jókai-Kódex. XIV-XV század*, Budapest.

Polák, V., 1951, Pôvod a význam slovenského slova *korčule*. – *Jazykovedný Sbornik Slovenskej Akadémie Vied a Umeni* 5: 187-189.

Prati, A., 1969, *Vocabolario etimologico italiano*, Roma.

Schubert, G., 1982, *Ungarische Einflüsse in der Terminologie des öffentlichen Lebens der Nachbarsprachen*, Wiesbaden.

Skok, P., 1971, *Etimologijski rječnik hrvatskoga ili srpskoga jezika*, vol. 1, Zagreb.

Sławski, F., 1974, Zarys słowotwórstwa prasłowiańskiego. – Sławski, F. (ed.): *Słownik prasłowiański*, vol. 1, Wrocław – Warszawa – Kraków: 43-141.

Stachowski, M., 2009, Eugen Helimskis Materialien zur Erforschung der ältesten slawisch-ungarischen Sprachkontakte. – *Studia Etymologica Cracoviensia* 14: 35-107.

Szádeczky Kardoss, L., 1927, *A székely nemzet története és alkotmánya*, Budapest [reprinted in 1993].

Zaicz, G. et al. (eds.), 2006, *Etimológiai szótár. Magyar szavak és toldalékok eredete*, Budapest.

Studia Etymologica Cracoviensia
vol. 14   Kraków 2009

William SAYERS (Ithaca)

BREWING ALE IN WALTER OF BIBBESWORTH'S
13 C. FRENCH TREATISE FOR ENGLISH HOUSEWIVES

The early medieval literatures of Britain, in English, Anglo-Norman French, Welsh, and Latin, make frequent references to the necessities of life, prime among which food, but always in passing. Something as common as brewing seldom rises to the level of narrative motif or an element of theme. Figurative use of household essentials such as food and clothing is often made in Christian homiletic works, but this offers little insight into process. Utilitarian writings, such as account books, do provide a basic vocabulary for mashing and brewing but these are often paratactic entries, unconnected among themselves. Nonetheless, such documentation often offers the first recorded instance of large blocks of medieval technical vocabulary. But well before the first true cook-books in vernacular languages of the fourteenth century, British literature does offer a little utilized source for the vocabulary in French and English of several domestic activities.

In the late thirteenth century the Essex knight Walter of Bibbesworth composed a *Tretiz* or treatise under the patronage of Dionisie de Munchensi, the mistress of vast estates in western Britain. Editor William Rothwell states that the work "was written in order to provide anglophone landowners in late thirteenth-century with French vocabulary appertaining to the management of their estates in a society where French and Latin, but not yet English, were the accepted languages of record."[1] The fictional addressee of the tract is, however, not the male landowner but rather the mistress of the house, *mesuer* in Anglo-Norman French, *housewif* as glossed in Middle English. The assumption of the work is that she will be prepared to pass along accurate French vocabulary to

---

[1] Walter of Bibbesworth 1990: 1. This edition, however welcome, is without lexical notes or glossary. In all, sixteen manuscripts of Walter's work have been preserved. Earlier editions include Wright 1909, which reproduces the text from British Library, Arundel 220, ff. 299-305, and Owen 1929, which publishes Cambridge University Library MS Gg.1.1. The Owen edition, with its many shortcomings, is now superseded by Rothwell's edition of the same manuscript.

her offspring.[2] Walter passes in review such specialized vocabularies as the terminology for the human body, clothing, collective terms for various domesti-
cated and wild animals and their vocalizations, fields and their crops. He then
addresses the brewing of ale. His objective is not so much lively description or
an explanation of techniques and processes as a simple communication of perti-
nent vocabulary. In one of the best preserved of the many manuscripts, the columns of rough-and-ready French verse have interlinear English glosses in red
ink.[3]

In this essay, the vocabulary of mashing and brewing in the French text and
English glosses is the object of a detailed examination. The passage may be
considered a lightly narrativized catalogue. One of the rules of this popular medieval sub-genre was that no term be mentioned more than once or twice. Context and the better known terms then assist us in addressing those more difficult
from our often imperfect knowledge of medieval technology. Given Walter's
objectives, terminology rather than techniques will have to be our chief concern,
although the bilingual nature of the treatise will permit some degree of cross-
illumination of the two cultural traditions. The possibility of lexical and/or technical borrowing will be explored, and the origins of the two fairly discrete
mashing and brewing vocabularies, Anglo-Norman French and Middle English,
will be examined. For example, do all the French terms simply derive from Latin
or Late Latin, or did the Franks introduce some Germanic words into Gallo-Romance? Similarly, are the Middle English terms all to be traced to Old English
or do some come from Norman French and, at a greater remove, the Old Danish
that the Northmen brought to the future Normandy and also to the Danelaw of
early medieval Britain? Here, it should be noted that etymology is no sure guide
to later meaning. Similarly, new technologies may generate or introduce appropriate new terminology, especially in the event of a technical transfer between
cultures. Conversely, an established technical term may persist, even when its
original referent has been superseded by new techniques and artifacts, so that
the old word wins a new signification. What is the historical depth of medieval
British brewing as recoverable from simple lexical evidence?[4]

In the following, the Anglo-Norman text is first given in full, with the interlinear English glosses moved to the right margin. Each of Walter's terms will

---

[2]   Walter names his patroness in his preface but, since Joan de Munchensi (her better
      known name) was a descendant of William the Marshall and her husband, William
      de Valence, was French-born, there can be little doubt about the family's linguistic
      competence in French. The stated aim of providing good French vocabulary for their
      offspring may then be a literary fiction.

[3]   We must allow for the possibility that the English glosses were not part of Walter's
      original conception and, however interesting, may reflect a second mind at work.
      The apparent equivalences must then not necessarily be seen as due to the author.

[4]   See Unger 2004.

be examined for its meaning, history, and origin.[5] The interface between French terms and English glosses will be addressed. Here, we must recognize that we have no assurance that the glosses are the work of the author of the verses. The verbal component of this vocabulary will be seen generally to have both general and narrower meanings, specific to brewing. With the exception of the names for the ingredients, the nominal component also tends to reflect the general Anglo-Norman vocabulary. This detailed examination will yield a full English translation of the passage, appended to this article. First, then, Walter's text, which begins with the subheading "Now the French for mashing malt and brewing ale".

Ore le fraunceis pur breser brece e bracer cerveise:
Puis ki desore suffist
Le fraunceis qe vous ai dist,
Ore ferreit bien a saver
Cum l'en deit breser e bracer   breser
A la manere ke hom fest serveise   5
Pur fere nos noces bien a ese.   kisses
Allumés, auncele, une frenole.   a keiex
Quant averas mangé de kakenole,   a cake of spices
En une cuve large e leez   fat
Cel orge la enfondrez,   10   stepe
E quant il est bien enfondré,
E le eauwe seit descouelé,   laden outh
Mountez dune cele haut soler,
Si le facez bien baler,   swepen
E la coucherez vostre blé   15
Taunt cum seit bien germee;   spired
E de cele houre apeleras
Breez qe einz blé nomaz,   malt

---

5   Lexicographical notes for Anglo-Norman French words are organized on this pattern: the head-word from *Anglo-Norman Dictionary* (*AND*), where other exemplification is usually found, followed by the Modern French (Mod.Fr.) form; proposed origin in classical Latin (Lat.), Late Latin (LLat.), or other languages, with hypothetical re-constructed forms marked *; reference to other French attestations in Tobler and Lommatzsch's *Altfranzösisches Wörterbuch* (TL); finally, the reference for discussion in *Französisches etymologisches Wörterbuch* (*FEW*). Some few words have also been treated by a work still in progress, *Dictionnaire étymologique de l'ancien français* (*DEAF*). For Walter's Middle English glosses, the pattern is: headword from *Middle English Dictionary* (*MED*), proposed origin in Old English (OE) or Old French (OFr.); finally, Modern English entry in *Oxford English Dictionary* (*OED*), with special reference to the etymological notes attached to entries.

Le breez de vostre mein movez
En mounceus ou est rengez,   20   rouwes
E puis le portés en une corbail   lepe
Pur enseccher au torrail,   kulne
Car corbail ou corbailloun
Vos servirunt tut a foisoun.
Puis serra le brez molu   25   grounden
E de eauwe chaude bien enbu.
Si le lessez descoure ataunt
Hors de keverel meintenaunt   mahissing fate
Taunt cum la bresceresce entent
Ki ele eit bersil a talent,   30   wort
E puis le berzize prendra   grout
De forment ou orge ki ele a,
E par le geeste e le berzille   berme worte
Dunt home plus se sutille,
Par dreit dever de bracerye.   35
Mes tut diviser ne sai jeo mie,
Mes tut issint de art en art
Attirez chescune part
Deskes vous eez bone serveise,
Dount home devient si ben a eise   40
Ki les uns en pernent taunt
Ke il enyverent meintenant.
Serveise fet miracles e merveilles:
De une chaundaile deus chaundailes:
Yveresce tent lais home a clerke;   45
Home mesconnu fet aver merke;
Yveresce fet hom fort chatoner;
Home aroé fet haut juper;   hose houten
Yveresce fet coyfe de bricoun
Rouge teint saunz vermeilloun,   50
E dunt dist home ki par seint Jorge
Trop ad il bu grece de orge.
A teles li auctour se repose,
Car parler veut de autre chose.[6]

Walter's title for this section plunges us into the problems of polyvalence,
homophony and homonymity, contextualized signification, and orthographical

---

[6]   Vv. 459-512 in Rothwell's edition.

variation (from word to word, and from continental French to Anglo-Norman French). Elsewhere in the treatise Walter disambiguates homonyms, e.g., various meanings of *litter* in the context of heating a baking-oven, and even coins pairs of words undocumented elsewhere, in this same instance *pail* for 'chaff' and *paille* for 'straw'.[7] Here *brece* refers to malt and *cerveise* to ale. *Bracer* (Mod. Fr. *brasser*) is the standard term for 'to brew' but Walter appears to creater a parallel term *breser* to cover the prior activities of grinding and infusing the malt produced from the germinated barley. Iconic for the multiple origins of brewing terminology is the origin of the very object of such domestic work: *cerveise* or ale. It is unglossed by the author and, unless this is an oversight, we may assume the word to have been well known. It is traced to Gaulish, the Celtic language spoken in pre-Roman Gaul, where a reflex of Celtic *curmi* 'ale' appears in Gallo-Latin as *ceruesia*, whence Old French *cerveise* with other Romance cognates.[8] See below for other key terms from the section title.

Walter provides a few bridging verses back to his previous topic, the dressing of flax and spinning of linen thread, then states that the housewife would do well to master the techniques of *breser* and *bracer* for the brewing of ale. The latter is found in such modern French terms as *brasser* 'to brew' and *brasserie*, originally the site of production, subsequently of consumption. This terminology focuses on the processing of the barley and malt, rather than on the end product, ale. The early French word for malt was *brais* (seen later in Walter's text as *breez*), derived from Latin *braces*, a term taken from Gaulish for a local grain, perhaps some kind of spelt.[9] Walter's *breser* 'to process malt' then reflects *breez* 'malt', while *bracer* points ahead to later forms of the more common term for 'to brew'. The author even glosses Anglo-Norman *breser* with *breser* in Middle English, although the word is not elsewhere attested, *breuen* and variants being the common terms.[10] Walter states that one of the objectives of brewing is to produce ale to enliven wedding feasts. The French term, *noces*, also referred to the wedding ceremony but this is unlikely to have featured food and drink. In Rothwell's edition this is glossed *kisses*. This could prompt thoughts of the kiss exchanged between bride and bridegroom, or of the *osculum*, the symbolic gift to the bride, but the manuscript reading has now been corrected to *ristes*, rites in Modern English.[11] Walter's next couplet (vv. 7-8) presents some problems but, as these are not relevant to brewing, they will not occupy us long. The context

---

[7]   This aspect of Walter's style is studied in William Rothwell 1994.

[8]   *AND*, *cerveise*; Mod.Fr. *cervoise*; < LLat. *ceruesia* < Gaul. *curmi*; Delamarre, 133; TL, 2.139, *cervoise*, *FEW*, 2.612, *cervesia*.

[9]   *AND*, *brais*; Mod.Fr. *brai*; < LLat. *braces* < Gaul. *bracis*; Delamarre, 85; TL, 1.1115, *brais*; *FEW*, 1.483, *brace*.

[10]   *MED*, *breuen*; < OE *breowan*; *OED*, *brew*.

[11]   I am grateful to an anonymous editorial reader of a draft note devoted to this crux for information on the most recent examination of the manuscript.

here still seems to be that of the wedding feast. *Allumés* are some kind of light-ing, whether torches or lamps; *frenole* is similarly a term for a rush-light, as the English gloss *keiex* attests. *Auncele*, and forms we might associate with it, is known only as a term for a young woman (cf. Eng. *ancillary*), a set of scales, and a font or stoup. Let us provisionally accept some large serving vessel filled with fresh ale among the torches and lights as part of the festive atmosphere. The next verse, "when you will have eaten a spice-cake" is plain enough, and might be associated with both wedding feasts and a thirst for ale.

We then come to the brewing process proper, which begins with malting the grain (vv. 8-20). The barley that will be used for ale-making is to be steeped in water in a large, deep vat. Old French *orge* 'barley' derives in linear fashion from Latin *hordeum*.[12] Its Middle English equivalent, *barli*, is not given. The vat, *cuve*, is not a utensil specific to brewing (< Latin *cupa* 'vat'; Middle English *fat*). Or we should perhaps say that the term is not restricted to malt processing, as is also the case for the verb *enfondrer* 'to sink, submerge', less analytic since less discrete in its meanings than the English gloss *stepe* 'steep'. When the bar-ley has been well steeped, the water is to be removed. Here there may be some tension between French terminology and English gloss. Walter says the water is to be *descouelé*, which we might translate as 'drained off', that is, removed by a natural flow, probably from the bottom. The gloss *laden outh* suggests removal from the top, although such a process cannot have been as effective as drainage. The brewster is then to go to a sunny upper room (*soller*) or loft, the floor of which is to be swept clean. The barley, here called *blé*, which originated as a general term for grain and then came to be used preferentially of wheat,[13] is to be spread (*coucher*) on the floor and left until it germinates (*germee, spired*).[14] As we shall see, the grain was probably laid down in rows or piles, in order to permit access for further treatment. From this point on, the grain is no longer called barley but rather malt (*breez*, see above). Like the other Middle English terminology met to date, *malt* is of native English origin.[15] The mounds of malt should be stirred (*mover*) by hand from time to time. *Mounceus* means mounds but the French verb *rengez* suggests that they were laid out in a grid pattern, hence English *rouwes*, rows.

When the germination process, aided by light and ventilation, is complete, the malt is moved to the next stage of processing (vv. 21-28). It should be carried

---

[12] *AND, orge*; Mod.Fr. *orge*; < Lat. *hordeum*, TL, 6.1254, *orge*; *FEW*, 4.234, *hordeum*.

[13] *AND, blé*; Mod.Fr. *blé*; < LLat. **blatum*; TL, 1.996, *blé*; *FEW*, 15.1.126, **blad*. Cf. Gaulish *blato-*, Delamarre, 78.

[14] Neither verb, *germer* in French, *spiren* in English, is specific to mashing and brewing, and they have clear Latin and Old English antecedents, respectively. On the former, see *DEAF*, G. 576.

[15] *MED, malt*; < OE *malt*; *OED, malt*.

in a basket, small or large according to circumstances, to be dried. Again, the French and English terms, *corbail/corbailloun* and *lepe*, are not specific to brewing. Nor is a special term used of curing or drying (*enseccher*). This is effected in an oast or grain-drying kiln. Walter's French term is *torrail*. This term is unrelated to Latin *furnus* or *fornax*, or Old French *four* in the general sense of oven. Nor does it mirror the English gloss *kulne*, which points ahead to Modern English *kiln*.[16] It is to be derived from Latin *torrere* 'to roast' and is then the most specific piece of equipment met thus far.[17] The term was, however, also used of lime-kilns. Walter's account is telescoped, with little reference to time intervals between the processing stages. The optimal time between the drying and use of malt is about three weeks.

The malt is then to be ground (*molu, grounden*).[18] How this may have differed from the regular milling of grain is left unexplained and Walter passes to the next stage, the addition of hot water. This infusion or mashing process is reflected in the French verb *enbeverer* 'to steep, soak', here seen in its reduced past participial form *enbu*. No equivalent English verb is named. Again the malt, now better called mash, is to be drained (*descoure* 'to run off', this too unglossed).

Up to this point, Walter is relatively easy to follow. Yet, the remainder of the passage offers both discontinuities in the brewing process and between the "French" and "English" steps, with the English terminology somewhat more specific than the French. A case in point is the *keverel* from which the mash is to be removed. This is a small *cuve* or vat (see above) and the terminology seems not process-specific, but the English gloss is *mahissing fate*, 'mashing vat' (the common modern term is *mash tun*). *Mashing* in this sense is a common Germanic brewing word and we can only regret the absence of its Anglo-Norman equivalent.[19] The brewster (*bresceresce*) must then determine whether she has sufficient *wort*.[20] We have seen how barley became malt. Now, just before the boiling and fermentation processes get under way, a new term is introduced. This is designated *bersil* in French and glossed *wort* in English. One verse later, *berzize* seems also used of the wort or *grout*, as it is here glossed.[21] Thus we have two pairs, *bersil/berzize* in Anglo-Norman and *wort/grout* in Middle English.

---

[16] *MED, kilen*; < OE *cylen*; *OED, kiln*.

[17] *AND, toraille*; Mod.Fr. *four* (substitution); < Lat. *torrere* 'to roast'; TL, 10.397; *FEW*, 13.2.107, *torrere*.

[18] *AND, moudre*; Mod.Fr. *moudre*; < Lat. *molere*; TL, 6.355, *moudre*; *FEW*, 6.3.29, *molere*; *MED, grinden*; < OE *grindan*; *OED, grind*.

[19] The terminology seems to have originated in the verbal notion *mashen* 'to mix ground malt and water', yielding the present phrase *mahissing fate* 'mashing vat'. *Mash* as a noun is a later development; *MED, mashinge*; < OE *mascan*; *OED, mash*.

[20] *AND, braceresse*; ModFr. *brasseuse*; *MED, wort*; < OE *wyrt*; *OED, wort*.

[21] *MED, grout*; < OE *grut*; *OED, grout*.

Bersil and congeners have not attracted the attention of etymologists. The word is found only in Walter's treatise and in some medical recipes, also of Anglo-Norman provenance. The explicit glossing in Walter and the pairing with ale in other texts leave no doubt as to meaning. This restricted distribution would argue against an origin in Gaulish, along with *cerveise* and *brais*, ale and malt, while raising the possibility of a loan from Old Norse, the Germanic languages of the Rhineland, even Old English. Its varied phonological contours do not hide its resemblance to known "barley" words, although even these have a curious distribution, *far* in Latin, *barr* in Old Norse, *bere* in Old English, with no representation in other continental Germanic. A form such as Old Norse *barlog* 'sweet wort' suggests a possible Scandinavian source for *bersil* but the more likely case is of a derivative, with typical Romance suffixation, of French and Norman *brais* 'malt', with the signification 'infused malt'.[22]

Walter's gloss *grout* is of interest since this term (now often written *gruit*, *grut*) was also used of herb mixtures added to the wort in order to bitter and flavor it, before the widespread use of hops. Here *grout* may reference both the malt and the additive, similarly coarsely ground, the basic meaning of the term.[23] Only at this point (v. 32) does Walter inform us that ale may be brewed of wheat or barley. Old French *forment* (Mod.Fr. *frument*) is used of the former,[24] *orge* of the latter (see the earlier note on *blé*, first grain generally, then wheat). But he offers no specifics as concerns the actual boiling of the wort or brewing. Walter then matches up two more pairs of specialized terms, *geeste* and *berzille* in French, glossed *berme* and *worte* in English. *Geeste* is the yeast that is added to the boiled wort (*berzille*) to initiate the fermentation process. The word *geeste* also appears to have deep historical roots and has been linked with Gaulish **jesta* 'yeast'.[25] Middle English *berme*, as a term for the froth or scum on the surface of fermenting ale and for brewer's yeast, is the development of Old English *beorma*.[26] It is evident that this would have been a yeast that floated on the top of the wort during fermentation and not a bottom yeast. At this point,

---

[22] *AND*, *bersil* (see also *bersise*); Mod.Fr. *moût* (substitution); < Norman *brais*; TL, 1.935, *bertiz*; *MED*, *wort*; < OE *wyrt*; *OED*, *wort*.

[23] Richard Unger (pers. comm.).

[24] *AND*, *frument*; Mod.Fr. *froment*; < Lat. *frumentum*; TL, 3.2111, *forment*; *FEW*, 3.828, *frumentum*.

[25] *AND*, *gest*; Mod.Fr. *levure* (substitution); < Gaul. **jesta*; TL, 4.296, *geste*; *FEW*, 5.35, **jesta*; *DEAF*, G.655. The last-named work would distinguish between a masculine form, loaned from Old English, and feminine forms, loaned from continental Germanic. The former transfer is the less probable.

[26] *MED*, *berme*; < OE *beorma*; *OED*, *barm*. If there is a distinction between the two Anglo-Norman terms, *bersil* and *bersize*, it might be that the latter is used of the wort after the yeast has been added, that is, when the fermentation process has begun. But the English glosses do not follow suit.

Walter retreats to a more general statment about brewing that suggests, as does his remark "But I can't comment on it all" (v. 36), that he had exhausted his technical vocabulary and was not concerned with the end stages of the process, e.g., clarifying the ale, putting it in casks, delivering it to consumers. Instead, Walter admonishes the brewster to complete successfully each of these final steps until she has a good ale.

He concludes with remarks on the effects of excessive drinking – miracles and marvels – none of which has lost its pertinence: sharpened wits, double vision, enhanced appreciation of one's own knowledge, social boldness, quadruped locomotion, loud speech, and finally a red face. Punning on *orge* 'barley' and *St. George*, he concludes by saying that people will say of the drunken man that "By St. George he has drunk too much of the fat (or cream) of the barley".

This section of Walter's treatise has yielded a modest vocabulary for the processing of malt and the brewing of beer. The Anglo-Norman French lexis is preponderantly of Gallo-Romance origin but some essential terms traceable to Gaulish. The more limited English vocabulary, on the other hand, is entirely of "native" origin, supporting conclusions drawn from other evidence that brewing had a long history in Britain before the Conquest. In comparison with Walter's disquisitions on baking and on flax and linen (where he stops short of the actual weaving process), his section on brewing gives a less full appreciation of the processes involved and also a less comfortable fit between French verse and English gloss.[27]

The easy glossing of French by English suggests that brewing in the late thirteenth century did not differ significantly on the two sides of the Channel, although the two vocabularies were discrete. Walter's lightly narrativized catalogue offers the first attestations in continuous prose (as distinct from simple interlinear glossing) of many of the French terms reviewed above. Written Middle English emerged from the shadow of Anglo-French in rather different fashion than did Old French from medieval Latin, but Walter's treatise also offers the first attested use of many of the Middle English words seen here.[28] The *Tretiz*, while scarcely a masterpiece of medieval didactic literature, is nonetheless a worthy, if understudied, forerunner to such later household manuals as the *Mesnagier de Paris* and, as concerns culinary arts, to such cookbooks of the next century as *The Forme of Cury* from cooks at the English royal court and Taille-

---

[27] See the companion pieces to the present article, William Sayers, Learning French in a Late Thirteenth-Century English Bake-House, and Flax and Linen in Walter of Bibbesworth's 13 c. French Treatise for English Housewives, both forthcoming.

[28] There is considerable variation among the Bibbesworth manuscripts, so that some few additional brewing terms in both French and English might be gleaned from the study of this largely unpublished material.

vent's *Viandier*.[29] Taken as a whole, Walter's work also poses important questions, little addressed here, on child-rearing and the social and supervisory networks of the English-speaking mistresses of rural estates in Britain in the last quarter of the thirteenth century.[30] From our perspective, there is also an underlying tension in the work, since, bilingual vocabulary aside, Walter doubtless knew less about the household matters on which he expounds, in particular the final stages of brewing ale, than his nominal addressee.[31]

Appendix

Now the French for mashing malt and brewing ale
Since the French that I have told you about will henceforth be sufficient [for dressing flax and spinning linen thread], now it would be good to know how to mash and brew in the process of making ale, as we do to make our wedding feasts enjoyable – with torches, serving bowls, and rush lights – and when you have eaten a spice-cake. In a deep and wide vat steep your barley and when it is well steeped and the water has been drawn off, go up then to that high loft and have it well swept out, and leave your grain spread out on the floor, until it has fully germinated. From that moment on you will call malt what was formerly called grain. Stir the malt in the piles where it is laid out with your hand, and then carry it in a basket in order to dry it in the oast (kiln), for the basket, big or little, will serve you amply. Then the malt is to be ground and well infused with hot water. Then let it drain a while, now outside the mashing vat, until the brewster sees that she has the wort as she wants it. Then she will take this grout, of wheat or barley, that she has, and with the barm and wort (by which people sharpen their wits) [she will carry out] the true duties of brewing. But I am not able to give you a full account. But thus, with one process after the other, complete each

---

[29] Walter of Bibbesworth's *Tretiz* was also incorporated in a larger work that is known under the title *Femina*. Here his interlinear English glosses are expanded to a full translation or paraphrase of the various French texts. Rothwell 1998 provides a general assessment of this composite and largely unstudied text. He has since published an excellent annotated online edition of one manuscript, *Femina* 2005, which also casts useful light back on Walter's text.

[30] While the point is made in this essay that Walter's interest for the history of the French and English terminology of the crafts and trades has largely been ignored, other scholars have seen the treatise as principally a pedagogical work. This prompted Rothwell's squib (1982), A Mis-Judged Author and His Mis-Used Text: Walter de Bibbesworth and His 'Tretiz'. For a more recent assessment of Walter's work in the sphere of second language acquisitions, see Kennedy 1998. The British author's relevance to the history of writing on food preparation is assessed in Hieatt 1982.

[31] On medieval didactic poetry generally, see the recent collective volume, *Calliope's Classroom* 2007.

stage until you have good ale, which makes people feel so good that some drink so much that they become drunk. Ale produces miracles and marvels, makes two candles out of one. Drunkenness turns a layman into a clerk; it gives an insignificant man a high profile. Drunkenness makes a man crawl; it makes a hoarse man cry aloud. Drunkenness gives you a fool's face, a red complexion without rouge. And this leads people to say that, by Saint George, he has drunk too much of the cream of the barley. With this, the author rests, for he will speak of other matters.

William Sayers
Department of Comparative Literature
Cornell University
Ithaca, NY 14853, USA
[ws36@cornell.edu]

References

Altfranzösisches Wörterbuch
   1925-2001 Tobler, Adolf, and Erhard Lommatzsch (comp.). Stuttgart: F. Steiner.
Anglo-Norman Dictionary
   1992   Rothwell, William, et al. (ed.). London: Modern Humanities Research Association. Anglo-Norman On-Line Hub, [http://www. anglo-norman.net/].
Calliope's Classroom
   2006   *Calliope's Classroom: Studies in Didactic Poetry from Antiquity to the Renaissance*. Harder, M. Annette, et al. (ed.). Paris and Dudley, Mass.: Peeters.
Dictionnaire de la langue gauloise
   2003   Delamarre, Xavier (comp.). 2nd ed. Paris: Editions Errance.
Dictionnaire étymologique de l'ancien français
   1974-   Balinger, Kurt, et al. (comp.). Québec: Presses de l'Université Laval; Tübingen: Niemeyer; Paris: Klincksieck.
Femina
   2005   *Femina: Trinity College, Cambridge MS B 14.40.* 2005. Rothwell, William (ed.). The Anglo-Norman On-Line Hub, [http://www. anglo-norman.net/texts/femina.pdf].
Französisches etymologisches Wörterbuch
   1928-   von Wartburg, Walther (ed.). Bonn, F. Klopp Verlag.

Hieatt, Constance B.
1982   'Ore pur parler del array de une graunt mangerye': The Culture of
            the 'Newe Get', circa 1285. *Acts of Interpretation: The Text in Its
            Contexts, 700-1600: Essays on Medieval and Renaissance Litera-
            ture in Honor of E. Talbot Donaldson.* Carruthers, Mary J, and
            Elizabeth D. Kirk (ed.). Norman, OK, Pilgrim, 219-33.

Kennedy, Kathleen E.
1998   Changes in Society and Language Acquisition: The French Lan-
            guage in England 1215-1480. *English Language Notes* 35: 1-19.

Mediae Latinitatis Lexicon Minus
2001   Niermeyer, J. F. (comp.). Leiden, Brill.

Middle English Dictionary
1952-2001 Kurath, Hans, et al. (comp.). Ann Arbor, Michigan: University of
            Michigan Press. [http://quod.lib.umich.edu.proxy.library.cornell.
            edu/m/med/].

The Oxford English Dictionary
1989   2nd ed. Oxford: Oxford University Press. *OED Online* [http://
            dictionary.oed.com/].

Rothwell, William
1998   The Place of *Femina* in Anglo-Norman Studies. *Studia Neophilo-
            logica* 70: 55-82.
1994   Of Kings and Queens, or Nets and Frogs: Anglo-French Homo-
            nymics. *French Studies* 48: 257-73.
1982   A Mis-Judged Author and His Mis-Used Text: Walter de Bibbes-
            worth and His 'Tretiz'. *The Modern Language Review* 77: 282-293.

Sayers, William
Forthcoming   Flax and Linen in Walter of Bibbesworth's 13 c. French
                Treatise for English Housewives. *Medieval Clothing and Textiles.*
Forthcoming   Learning French in a Late Thirteenth-Century English Bake-
                House. *Petits Propos Culinaires.*

Unger, Richard W.
2004   *Beer in the Middle Ages and Renaissance.* Philadelphia: Univer-
            sity of Pennsylvania Press.

Walter of Bibbesworth
1990   *Le Tretiz.* Rothwell, William (ed.). London: Anglo-Norman Texts
            Society.
1929   *Le Traité de Walter de Bibbesworth sur la langue française.*
            Owen, A. (ed.). Paris: Presses Universitaires de France.
1909   *Tretiz. Femina.* Wright, W. (ed.). London: Roxburghe Club.

Studia Etymologica Cracoviensia
vol. 14   Kraków 2009

Kenneth SHIELDS, Jr. (Millersville)

"UNITY IN APPARENT DIVERSITY":
ITS IMPLICATIONS FOR
HISTORICAL/COMPARATIVE LINGUISTICS

At the heart of historical linguistic analysis is the comparative method, which utilizes correspondence sets consisting of cognate items whose formal properties are systematically observed in order to reconstruct the original etyma from which the cognates evolve. The key concept underlying the method is that of "formal correspondence," or the etymological parallelism of the overt historical manifestations of the original etymon (see, e.g., Fox 1995: 57-91). However, in a number of recent publications (e.g., Shields 1999, 2000), I have pointed out that historical linguists need to take note of another type of comparative analysis – which I have termed "unity in apparent diversity" – involving "the existence of a common underlying process with different overt [formal] results" in related languages (Shields 1999: 29). That is, related lects may show different formal manifestations of a morpho-syntactic process which they have inherited from their common proto-language. The identification of such a process through systematic comparison can result in insights into the structure of the proto-language which are as significant as information derived through the classic comparative method. In this brief paper I wish to discuss further the implications of "unity in apparent diversity" for historical/comparative linguistic theory.

I shall begin my remarks by pointing out a few examples of such processes within the Indo-European language family. First of all, I have argued that "the appearance of specifically non-singular constructions was rather late in the evolution of the Indo-European language" (1982a: 63; cf. Shields 1992: 13-16) and that the bifurcation of the non-singular category into dual and plural is later still (cf. Shields 2004). In regard to verb conjugation, Lehmann (1974: 201-202) "also suggests that the appearance of a special inflectional non-singular was a late development, principally dating from the time when the various dialects had begun to emerge as autonomous entities. He says: 'The system of verb endings clearly points to an earlier period in which there was no verbal inflection for number .... For the dual and the plural endings are obviously defective. We cannot reconstruct endings in these two numbers which are as well supported as are those of the singular, except for the third plural'" (Shields 1992: 13-14). Lehmann (1993: 174-175) reiterates this point when he emphasizes that "the differences among dialects in the endings for the first and second plural indicate ... that each of the first and second plural forms was independently developed in the dialects" (cf. also Adrados 1985: 31-32, 36-37). However, I have maintained that despite the formal differences in attested dialectal non-singular verbal suffixes, a common derivational process is at work in them all, which is probably inherited from late Indo-European when the non-singular category was being extended consistently in conjugation. In short, "it seems to me that the non-singular verbal suffixes are merely the singular ones with non-singular markers attached. For example, the first person plural suffix *-mes (Skt. -mas, Dor. -mes) can be interpreted as first person (singular) *-m plus the non-singular suffix *-(e/o)s (cf. Gk. pód-es 'feet'), while *-men (Gk. -men, Hitt. -men) shows *-m plus the non-singular marker *-(e/o)n (cf. Toch AB riñ 'cities'), about which I have written extensively (cf., e.g., Shields 1982a: 63-70, 1985: 190-191, 1991/2: 76-77, 1992: 65-67). Even Skt. -ma may be analyzed as *-m plus the non-singular ending *-e (cf. Gk. mētér-e 'two mothers,' OIr. rig < *rēg-e 'two kings'; cf. Shields 1982b, 1992: 66)" (Shields 1997a: 108). The original lack of contrast between dual and plural – a lack most obviously attested in Hittite – explains how the suffix *-e is manifested with both dual and plural signification in the dialects (cf. Shields 1997a: 107-108). The central point here is that a systematic comparison of the non-singular verbal suffixes of the early Indo-European dialects reveals a common process in their derivation – the affixation of an emerging non-singular marker to the appropriate singular personal suffix. The striking formal differences among the dialects – emphasized so strongly by Lehmann – are muted to a large degree by the existence of the common means of derivation apparently available in the proto-language itself.

As a second example of "unity in apparent diversity," I wish to cite the formation of the nominal o-stem genitive. Once again, there is great variation in attested dialectal forms. For example, in the singular number, the suffix *-ī is found in Italic (Lat. -ī) and Celtic (OIr. -i), although Faliscan and Oscan-Umbrian show the same *-osyo which is characteristic of Sanskrit and Greek (Falisc. -osio, Osc.-Umb. -eis, Ved. -a-sya, Hom. -o-io) and Celtiberian preserves a form in -o (< *-o-o, cf. Shields 2005: 236-238) . In Germanic *-e-so (Go. -is) has currency. In the plural a form in *-on or *-ōn (< *-o-on) is widely distributed (Lat. -um, Gk. -ōn, Skt. -ām, OE -a), but Baltic and Slavic utilize *-ād (Lith. -o, OCS -a, cf. Shields 2001) in the same function, while within Germanic, Gothic employs *-ē (Go. -ē) as the o-stem genitive plural desinence. In a series of articles (Shields 1991, 1997b, 2000, 2001, 2005), I have pointed out that each of these variant endings can be derived from a corresponding deictic particle easily reconstructed for Indo-European on an independent basis or from a contamination of these deictic particles. Among the relevant deictics are *(e/o)s, *(e/o)n, *(e/o)t, *ē, *ā, *ī, *i, and *e/o. In short, then, comparative data would indicate that late Indo-European utilized a process of affixing deictic particles to o-stem nominal forms as a means of creating genitive constructions, with the dialects themselves manifesting different deictic elements in this process. This derivational process is consistent with Lyons' (1968: 550, 1971: 388-395) and Clark's (1978: 117-118) acknowledgment of an etymological connection between possessive and locative formations in many languages. Since, as I indicated earlier, the inflectional expression of number was not consistently applied in late Indo-European, as the interchangeable number value of the Hittite genitive suffixes in -aš and -an clearly indicates, the deictics which came to mark the genitive case function were originally indifferent to number specification (cf. Shields 1997b: 240-241).

As a final example of the "unity in apparent diversity" phenomenon, I would like to refer to Lehmann's analysis (1998) of the origin of the relative pronouns in *kʷe/i- and *yo-. As Szemerényi (1996: 210) notes, "to the group which uses *kʷi-/*kʷo- as a relative belong Anatolian, Tocharian, Italic, later also Celtic and Germanic [e.g., Hitt. kwiš, Lat. quis]. Another group comprising Aryan, Greek, Phrygian, and Slavic uses *yo- ... as the relative [e.g., Skt. yás, Gk. hós]." Acknowledging his scholarly debt to Justus (1976), Lehmann (1998: 399-400) describes the common process which underlies the formal differences evident in the dialects: "Sketching the development of relative clauses from the OV stage of Indo-European, we assume for the oldest period the particles *kʷe and *yo that were suffixed to the preceding word in order to single it out. In this sense they were used to conjoin words, indicating that the suffixed word was to be interpreted together with the word or words preceding it. This is the use that was maintained with the meaning 'and, also'. They were then used to highlight focal elements. This use survived in Baltic and Slavic, where it led to the definite form of the adjective .... When used in the first of two successive clauses, forms of the particles indicated that the second clause included a semantic item that was modified by an element in the first. Such first clauses correspond to the subordinate clauses that are referred to as relative. Nouns as focussed elements in the first or relative clause could be repeated or referred to in the second by an anaphor. When the early dialects were modified to VO structure, the clause with the focussing element was placed after the noun that was modified in the principal clause. The focussing element singled out the item referred to and became a relative pronoun." Lehmann (1998: 400) admits that one can only speculate about why one group of dialects attests one original particle in relative pronoun function while another group attests a different one in this capacity, but he remains confident that the common evolutionary process in which these particles participated potentially explains a great deal about the morpho-syntax of the proto-language itself.[1]

So, then, what are the implications of "unity in apparent diversity" for historical linguistic analysis? Most obviously, the recognition of the phenomenon has the potential of identifying categories or constructions in a proto-language which had begun to emerge at the time of the divergence of the original speech community since it implies that the proto-language had developed the means but not the precise forms for expression of those categories or constructions. Thus, just as the classic comparative method utilizes correspondence sets of genetically equivalent forms as the basis for postulating etyma in the proto-language at the time when these etyma began to undergo divergent development, so the comparison of parallel morpho-syntactic constructions in related languages in order to identify common processes in their derivation leads to insights into the structure of the proto-language just prior to its dialectalization. The primary difference between the approaches is that the first is form-based and the second is process-based. However, I must admit that it can be difficult to assess whether the common processes manifested by related languages are the result of inheritance or independent but parallel development because many developmental processes which languages undergo constitute what Fox (1995: 194-195) calls "'laws' of language development," or "general principles of change" which have a basis in language typology rather than genetic relationship. Among the examples cited above, the development of possessive constructions from "locational" deictics has been identified as such a general typological principle of language evolution.[2] Thus, in order to maximize the utility of process-based comparison, it becomes necessary to differentiate more precisely between genuinely universal evolutionary processes and those which are more restricted in applicability. In essence, what I am advocating here is a distinction along the lines of what Dressler (2003) calls "universal, system-independent" naturalness/markedness and "system-dependent" naturalness/markedness. Such a distinction "establishes deductively degrees of universal preferences" in the context of linguistic structure and change (Dressler 2003: 463). Of course, the less universal

---

[1]   The number of different forms participating in this process may have actually been larger. Lehmann (1998: 400) explains: "The proto-language, then, included at least two particles with the meaning 'and, also' that were used to focus elements, and thereupon as relative markers. Watkins has identified a third that came to be so used in one of the Old Irish relative patterns: *de (1963: 26-28). Another that might have been developed as relative marker was *u (Pokorny 1959: 74); maintained in Skt. u, it has among other uses a focussing function, as Klein notes in probably the most extensive study of any of the particles (Klein 1978)."

[2]   In the third example, the reinterpretation of the particle as a relative pronoun would not seem to be a necessary development, although universals of word order typology are likely responsible for making the reinterpretation a possibility.

the process, the less likely it can be associated with independent but parallel development in related lects. Until typological theory establishes more definitively the universal nature of various "'laws' of language development," some caution must be exercised in drawing definitive conclusions from "unity in apparent diversity."

A second but less significant qualification of the utility of process-based comparison involves the fact that a number of related languages can simply substitute new forms for an original proto-form, giving the impression that the related lects originally shared only process, not form. Such a problem is inherent, too, in the classic comparative method itself when innovation has taken place in all or nearly all of the languages being compared; in such a situation "reconstruction of the original state of affairs in the proto-language is therefore not possible" (Fox 1995: 73).

In the final analysis, linguistic reconstruction always remains a highly speculative enterprise (cf. Shields 1992: 1-3) despite many valuable refinements in its methodology since its inception in the nineteenth century. It is within the context of offering another methodological refinement that I submit for consideration the principle of "unity in apparent diversity."

Kenneth Shields, Jr.
Millersville University
English Department
P.O. Box 1002
Millersville, PA 17551-0302, USA

References

Adrados, F.
  1985. "Der Ursprung der grammatischen Kategorien des Indoeuropäischen," [in:] B. Schlerath & V. Rittner (eds.); *Grammatische Kategorien: Funktion und Geschichte*, 1-46, Wiesbaden: Ludwig Reichert.
Clark, E.
  1978. "Locationals: Existential, Locative, and Possessive Constructions," [in:] J. Greenberg, C. Ferguson & E. Moravcsik (eds.); *Universals of Human Language*, vol. 4, 85-126, Stanford: Stanford University Press.
Dressler, W.
  2003. "Naturalness and Morphological Change," [in:] B. Joseph & R. Janda (eds.); *The Handbook of Historical Linguistics*, 461-471, Malden, MA: Blackwell Publishing.

Fox, A.
   1995. *Linguistic Reconstruction: An Introduction to Theory and Method,*
          Oxford: Oxford University Press.
Justus, C.
   1976. "Relativization and Topicalization in Hittite," [in:] C. Li (ed.); *Subject
          and Topic,* 215-245, New York: Academic Press.
Klein, J.
   1978. *The Particle* u *in the Rigveda,* Göttingen: Vandenhoeck & Ruprecht.
Lehmann, W.
   1974. *Proto-Indo-European Syntax,* Austin: The University of Texas Press.
   1993. *Theoretical Bases of Indo-European Linguistics,* London: Routledge.
   1998. "Explanation of Syntactic Changes in Late Indo-European by Use of
          Universals," [in:] J. Jasanoff, H. C. Melchert & L. Olivier (eds.); *Mír
          Curad: Studies in Honor of Calvert Watkins,* 391-404, Innsbruck: In-
          stitut für Sprachwissenschaft der Universität Innsbruck.
Lyons, J.
   1968. "Existence, Location, Possession, and Transitivity," [in:] B. Van Root-
          selaar & T. Staal (eds.); *Logic, Methodology, and Philosophy,* vol. 3,
          495-509, Amsterdam: Benjamins.
   1971. *Introduction to Theoretical Linguistics,* Cambridge: Cambridge Uni-
          versity Press.
Pokorny, J.
   1959. *Indogermanisches etymologisches Wörterbuch,* vol. 1, Bern: Francke.
Shields, K.
   1982a. *Indo-European Noun Inflection: A Developmental History,* University
          Park: Penn State Press.
   1982b. "On the Origin of the Greek Nominative-Accusative Dual Suffix *-e,*"
          Živa Antika 32, 27-32.
   1985. "Speculations about the Indo-European Cardinals, 5-10," *Diachronica*
          2, 189-200.
   1991. "Comments about the *o*-Stem Genitive of Indo-European," *Histori-
          sche Sprachforschung* 104, 52-62.
   1991/92. "The Emergence of the Non-Singular Category in Indo-European,"
          Lingua Posnaniensis 34, 75-82.
   1992. *A History of Indo-European Verb Morphology,* Amsterdam: Benjamins.
   1997a. "On the Pronominal Origin of the Indo-European Athematic Verbal
          Suffixes," *Journal of Indo-European Studies* 25, 105-117.
   1997b. "The Gothic Genitive Plural in *-ē* Revisited," *American Journal of
          Germanic Linguistics and Literatures* 9, 239-249.
   1999. "Sanskrit Dative Singular *-āya* and Its Indo-European Connections,"
          Historische Sprachforschung 112, 26-31.

2000. "Indo-European *o*-Stem Genitives in *-ī," *Lingua Posnaniensis* 42, 145-150.

2001. "On the Origin of the Baltic and Slavic *o*-Stem Genitive Singular Suffix *-ād," *Baltistica* 36.2, 165-171.

2004. "The Emergence of the Dual Category in Indo-European: A 'New Image' and Typological Perspective," *Indogermanische Forschungen* 109, 21-30.

2005. "On the Indo-European Genitive Suffix *-e/o," *Emerita* 73, 233-239.

Szemerényi, O.

1996. *Introduction to Indo-European Linguistics*, Oxford: Oxford University Press.

Watkins, C.

1963. "Preliminaries to a Historical and Comparative Analysis of the Syntax of the Old Irish Verb," *Celtica* 6, 1-49.

Studia Etymologica Cracoviensia
vol. 14   Kraków 2009

Heinrich WERNER (Bonn)

ZUR ETYMOLOGIE DES NAMENS *Sibir* 'SIBIRIEN'

In der Fachliteratur gibt es bis zu fünf, sechs unterschiedliche Versionen der Herkunft des Namens *Sibir* 'Sibirien' (Vasmer 1971/3: 616; Anikin 2000: 493-494), die bislang alle umstritten bleiben. Unumstritten ist nur die Tatsache, daß der Name auf die alte Bezeichnung der Hauptstadt des westsibirischen tatarischen Khanats *Sibir* (später *Isker*) an der Tobolmündung am Irtysch zurückgeht: der Name wurde allmählich von der Stadt auf das Khanat und später auf alle Gebiete östlich vom Ural übertragen.

Es handelt sich ganz offensichtlich um ein Ethnonym, obwohl man versuchte, wie z.B. in Ramstedt 1935: 362, den Namen aus mong. *siber* 'sumpfiges Walddickicht', kalm. *šiwr̥* 'feuchte, sumpfige Waldfläche' zu erklären, woraus auch die türkischen Bezeichnungen entstanden sein sollen (übrigens wollte man den Namen *Sibir* mit türk. *sapmak* 'vom Weg abkommen' und mit chant. *syb-* 'Bach' + *-ir* < türk. *-jir* 'Erde' verbinden, s. Vasmer 1971/3: 616; Anikin 2000: 493).[1] Mit dem ursprünglichen Ethnonym kann dagegen chant. *sipər məɣ* 'Sibirien' verbunden werden, was aber an und für sich kein Beweis für die ugrische Herkunft des Ethnonyms *Sibir* ist.

Nach den Sagen der westsibirischen Tataren wurde der betreffende Name von der vortürkischen Bevölkerung der Region hinterlassen, worunter man zuweilen eben die ugrische Bevölkerung vermutet. Es ist aber so, daß dieses Ethnonym ganz offensichtlich mit den historischen Sabiren verbunden ist, die in den Quellen als ein Hunnenvolk erwähnt werden und im 5.-6. Jahrhundert n.Chr. den Höhepunkt ihrer Macht erreichten, nachdem sie unter dem Druck der Awaren bis ans Kaspische Meer vorgedrungen waren und im Nordkaukasus von der Wolgamündung bis zu Derbend ihr Reich gegründet hatten. In Artamonov 1962: 66 und Gumiljov 1998/2: 266-267, aber auch schon früher in Inostrancev 1926,

---

[1] Kaum annehmbar ist auch der Versuch in Vasilevič 1966: 338, ewenk. *Sivîr* 'Sibirien' mit dem Namen der sabinischen Vorfahren *sivei* zu verbinden, da die ewenk. Bezeichnung eindeutig aus dem Russischen stammt (Anikin 2000: 494).

vermutete man unter den Sabiren sibirisch-ugrische und samojedische Stämme.[2]
Beides ist fraglich, und zwar aus folgenden Gründen: die ugrischen Stämme
kamen erst nach dem 11.-12. Jahrhundert über den Ural nach Sibirien (Decsy
1965: 217-218; Rombandeeva 1976: 230), und die Samojeden hatten ihre
Wohnsitze, wie die Verbreitung ihrer Toponyme zeigt, vorwiegend im Stromgebiet des Ob und östlich davon, nicht aber im Stromgebiet des Irtysch. In Hajdu
1953: 88-89 wird angenommen, daß der Mittelpunkt der samojedischen Wohn-
plätze, von dem sie sich um die Zeitwende ausgebreitet hätten, am Irtysch zu
suchen sei. Die jüngsten Forschungsergebnisse auf dem Gebiet der sibirischen
Toponymik (Maloletko 2000) zeigen aber, daß im Stromgebiet des Irtysch vorwiegend Toponyme jenissejischer Herkunft verbreitet sind. Auch wenn samojedische Toponyme im Gebiet zwischen dem Irtysch und Ob vorkommen, so sind
sie im Vergleich zu den jenissejischen später hinterlassen worden (Duľzon
1961). Eine jenissejisch-samojedische Symbiose in diesem Gebiet ist aber nicht
auszuschließen (s. Hajdu 1953, Helimski 1982).

Man könnte das Ethnonym *Sibir*, das in einer ganzen Reihe von phonetischen Varianten vorkommt (*Sabir, Savir, Saber, Saver, Sabar, Savar, Seber,
Sever, Sebur, Sipyr, Sapir, Syvyr, Sivir, Sipir, Šibir, Soper* u.a.), aus einer iranischen Quelle herleiten,[3] wenn man wenigstens die Situation der Sauromaten
und Sarmaten berücksichtigt, deren Herrschaft sich bis ins Stromgebiet des Tobol erstreckte. Dabei handelt es sich aber wiederum um die vorugrische Bevölkerung der Region, die den Namen bewahrt hat.

Bekanntlich vermutete man schon in Patkanov 1897-1900, daß die "Bur-
gen" und "Festungen" im Wohngebiet der Irtysch-Ostjaken (d.h. der Ugrier –
H.W.) auf die ehemalige einheimische Bevölkerung der Region zurückzuführen
sind: "Ob die Ostjaken selbst alle Erdfestungen errichtet haben, ist uns unge-
wiss. Es scheint uns nicht unmöglich zu sein anzunehmen, daß sie dieselben
oder vielleicht einen Teil derselben von den ehemaligen Aborigenen des Landes
(*Sâbaren, Șiḇiren; Âr-Jach*), von denen wir allerdings bis jetzt fast nichts wissen, geerbt haben." Unter dieser vorugrischen Bevölkerung, die zuweilen auch
als Volk der Tschuden (russ. *чудь*) bezeichnet wurde (Castren 1856: 57), vermutete J. Ph. von Strahlenberg die asiatischen Skythen (Strahlenberg 1730:
313). Wer waren aber diese vorugrischen Sabiren oder Tschuden wirklich?

Der Name *Sabir* (*Sibir*) taucht schon in den alten Quellen im 2. Jahrhundert n.Chr. auf (die Σαυαροι des Ptolemaeus). In Feist 1928: 31, Anm. 3 ver-

---

[2]   In Artamonov 1962 und Gumiljov 1998/2 stützt man sich vorwiegend auf Černecov
      1941 und Černecov 1953: 238, wo es sich um die Vorfahren der Wogulen handelt;
      in der Tat geht es eigentlich dabei um die vorugrische Bevölkerung der Region, wor-
      unter man die Sabiren vermuten sollte.

[3]   Nicht aber im Sinne von O. Szemerényi < altpers. *asabāra-* < **aśu̯a-bāra* 'Reiter'
      (s. Anikin 2000: 494).

sucht man ihn mit den *Sěverъ*-Slawen in Osteuropa und in Lunin 1998: 402 sogar mit dem Flußnamen *Severskij Donez* zu verbinden, und in diesem Fall wären slaw. *Sever* 'Nord' und *Sabir* (*Sibir*) 'Sibirien' auf eine und dieselbe Quelle zurückzuführen. Dies wird in Vasmer 1971/3: 589 zu Recht abgelehnt, weil sich das baltisch-slawische Wort für 'Nord' (vgl. russ. *Sever* 'Nord', aslaw. *sěverъ*, ukrain. *siver* 'Kälte', russ. dial. *siver* 'Nordwind', lit. *šiaurys* 'Nordwind', *šiaurė* 'Norden', *šiaurus* 'eiskalter (Wind)', lat. *caurus* 'nordwestlicher Wind' usw.) nach A. Erhart (s. "Sborník prací Filosofické fakulty Brněnské university", 6 [A 5], Brno, S. 5) eindeutig mit idg. **seu-*, aind. *savya-* 'link(er)' verbinden läßt, und zwar mit derselben semantischen Begründung wie aind. *purva-* 'vorderer/östlicher', *pasca-* 'hinterer/westlicher', *daksina-* 'rechter/südlicher'. Diese Vorstellungen von den vier Himmelsrichtungen, welchen die uralte Solarorientierung zugrunde liegt, gibt es übrigens auch bei anderen Völkern Eurasiens, z.B. bei den Jenissejern: so wird bei den Keten die östliche Seite im Zelt auch als die vordere und die reine betrachtet, denn im östlichen Teil des Himmels befindet sich *Es*, der Himmelsgott; entsprechend ist die westliche Seite auch die hintere, die südliche die rechte und die nördliche die linke.

Daß es sich im Falle der *Σαυαροι* von Ptolemaeus im 2. Jahrhundert um andere Sabiren handelt als die sibirischen, ist kaum zu glauben; man beachte, wie schon erwähnt, daß sich die sarmatischen Gebiete bis zum Irtysch erstreckten, und bestimmte Gruppen der Irtysch-Sabiren konnten bereits vor den Hunnen im Stammesbund der Sarmaten nach Osteuropa gekommen sein. Und daß sich die Sabiren später an dem Stammesbund der Hunnen beteiligten, ist auch nicht zu bezweifeln, da sie als Hunnenvolk bekannt waren und sogar nach der Hunnenepoche im 5.-6. Jahrhundert, als sie ihr eigenes Reich im Nordkaukasus gegründet hatten, in den Quellen ein Hunnenvolk blieben[4] (Näheres hierzu s. weiter unten).

In Pritsak 1989: 275-280 versuchte man den Namen *Sibir* mit den asiatischen *Hsien-pi* zu verbinden, die vermutlich 370 n.Chr. das Stromgebiet des Irtysch und Tobol erreichten: "The Hsien-pi Mu-jung stayed there for about a hundred years (370-460), and their impact was significant enough to attach their own political name to the territory, Hsien-pi (**Säbi-r*)." Diese Übertragung des Namens *Hsien-pi* auf das entsprechende westsibirische Territorium erklärt O. Pritsak folgendermaßen: "The old pronunciation of the Chinese characters *Hsien-pi* was **siem-bi*, i.e., **säbi*. The final *-r* (in the name *Säbi-r*) is the well-known Altaic collective suffix attested to in both the Hunnic and (proto)Mongolian lin-

---

[4] Außer dem Ethnonym *Sabir* (*Sibir*) kann man noch die Namen auf *-ir* der ebenfalls "hunnischen" Stämme *Akatz-ir* und *Altzig-ir* nennen, die neben den Sabiren erwähnt werden (Artamonov 1962: 84), also drei Namen, die typische Bahuvrîhi-Komposita darstellen. Die Versuche, den Namen *Akatzir* aus den türkischen Sprachen zu erklären (s. Artamonov 1962: 55-56; Altheim 1969: 111), bleiben fraglich.

guistic families; the Turkic correspondence was -z ... The development *ä > i* in the first syllable (**Säbir > Sibir*) already reflects the typical Volga vocalic shift which look place in Volga-Turkic during the period of the Golden Horde (13th-14th century)."

Bei dieser Deutung des Namens *Sibir* sind wenigstens zwei Schwierig-keiten so gut wie unüberwindbar: 1) die zeitliche Lücke von 200 Jahren seit der ersten Erwähnung der Σαναροι von Ptolemaeus im 2. Jahrhundert bis zur ver-mutlichen Beherrschung Westsibiriens durch die Hsien-pi 370-460 n.Chr.; 2) die umstrittene phonetische Erklärung des Wandels *Hsien-pi > *säbi* (anstatt **sänbi*) > *Sabir > Sibir*.

Es gibt keine weiteren Hinweise über die ethnische Identität der Sabiren. Dargestellt werden sie als ein zahlreiches, starkes, kriegerisches Volk, erwähnt werden ihre guten Belagerungsanlagen und ihre Kriegslager im Wald, die aus Zelten bestanden und mit dauerhaftem Pfahlzaun umgeben waren. Das Volk be-stand aus mehreren selbständigen unabhängigen Gentes, angeführt von Häupt-lingen, die in jedem Fall selbst über Krieg oder Frieden entschieden. Im Notfall (z.B. bei Gefahr und Krieg) schlossen sich die Gentes zu einem einheitlichen Stamm zusammen (Artamonov 1962: 74).

Da die ugrische oder samojedische Abstammung der Sabiren (Sibiren) aus obengenannten Gründen abgelehnt werden muß, versuchte ich die Herkunft dieses Volkes in Werner 2007 mit den Westjenissejern zu verbinden. Auf jeden Fall läßt sich m.E. diese Version viel besser begründen als die ugrische und sa-mojedische oder auch die alttürkische (bzw. hunnische). Die erste Frage aber, die dabei zu klären ist, betrifft die Übertragung des Ethnonyms *Sabir* (*Sibir*) ira-nischer Herkunft auf die Jenissejer.

Daß nomadische Viehzüchter iranischer Herkunft seit jeher größere Gebie-te Westsibiriens beherrschten, ist kaum zu leugnen, merkwürdig ist aber, daß sie hier, vor allem im Stromgebiet des Irtysch, dem Ausgangsgebiet der Sabiren, keine Toponyme hinterlassen haben: die historischen Toponyme der Region auf *-ses, -sis, -sas, -tes, -tis, -tas, -zes, -zas, -cas, -sim, -tym, -igaj, -lat, -get, -gat* lassen sich in der Regel nur aus den Jenissej-Sprachen erklären (Dul'zon 1959; Dul'zon 1963; Maloletko 2000) und sind also jenissejischen Ursprungs. Diese Tatsache läßt vermuten, daß das Volk der historischen Sabiren infolge einer lan-gen Symbiose zwischen den eingewanderten nomadischen iranischen Viehzüch-tern und der einheimischen jenissejischen Bevölkerung entstand[5] und durch die

---

[5]   Eine andere Ethnogenese der Sabiren vermutet man in Gumiljov 1998/1: 324: hier geht man davon aus, daß sie durch die Vermischung der westlichen Dinglinger mit den Obugriern entstanden sind. Wie gezeigt, kamen die Obugrier erst nach dem 11.-12. Jahrhundert nach Westsibirien und konnten an der Ethnogenese der Sabiren nicht beteiligt gewesen sein. Und nach der Hypothese von Aristov – Grumm-Grži-majlo sollte man unter den Westdinglingern Westjenissejer vermuten.

Sprache sowie mehrere ethnische Züge dieser einheimischen Bevölkerung geprägt war, auch wenn die Jenissejer dabei von ihrer ursprünglichen aneignenden
Jäger- und Fischerkultur zur Viehzüchterkultur wechselten. Die herrschende ira-
nische Schicht ist in der einheimischen Bevölkerung aufgegangen, hinterließ
aber einige Ethnonyme und einige weitere Iranismen (s. Stachowski 2006).

Nach den Charakteristika der jenissejischen Protokultur (Werner 2006), die
sich auf Grund des Wortschatzes und der Mythen feststellen lassen, hat man es
im Falle der jenissejischen Urbevölkerung Westsibiriens mit typischen Jägern,
Fischern und Sammlern der südsibirischen Bergtaiga zu tun, die den personifi-
zierten Himmel *Es*, die höchste Gottheit, und die Mutter-Erde *Baŋam* verehrten.
Ob es unter den Urjenissejern auch Viehzüchter gegeben hat, bleibt fraglich.
Ihre Beteiligung an den archäologischen Viehzüchterkulturen Sibiriens wie der
Karassuk-Kultur oder der Andronowo-Kultur (Maloletko 2000: 190-224) ist aber
dadurch nicht auszuschließen, denn ein Teil von ihnen konnte infolge enger
Kontakte oder sogar einer Art Symbiose mit den eingewanderten nomadischen
Viehzüchtern die Lebensart der letzteren übernommen haben. Bei den Sabiren
trifft es zu, denn die sabirische Horde, die ihr eigenes Reich im Nordkaukasus
gegründet hatte, bestand vor allem aus Viehzüchtern.

Außer dem Ethnonym *Sabir* kann man noch auf *Ir*, *Ar* und *As* hinweisen,
die ebenfalls iranischen Ursprungs sind (siehe Artamonov 1962: 357-360; Altheim 1969: 55-58) und von denen das Ethnonym *Ar* in der Selbstbezeichnung
der jenissejischen *Arinen* und *As* in der der jenissejischen *Assanen* erhalten geblieben sind. In diesem Zusammenhang ist auch noch auf das vorugrische Volk
Ar-Jach (wörtl. *Ar*-Volk) im Stromgebiet des Wasjugan (Wohngebiet der Chan-
ty) hinzuweisen, dessen Name *Ar* ganz offensichtlich mit den jenissejischen
Arinen identisch ist.[6]

Daß die erwähnte Symbiose zur Assimilation nicht der entsprechenden
westjenissejischen Bevölkerung, sondern der iranischen Nomaden führte, ist
dadurch zu erklären, daß die Jenissejer hier in der überwältigenden Mehrzahl
waren. Das läßt sich daraus schließen, daß nur ein zahlreiches, starkes und kriegerisches Volk seine Toponyme von der Nordmongolei im Osten bis zu Osteuropa im Westen hinterlassen konnte.[7] Höchstwahrscheinlich handelt es sich
im Falle der Sabiren um die Protoarinen, denn auch in späterer Zeit galten ihre
Nachkommen, die jenissejischen Arinen, als mächtig und sehr kriegerisch (vgl.
die Bemerkungen über die ehemalige Macht, den Reichtum und Einfluß der

---

[6]   Die Verbindung mit den jenissejischen *Arinen* bekräftigen in diesem Fall die örtli-
      chen Toponyme auf *-igaj*, die sich aus dem ar. *ikai* 'Fluß' erklären lassen (Maloletko
      2000: 128).

[7]   Näheres zu dieser Verbreitung der jenissejischen Toponyme in Westsibirien siehe in
      Maloletko 2000.

Arinen in Sibirien in Castren 1860: 375); wie bekannt, sind die Arinen erst im 17.-18. Jahrhundert endgültig unter anderen Völkern Sibiriens aufgegangen.

Nach Dul'zon 1962: 74 verbreiteten sich die Jenissejer historisch vorzugsweise in westliche und nordwestliche Richtung, und die Avantgarde bestand dabei aus Arinen. Als jenissejisches Ausgangsgebiet betrachtete A. P. Dul'zon Südsibirien zwischen dem Oberlauf des Jenissej und des Irtysch, und als westliches Gebiet ihrer Expansion nannte er das Stromgebiet des Irtysch.

Hier sollte man auch an die Hypothese von Aristov 1897 und Grumm-Gržimajlo 1909 erinnern, wonach die Jenissejer als direkte Nachkommen des Ding-ling-Volkes der südsibirischen Bergtaiga zu betrachten sind, welche in den altchinesischen Chroniken eben als ein sehr kriegerisches, zahlreiches und lebensfähiges Volk von Jägern, Fischern und Sammlern beschrieben sind.

Man kann also davon ausgehen, daß eben die Jenissejer die uralte einheimische Bevölkerung im Stromgebiet des Irtysch darstellten, und einen genaueren Hinweis auf die chronologische Zeitspanne ihres Aufenthaltes in diesem Gebiet in früherer Zeit geben etliche jenissejisch-indogermanische Wortparallelen (Werner 2007: 18-23; vgl. auch Gamkrelidze/Ivanov 1984/2: 939). Genauso wie indogermanische Entlehnungen zu jener Zeit in die finnisch-ugrischen Dialekte kamen (Jacobsohn 1923; vgl. auch Gamkrelidze/Ivanov, ebd., 921-940), konnten auch jenissejisch-indogermanische Wortparallelen wie z.B. die folgenden entstanden sein:

PJ *qip^hə/*qəp^hə 'Handel/Verkauf', 'handeln/verkaufen': jug. χip, ket. qi·, kot. hapi ds.; ar. (H) kobolsom 'ich kaufe', ulkobu 'ich verkaufe';
    vgl. heth. ḫappar- 'Handel', 'Preis'; ḫapparāi 'verkaufen', ḫappinaḫḫ 'Reichtum'; wahrscheinlich handelt es sich um ein Wanderwort, das mit der Verbreitung des Handels verbunden war; vgl. auch anord. kaupa, got. kaupōn 'Handelsgeschäfte treiben' (> aslaw. koupiti 'kaufen');

PJ *p^hənəŋ 'Sand' (ket. hʌneŋ, jug. fʌniŋ, ar. phin'aŋ/fin'aŋ, pump. pinniŋ ds.);
    idg. *pēs-/*pēns- 'Sand', 'Staub' (aind. pāṁsuká-, awest. pąsnu-š 'Staub, Sand', aslaw. pěsъkъ 'Sand');

PJ *p^hʌl- 'Sämischleder' (< 'Fell'), ist als ket. hʌl-, jug. fʌl-, kot. fal(aŋ)- in Komposita belegt: ket. hʌlat, jug. fʌlat 'Sämischleder'/'Oberbekleidung aus Sämischleder' < ket. hʌl + qa²t 'Parka, Pelz, Mantel', jug. fʌl + χa²t 'Parka, Pelz, Mantel' (vgl. auch ket. esta hʌlat, jug. ezda fʌlat 'Himmelsgewölbe', wörtl. 'Gottes Oberbekleidung aus Sämischleder');
    germ. *fella (ahd. vēl/vēll, ags. fēll, anord. fjall, engl. fell, got. fill in filleins 'ledern') 'Haut von Mensch und Tier' < vorgerm. *pello- < *pelno- (griech. pella, lat. pellis) 'Haut, Leder';

PJ *p^hʌl(əŋ)-sei 'nähen': ket. hʌlsej, jug. fʌlsej, kot. falaŋše 'nähen', wörtl. vielleicht ein Kompositum 'Sämischleder nähen' < ket. hʌl-, jug. fʌl-, kot. falaŋ- + ket. -sej, jug. -sej, kot. -šel/-če 'nähen';

zu jen. *-sei, -sej, -še* 'nähen' vgl. idg. **si̯ū-* 'nähen': lit. *siūti,* got. *siujan*
'nähen' usw.;

PJ **dinə* 'Tanne': ket. *di·n',* jug. *din,* kot. *tîni/tini,* ar. *tin,* ass. *tin* 'Tanne';
idg. **dhanu-/*dhonu-* 'Bezeichnung einer Baumart'; aind. *dhánvan-, dhánu-,*
dhánus 'Bogen', *dhanvana* 'ein bestimmter Fruchtbaum'; germ. **danwō-*
(asächs. *danna,* mnd. mnl. *danne,* ahd. *tanna,* mhd. *tanne*) 'Tanne'; germ.
*dannio- (asächs. anfr. *dęnnia,* nnl. *den*) 'Fichte' (Kluge 1975: 769; Pokorny 1959: 234);

PJ **du²* (< **dug*) 'Rauch' (ket., jug. *du²,* ar. *t'u,* ass., kot. *tu/tug,* pump. *dukar*
ds.);
idg. **dhem-/*dhemə-* ds. (heth. *tuḫḫ-u̯ai,* ahd. *toum,* lat. *fūmus,* aind. *dhū-*
mas, lit. *dū̆mai,* russ. *dim* ds.; heth. *tuḫḫima* 'Atemnot', 'Erstickung');

PJ **tʰum* 'schwarz': ket. *tu·m,* jug. *tum,* kot. (C) *tʰum* ds.; ar. *t'ūma,* ass. *tuma,*
imb. *túemam,* pump. *tuma* 'es ist schwarz (grau)';
idg. **tem(ə)-* 'dunkel': lat. *temere* 'blindlings', aind. *támas-* 'Dunkel, Fin-
sternis', *tamasá-* 'dunkelfarbig', lit. *tamsùs* 'dunkel, schwarz', lit. *tamsà,*
aslaw. *tĭma,* ahd. *dëmar* 'Dämmerung', air. *temel* 'Fisternis', isl. *þāmaðr*
'dunkel', mir. *teim, temen* 'dunkel, grau' (Pokorny 1959: 1063);

PJ **qo²p* 'Fußsohle': jug. *χɔ²p,* ket. *bulap* (< *bu·l* 'Fuß' + *qɔp*), kot. *pulap* (<
pul 'Fuß' + *hop*) 'Fußsohle'; sket. *qɔpku* 'mittlerer Teil der Fußsohle' <
qɔ²p 'Fußsohle' + *ku·* 'Öffnung';
idg. **k̂ăpho-/*k̂ŏpho-*: aind. *śaphá-* 'Huf, Klaue', awest. *safa-* 'Huf des
Pferdes'; ags. asächs. afries. *hōf,* anord. *hōfr,* ahd. *huof,* schwed. *hof,* dän.
hov, engl. *hoof,* nl. *hoef* 'Huf';

PJ **tʰʌ²q* 'Finger'/'Zehe': ket. *tʌ²q,* jug. *tʌ²χ,* kot. *tʰok/tʰox/tʰog,* pump. *tok* ds.;
germ. **taixw-* 'Zehe': ags. *ta(he),* afries. *tāne,* anord. *ta,* dän. *taa,* engl. *toe,*
schwed. *tå,* ahd. *zē(c)ha,* mhd. *zēhe,* mnl. *tē(n);*

PJ **tʰigə* 'Kuh': kot. (C) *tʰigä/tʰi²ä,* ar. *t'ūja,* ass. *tig/tik* 'Kuh' (vielleicht mit
ursprünglicher allgemeiner Bedeutung 'Melktier'?); ar. *t'ugal/tügal,* ass.
tigvu 'Kalb';
germ. **tika* (?): norw. dial. *tikka* 'Ziege', schwed. *ticka* 'Muttertier von
Ziege/Schaf', ahd. *ziga,* mhd. *zige* 'Ziege';[8]

PJ **qu²s,* **qu²t* 'Birkenrindezelt': ket. *qu²s,* jug. *χu²s,* ar. *kus,* ass. *huš/hiš,* kot.
huš/hûš, pump. *hu-kut;*
germ. **hūs-* 'Haus', 'Behausung': ahd. asächs. ags. anord. *hūs* ds., got.
gud-hūs 'Tempel'; in Gamkrelidze/Ivanov 1984/II: 939 germ. *hūs* < jen.
qu²s, in Stachowski 1997/2: 231 < gtü. **kōš/*kuš* 'Zeltlager' < 'zusam-
mengetan'/'Nomadenkarawane' (vgl. atü. *köč* 'Nomadenlager');

---

8 Damit läßt sich, wie in Gamkrelidze/Ivanov 1984: 586 vermutet, armen. *tik* 'Wein-
schlauch' und idg. **t'igᵉ*- zusammenstellen. Vgl. auch atü. *tekä* 'Ziegenbock', mo.
tex 'Steinbock'.

PJ *qɔləp 'Hälfte' > 'Seite', 'Gegend (Land)': ket. qolep, jug. χɔlap, kot. holap,
    Pl. holapaŋ; nket. (mit Metathesis) pelaq (> selk. pelaq) ds.;
    germ. *halƀ- 'Teil, Seite, Hälfte': got. halba, anord. halfa, ahd. halba; vgl.
    Adj.: got. halbs, ahd. halb, asächs. afries. mnl. half, ags. healf, anord. halfr;
PJ *Pʰərgən, jug. Firginʲ 'Waldhexe';
    anord. Fjǫrgyn 'Mutter des Thor-Gottes', 'Göttin Erde'. Der Name wird
    etymologisch mit got. fairguni 'Berg' (heth. peruna 'Fels', aind. parvata-
    'Berg') verbunden. Auf der anderen Seite vergleicht man diesen Namen
    mit idg. *Per(k) 'Donnerschleuderer', worauf lit. Perkūnas, lett. Perkūns,
    slav. Perun 'Gott des Donners, Blitzes und Regens' und lit. Perkūnija
    'Frau des Perkūnas' zurückgehen;
PJ *as/*es 'Gott/Himmel': ket. e·s, jug. es, kot. êš, ar. es/eš 'Himmel/Gott';
    anord. âs, Pl. æsir 'Ase/As-Gott';
ket. Imlʲa 'weiblicher unterirdischer Geist'; vgl. die alte ketische Imlja-Gens,
    von welcher der ketisch-jugische Familienname Imljakov(a) abstammt (s.
    Alekseenko 1967: 33). In Helimski 1982: 240-241 wird ket. Imlʲa mit selk.
    imilʲa 'Großmutter', 'Tante' verglichen;
    anord. Embla 'die erste [vom As-Gott geschaffene] Frau'.

Zu dieser Zeit mußten die Indogermanen (vielleicht die sogenannten "alt-
europäischen" Indogermanen, s. Gamkrelidze/Ivanov, ebd., 943-957), Viehzüchter der osteuropäischen, nordkaukasischen und westsibirischen Steppenzone, als
Nachbarn nördlich von sich die Ugrofinnen und östlich vom Südural bis zum
Stromgebiet des Irtysch die Westjenissejer gehabt haben. In beiden Fällen
können nur die Wortparallelen die ehemaligen Kontakte bezeugen, und wenn
die ugrofinnisch-indogermanische Kontaktzone höchstwahrscheinlich in Osteuropa zwischen dem Stromgebiet der Wolga und dem Ural zu suchen ist, kann
für die entsprechende älteste jenissejisch-indogermanische Kontaktzone das Gebiet zwischen dem Südural und dem Stromgebiet des Irtysch in Frage kommen,
weil sich bis hierher die Verbreitung der Toponyme jenissejischer Herkunft beobachten läßt. Eben diese Urjenissejer kann man als Vorfahren derjenigen betrachten, die später vermutlich an den Stammesbünden der Skythen, Sauromaten, Sarmaten, Alanen und Hunnen unter dem Namen Sabiren teilgenommen
haben.
    Hier komme ich noch einmal auf die Frage der Beteiligung der Sabiren am
Hunnenbund zurück. Da die Sabiren in den Quellen als ein hunnischer Stamm
bezeichnet werden, kann man das Problem ihrer Zugehörigkeit zu den Hunnen
nicht umgehen.
    Wie bekannt, konnte nach der Version von Inostrancev 1926, Gumiljov
1960, Artamonov 1962 ein Teil der nördlichen Xiongnu in der Mitte des 2. Jahrhunderts n.Chr. ihrem Verfolger, dem Hsien-pi-Volk, entkommen, konsolidierte

um sich die westsibirische ugrische und samojedische Bevölkerung und bildete im Laufe von zwei Jahrhunderten (von der Mitte des 2. bis zur Mitte des 4. Jahrhunderts) jenen Völkerbund, der unter dem Namen der *Hunnen* in die Geschichte eingegangen war. Nach einer anderen Version haben die europäischen Hunnen mit den Xiongnu Zentralasiens nichts zu tun: man sollte sie als alttürkische Stämme betrachten, die vom nordöstlichen Iran als Ausgangsgebiet gekommen waren (Maennchen-Helfen 1945; Altheim 1969). Wie dem auch sei, man sollte in beiden Fällen von einem Völkerbund ausgehen, der in den ersten Jahrhunderten n.Chr. vor dem großen Vorstoß nach Westen im 4. Jahrhundert in den Steppengebieten Westsibiriens und Osteuropas entstand. Die anführende Schicht in diesem Völkerbund bestand höchstwahrscheinlich aus asiatischen Nomaden, die Hauptmasse der mitgerissenen Stämme stellte aber die einheimische Bevölkerung Westsibiriens dar. Es konnten aber, wie bereits erwähnt, keine westsibirischen Ugrier oder Samojeden, sondern nur Westjenissejer gewesen sein. Eben daher kommt die Bezeichnung der Sabiren (übrigens auch der *Akatzien* und *Altzigiren*) als hunnische Stämme.

Das obenerwähnte Ethnonym *Ir* kommt nur in Komposita vor, und zwar in den "hunnischen" Stammesnamen auf -*ir* – *Sabir, Akatzir, Altzigir*. Eigentlich könnten diese Namen als *Sab*-(Sippe), *Akatz*-(Sippe) und *Altzig*-(Sippe) des *Ir*-Volkes gedeutet werden, um so mehr, als daß die zwei letzteren Namen immer neben den *Sabiren* erwähnt werden (Artamonov 1962: 84). Dasselbe Ethnonym *Ir*- findet sich im Namen des Irtyschflusses: *Ir-tyš < Ir* + jenis. -*tis/-tys* (oder auch -*tes, -tas, -cas, -ces, -cis, -ses, -sis* usw.) 'Fluß', also wörtlich 'Fluß der *Irer* (des *Ir*-Volkes)'; *Ir* ist offensichtlich in den Bahuvrîhi-Komposita *Sab-ir, Akatz-ir, Altzig-ir* als Grundwort und im Kompositum *Ir-tyš* als Bestimmungswort zu betrachten.

Der Name *Irtyš* wird in der Fachliteratur unterschiedlich gedeutet (s. Popova 2000). Er kommt schon als *Ärtis* in den orchon-jenissejischen Runeninschriften vor. Auf Grund des Kirgisischen will man den Namen aus *ir* 'Erde' + *tyš* 'graben, scharren, wühlen', also als 'Erdwühler' deuten. Genauso wird die kasachische Variante *Jertis* erklärt; beide Deutungen sind ohne Zweifel ein Fall der Volksetymologie, da die Namen der sibirischen Flüsse nach einem ganz anderen semantischen Modell gebildet sind (siehe Maloletko 2000). Nach A. P. Dulzons Auffassung sollte man in diesem Fall -*tyš* < jenis. -*tis* < -*cis* < -*sis/-ses* 'Fluß' herleiten, eine Deutung, die auch in Popova 2000 geteilt wird. Umstritten bleibt aber die Deutung des *ir*-Elements. Nach V. N. Popova handelt es sich um die idg. Wurzel *ir-* < **ar-* 'fließen', und bei Berücksichtigung einer iranischen Quelle für *ir-* sollte man *Ir-tyš* als (russ.) 'бурный, стремительный поток' (wörtl. 'ungestüme Sturzflut' oder 'stürmischer, ungestümer Strom') übersetzen.

Hier kann man, wie oben schon erwähnt, tatsächlich von einer indogermanischen (eigentlich iranischen) Quelle ausgehen, aber nicht von *ir-* 'fließen', sondern vom Ethnonym *Ir*, welches neben *Ar* und *As* erwähnt wird (Artamonov 1962: 357-360; Altheim 1969: 55-58): idg. *airya-* 'rechtmäßig, edel' > 'Arier', die Bezeichnung der Einwanderer auf persischem und indischem Boden mit weiterer Entwicklung des entstandenen Volksnamens zum Ländernamen awest. *airyanam* > gegenwärtig *Iran*. Aus dieser Sicht ist der Name *Irtyš* < *Ir* '*Ir*-Volk' + jenis. *-tes/-tis* (*-ces*, *-ses*) 'Fluß', also 'Fluß des Volkes der Irer', eine analoge Bildung wie der Name des ossetischen Flusses *Ardon* < *Ar* '*Ar*-Volk' + *don* 'Fluß', wörtlich 'Fluß der Arier' oder 'Fluß des *Ar*-Volkes'. Von den Nomaden-völkern iranischer Herkunft, z.B. im Rahmen des Sarmatenbundes, konnte das Ethnonym in phonetischen Varianten *Ir*, *Ar*[9] auf die einheimische (jennissejische) Bevölkerung im Stromgebiet des Irtysch übergegangen sein. Derartige Entste-hung der Selbstbezeichnung der Arinen *Ar* (chant. *Ar-Jach* 'Volk Ar'), der früh verschwundenen *Ir*-Jenissejer und der jennissejischen *As/Assan* 'Assanen' ist wahrscheinlich, wenn man von dem heutigen Forschungsstand ausgeht, die ein-zig mögliche Erklärung dieser jennissejischen Ethnonyme.[10]

Was die späteren historischen Kontakte der Jenissejer zu anderen Völkern Westsibiriens anbetrifft, so scheinen Kontakte mit türkischen, samojedischen und sibirisch-ugrischen Völkern unumstritten zu sein. Für das hier erörterte Pro-blem der Herkunft des Namens *Sibir* sind die jennissejisch-ugrischen Kontakte von besonderem Interesse, denn eben diese Kontakte bestätigen neben den Top-onymen die Annahme, daß die vorugrische Bevölkerung im Stromgebiet des Irtysch aus Jenissejern bestand. Auf diese Kontakte weisen jennissejisch-ugrische Wortparallelen wie die folgenden hin:

PJ *atə* 'nicht' (Verbot): ket. jug. *at/ata*, *atn* (< *at qa·n*) 'nicht' (beim Verbot vor Imperativformen), wog. *at* ds.;

PJ *epʰəl*: jug. εſɨr, ket. ε:l 'Preiselbeere', wog. *äpərəχ*, *äpərjəχ*, *äpəχ*, *äpra* 'Erdbeere', ung. *eper(j)* 'Erd-, Maulbeere';

PJ *ikaj/*igaj* 'kleinerer Fluß', ar. (Helimski 1986) *ikai* 'Fluß', kot. (Castren 1858) *egîg/egîx* 'Fluß-arm'; obugr. *igaj* 'kleinerer Fluß' (kommt in mehre-ren Toponymen vor);

PJ (W) *ʔ(H)oksi, PJ (S) *ʔɔksi (~ x-) 'Baum'; PJ (W) *(H)aʔq, PJ (S) *xaʔq 'Bäume': ket. *o·ks* (Pl. *aʔq*), jug. *oksɨ* (Pl. *aʔχ*) 'Baum'; obugr. *jux* ds.;

---

9   Zur idg. (iranischen) Quelle der Ethnonyme *Ir*, *Ar*, *Ass* bei den Alanen und über die *Ir*- und *Oss-/Ovs*-Osseten s. Altheim 1969: 58-59.

10   Über andere spekulative Deutungen des Ethnonyms *Ar*, die mit tü. *arï* 'Biene', 'Hor-nisse', und des Ethnonyms *As/Assan*, die mit jenis. *asa* 'Teufel' verbunden sind, s. Werner 2005: 68, 122. Spuren in Form von Ethnonymen haben die Arinen ihrerseits bei anderen sibirischen Völkern hinterlassen, z.B. das Ethnonym *Ara* (*Aara*) bei den Chakassen.

PJ *qep/*qa²p 'Boot aus Birkenrinde', ket. qap/qa²p, jug. χap/χa²p ds., kot. (C) xep/xêp/qep 'Boot', ass. (M) xaip ds., ar. (VW) ƚʲulap < *ƚʲul-χap 'Schiff'; Helimski 1982, 28 vgl. mit mans. xâp 'Kahn';

PJ *pʰʌnəŋ 'Sand, Asche': ket. hʌneŋ, jug. fʌniŋ, ar. pʰinʲaŋ/finʲaŋ/finnʲaŋ, jen. (Fischer) poaniŋ, pump. pinniŋ/feniɡ 'Sand'; kot. fenaŋ/pʰenaŋ, funaŋ 'Asche'; chant. pān 'Sand';

PJ *qe²s 'Sandbank', 'Sandufer': ket. qɛ²s, jug. χɛ²s ds., ar. qes 'Stein', wog. χɤs 'Sand';

PJ *set/*tet 'Fluß': ket. se·s, jug. ses, kot. šet, ar. sat ds., eed.-ket. (Mes) šöš 'kleiner Fluß'; wog. sōs 'Fluß';

PJ *se²ələ 'Rentier': sket. sɛl, nket. sɛ:li, jug. sɛʰ:r, pump. salat, ar. sin (Pluralform) 'Rentier', kot. šeli/šele 'Wild'; wog. sāli 'Rentier';

PJ *pʰestəp 'Vielfraß' (Tier): ar. pʰhjastap, ass. pestáp, kot. (M) peštap, kot. (C) feštap/pʰeštap ds.; wog. pašxer/pašker 'Vielfraß' (Tier), vgl. auch das wogulische Pāstər-Geschlecht (Altheim 1969: 235-237);

PJ *tʰo²əqə 'eine Entenart': sket. tɔʁ, nket. tɔ:ʁe, jug. tɔʰ:χ, kot. altʰax (< al + tʰax) 'Quakerente'; wog. toχ 'anas clypeata' u.a.;

Kott (Castren 1858) hanaŋ, pl. hanaŋan/hanakŋ 'Ufer'; Helimski 1982: 69 vergleicht Kott hanaŋ mit chant. kanəŋ ds.;

OKet qopta > Ket qɔpta (Pl. qɔ́ptaŋ/qɔpta:ŋ) 'verschnittener Ochse'; PJ (Starostin) *qopt- (~ χ-, -ɔ-) id. (?); Bouda 1957 vgl. mit nen. hâbt(a), obugr. χopt ds.

Von besonderem Interesse sind die in Maloletko 2000: 6-8 gebrachten obugrisch-kaukasischen Wortparallelen, bei denen sich die meisten aus den Jenissej-Sprachen erklären lassen; daß könnte bedeuten, wenn die angeführten Wortparallelen korrekt sind, daß die entsprechenden kaukasischen und obugrischen Wörter aus einer und derselben Quelle stammen, und zwar aus dem Sabirischen, auch wenn chronologisch der sabirisch-kaukasische Kontakt[11] im 5.-6. Jahrhundert viel früher stattfinden konnte als der sabirisch-ugrische nach dem 11.-12. Jahrhundert (?). Vgl.

obugr. igaj 'kleinerer Fluß'; ar. (Helimski) ikai 'Fluß', kot. (C) egîg/egîx 'Flußarm';[12] Cez uʒʊy, Xwarši exy, Hunzib ɔxy, Hinux uxy, exe 'Fluß';

---

[11] Übrigens sollen die nordkaukasischen Sabiren nach dem Untergang ihres Reiches in den nordkaukasischen Völkern aufgegangen sein (s. Gumiljov 1998/1: 324).

[12] Das Wort igaj kommt in einer Reihe von ugrischen Flußnamen im Stromgebiet des Wasjugan (linker Nebenfluß des Ob) vor: Altym-igaj, Vare-igaj, Vilan-igaj, En-igaj, Elle-Kulun-igaj, Ipaly-igaj, Kalap-Igaj, Kalman-igaj, Tomul-igaj u.a. (Maloletko 2000: 95). Der Autor vermutet, daß diese Hydronyme arinischer Herkunft sind, vom Volk Ar-Jach hinterlassen wurden, welches sich mit den Protoarinen identifizieren läßt.

obugr. *jux* 'Baum'; PJ (W) **(H)oksi*, PJ (S) **ʔɔksi* (~ *x-*), Pl. (W) **(H)aʔq*, (S) **xaʔq* 'Baum': ket. *o·ks* (Pl. *aʔq*), jug. *oksɨ* (Pl. *aʔχ*) 'Baum'; kot. (C) *atči/ atče*, Pl. *âx/ax, ak* ds., kot. (M, Kl, W, VW) *ak* 'Wald'; pump. (W, VW, Kl) *hóxon* 'Baum', 'Wald'; Rutul *uyx* 'Birke', Hunzib *p-ыxy* 'Pappel', Andi *б-exy* 'Birke', Awar *p-ox* 'Hain';[13]

obugr. *amp* 'Hund'; ket. *äba/äva*, Pl. *äbaŋ/ävaŋ* 'Hundehütte'; Lezgisch *ампа* 'Hund';

obugr. *vala* 'Stelle', vgl. im Wasjugan-Dialekt: *vač-vala* 'Ort/Stelle einer Stadt'; ket. *bal* 'Zwischenraum'; in der Regel kommt nur die Lokativform *balga* als Postposition 'zwischen' vor; ket. *áqna bálga* 'zwischen Bäumen', *dɛŋna balga* 'unter Menschen'; ket. Pl. *balaŋ* ds.: *aqna balaŋga* 'zwischen Bäumen'; jug. *bar/baʔr*, Pl. *bárɨŋ* ds.; meist kommt die jug. Pluralform *barɨŋ* und die Lokativform *bargej* als Postposition 'zwischen' vor: jug. *áχna bárɨŋ* 'zwischen Bäumen', *dʲɛŋna barɨŋ* 'unter Menschen'; Lak *шара-валу* 'Dorf' (*-валу* ist ein Derivationssuffix?);

obugr. *pelʲa/pelä* 'Berg', 'Hügel', 'längliches niedriges Plateau'; PJ **qoləp* 'Seite'/'Hälfte' (> 'Gegend, Land'); ket. *qɔlep*, jug. *χɔlap*, kot. *halap* ds.; vgl. ket. *ətna qɔlep* 'unser Land', *bɨlda qɔlamsʲadɨŋta* 'in allen Ländern'; nket. auch *pelaq* (durch Metathesis < *qolep*) ds., vgl. selk. (C) *pälek/peläŋ*, kam. *älek*, kar. *päläŋ*, jur.-sam. (C) *pealea* 'Hälfte';[14] Godoberi *бел*, Botlix *беял*, Çamalal/Kryz *бел*, Andi *бил* 'Berg';

obugr. *ink* 'Wasser'; ket. *ə·n se·s* 'Fluß mit ruhiger Strömung', *ʌnl* 'kleine Bucht' < *ʌn/ə·n* 'ohne Strömung' + *u·l* 'Wasser'; vgl. ket. *qɨ·n'*, jug. *χɨ·n* 'Strömung' < ket. *qä*, jug. *χɛʔ* 'groß'/'sehr' + *ʌn/ə·n* 'ruhiges (Wasser/Strömung)'; Axwax *инхе*, Hunzib *энху* 'Wasser';

obugr. Hydronyme auf *-lat* 'Fluß' (?): *Sa-lat, A-lat, Og-lat, Aj-Kyŋ-lat, Aŋk-lat, Vy-lat, Sam-lat, Ka-lat, Ju-lat, Ači-lat, Kuda-lat* u.a. gehen nach A. M. Maloletko auf die Zeit des Volkes *Ar-Jach* zurück, welches sich höchstwahrscheinlich mit den Protoarinen identifizieren läßt; Proto-Dagh. **lölöd/ *löad* 'Wasser', Arči *löat* 'Meer', Lezgisch *lat* 'Tränkrinne'; das Wort läßt sich vielleicht nach Maloletko 2000: 138-142 unter bestimmtem Vorbehalt als jenissejisch deuten, da es als Appellativum der Hydronyme in Arealen mit jenissejischen Toponymen vorkommt; man kann es entweder mit ket. *lɨʔt*, jug. *lɨʔtʲ* 'Berg'/'Plateau' vergleichen oder auf FPJ **λat* 'Fluß' (vgl.

---

[13] Die Präfixe sind in den Daghestansprachen Anzeiger der entsprechenden Nominalklasse.

[14] Auf Grund der ketischen Varianten dieses Wortes *qolep, pelaq* läßt sich eindeutig eine Metathesis beobachten, und während die Variante **qolep* in den meisten Jenissej-Sprachen vorkommt, wird in den samojedischen Sprachen die Variante **paleq* gebraucht. Vgl. die Wortparallelen **haleb* in den germanischen und **pol-* (russ. *pol-*, *polovina*) in den slawischen Sprachen.

pump. *-tat/-tet*, ar. *-sat/-set* 'Fluß') mit einem lateralen Geräuschlaut im Anlaut zurückführen, der in den belegten Jenissej-Sprachen in einen *l-*, *t-* oder *s*-Laut übergegangen ist (Werner 2005: 218-224).

Heinrich Werner
Herrstr. 195
D – 53111 Bonn

Literatur

Alekseenko, E. A. (1967): *Kety. Istoriko-ètnografičeskie očerki.* Leningrad.

Altheim, F. (1969): *Geschichte der Hunnen*, Bd. 1, 2. Aufl. Berlin (1. Aufl. 1959).

Anikin, A. E. (2000): *Etimologičeskij slovař russkich dialektov Sibiri*, 2-e izdanie. Moskva – Novosibirsk.

Aristov, N. A. (1897): *Zametki ob ètničeskom sostave tjurkskich plemjon i narodnostej.* Sankt-Peterburg.

Artamonov, M. I. (1962): *Istorija chazar.* Leningrad.

Bouda, K. (1957): Die Sprache der Jenissejer: Genealogische und morphologische Untersuchungen. – *Anthropos*, Bd. 52/1-2: 65-134.

Castren, M. A. (1856): *Reiseberichte und Briefe aus den Jahren 1845-1849.* Sankt Petersburg.

Castren, M. A. (1858): *Versuch einer jenissei-ostjakischen und kottischen Sprachlehre nebst Wörterverzeichnissen aus den genannten Sprachen.* Sankt Petersburg.

Castren, M. A. (1860): *Putešestvie po Laplandii, Severnoj Rossii i Sibiri (1838-1844, 1845-1849).* – Magazin zemlevladenija i putešestvij, t. VI. Moskva.

Černecov, V. N. (1941): Problemy zaselenija Severo-Zapadnoj Sibiri po dannym paleoantropologii. – *Kratkie soobščenija Instituta material'noj kul'tury*, vyp. 9: 14-28.

Černecov, V. P. (1953): *Ust'-polujskoe vremja v Priobje.* – Materialy i issledovanija po archeologii SSSR, 35.

Decsy, Gy. (1965): *Einführung in die finnisch-ugrische Sprachwissenschaft.* Wiesbaden.

Duľzon, A. P. (1959): Ketskie toponimy Zapadnoj Sibiri. – *Učenye zapiski Tomskogo pedagogičeskogo instituta*, 18. Tomsk: 91-111.

Duľzon, A. P. (1961): Slovarnye materialy XVIII v. po ketskim narečijam. – *Učenye zapiski Tomskogo Pedagogičeskogo instituta. Lingvističeskie nauki*, t. XIX, vyp. 2. Tomsk: 152-189.

Duľzon, A. P. (1961): Dorusskoe naselenie Zapadnoj Sibiri. – *Voprosy istorii Sibiri i Daľnego Vostoka*. Novosibirsk: 361-371.

Duľzon, A. P. (1962): Drevnie peredviženija ketov po dannym toponimiki. – *Izvestija Vsesojuznogo geografičeskogo obščestva*, t. 94. Leningrad: 474-482.

Duľzon, A. P. (1963): Etničeskij sostav drevnego naselenija Zapadnoj Sibiri po dannym toponimiki. – *Trudy XXV Meždunarodnogo kongressa vostokovedov*, t. 3. Moskva: 289-295.

Feist, S. (1928): Die Ausbreitung des indogermanischen Sprachstammes über Nordeuropa in vorgeschichtlicher Zeit. – *Wörter und Sachen. Kulturhistorische Zeitschrift*, Bd. 11: 31-35.

Gamkrelidze, T. V. / Ivanov, V. Vs. (1984): *Indoevropejskij jazyk i indoevropejcy*, I-II. Tbilisi.

Grumm-Gržimajlo, G. E. (1909): Belokuraja rasa v Srednej Azii. – *Russkoe geografičeskoe obščestvo (zapadnoe otdelenie)*, t. 34: 163-188 (s. denselben Aufsatz in: Gumiljov 1998/1: 340-352).

Grumm-Gržimajlo, G. E. (1926): *Zapadnaja Mongolija i Urjanchajskij kraj*, II. Leningrad.

Gumiljov, L. N. (1960): *Chunnu. Sredinnaja Azija v drevnie vremena*. Moskva.

Gumiljov, L. N. (1998/1-2): *Sočinenija*, t. 9-10. *Istorija naroda Chunnu*. Moskva.

Hajdu, P. (1953): Die ältesten Berührungen zwischen den Samojeden und den jenisseischen Völkern. – *Acta Orientalia* 1953/3: 73-101.

Helimski, E. A. (1982): Keto-Uralica. – *Ketskij sbornik. Antropologija, ětnografija, mifologija, lingvistika*. Leningrad: 238-250.

Helimski, E. A. (1986): Archivnye materialy XVIII v. po enisejskim jazykam. – *Paleoaziatskie jazyki*. Leningrad: 179-212.

Inostrancev, K. A. (1926): *Chunnu i gunny*. – Trudy tjurkologičeskogo seminarija, t. XVII. Leningrad.

Jacobsohn, H. (1923): *Arier und Ugrofinnen*. Göttingen.

Kluge, F. (1975): *Etymologisches Wörterbuch der deutschen Sprache*, 21. unveränderte Auflage. Berlin – New York.

Lunin, B. V. (1998): Vtorženie gunnov v Podońje – Priazóvje. – L. N. Gumiljov, *Istorija naroda Chunnu*, II: 394-415.

Maenchen-Helfen, O. (1945): Huns and Hsiung-nu. – *Byzantion*, t. XVII: 222-243.

Maloletko, A. M. (2000): *Drevnie narody Sibiri*, t. II. Kety. Tomsk 2000.

Patkanov, S. (1897): *Die Irtysch-Ostjaken und ihre Volkspoesie*. Sankt Petersburg.

Pokorny, J. (1959): *Indogermanisches etymologisches Wörterbuch*. Bern – München.

Popova, V. N. (2000): Areaľno-retrogressivnyj metod A. P. Duľzona v issledo-vanii substratnoj toponimii. – *Voprosy jazykoznanija*, 2000/3: 50-54.

Pritsak, O. (1989): The origin of the name *Sibir*. – *Asiatische Forschungen*, Bd. 108: *Gedanke und Wirkung*. Festschrift zum 90. Geburtstag von Nikolaus Poppe. Wiesbaden: 271-280.

Ramstedt, G. J. (1935): *Kalmückisches Wörterbuch*. Helsinki.

Rombandeeva, E. I. (1976): Mansijskij jazyk. – *Osnovy finno-ugorskogo jazy-koznanija*, 1976: 229-239.

Stachowski, M. (1997): Altaistische Anmerkungen zum "Vergleichenden Wör-terbuch der Jenissej-Sprachen". – *Studia Etymologica Cracoviensia*, vol. 2. Kraków: 227-239.

Stachowski, M. (2006): Persian loanwords in 18th century Yeniseic and the problem of linguistic areas in Siberia. – *In the Orient where the Gracious Light...* Satura orientalis in honorem Andrzej Pisowicz. Kraków: 179-184.

Starostin, S. A. (1995): Sravniteľnyj slovaŕ enisejskich jazykov. – *Ketskij sbor-nik. Lingvistika*. Moskva: 176-315.

Strahlenberg, P. J. von (1730): *Das nord- und östliche Theil von Europa und Asia*. Stockholm 1730.

Vasilevič, G. M. (1966): *Istoričeskij foľklor évenkov*. Moskva – Leningrad.

Vasmer, M. (1964-1973): *Russisches etymologisches Wörterbuch*, Bde 1-4, Russische Ausgabe. Moskva.

Werner, H. (2005): *Die Jenissej-Sprachen des 18. Jahrhunderts*. = Veröffentli-chungen der Societas Uralo-Altaica, Bd. 67. Wiesbaden.

Werner, H. (2006): *Die Welt der Jenissejer im Lichte des Wortschatzes (Zur Re-konstruktion der jenissejischen Protokultur)*. = Veröffentlichungen der So-cietas Uralo-Altaica, Bd. 69. Wiesbaden.

Werner, H. (2007): *Die Glaubensvorstellungen der Jenissejer aus der Sicht des Tengrismus*. = Veröffentlichungen der Societas Uralo-Altaica, Bd. 73. Wiesbaden.

Studia Etymologica Cracoviensia
vol. 14   Kraków 2009

Krzysztof Tomasz WITCZAK (Łódź)

A WANDERING WORD FOR 'HARDENED IRON, STEEL'
A STUDY IN THE HISTORY OF CONCEPTS AND WORDS

Eugen Helimski's collected works (2000) strongly demonstrate that the late scholar represented the so-called "Wörter und Sachen" school, his methodology relying on investigating the history of words, concepts, and cultural innovations from the Nostratic age to the modern times. This paper, written in adherence to this model of reasoning, shall be my own contribution dedicated to the memory of Prof. Eugen Helimski.

1. Introduction

The distribution of the Turkish term for 'steel' (cf. North Turkish *bulat*, Kipchak *bolat*, Kum. *bolat*, Azerbaidjan *polat*, Alt. Tel. Leb. *polot*) exemplifies the complex problem of the origin of a bundle of words. The noun also appears in Mongolic (cf. Mongol *bolot*, *bold* 'steel') and Semitic (cf. Arabic *fūlād* 'steel', Syriac *pld* 'id.'). Furthermore, it is attested in the Caucasian area, e.g. Georgian *poladi*; Chechen *bolat*, Arm. *p'ołovat'*, *połp'at'* 'steel', Ossetic *bolat* 'steel, damascean steel / сталь, булат' (Abaev 1958: I 265). The term in question is not limited to Ossetic, but also occurs in numerous other Iranian languages, cf. Pahlavi *pūlāvat*, *pūlāfat*, *pūlāft* 'steel', NPers. *pūlād* 'id.' (Horn 1893: 75, No. 310); Kurdish *pūlā*, *pīlā*; Pashto *pōlād*, Baluchi *pulād*, *pūlāt*.

The word is not unknown in Central and Eastern Europe, see Polish *bułat* 1. 'wysokogatunkowa stal', 2. 'miecz perski zakrzywiony, szabla turecka z szeroką głownią, zrobiona z takiej stali; tarcza', *bułatowy* or *bułatny* adj. 'zrobiony ze stali damasceńskiej' (Stachowski 2007: 66-67), *bułat* 1. 'stal perska, polerowana', 2. 'szeroka szabla turecka, perska', *bułatowy* or *bułatny* adj. 'stalowy' (Bańkowski 2000: I 95); Old Czech *bulát* 'steel; sword' (Machek 1957: 51); Old Russ. *булатъ* 'hardened better steel; sword, knife', Russian *булáт* 'a kind of steel; blade made from steel / сорт стали, стальной клинок' (Preobraženskij 1910-1914: 52 [90]; Vasmer 1986: I 238); Ukrainian *булáт* 'a kind of excellent steel'; Romanian *bulát* n. 'nóż (bednarski) / (cooper's) knife'.

It is evident that similar forms are widely disseminated throughout Central Asia, the Caucasus, the Near East and Central-Eastern Europe. Not infrequently, determining which language is the borrower and which the donor causes severe difficulties.

According to most scholars, the source form for this wandering word is Classical Persian *pūlād* 'steel' (Tokarski 1980: 97; Vasmer 1986: 238; Bańkowski 2000: 95). Taking into account the opinions of earlier etymologists, Preobraženskij (1910-1914: 52) claims Old Russ. *булатъ* to be a borrowing from a Persian source via Turkish. Abaev (1958: 265) seems reluctant to accept this idea, stating that 'the original source has yet to be established' ('Первоисточник не установлено'), but simultaneously he indicates that the Ossetic appellative, as well as the Slavic forms, must be borrowed from a Turkish source.

2. Pahlavi *pūlāvat*, New Persian *pūlād* 'steel' and Sanskrit *pāraśava-* 'iron': is there any connection between them?

The Pahlavi term for 'steel', *pūlāvat, pūlāfat, pūlāft*, borrowed into Arm. *p'oɫovat', poɫp'at'* 'id.', must be considered as the source of Classical Persian *pūlād* 'steel'. Most Iranian forms, including Kurdish *pūlā, pīlā*; Pashto *pōlād*, Baluchi *pulād, pūlāt*, seem to be borrowed from a Persian source, as does the Turkish term for 'steel'. The remaining forms are nothing else but loanwords from a Turkish source. This is why our analysis should return to the Pahlavi and New Persian appellatives.

According to the best knowledge of mine, the Pahlavi term for 'steel' originally contained the Indo-Iranian suffix *-vat-* (< IE *-wn̥t-*), denoting the abundance of what is expressed by the basic element. It is, however, largely unclear what is the base of the West Iranian archetype. In my opinion, it might be Old Persian *pāraθu-* or *pāraθava-*, cf. OInd. *pāraśava-* m./n. 'iron' (lex.), usually adj. 'pertaining to iron; made of iron'.

The development of OPers. *-rθ-* (= OInd. *-rś-* or *-rth-*) to NPers. *-hl-* and *-l-* is well-known in the West Iranian area (Hübschmann 1895: 194-196, 207-208), cf. NPers. *pahlav* 'hero' < OPers. *parθava-* 'Parthian', AGk. *Πάρθοι* 'Parthians', Arm. *Pahlav* (Horn 1893: 76; Hübschmann 1895: 207); NPers. *pahlū* 'Seite, Stadt', Pahlavi *pahlūk, pahrūk* 'Seite' < OPers. *parθu-*, Avestan *parᵊsu-* f. 'rib / Rippe', also *pərəsu-* f. 'Rippe, Brustseite', cf. OIr. *parśu-* f. 'rib, curved knife, sickle' (Horn 1893: 76; Hübschmann 1895: 213, 241); NPers. *hamāl* 'der Gleiche, Genosse, Kamerad' < *hamahl* < OPers. *hamarθa-*, cf. OInd. *samartha-* adj. 'appropriate, capable' (Hübschmann 1895: 207-208); NPers. *pul*, Pahlavi *puhl, puhr* 'bridge / Brücke' < OPers. *pr̥θu-*, Av. *pərətu-*, Kurd. *purd* 'id.' (Horn 1893: 76; Hübschmann 1895: 195, 278), cf. Lat. *portus* (*u-stem*) 'port, harbour, haven, refuge'; NPers. *čil, čihil* 'fourty / vierzig' < OPers. **čaθvr̥θat-* '40', cf. OInd. *catvāriñśat-* '40' (Horn 1893: 101; Hübschmann 1895: 207).

The suggested derivation of initial *pūl-* or *pūlā-* from Old Persian **pāraθu-* or **pāraθava-* is possible from the phonological point of view, especially if a short vowel in the medial position was syncopated. However, other Iranian nouns (e.g. Kurdish *pūlā, pīlā*; Pashto *pōlād*, Baluchi *pulād, pūlāt* 'steel') cannot be treated as related. They must be viewed as borrowings from a New Persian source, as might be expected on account of the great similarity between the attested forms.

The semantic value of the suffix **-vat-* ('full of') clearly demonstrates that 'steel' in West Iranian was perceived as 'containing a lot of iron'. It is relatively certain that the Old Persian **pāraθu-vat-* or, alternatively, **pāraθava-vat-* 'steel' (orig. 'full of iron') was an innovational formation, derived from the Indo-Iranian archetype **pāraću-* m. (*u*-stem) 'iron' and **pāraćava-* (orig. *o*-stem) 'iron', adj. 'pertaining to iron'. The latter archetype is confirmed by OInd. *pāraśava-* adj. 'made of iron / eisern', *sarva-pāraśava-* adj. 'ganz eisern', *pāraśavaḥ* m., *pāraśa-vam* n. 'iron / Eisen' (lex.). The correspondence between OPers. θ (= Awest. *s*) = OInd. *ś* (< Indo-Iranian **ć* < IE **k̂*) is perfect as far as the phonological rules are concerned. The phonetic and semantic aspects are unassailable as well.

3. The Mycenaean Greek for 'meteoritic iron'

In my earlier article (Witczak 2000a: 53-61) I reviewed the evidence for the Mycenaean Greek term *pa-ra-ku**, which denotes a kind of metal or semiprecious stone used for decorating wooden objects, especially utensils and pieces of furniture. It appears as *pa-ra-ku-we, pa-ra-ke-we* (instr. sg. in PY Ta 642, Ta 714, Ta 715) and *pa-ra-ku-we-jo* (an adjective in KN Sp 4451). However, a pair of tyres (*wo-ra-e*), used for binding chariot wheels and described simply as *pa-ra-ku-we-jo* 'made of *pa-ra-ku*', is mentioned in the tablet KN Sp 4451. Chariot wheels were bound by hard and durable metals, especially bronze (most frequently) or silver (once in PY Sa 287).

Aura Jorro (1993: 83) mentions the following interpretations of *pa-ra-ku** proposed so far:
(1) 'silver' (H. Mühlenstein; W. Merlingen; V. Karageorghis);
(2) 'emerald' (M. Ventris; V. Georgiev; L. A. Stella; J. L. Melena);
(3) 'zinc' (A. Heubeck);
(4) 'niello' (J. Chadwick);
(5) 'tin' (L. R. Palmer);
(6) 'iron' (V. V. Ivanov; V. P. Kazanskene, N. N. Kazanskij);
(7) 'foil, sheet of metal' (F. Householder);
(8) 'electron, pale gold, mixture of gold and silver' (M. Lejeune; D. H. F. Gray);

(9) 'amber' (M. S. Ruipérez);

(10) 'a precious stone used as a seal' (M. D. Petruševski; C. J. Ruijgh).

I rejected a number of interpretations (e.g. EMERALD, NIELLO, AMBER), as the substance called *pa-ra-ku** was used for manufacturing metal rims (tyres) of chariot wheels. Indeed, the tablet KN Sp 4451 contains the following text: *wo-ra-e, pa-ra-ku-we-jo* *253 2['two tyres made of *pa-ra-ku*'. It is beyond doubt that *pa-ra-ku** must represent a hard and durable metal and not a precious substance or stone. This metal must have been different than GOLD (Myc. Gk. *ku-ru-so*), SILVER (Myc. Gk. *a-ku-ro*), COPPER (Myc. Gk. *ku-wa-no*?), LEAD (Myc. Gk. *mo-ri-wo-do*?) or BRONZE (Myk. Gk. *ka-ko*). Thus, I discussed three of the remaining suggested possibilities: ZINC, TIN and IRON (Witczak 2000a: 57-58).

Unfortunately, Heubeck's proposal must be abandoned, zinc being a rather delicate metal, not suitable for the production of rims. It was by no means easily available in the ancient times, and even brass, produced by mixing copper and zinc, was unknown in antiquity.

Tin was known in the Mycenaean age, but there are no records of its use for producing tyres for chariot wheels. Being a rather soft metal, it was not appropriate for manufacturing wheel rims. Furthermore, tin and copper were not "normally employed in their pure forms, but alloyed in a mixture of up to ten percent tin to make bronze" (Chadwick 1976: 139).

The interpretation of *pa-ra-ku** as IRON seems the most probable in view of the Mycenaean evidence as a whole. In the middle of the second millennium BC, iron was considered a precious, ornamental metal. Two Soviet scholars (Kazanskene, Kazanskij 1986: 66) give the following argument for such an identification:

> Во всех контекстах *pa-ra-ku* предшествует золоту. Можно думать, что этот металл был более редким, чем золото. Во II тыс. до н.э. самым ценным металлом было железо (ср. амулет из железа на груди Тутанхамона и золотой гроб этого фараона). Кажется возможным сопоставить мик. *pa-ra-ku* с хеттским (из хаттского) *ha-pa-al-ki-* 'железо'. / In all contexts *pa-ra-ku* precedes gold. One could think that this metal was rarer than gold. In the 2nd millennium BC, iron was the most precious metal (cf. the iron amulet on Tut-Ankh-Amon's breast [sic!] against the golden coffin in which the pharaoh was buried). It seems possible to compare Myc. Gk. *pa-ra-ku* with Hittite (from Hattic) *ha-pa-al-ki-* 'iron'. (Kazanskene, Kazanskij 1986: 66)

Sir Colin Renfrew, the well-known British archaeologist, declared that "Iron is rare in the Mycenaean period, but there are a few occurrences including the bezel of a ring of the fifteenth century BC from Chamber Tomb 7 at Aidonia"

(Renfrew 1998: 244; see also Demakopoulou 1996: 50, No. 19). A different finding of an iron meteorite (9 kg chunk, saw marks) originates from the Minoan palace of Hagia Triada (Crete, ca. 1600-1500 BC), though Buchwald (2005: 24) claims it as somewhat suspect.

It should be emphasized that bronze was the major metal in the Mycenaean period, as well as in the Homeric epic. However, Homer's description of the athletic competition in honour of the fallen Patroclus (*Ilias* XXIII, lines 826-835) clearly demonstrates that iron was a rare metal, but a better one, having a very high value. Though iron was a rare metal in Greece in the period of the Troyan war, Homer refers to iron as many as 51 times: 22 times in his *Ilias* and 29 times in his *Odyssey* (Buchwald 2005: 88).

The suggested meaning '(± meteoritic) iron' was confirmed by identifying Myc. Gk. *pa-ra-ku* with Sanskrit *pāraśava-* m./n. 'iron' and Hittite *ḫapalki* n. 'iron' (Witczak 2000a: 58-60; 2000b: 189).

4. Lexical evidence

It is universally believed that Indo-European possessed no word for 'iron' (Gamkrelidze, Ivanov 1984: 710; Mallory, Adams 1997: 313-314). Below, I would like to discuss the problem afresh in order to establish whether this opinion is correct or not. If a cognate term for 'iron / steel' is attested in Old Iranian and Old Persian (really in Pahlavi and Classical Persian), then we must take into account the possibility that iron (especially meteoritic iron) was known in the late Indo-Iranian age. It seems possible to adduce further linguistic facts and words which may go back to the late Indo-European epoch. Needless to say, the terms for 'iron' and especially for 'steel' frequently belong to the so-called "Wanderwörter", for which reason I shall enhance this study with some additional notes on the origin and etymology of the bundle of words in question.

Let us review the linguistic evidence.

A. Sanskrit *pāraśava-* m./n. 'iron' (lex.)

According to Mayrhofer (1976: 257), the Sanskrit words *pāraśava-* adj. 'made of iron / eisern', *sarva-pāraśava-* adj. 'ganz eisern', also *pāraśava-* m., *pāraśavam* n. 'iron / Eisen' (lex.), are perhaps derived from OInd. *paraśúḥ* m. 'hatchet, axe, battle-axe' ("Vielleicht Ableitung von *paraśúḥ*"). The vṛddhi formation (note the long -*ā*- in the first syllable) is theoretically acceptable, but far from certain. The semantic development 'axe' > 'iron axe' > 'made of iron' > 'iron' is not unthinkable, but the change is usually attested as occurring in the opposite direction. Therefore, the most plausible assumption is that Sanskrit *pāraśava-* (functioning both as an adjective and a noun) indicates an earlier *u*-stem.

OInd. *paraśúḥ* m. 'hatchet, axe, battle-axe' (also *parśuḥ* in epic), Pali *para-su-*, Hindi *pharsā* 'id.' and some Iranian cognates (cf. Yazghulami *parus* 'axe', Parachi *pašö* 'id.' < Iran. **parasu-*; Ossetic *færæt* 'axe, hatchet', Khotan Saka *paḍa* 'axe' < Scythian or Old Persian **paraθu-*) represent IE **peleḱus* m. 'hatchet, axe, battle-axe', cf. Gk. πέλεκυς m. 'sacrificial axe, battle-axe' (Wüst 1956). If the Sanskrit adjective *pāraśava-* ('made of iron') is, in fact, a vṛddhi formation created on the basis of the well-known Old Indic term for 'hatchet, axe, battle-axe' (*paraśúḥ*), we should derive this adjective from an alleged Indo-European archetype **pēleḱewo-* [sic!].

An alternative interpretation was proposed by S. Sen, who treats *pāraśava-* as an "Ableitung" from Indic **parśava-* (= Old Persian *parθava-* 'Parthian') with the original meaning '[the metal] imported from Parthia'. It is certain that the plural form *pāraśavāḥ* denotes an ethnonym or a tribal name, but the connection with the name of the Persians is "ganz unsicher" (according to Mayrhofer 1976: 257). It is better to treat the appellative for 'iron' and the ethnonym separately.

B. Pahlavi *pūlāvat*, *pūlāfat*, *pūlāft* 'steel', NPers. *pūlād* 'id.'

The two terms in question must stem from Old Persian **pāraθu-vat-* or **pāraθava-vat-* 'steel' (orig. 'full of iron'). The similarity to OInd. *pāraśava-* m. 'iron' (lex.), adj. 'pertaining to iron', *sarva-pāraśava-* adj. 'ganz eisern' is evident and quite striking, even though the Old Persian formation is not completely identical. It is worth emphasizing that the phonological correspondence is complete (note that OPers. *θ* is here related to OInd. *ś*) and the meaning ('iron / steel') is well-established.

C. Mycenaean Greek *pa-ra-ku** '± meteoritic iron'

The Mycenaean Greek term in question is safely attested as *pa-ra-ku-we*, *pa-ra-ke-we* (instr. sg. in PY Ta 642, Ta 714, Ta 715) and it is seen in an adjective *pa-ra-ku-we-jo* (in KN Sp 4451) as well. This term refers to a precious material, probably a metal, used in the decorative techniques. However, in the tablet KN Sp 4451, a pair of tyres (*wo-ra-e*) is mentioned, apparently used for binding chariot wheels and described simply as *pa-ra-ku-we-jo* 'made of *pa-ra-ku*'. As has already been said, the usual materials used for binding chariot wheels were bronze or silver. This is why the meaning 'iron', suggested e.g. by Kazanskene and Kazanskij (1986: 66) and Witczak (2000a; 2000b: 189), seems most convincing.

The Mycenaean Greek name *pa-ra-ku* (presumably denoting 'meteoritic iron') was forgotten in the post-Mycenaean times. There is no noun in Classical Greek corresponding to it either phonetically or semantically. The loss of this ancient appellative might have been caused by the fact that the Greeks soon lost interest in meteoritic iron, the new iron-based technology (together with a new name of the smelted iron, AGk. σίδηρος) having been introduced to Greece.

D. Hittite *ḫapalki* n. 'iron'

Friedrich (1991: 350) lists Hittite *ḫapalki-* (*apalki-*) 'Eisen' with the following comment: "Nichtidg. Wort unbekannter Herkunft". The noun also appears in Hattic and Hurrian texts (cf. Hattic gen. sg. *ḫa-pal-ki-ya-an*; Hurr. *ḫa-pal-ki*, *a-pal-ki*) and in some Neo-Babylonian sources as *ḫabalginnu*. According to Puhvel (1991: 117-118), "*ḫapalki-* as a metal word seems centered on Anatolia (first attested in Hattic)", suggesting that more "remote cognates" occurred in Ancient Greek as χάλυψ (gen. sg. χάλυβος) m. 'hardened iron, steel', adj. 'made of iron' (by a metathetical deformation). Other scholars suggest that "the Hittite form *(ḫ)apalki-* bears only the most tenuous similarity" to Greek χαλκός 'bronze' (Adams, Mallory 1997: 314). Both Greek χάλυψ (gen. sg. χάλυβος) m. 'hardened iron, steel' and χαλκός 'bronze' may be viewed as borrowings from an Anatolian source.

Hitt. *ḫapalki* n. 'iron' seems phonetically similar to OInd. *pāraśava-* m./n. 'iron' (lex.), NPers. *pūlād* 'steel' and Myc. Gk. *pa-ra-ku* 'meteoritic iron' (as if from IE *pālaku-). Although the meaning is firmly established ('iron' / 'steel' in all the cases), the difference consisting merely in the replacement of the *i*-stem in Hittite by the *u*-stem in Greek (and Indo-Iranian), the phonological similarity may be fortuitous. The initial element *ḫa-* may be a "strengthening" prefix (Witczak 2005: 365). According to Sturtevant's rule (law), medial *-p-* in Hittite appears to reflect a voiced stop (IE *b* or *bh*), whereas the geminate *-pp-* indicates a voiceless stop (IE *p*). Thus, the Anatolian form, although it resembles the Indo-Iranian and Mycenaean Greek words, cannot be treated as entirely identical. There seem to be two possible conclusions: either the Hittite term for 'iron' is not related to the Indo-Iranian and Greek names, or all the terms are borrowed from an unknown source.

E. Lusitanian *pālaga* f. 'a clot of gold', dimin. *pālacurna* f. 'a small clot of gold; golden sand'

Both lexemes are registered by Pliny the Elder (*Hist. Nat.* XXXIII 77: "inveniuntur ita massae, nec non in puteis, et denas excedentes libras: *palagas*, alii *palacurnas* ... vocant"). The former item (Lus. *palaga*), representing an innovative formation (the feminine *ā*-stem replaces here the original *u*-stem), displays the characteristic lenition of the original *-k-* to *-g-* (Witczak 2005: 364). The latter appellative seems to be a diminutive form, derived from an *u*-stem archetype *pālaku-* by means of an unusual suffix *-rna* (as if from *-snā*). It is highly probable that the Lusitanian forms in question derive from the same archetype which Myc. Gk. *pa-ra-ku* 'meteoritic iron' and OInd. *pāraśava-* seem to go back to. The semantic difference ('gold' vs. 'iron') can be accounted for by the interchange of the value of both metals. In the so-called Bronze Age, iron was a metal more precious than gold. In the Iron Age, gold became the most valuable metal; hence, the change of 'a clot of iron' to 'a clot of gold' is easily explainable from the perspective of time.

F. Tocharian B *pilke** (n.) 'copper', *pilkesse* adj. 'pertaining to copper'

Adams (1999: 387) believes Toch. B *pilke* 'copper' to represent a derivative of the verbal root ^{3}*pälk-* 'to burn' with its original semantics: '[something that looks like] burning, shining, brilliant'. According to Adams (1999: 378), the Tocharian AB verb ^{3}*pälk-* 'to burn, torture' and its homonym ^{2}*pälk-* 'to shine, illuminate' reflect the zero grade of the Indo-European root **bhelg-* : **bhleg-*, cf. Greek φλέγω 'to burn, singe, ignite', Lat. *fulgeo* intr. 'to flash, lighten, shine'.

Phonetically, the Tocharian B word for 'copper' resembles the above-mentioned terms for 'iron' (or 'steel' or 'gold'). Despite the fact that the consonants *p*, *l* and *k* seem completely identical with those in Hittite *(ḫ)apalki*, Myc. *pa-ra-ku* [*pālaku-*] and Lus. *palaga/palacurna*, the phonological similarity may be fortuitous. All IE stops became voiceless in Tocharian, as well as in Hittite, thus the Anatolian and Tocharian nouns in question may go back to a common archetype containing voiced stops. The divergent meaning 'copper' in Tocharian is noteworthy as well.

5. The phonological analysis of the discussed words

The phonological correspondences existing between the terms A-F are presented below in table 1.

languages	IE *p	IE *$\bar{a}$	IE *l	IE *$\breve{a}$	IE *$\hat{k}$	stems	notes
Sanskrit	p	$\bar{a}$	r	a (short)	$\acute{s}$	ewo-stem, orig. u-stem	
Persian	p	$\bar{u}$ (< *$\bar{a}$)	*r	syncope	*θ	u-stem or ewo-stem	$l < $*$r\theta$
Mycenaean Greek	p	a	r or l	a	k	u-stem	
Hittite	p	a	l	–	k	i-stem	(ḫ)a-prefix
Lusitanian	p	a	l	a	c or g	ā-stem (and u-stem)	
Tocharian B	p	i	l	–	k	unknown (o-stem?)	

Table 1: Analysis of phonological correspondences

The Indo-European stops *p and *$\hat{k}$ demonstrate uniform, exact and expected reflexes. The initial labial stop *p*- is constant in all the compared nouns, although we should remember that the Mycenaean Greek transliteration is hardly exact (the syllabogram *pa* may also render *pha*, but not *ba*), the Tocharian evidence is uncertain (*p* can represent not only IE **p*, but also **b* or **bh*) and Hittite -*p*- seems somewhat dubious (of course, if we accept Sturtevant's rule, according to which the voiceless labial **p* in an intervocalic position is indicated by -*pp*- in Hittite).

The Indo-European phoneme **k̂* is regularly represented by Sanskrit *ś*, Old Persian **θ* (established by the New Persian phoneme *l* < **rθ*) and -*k*- in the so-called centum languages. Albeit the centum evidence is relatively strong, alternative possibilities also exist. The Linear B syllable sign *ku* may be read not only as Greek κυ, but also γυ or χυ. The Lusitanian forms *palaga* and *palacurna* display the variation *c ~ g*. The data from Hittite and Tocharian B are also ambiguous, as the voiceless stop -*k*- in both these languages may represent not only **k / *k̂*, but also **g / *ĝ* and **gh / *ĝh*.

The liquid **l* is regularly continued by *r* (in Indo-Iranian) and *l* (in the remaining Indo-European languages). The syllable sign *ra* in the Linear B script belongs to the *r*-series, which could represent two Greek phonemes – λ or ρ. In this particular case, the first possibility is preferable.

A number of intricate problems are connected with the vowels. The Indo-Iranian forms hint towards a long vowel in the initial syllable, the quality of which is unknown (Indo-Iranian **ā* may go back to IE **ā*, **ē* and **ō*). The Mycenaean Greek and Lusitanian forms clearly point to the vowel *a* (due to the ambiguities of the Linear B script, it is uncertain whether a long or a short vowel is indicated). The vowel -*a*- in Hittite is ambiguous as well. The Tocharian vowel -*i*- would require an additional explanation, which cannot be given here.

The second vowel -*a*- is consistently short and preserved as such in Sanskrit, Greek and Lusitanian. The short vowel in the Persian form was lost by syncope. The Hittite and Tocharian words display nothing between the liquid -*l*- and the guttural -*k*-, therefore the short vowel must have been lost earlier.

The related terms show a number of different stems (namely, *ā*-, *i*-, *o*- and *u*-stems). The *u*-stem seems the most archaic and original. It was preserved intact in Mycenaean Greek. The Persian root vocalism *ū* (< **ā*) is caused by the *u*-umlaut, while the *o*-stem of the Sanskrit term *pārasava*- developed secondarily from the original *u*-stem. Lusitanian *palaga* appears as a feminine *ā*-stem, but the diminutive form *palacurna* indicates an earlier *u*-stem. The original stem in Tocharian B *pilke** is unclear, though an *o*-stem seems preferable. The *i*-stem in Hittite is completely isolated, but it might, theoretically, be more archaic than the *u*-stem. The palatalized guttural stop **k̂* can be easily explained by the influence of the front vowel **i* (and not **u*).

The greatest difficulty in establishing the Indo-European origin of the discussed bundle of words is connected with the fact that the word in question appears to contain a double *a*-vocalism. The vowel $*\bar{a}$ frequently originates from the combination of the primitive vowel $*e$ and the laryngeal $*H_2$, but this possibility seems to be excluded by the Hittite data.[1] Additionally, the short vowel $*\breve{a}$ is relatively rare in Indo-European; in fact, it is labeled as 'foreign' by most researchers (e.g. Kuryłowicz 1956: 174-195; Lubotsky 1989: 53-66). Hence, these 'vocalic' arguments may be a strong indication of a non-Indo-European origin of the words. The reconstructed archetype $*p\bar{a}la\hat{k}\text{-}u\text{-}$ is etymologically unclear, not appearing to be motivated by a verbal or adjectival root. Consequently, I accept the hypothesis that it was borrowed from an external source in the relatively late phase of the Indo-European community.

6. Remarks on the primitive semantics of IE $*p\bar{a}la\hat{k}\text{-}u\text{-}$

A number of terms for 'iron' (and related metals) have been discussed above; the conclusion reached is that an Indo-European noun $*p\bar{a}la\hat{k}\text{-}u\text{-}$ may be reconstructed at least for the late phase of the existence of the Indo-European community. In my opinion, the differentiation of the Indo-European community began in the second half of the sixth millennium BC. Geographical factors (ca. 5600 BC – Black Sea Deluge) triggered the emergence of two Indo-European subgroups: Anatolian and European (Witczak 2006). It is conceivable that the language identity of the Indo-Europeans was preserved until the third millennium BC.

Yener (2000: 1) indicates that the use of metals (in Anatolia) and smith's metallurgical knowledge are very archaic: "The earliest occurrences of metal objects date to the Aceramic Neolithic (8th millennium BC), the beginning of settled farming communities and animal and plant domestication. [...] The aceramic site of Çayönü, dated by radiocarbon to c. 7250-6750 BC, attests to this precociousness with an astonishing 4,000 malachite and native copper artifacts. Malachite was mostly used for beads, whereas other copper metal artifacts such as pins and awls were annealed and work hardened; one object had a high trace level of arsenic, suggesting the use of native ores as natural alloys". Discussing the transformations in metal technology in the Chalcolithic Period (c. 5500-3000 BC) he informs the readers that "Metallurgy appears to be an empirical and experimental art prior to this time" (Yener 2000: 25). It is obvious that the Indo-European tribes, especially these which settled in Anatolia and the Balkan area, were able to know and name metals (including silver, gold, copper, lead, zinc, tin, and iron), as well as to prepare and use some metal artifacts.

---

[1] The conclusion may be quite different if we adopt the assumption that the Hittite name for 'iron', *(h)apalki*, derives from *pahlaki* by a metathesis of consonants. Note that the Hittite term *ahlipaki*, denoting a kind of metal or semi-precious stone, was considered by E. Neu (1982: 140-141) to be a metathesized variant of *(h)apalki*. See also Puhvel (1991: 117).

The semantic value of the Indo-European metal term *pālak̂-u- cannot be established with certainty. The above-discussed forms appear to point to the meaning 'iron'. It must be emphasized, however, that iron-working in general does not emerge until after 2000 BC, when it first appears in eastern Anatolia. From there, it seems to have spread throughout Asia, the Near East and across Europe, generally after 1000 BC. The new iron technology reached Greece by 1000 BC and the Italian Peninsula shortly thereafter, diffusing through Central and Western Europe by about 800 BC, and finally reaching Britain by about 500 BC. This chronology of the spread of iron-working hardly confirms the supposition that the reconstructed archetype *pālak̂-u- was already in use in the third millennium BC. According to Martin E. Huld and J. P. Mallory, the "diffusion of the new iron-based technology would date to a period long after the dissolution of PIE and it occasions no surprise that there is no common word for this metal between IE stocks other than occasional loans" (Mallory, Adams 1997: 314).

The linguistic material from six Indo-European branches enables us to question the traditional belief that there was no common word for iron in Indo-European. Thus, the semantic aspect of the reconstructed form should be reviewed anew.

The semantic relations between the relevant forms are given below in table 2.

languages	forms	gender	meaning
Sanskrit	*pāraśavam, -aḥ*	neuter or masculine	iron
Persian	*pūlāvat, pūlād*	unclear	steel
Mycenaean Greek	*pa-ra-ku**	unclear (perh. masc.)	± meteoritic iron
Hittite	*(ḫ)apalki*	neuter	iron
Lusitanian	*pālaga, pālacurna*	feminine	clot of gold / small clot of gold
Tocharian B	*pilke**	neuter	copper
Indo-European	**pālak̂-u-*	neuter (?)	± iron, esp. meteoritic iron

Table 2: Analysis of semantic relations

The Lusitanian forms with the meaning 'a clot of gold' (instead of 'a clot of iron') are especially valuable, having originated during a time in which iron was more precious than gold, i.e. the Bronze Age. In the Iron Age, iron became common and gold replaced it as the most costly metal. Therefore, the creation of *pālak̂-u- indubitably preceded the coming of the Iron Age. Nevertheless, many archaeologists claim that iron (especially meteoritic) was known and used much earlier. There are occasional findings of (meteoritic) iron objects dating from the fifth millennium BC (e.g. 3 small balls from Tepe Sialk, North Iran, ca. 4600-4100 BC), the fourth millennium BC (e.g. 9 beads from El Gerzeh, Egypt, before 3000 BC) and the third millennium BC (e.g. a macehead in treasure L from Troy, Anatolia, 2600-2400 BC), see Buchwald (2005: 24, table 1.5), who lists 13 cases from the Middle East, including an iron battle axe from Ras Shamra (Syria, 1450-1350 BC) and an iron dagger with gold haft, a headrest, 16 miniature chisels from Tut-Ankh-Amon's grave (Egypt, ca. 1350 BC).

I reckon that it may be proved on the basis of the linguistic material that the Indo-Europeans were acquainted with some iron objects in the third millennium BC. Meteoritic iron, as the hardest metal, must have been known to most Indo-European tribes, which borrowed its name from some unknown language.

7. Conclusions

The Indo-Europeans borrowed the term for 'meteoritic iron', *$pālak̑-u-$, from an external source. It was used to denote the most precious and hardest metal during the Bronze Age and the earlier times. The traces of this Indo-European noun were preserved in six branches of Indo-European (from Indic, Iranian, Tocharian and Anatolian in Asia through Greek in the South Europe to Lusitanian in the West Europe). The Old Persian form *$pāraθu-$ (or *$pāraθava-$) 'iron' became a basis for creating the name for 'steel' (OPers. *$pāraθu-vat-$, originally 'full of iron'), attested as $pūlāvat$, $pūlāfat$, $pūlāft$ in Pahlavi and as $pūlād$ 'steel' in Classical Persian. The Pahlavi name was borrowed into Armenian, whereas the New Persian form $pūlād$ gave rise to an oriental "Wanderwort" for 'hardened iron, steel', which is to be found in the Semitic, Caucasian, Mongolian and Turkish vocabulary. This wandering term reached Eastern and Central Europe (cf. Old Russ. булатъ 'hardened better steel; sword, knife', Russian булát 'a kind of steel; blade made from steel'; Ukrainian булáт 'a kind of excellent steel'; Polish bułat; Old Czech bulát 'id.'; Romanian bulát n. 'cooper's knife') via Turkish.

Krzysztof Tomasz Witczak
Uniwersytet Łódzki
Zakład Językoznawstwa i Indoeuropeistyki
ul. Lipowa 81, IV p.
PL – 90-568 Łódź
[ktw@uni.lodz.pl; ktw2006@wp.pl]

References

Abaev V. I., 1958, *Историко-этимологический словарь осетинского языка* [Historical and Etymological Dictionary of the Ossetic Language], vol. 1, Moskva, Leningrad: Izdatel'stvo Akademii Nauk SSSR.

Adams D. Q., 1999, *A Dictionary of Tocharian B*, Amsterdam – Atlanta: Rodopi.

Aura Jorro F., 1993, *Diccionario micénico*, vol. 2, Madrid: Consejo Superior de Investigaciones Científicas.

Bańkowski A., 2000, *Słownik etymologiczny języka polskiego* [Etymological Dictionary of the Polish Language], vol. 1 (A-K), Warszawa: Wydawnictwo Naukowe PWN.

Buchwald V. F., 2005, *Iron and Steel in Ancient Times* (Historisk-filosofiske Skrifter 29), Copenhagen: The Royal Danish Academy of Sciences and Letters.

Chadwick J., 1976, *The Mycenaean World*, Cambridge – London – New York – Melbourne: Cambridge University Press.

Demakopoulou K., 1996, *The Aidonia Treasure*, Athens: National Archaeological Museum.

Friedrich J., 1991, *Kurzgefasstes hethitisches Wörterbuch. Kurzgefasste kritische Sammlung der Deutungen hethitischer Wörter*, Heidelberg: Carl Winter Universitätsverlag.

Gamkrelidze T. V., Ivanov V. V., 1984, *Индоевропейский язык и индоевропейцы. Реконструкция и историко-типологический анализ праязыка и протокультуры*, vol. 1-2, Tbilisi: Izdatel'stvo Tbilisskogo Universiteta. (English version: *Indo-European and the Indo-Europeans. A Reconstruction and Historical Analysis of a Proto-Language and Proto-Culture*, vol. 1-2 [Trends in Linguistics. Studies and Monographs 80], Berlin – New York 1994-1995: Mouton de Gruyter.)

Helimski E., 2000, *Компаративистика, уралистика: лекции и статьи* [Comparative and Uralic Studies: Lectures and Articles], Moskva.

Horn P., 1893, *Grundriss der neupersischen Etymologie*, Strassburg: Verlag von Karl J. Trübner.

Hübschmann H., 1895, *Persische Studien*, Strassburg: Verlag von Karl J. Trübner.

Kazanskene V. P., Kazanskij N. N., 1986, *Предметно-понятийный словарь греческого языка. Крито-микенский период* [Thematic-Notional Dictionary of the Greek Language. A Creto-Mycenean Period], Leningrad: Izdatel'stvo «Nauka».

Kuryłowicz J., 1956, *L'apophonie en indo-européen* (Prace Językoznawcze nr 9), Wrocław: Zakład im. Ossolińskich, Wydawnictwo PAN.

Lubotsky A., 1989, Against a Proto-Indo-European Phoneme *a*, in: Th. Venne-mann (ed.), *The New Sound of Indo-European. Essays in Phonological Reconstruction* (Trends in Linguistics. Studies and Monographs 41), Berlin – New York: Walter de Gruyter & Co., pp. 53-66.

Machek V., 1957, *Etymologický slovník jazyka českého a slovenského* [Etymological Dictionary of the Czech and Slovak Languages], Praha: Nakladatelství Československé Akademie Věd.

Mallory J. P., Adams D. Q., 1997, *Encyclopedia of Indo-European Culture*, London – Chicago: Fitzroy Dearborn Publishers.

Mayrhofer M., 1976, *Kurzgefaßtes etymologisches Wörterbuch des Altindischen*, B. II, Heidelberg: Carl Winter Universitätsverlag.

Neu E. (ed.), 1982, *Investigationes philologicae et comparativae. Gedenkschrift für Heinz Kronasser*, Wiesbaden: Otto Harrassowitz.

Preobraženskij A. G., 1910-1914, Этимологический словарь русского языка [Etymological Dictionary of the Russian Language], vol. 1 (A-O), Moskva: Tipografia G. Lissnera i D. Sovko. (Reprinted in 1958 in Moskva: Gosudarstvennoe izdateľstvo inostrannych i nacionaľnych slovarej.)

Puhvel J., 1991, *Hittite Etymological Dictionary*, vol. 3: words beginning with H, Berlin – New York: Mouton de Gruyter.

Renfrew C., 1998, Word of Minos: the Minoan Contribution to Mycenaean Greek and the Linguistic Geography of the Bronze Age Aegean, *Cambridge Archaeological Journal* 8(2), 1998, pp. 239-264.

Sharypkin S., 2000, *Miscellanea Mycenaea* ("Do-so-mo" vol. 1), Olsztyn: Zakład Historii Starożytnej i Kultury Antycznej Uniwersytetu Warmińsko-Mazurskiego w Olsztynie.

Stachowski S., 2007, *Słownik historyczny turcyzmów w języku polskim* [A Historical Dictionary of Turkish Borrowings in Polish], Kraków: Księgarnia Akademicka.

Tokarski J. (ed.), 1980, *Słownik wyrazów obcych PWN* [PWN Dictionary of Foreign Words], Warszawa: Państwowe Wydawnictwo Naukowe.

Vasmer M., 1986, Этимологический словарь русского языка [Etymological Dictionary of the Russian Language], vol. 1 (A-Д), 2nd edition, Moskva: "Progress".

Witczak K. T., 2000a, Mykeńska nazwa żelaza (*pa-ra-ku*) i jej indoeuropejska geneza [Mycenaean Greek Term for 'Iron' (*pa-ra-ku*) and Its Indo-European Origin], in: Sharypkin S. (2000), pp. 53-61.

Witczak K. T., 2000b, Metale i wytwory metalowe w kulturze ludów indoeuropejskich [Metals and Metal Artifacts in the Culture of the Indo-European Tribes], in: *ΕΙΔΩΛΟΝ. Kultura archaiczna w zwierciadle wyobrażeń, słów i rzeczy*, ed. by H. Van den Boom, A. P. Kowalski, M. Kwapiński, Gdańsk: Wyd. Bernardinum, pp. 177-193.

Witczak K. T., 2005, *Język i religia Luzytanów. Studium historyczno-porów-nawcze* [The Language and Religion of the Lusitanians. A Historical-Comparative Study], Łódź: Wydawnictwo Uniwersytetu Łódzkiego.

Witczak K. T., 2006, Dyferencjacja języków indoeuropejskich [The Differentiation of the Indo-European Languages], a paper presented at the conference *Językoznawstwo historyczne i typologiczne. W 100-lecie urodzin profesora Tadeusza Milewskiego* (Kraków, 12-13 XII 2006).

Wüst W., 1956, Idg. *péleku-* 'Axt, Beil'. Eine paläo-linguistische Studie, *Annales Academiae Scientiarum Fennicae*, Ser. B., 93, Helsinki, pp. 1-145.

Yener K. A., 2000, *The Domestication of Metals. The Rise of Complex Metal Industries in Anatolia*, Leiden – Boston – Köln: Brill.

Studia Etymologica Cracoviensia
vol. 14   Kraków 2009

Robert WOODHOUSE (Brisbane)

THREE GERMANIC ETYMA REQUIRING PIE *b?

1. Among the evidence adduced by Patri (2005) for the purpose of casting doubt on the validity of Winter's law in Slavic[1] are three items allegedly reflecting PIE *-b- allegedly guaranteed by Proto-Germanic (PGm.) *-p- in
(1) PGm. *deupaz* 'deep', cf. Proto-Slavic (PSl.) *dъbno > *dъno 'bottom', Lith. *dubùs* 'deep', etc. (p. 274),
(2) OIcel. *drepa* 'strike, knock', OHG *treffan* 'hit, touch', cf. PSl. *drobiti 'smash, crush' (p. 277),
(3) OIcel. *happ* 'good luck, success', cf. PSl. *kobъ 'augury, prophesy, sorcery, etc.' (p. 277).
Whatever the final ruling on Winter's law may eventually be, the difficulties surrounding PIE *b are well known. Consequently caution should surely be exercised in proposing any reconstruction requiring this alleged PIE phoneme.

That the PIE *b reconstructed by Patri and some others (e.g. Uhlich 1995; Levickij 2000-2001, 1: 132, 4: 64 s.v. *deup-*) for the above Germanic items may be only apparent and not a foregone conclusion emerges from the fact that there is a substantial group of PGm. lexica containing PGm. simplex medial voiceless stop – particularly when following a long vowel or a diphthong – that can be etymologically related to other items having the corresponding PGm. geminate, usually following a short vowel. The PGm. voiceless stop in these cases does not necessarily continue a PIE media, but can reflect instead the PIE tenuis or aspera. These developments, for which Kortlandt (1991: 1) has proposed reviving the name Kluge's law, are believed to have taken their original point of departure in clusters of stop + *n that underwent lenition in PGm. by Verner's law (on the matter of the lenition see Woodhouse 2003: 215-221).[2]

2. The easiest case to deal with is that of PGm. *deupaz*. Lühr, to whom we are indebted for the most detailed recent (1988) discussion of the whole question, in fact includes PGm. *deupaz* in this group (p. 232f.), connecting the word

---

[1]   I hope to publish a full examination of Patri's other counterevidence on another occasion.
[2]   Note that in the latter reference there is a misprint in the table on p. 218: the asperae column for stage VIIIb should read "D'n/TT" (not "D'/TT").

with MHG *topf* 'olla', etc. (< PGm. **dupōn-*, **dupp-*), and proposing that the ancestral root should be reconstructed "womöglich" with PIE **bʰ*, not PIE **b*.

The proposition that **deupaz* belongs with this group can be supported by the several cognates with **n*-suffixes in other languages, e.g. the PSl. one cited above, Latv. *dubens* 'bottom', OIr. *domain* 'id.', Welsh *dwfn* 'id.', Breton *don* 'id.' (Vasmer/Trubačev 1986-1987 s.v. *dno*; Stokes/Bezzenberger 1894 [1979]: 153).

The proposition that the Baltic and Slavic words in question should be reconstructed with medial PIE **bʰ* (and not PIE **b*) is of course not new. Thus, for example, although Young (1990: 150), relying on Pokorny (1959), continues to write **dheub-*, **dheup-* for the PIE original of the Baltic cognates, Illič-Svityč (1979: 106) writes the etymon **dhubhnóm*, a form that probably goes back to the 1963 Russian language original (which regrettably I have not seen) and Trubačev (1978: 175f.) writes it once **dhub(h)-nom* but thereafter refers to the root as **dheubh-/*dhubh*. All that seems to be lacking is a plausible IE etymon.

I think this lack can be overcome as follows.

Trubačev (ibid.) draws attention to the possibility of a connection between PSl. **dъ(b)no* and PSl. **dъbrъ* 'valley, etc.' and may be right in supposing that this is due to contamination by **dъbno* of a word or words based on PIE **duwō* 'two' and directly comparable with Armen. *erkin* 'sky' and *erkir* 'earth', though it is the connection between PSl. **dъ(b)no* and **dъbrъ* that is chiefly of interest here. Some Slavic cognates of the latter, such as Russ. *debri* 'impenetrable forest', Ukr. *debri* 'id.', older Pol. dial. *dziebra* 'valley between mountains', suggest a parallel form **dъbrъ*, and the existence of these parallel forms in Slavic seems itself to be paralleled by the Latv. variants *dibens*, *dibins* beside *dubens* 'bottom'. At all events, while 'valleys' are no doubt features having considerable depth, it is also true they are generally in shadow for longer periods than are mountain tops and plains at similar latitudes. And the presence of meanings such as that of Russ. *debri*, 'impenetrable forest', a landscape generally associated with darkness, also contributes to a connection I would like to propose between the concepts 'deep' and 'dark'. The connection seems to be particularly strong in Germanic, cf. Eng. *a deep and dark mystery*, especially in the colour terminology of at least English,[3] NHG (*tief* and *dunkel*), Dutch (*diep* and *donker*) and Swedish (*djup* and *mörk*).[4]

---

[3]   Cf. relevant lexicographic treatments of these meanings of *dark* and *deep*, respectively in Gove (1961 [1966], s.vv.): "**dark** ... **2a** ... *specif. of color* : of low or very low lightness" and "**deep** ... **3** ... **h** ... *of color* : high in saturation and low in lightness : vivid and dark".

[4]   I note also that in Daphne Rusbridge's English singing translation of the famous "silver moon" aria in Dvořák's opera *Rusalka* the phrase *na nebi hlubokém*, literally 'in the deep sky' is rendered "upon the deep dark sky" (see Dvořák 1972: 46).

These considerations suggest that a connection may be seriously enter-
tained between PGm. *deupaz with Irish *dub* 'black', Gk. τυφλός 'blind', PGm.
daubaz 'deaf, stupid' (OHG *toub*, Goth. *daufs*, etc.; cf., e.g. Chantraine 1968-
1980 s.v. τύφομαι; Frisk 1960-1970 s.v. τυφλός).

3. Opinions vary as to whether OIcel. *drepa* 'strike, knock', OHG *treffan*
'hit, touch', etc., are related to Goth. *ga-draban* 'hewn (out of rock)', de Vries
(1977 s.v.), e.g., being in favour, Kluge/Seebold (1995 [1999] s.v.), e.g., against.[5]
This latter position is clearly based on Seebold's proposal that Goth. *gadraban*
is an error for **gagraban* (noted by Patri 2005: 277; Zehnder LIV²: 153), an
idea that can hardly be maintained since there are three weighty arguments
against it.

First, all the genuine instances of Goth. *graban* and its compounds are
translations of Gk. σκάπτω 'dig' or ὀρύσσω 'dig' and its compounds, whereas
gadraban translates the perfect medio-passive participle of λατομέω 'quarry
rock'. Secondly, if it is an error, then it is a very puzzling one: if no such word
exists why would the scribe have written it? There is no other word in the immediate vicinity of Mark 15:46 containing the sequence *dr*. Thirdly, if there had
been an error at this point we might well expect it to be the reverse of what is
attested, i.e. that the scribe would have written **gagraban* instead of *gadraban*
both because dittography is a common enough source of error and because such
an act would also seem to involve replacing a somewhat infrequent and perhaps
technical term with a more everyday one. I conclude therefore that *gadraban* is
genuine and can be used to vouch for the Kluge's law origin of the *p in OIcel.
drepa, etc.

Further, it is clear that there is nothing new about the belief that simplex
Germanic *p after a short syllabic nucleus can be transferred or backformed
analogically from the geminate. Thus Lühr (1988: 236, 238, 239, etc.) finds this
the origin of PGm. *p beside *pp in, e.g.: OHG *scaf, scaffo* beside *scapf, scapfo*
(names of various kinds of vessels); OE *scypen* 'stall' beside OHG *scopf* 'barn';
OIcel. *skypill* 'kind of headgear' beside MHG *schopf, schopfe* 'head hair, etc.';
and so on. Kluge/Seebold (1995 [1999] s.vv.) find NHG *schaffen* 'create' to be
related to NHG *Schöpfer* 'creator' and to Lith. *skõpti* (also *skõbti*) 'hollow,
gouge', Gk. σκέπαρνον 'carpenter's axe or adze' and, while not claiming any
direct relationship between NHG *hoffen* 'hope' and *hüpfen* 'hop', nevertheless
adduce for both without comment Sommer's idea that both derive from an inter-
jection *hup signalling an upward movement, proposing in addition a connection
of *hoffen* with Gk. κύπτω 'bow, bow the head' (< *kupyō or *kubʰyō, Frisk
1960-1970 s.v.; Chantraine 1968-1980 s.v.), so that for neither *schaffen* nor *hof-*

---

[5]   These authors (ibid.) also implicitly reject the proposed connection with PSl. *drobiti*
       with their judgement: "Ohne brauchbare Vergleichsmöglichkeit".

fen is an etymon containing PIE **b* proposed. Consequently neither is there any need to entertain such an etymon for NHG *treffen*, OIcel. *drepa* and the connection of these with Goth. *ga-draban* and PSl. **drobiti* 'smash, crush' can be upheld without, in the case of the latter, any soul-searching vis-à-vis Winter's law.

4. With respect to OIcel. *happ* 'good luck, good fortune, success', de Vries (1977 s.v.) is undecided whether the geminate derives from **mp*, which is represented in Swed. *hampa sig* 'happen' or is due to affectivity, but leans towards the latter. Since 'good luck' is supportive of the person who possesses it, it seems not too far-fetched to suppose a connection with Ved. *skabhnā́ti* 'support', Lat. *scamnum* 'bench, stool, throne', which supply the evidence for the nasal suffixation needed to support derivation of the Germanic geminate from PIE **-bʰn-*, as well as the *s*-mobile that explains the simultaneous presence of a tenuis and an aspera in the root of the Germanic words and other suggested cognates,[6] such as OIr. *cob* 'victory' (a fortunate outcome), ORuss. *kobъ* 'good fortune, success; sign of fortune, portent; fortune telling by portents; belief system, teaching; faith'; and OCS *kobъ* 'faith (?)'.[7] Since fortune in the sense of destiny is something one cannot shake off, we have an obvious connection to Lith. *kabùs* 'tenacious, prehensile' (Orel 2003: 161 s.v. **xappan*) and Avestan *fra-scinbaiiōiṯ* 'soll befestigen' (Kümmel LIV²: 549).[8] The Avestan word and the Ved. aorist *skambhur* also support the nasalized Swedish form cited above. Kümmel (ibid.) tentatively reconstructs the PIE root as **skebʰH-*.

5. Thus it has proved possible to support respectable IE etymologies not containing PIE **b* for all three of our Germanic etyma. Consequently there are no convincing grounds, theoretical or practical, for reconstructing any of them with PIE **b*.

---

[6]   The tectal variation in Ved. *śárdha-* 'crowd, might', Gk. κόρθυς 'heap', PSl. **čerda* 'series, row, herd', Goth. *hairda* 'herd, flock', etc. (Orel 2003: 170) suggests that this too should be reconstructed as PIE **skerdʰ-*.

[7]   According to Sadnik/Aitzetmüller (1955 s.v.), the word only occurs in Suprasliensis, twice (46: 24; 147:7 in Severjanov's 1904 [1956] edition), and on both occasions in an instruction that the interlocutor state his *kobъ*. The answer each time is *krъstijan(ъ že) jesmъ* '(well) I am a Christian'. Vasmer/Trubačev (1986-1987 s.v.) gloss the OCS word οἰωνοσκοπία 'divination' (literally 'watching a large (?) bird'), which does not seem to suit the contexts in which it is attested.

[8]   Note that Vasmer/Trubačev (1986-1987 s.v. *kobʹ*) are doubtful about Uhlenbeck's proposed connection with Ved. *kābavás*, the name of an evil spirit, and are silent about the connection mentioned by Sadnik/Aitzetmüller (1955: 250) with Cz. *koba* 'raven' which is specifically rejected by Machek (1957 s.v. *koba 1*).

Robert Woodhouse
School of Languages and Comparative Cultural Studies
University of Queensland
Brisbane QLD 4072, Australia
[r.woodhouse@uq.edu.au]

References

Chantraine, Pierre, 1968-1980, *Dictionnaire étymologique de la langue grecque: histoire des mots*, 4 vols., Paris: Klincksieck.

de Vries, Jan, 1977, *Altnordisches etymologisches Wörterbuch*, 2. verbesserte Aufl., Leiden: E. J. Brill.

Dvořák, Antonín, 1972, *Rusalka*, op. 114, text Jaroslav Kvapil, übersetzt von Robert Brock, translated by Daphne Rusbridge, klavírní výtah / Klavierauszug / vocal score Karel Šolc, Prague: Supraphon.

Frisk, Hjalmar, 1960-1970, *Griechisches etymologisches Wörterbuch*, 2 vols., Heidelberg: Carl Winter.

Gove, Philip B., 1961 [1966], *Webster's third new international dictionary of the English language unabridged*, Springfield, Massachusetts: Merriam-Webster.

Illič-Svityč, V. M., 1963, *Imennaja akcentuacija v baltijskom i slavjanskom: sud'ba akcentuacionnyx paradigm*, Moscow: Institut slavjanovedenija AN SSSR.

— = Illich-Svitych, V. M., 1979, *Nominal accentuation in Baltic and Slavic*, tr. Richard L. Leed and Ronald F. Feldstein, Cambridge, Mass. / London, UK: MIT Press.

Kluge/Seebold = Kluge, Friedrich, 1995 [1999], *Etymologisches Wörterbuch der deutschen Sprache*, 23. erweitete Aufl. bearbeitet von Elmar Seebold. Berlin / New York: Walter de Gruyter.

Kortlandt, Frederik, 1991, Kluge's law and the rise of Proto-Germanic geminates, *Amsterdamer Beiträge zur älteren Germanistik* 34: 1-4.

Kümmel, Martin: see LIV^2.

Levickij, V. V., 2000-2001, *Ètimologičeskij slovaŕ germanskix jazykov*, 1-4, Černovcy, Ukraine: Ruta.

LIV^2 = 2001, *Lexikon der indogermanischen Verben: die Wurzeln und ihre Primärstammbildungen*, unter Leitung von Helmut Rix, bearbeitet von Martin Kümmel, Thomas Zehnder, Reiner Lipp, Brigitte Schirmer, 2. erweiterte und verbesserte Aufl. bearbeitet von Martin Kümmel und Helmut Rix, Wiesbaden: Dr. Ludwig Reichert.

Lühr, Rosemarie, 1988, *Expressivität und Lautgesetz im Germanischen*, Heidelberg: Carl Winter.

Machek, Václav, 1957, *Etymologický slovník jazyka českého a slovenského*, Prague: Československá akademie věd.

Orel, Vladimir, 2003, *A handbook of Germanic etymology*, Leiden: E. J. Brill.

Patri, Sylvain, 2005, Observations sur la loi de Winter, *HS* 118: 269-293.

Pokorny, Julius, 1959, *Indogermanisches etymologisches Wörterbuch*, 1, Munich/Berne: A. Franck.

Sadnik, L., and Aitzetmüller, R., 1955, *Handwörterbuch zu den altkirchenslavischen Texten*, Heidelberg: Carl Winter / The Hague: Mouton.

Severjanov, 1904, *Supraslʹskaja rukopiś*, St. Petersburg: Otd. russk. jaz. i slov. Imp. AN [1956 repr., Graz: Akad. Druck u. Verlagsanstalt].

Stokes, Whitley, and Bezzenberger, Adalbert, 1979, *Wortschatz der keltischen Spracheinheit*, 5th ed. (originally Part 2 of August Fick, *Vergleichendes Wörterbuch der indogermanischen Sprachen*, 4th ed. 1894), Göttingen: Vandenhoeck & Ruprecht.

Trubačev, O. N., 1978, *Ètimologičeskij slovaŕ slavjanskix jazykov: praslavjanskij leksičeskij fond*, 5, Moscow: Nauka.

Uhlich, Jürgen, 1995, Altirisch *domun* 'Welt; Erde' und *domain* 'tief', *HS* 108: 278-289.

Vasmer/Trubačev = Fasmer, Maks, and Trubačev, O. N., 1986-1987, *Ètimologičeskij slovaŕ russkogo jazyka*, 2nd ed., 4 vols., Moscow: Progress.

Young, Steven R., 1990, Baltic diphthongal bases and Winter's law, *HS* 103: 132-154.

Woodhouse, Robert, 2003, Gothic *siuns*, the domain of Verner's law and the relative chronology of Grimm's, Verner's and Kluge's laws in Germanic, *PBB* 125: 207-222.

Zehnder, Thomas: see LIV[2].